Junior Certificate

Higher Level Paper 1

Mathematics

Michelle Kelly and Gillian Russell

Edco

The Educational Company of Ireland

Published 2017

The Educational Company of Ireland
Ballymount Road
Walkinstown
Dublin 12

www.edco.ie

A member of the Smurfit Kappa Group plc

ISBN: 978-1-84536-757-2

Book design: Liz White Designs

Cover design: Identikit

Layout: Compuscript

Editors: Sam Hartburn, Gwynneth Drabble

Illustrations: Compuscript

Proofreaders: Stephen Cashmore, Eric Pradel

For permission to reproduce photographs, the authors and publisher gratefully acknowledge the following: Shutterstock.

CONTENTS

Introduction

This book covers the material required for Paper 1 of the Junior Certificate Higher Level Mathematics examination.

Each chapter contains the essential key information required for that given topic. There are detailed revision notes and well-explained examples throughout the chapter. Along with this, we provide a comprehensive Exercise section complete with detailed Solutions in each chapter. These questions range from simple to exam-style questions.

It is extremely important to note that any topic covered on the Junior Certificate syllabus can appear on either Paper 1 or Paper 2 of the exam. This is why we have, where appropriate, indicated any links between chapters within the same book, but also chapters which are linked across both books.

Study tips

- When studying maths, we need to just roll up our sleeves and actually solve some maths problems. Practise, practise, practise!
- After you make a mistake, which we all do, it is important to review and understand where you went wrong in the problem. This is why we have included complete detailed solutions to all our exercises.
- *Understanding* the mathematical process is more important than *memorising* the process.
- Getting the most from your study sessions will require concentration. This is why we suggest a distraction-free zone.
- We recommend that you create a bank of notes with key points such as terminology, definitions and the basic concepts. You will see these throughout our chapters in coloured boxes.
- It is important to study all topics – not just the topics you like.

We would like to wish you every success in your study of Mathematics.

Michelle Kelly and Gillian Russell

Number

1

Learning objectives

In this chapter you will learn about:

- Natural numbers
- Integers
- Rational numbers
- Irrational numbers
- Real numbers
- The order of operations.

Natural numbers

Natural numbers are positive whole numbers, often associated with counting. Thus, they are also known as counting numbers.

They are represented on a number line as shown below:

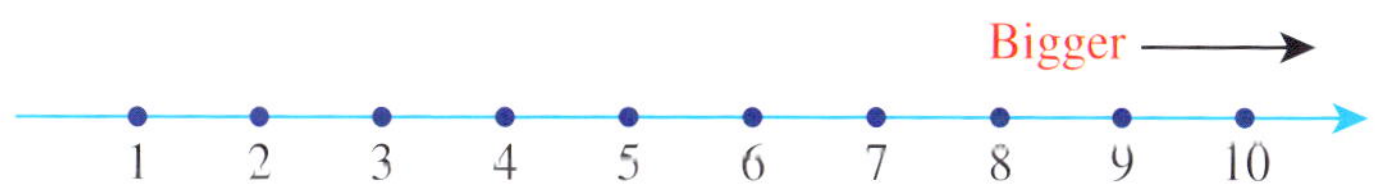

Note: as the arrow moves to the right the numbers get bigger.

Points to note

The natural numbers, ℕ

- ℕ = {1, 2, 3, ...}.
  The dots indicate that the numbers go on forever (they are infinite).
- They are the set of the positive whole numbers.
- The set of natural numbers **excludes zero**.
- The number set for natural numbers is given in the *Formulae and Tables* booklet.
- Examples of natural numbers include: 3, 9, 108.

Natural number operations

Key Terminology

Operation	Meaning	Examples
Addition	To find the **sum** or **total** of a set of numbers.	$6 + 9 = 15$ $24 + 37 + 42 = 103$
Subtraction	To find the **difference** between numbers.	$20 - 9 = 11$ $59 - 21 = 38$
Multiplication	To find the **product** of a set of numbers.	$4 \times 8 = 32$ $5(9) = 45$
Division	To find the **quotient** of a set of numbers.	$88 \div 8 = 11$ $\frac{140}{7} = 20$
Powers	Powers indicate how many times the base number is multiplied by itself.	$4^2 = 4 \times 4 = 16$ $5^4 = 5 \times 5 \times 5 \times 5 = 625$

Factors

To get the **factors** of a given number we need to find all the numbers that divide evenly into that number.

Example

Number	5	18	22
	1×5	1×18 2×9 3×6	1×22 2×11
Factors	1, 5	1, 2, 3, 6, 9, 18	1, 2, 11, 22

Prime numbers

A **prime number** is a natural number that can be divided evenly only by 1 and itself. Prime numbers have two factors only.

The first 37 primes are: 2, 3, 5, 7, 11, 13, 17, 19, 23, 29, 31, 37, 41, 43, 47, 53, 59, 61, 67, 71, 73, 79, 83, 89, 97, 101, 103, 107, 109, 113, 127, 131, 137, 139, 149, 151, 157

Prime factors

The prime factors of a given natural number are the factors of that number which are prime numbers.

Top Tip

To determine the prime factors of a given number, follow these steps:

1. Divide by the smallest prime number that divides in evenly.
2. Keep dividing by this prime number until it no longer divides in evenly.
3. Divide by the next highest prime number that divides in evenly.
4. Again, keep dividing by this prime number until it no longer divides in evenly.
5. Keep repeating these steps until you get the answer 1.
6. Write out these prime factors and show that when all the factors are multiplied by each other they give the original number.

Example

What are the prime factors of 1240?

Solution

- Step 1 to Step 5:

  Keep dividing by prime numbers until you get the answer 1:

2	1240
2	620
2	310
5	155
31	31
	1

Note: the prime numbers 3, 7, 11, 13, 17, 19, 23 and 29 do not divide evenly into 1240.

- Step 6:

  Write out the prime factors and show that when all the factors are multiplied by each other they give the original number.

  Therefore $1240 = 2^3 \times 5 \times 31$ (Always check your answers with a calculator.)

Composite numbers

A **composite number** is a number that can be divided evenly by a number other than 1 and itself. A composite number has more than two factors.

The first 46 composite numbers are: 4, 6, 8, 9, 10, 12, 14, 15, 16, 18, 20, 21, 22, 24, 25, 26, 27, 28, 30, 32, 33, 34, 35, 36, 38, 39, 40, 42, 44, 45, 46, 48, 49, 50, 51, 52, 54, 55, 56, 57, 58, 60, 62, 63, 64, 65

Lowest common multiple (LCM)

The **lowest common multiple (LCM)** is the smallest positive number that is a multiple of two or more given numbers.

Top Tip

There are a number of methods to find the LCM. Two of these methods are described below.

Method 1

To find the LCM, follow these steps:

1 List a set of multiples for each number given.

2 Continue until the same number appears in each list. This is the LCM.

Method 2

To find the LCM, follow these steps:

1 Write each number as a product of its prime factors.

2 For each **different** prime number in all of the given numbers in the question:

- Count how many times that prime number appears
- For each prime number, write down the largest of these counts.

3 The LCM is the product of all the prime numbers written down.

Example

A light show has red lights that flash every 20 seconds, blue lights that flash every 35 seconds and orange lights that flash every 42 seconds. If they all start flashing at the same time, how long will it be before they flash together again?

Solution (using Method 2)

1 Write each number as a product of its prime factors.

$20 = 2 \times 2 \times 5$

$35 = 5 \times 7$

$42 = 2 \times 3 \times 7$

2 Write down each prime factor to its highest power, for each composite number given in the question.

$20 = 2 \times 2 \times 5 = \boxed{2^2} \times \boxed{5}$

$35 = 5 \times \boxed{7}$

$42 = 2 \times \boxed{3} \times 7$

The common prime factors to their highest powers are: 2^2, 3, 5 and 7.

3 To get the LCM, multiply all these prime factors.

LCM is $2^2 \times 3 \times 5 \times 7 = 420$.

This means that it will take 420 seconds (7 minutes) until the three lights flash at the same time again.

Highest common factor (HCF)

The **highest common factor (HCF)** is the largest number that divides evenly into two or more given numbers.

Top Tip

There are a number of methods to find the HCF. Two of these methods are outlined below.

Method 1

To find the HCF, follow these steps:

1 List all the factors for each of the numbers given. (Use a calculator to do this.)

2 Choose the highest factor that appears in every list.

Method 2

To find the HCF, follow these steps:

1 Find the prime factors of each number.

2 Write each number as a product of its prime factors.

3 Choose the common prime factors with the lowest power.

4 To get the HCF, multiply the common prime factors with the lowest power.

Example

A shop has 390 pens, 585 markers and 715 pencils. Each product is sold in a pack which contains the same number of each item. What is the largest number of packs that the shop can make?

Solution (using Method 2)

1 Find the prime factors of each number.

$$\begin{array}{r|r} 2 & 390 \\ \hline 3 & 195 \\ \hline 5 & 65 \\ \hline 13 & 13 \\ \hline & 1 \end{array} \qquad \begin{array}{r|r} 3 & 585 \\ \hline 3 & 195 \\ \hline 5 & 65 \\ \hline 13 & 13 \\ \hline & 1 \end{array} \qquad \begin{array}{r|r} 5 & 715 \\ \hline 11 & 143 \\ \hline 13 & 13 \\ \hline & 1 \end{array}$$

2 Write each numbers as a product of its prime factors.

$390 = 2 \times 3 \times 5 \times 13$

$585 = 3^2 \times 5 \times 13$

$715 = 5 \times 11 \times 13$

3 Choose the common prime factors with the lowest power.

$390 = 2 \times 3 \times \boxed{5} \times \boxed{13}$

$585 = 3^2 \times \boxed{5} \times \boxed{13}$

$715 = \boxed{5} \times 11 \times \boxed{13}$

The common prime factors with the lowest powers are 5 and 13.

4 To get the HCF, multiply the common prime factors with the lowest power.

HCF $= 5 \times 13 = 65 \Rightarrow$ the largest number of packs that can be made is 65.

Integers

The set of **integers** contains **zero** and all **whole** positive and negative numbers.

They are represented on the number line as shown below:

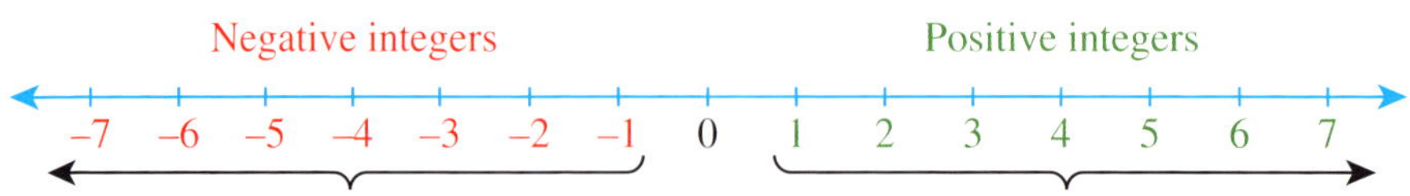

As shown on the number line:

- Integers to the right of zero get bigger the further you move away from zero.
- Integers to the left of zero get smaller the further you move away from zero.

Points to note

The integers, $\mathbb{Z}$

- $\mathbb{Z} = \{\dots, -2, -1, 0, 1, 2, \dots\}$
- Integers are the set of all the positive and negative whole numbers including 0.
- The number set for integers is given in the *Formulae and Tables* booklet.
- The set of natural numbers is a subset of the integers. So, $\mathbb{N} \subset \mathbb{Z}$.

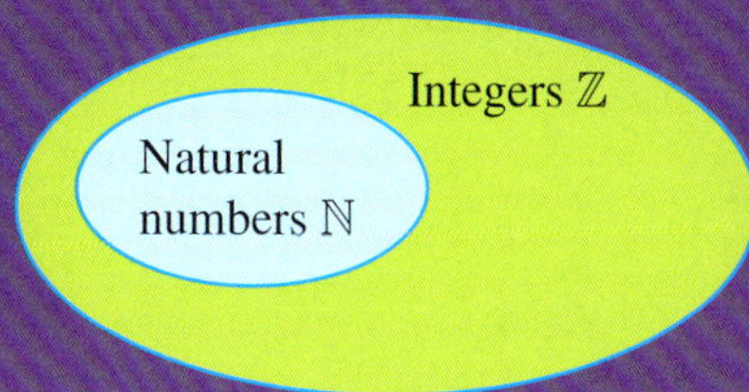

Integer operations

Addition and subtraction	
If the signs are the same, add and use the common sign.	**If the signs are different, subtract and use the sign of the bigger number.**
$6 + 7 = 13$	$6 - 7 = -1$
$-6 - 7 = -13$	$7 - 6 = 1$

Multiplication and division			
Like signs give plus.		**Unlike signs give minus.**	
$6 \times 7 = 42$	$\frac{42}{6} = 7$	$6(-7) = -42$	$\frac{-42}{6} = -7$
$(-6) \times (-7) = 42$	$\frac{-42}{-6} = 7$	$(-6) \times 7 = -42$	$\frac{42}{-6} = -7$

Quick rule	
Multiplication	**Division**
$(+) \times (+) = (+)$	$(+) \div (+) = (+)$
$(-) \times (-) = (+)$	$(-) \div (-) = (+)$
$(-) \times (+) = (-)$	$(-) \div (+) = (-)$
$(+) \times (-) = (-)$	$(+) \div (-) = (-)$

Example

Evaluate each of the following:

(a) $(-4) + 3 + (-7) + 5$ **(b)** $2 + 9 + (-8) + (-9) + 6$ **(c)** $-2 \times 2 \times (-1) \times (-3)$

Solution

(a) $(-4) + 3 + (-7) + 5$ Work from left to right, adding the first two terms: $(-4) + 3$.

$= -1 + (-7) + 5$ Continue working from left to right, adding two terms at a time.

$= -8 + 5$

$= -3$

(b) $2 + 9 + (-8) + (-9) + 6$ Work from left to right, adding two terms at a time.

$= 11 + (-8) + (-9) + 6$

$= 3 + (-9) + 6$

$= -6 + 6$

$= 0$

(c) $-2 \times 2 \times (-1) \times (-3)$ Work from left to right, multiplying two terms at a time.

$= -4 \times (-1) \times (-3)$

$= 4 \times (-3)$

$= -12$

Rational numbers

A **rational number** is any number that can be written as a **ratio**, which means it can be written as a **fraction**.

Examples of rational numbers include: $\frac{2}{1}, \frac{1}{3}, -\frac{4}{5}$ and $\frac{13}{7}$.

Two of the common shapes generally used to represent fractions are circles and rectangles.

Fraction	Circle	Rectangle
$\frac{1}{2}$	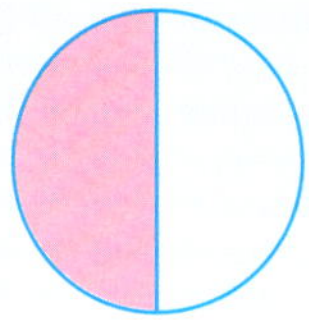	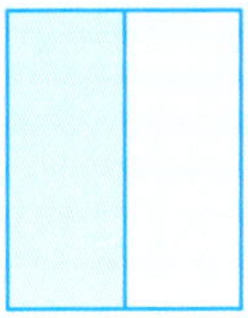

$\frac{1}{4}$

$\frac{4}{6}$

$\frac{2}{8}$

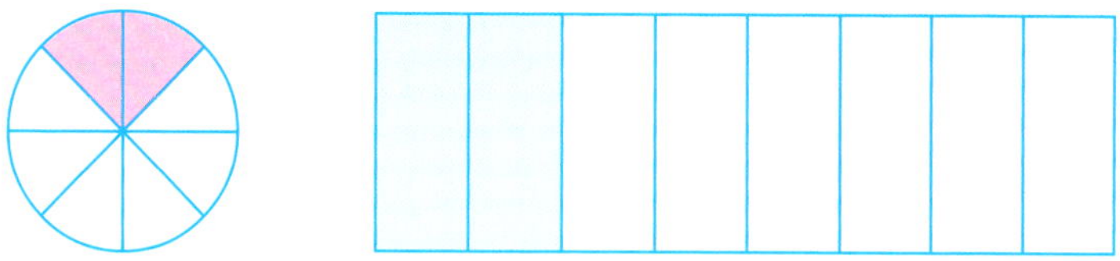

Every whole number is a rational number, because any whole number can be written as a fraction.

For example: 10 can be written as $\frac{10}{1}$, 82 can be written as $\frac{82}{1}$, and 3867 can be written as $\frac{3867}{1}$.

Points to note

Rational numbers, $\mathbb{Q}$

- $\mathbb{Q}$ = the set of numbers which can be written in the form $\frac{p}{q}$, where p and $q \in \mathbb{Z}$, and $q \neq 0$.
- The number set for rational numbers is given in the *Formulae and Tables* booklet.
- The decimal form of a rational number is either a terminating or repeating decimal.
- A terminating decimal is a decimal that contains a finite number of digits: for example, 36·8, 0·125 and 4·5.
- Repeating decimals are decimals that contain an infinite number of digits: for example, 0·333.... and 7·689 689...
- The natural numbers and integers are subsets of the set of rational numbers. So, $\mathbb{N} \subset \mathbb{Z} \subset \mathbb{Q}$.

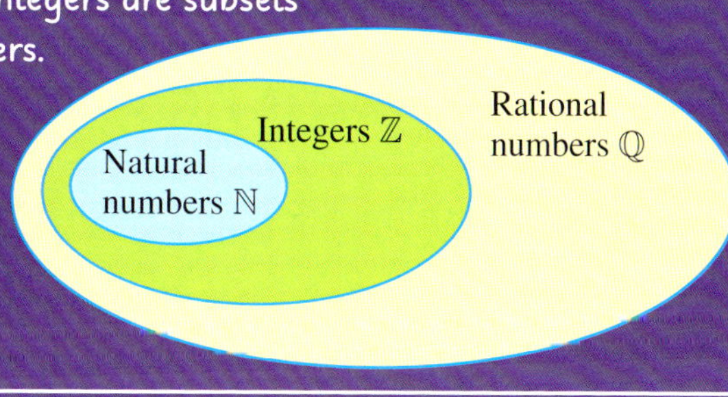

Types of fractions

Proper fractions	Improper fractions	Mixed fractions
The numerator is smaller than the denominator so the fraction is always less than 1.	The numerator is bigger than the denominator so the fraction is always greater than 1.	Always contain an integer and a proper fraction.
Examples	**Examples**	**Examples**
$\frac{1}{4}$, $-\frac{6}{7}$ and $\frac{23}{25}$	$\frac{6}{5}$, $-\frac{8}{3}$ and $\frac{38}{31}$	$2\frac{1}{5}$, $-4\frac{3}{8}$ and $10\frac{2}{9}$

Equivalent fractions

- **Equivalent fractions** are fractions that have the same value but look different.
- To find equivalent fractions of a given fraction, we can multiply or divide the numerator and denominator by the same number.

For example, the following fractions are equivalent fractions as they all represent the same value.

$$\frac{1}{2} = \frac{2}{4} = \frac{3}{6} = \frac{4}{8}$$

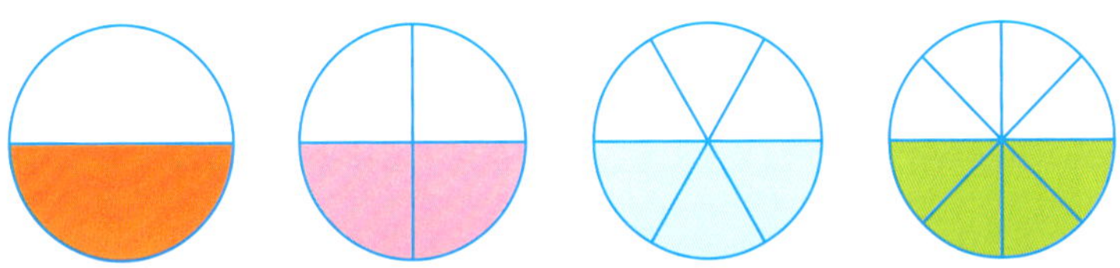

Example

Find the missing numbers in the equivalent fractions given:

(a) $\frac{5}{7} = \frac{45}{\square}$ **(b)** $\frac{72}{96} = \frac{\square}{12}$

Solution

(a) $\frac{5}{7} = \frac{45}{\square}$ What number multiplied by 5 gives 45? Answer: 9.

$\frac{5 \times 9}{7 \times 9} = \frac{45}{\square}$ Multiply numerator and denominator by 9.

$\frac{5 \times 9}{7 \times 9} = \frac{45}{\boxed{63}}$

(b) $\frac{72}{96} = \frac{\square}{12}$ What number divides into 96 to give 12? Answer: 8.

$\frac{72 \div 8}{96 \div 8} = \frac{\square}{12}$ Divide numerator and denominator by 8.

$\frac{72 \div 8}{96 \div 8} = \frac{\boxed{9}}{12}$

Example

Investigate whether the fractions $\frac{4}{7}$, $\frac{12}{21}$ and $\frac{28}{49}$ are equivalent.
Explain your answer.

Solution

Check:

Is $\frac{4}{7} = \frac{12}{21}$?

Yes, as $\frac{4 \times 3}{3 \times 3} = \frac{12}{21}$

Is $\frac{4}{7} = \frac{28}{49}$?

Yes, as $\frac{4 \times 7}{7 \times 7} = \frac{28}{49}$

Therefore, the fractions $\frac{4}{7}$, $\frac{12}{21}$ and $\frac{28}{49}$ are equivalent.

The reciprocal

The **reciprocal** of a number is found by dividing 1 by the given number.

The general rule is shown in this table.

General number	Reciprocal
a	$1 \div a = 1 \times \frac{1}{a} = \frac{1}{a}$
$\frac{a}{b}$	$1 \div \frac{a}{b} = 1 \times \frac{b}{a} = \frac{b}{a}$

Quick rule: Simply turn the fraction upside down.

Number	$\frac{3}{5}$	$-\frac{7}{4}$	$16 = \frac{16}{1}$	$\frac{1}{15}$	$\sqrt{2}$	$-6 = -\frac{6}{1}$
Reciprocal	$\frac{5}{3}$	$-\frac{4}{7}$	$\frac{1}{16}$	$\frac{15}{1} = 15$	$\frac{1}{\sqrt{2}}$	$-\frac{1}{6}$

Rational number operations

Addition and subtraction

When adding or subtracting fractions **without** the aid of a calculator, follow these steps:

1. Find the lowest common multiple of the denominators (LCM).
2. Rewrite each fraction as an equivalent fraction with this denominator.
3. Add or subtract the numerators of the fractions to get your answer.

Example of addition	Example of subtraction
$\frac{2}{5}+\frac{2}{3}$ (LCM = 15)	$\frac{5}{7}-\frac{1}{4}$ (LCM = 28)
$=\frac{3(2)}{15}+\frac{5(2)}{15}$	$=\frac{4(5)}{28}-\frac{7(1)}{28}$
$=\frac{6}{15}+\frac{10}{15}$	$=\frac{20}{28}-\frac{7}{28}$
$=\frac{6+10}{15}$	$=\frac{20-7}{28}$
$=\frac{16}{15}=1\frac{1}{15}$	$=\frac{13}{28}$

Multiplication	Division
Multiply the first numerator by the second numerator, and multiply the first denominator by the second denominator.	Multiply the first fraction by the reciprocal of the second fraction.
Example	**Example**
$\frac{2}{5}\times\frac{3}{7}=\frac{2\times 3}{5\times 7}=\frac{6}{35}$	$\frac{5}{9}\div\frac{2}{7}=\frac{5}{9}\times\frac{7}{2}=\frac{35}{18}$

Example

A teacher gives her class the following sum to do **without** using a calculator.

$\frac{1}{6}+\frac{5}{9}=?$

Some of the students give the answer $\frac{1}{6}+\frac{5}{9}=\frac{6}{15}$, which is incorrect.

(a) Explain what the students did wrong.

(b) Find the correct answer.

Solution

(a) The students just added the numerators and the denominators, which is incorrect. They should have found a common denominator first.

(b) $\frac{1}{6}+\frac{5}{9}$ (LCM = 36)

$=\frac{6(1)}{36}+\frac{4(5)}{36}$

$=\frac{6}{36}+\frac{20}{36}$

$=\frac{6+20}{36}=\frac{26}{36}=\frac{13}{18}$

Example

Jack got some money for his birthday. He decides to spend $\frac{2}{5}$ of his money on computer games, save $\frac{1}{3}$ and spend $\frac{1}{2}$ of the remainder on new clothes. What fraction of his money has Jack spent on new clothes?

Solution

(If a sum has more than one calculation, do them one at a time.)
He spends $\frac{2}{5}$ on computer games. This means the remainder is: $1-\frac{2}{5}=\frac{3}{5}$
He saves $\frac{1}{3}$ so the amount remaining now is: $\frac{3}{5}-\frac{1}{3}=\frac{9}{15}-\frac{5}{15}=\frac{4}{15}$
He then spends $\frac{1}{2}$ of the remainder on new clothes: $\frac{1}{2}\times\frac{4}{15}=\frac{4}{30}=\frac{2}{15}$
This means he has spent $\frac{2}{15}$ of his money on new clothes.

Irrational numbers

An **irrational number** is any number that cannot be written as a fraction. However, irrational numbers can be written as decimals that neither terminate nor repeat.

Examples of irrational numbers include: $\sqrt{2}, \sqrt{3}, \sqrt{5}, \sqrt{7}, \pi$.

Points to note

The set of irrational numbers, $\mathbb{R}\backslash\mathbb{Q}$

- $\mathbb{R}\backslash\mathbb{Q}$ = the set of numbers which **cannot** be written in the form $\frac{p}{q}$, where p and $q \in \mathbb{Z}$, and $q \neq 0$. (This is **not** the set of the rational numbers given in the *Formulae and Tables* booklet. You do **not** need to learn this, you just need to know where to find the information).
- The roots of all prime numbers are irrational numbers.
- The sets of rational numbers, integers and natural numbers are **not subsets** of the irrational numbers. So $\mathbb{N} \subset \mathbb{Z} \subset \mathbb{Q} \not\subset \mathbb{R}\backslash\mathbb{Q}$.

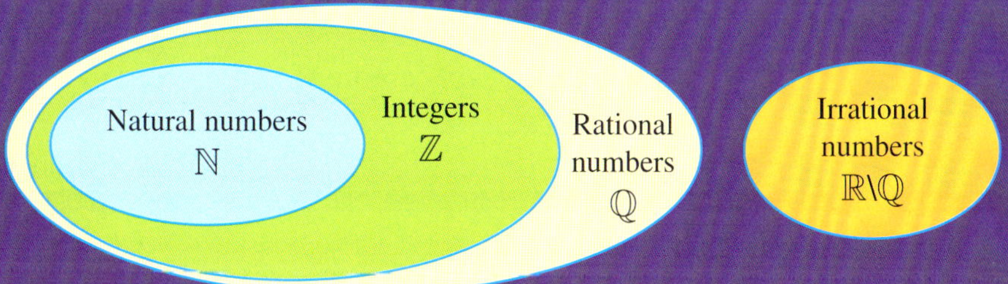

Surds

A **surd** is just another name for a root of a number that is an irrational number.

For example, $\sqrt{9} = 3$ is **not** a surd as it can be written as a rational number, but $\sqrt{2} = 1{\cdot}414\ 213\ 562\ 37\ldots$ is a surd as it is an irrational number.

Surds have a decimal which goes on forever without repeating.

Number	Decimal	Surd?
$\sqrt{2}$	1·414 213 562 37…	Yes
$\sqrt{4}$	2	No
$\sqrt{7}$	2·645 751 311 06…	Yes
$\sqrt{\frac{1}{16}}$	$\frac{1}{4} = 0{\cdot}25$	No
$\sqrt{\frac{3}{5}}$	0·774 596 6692...	Yes

Simplifying expressions involving surds

Points to note

Surd rules	Meaning	Example
$\sqrt{ab} = \sqrt{a} \times \sqrt{b}$	Factorise the number that has been rooted and multiply the root of each factor.	$\sqrt{45} = \sqrt{9 \times 5}$ $= \sqrt{9} \times \sqrt{5}$ $= 3\sqrt{5}$
$\sqrt{a} \times \sqrt{a} = a$	The root of a number multiplied by itself is equal to the number.	$\sqrt{2} \times \sqrt{2} = 2$
$3\sqrt{a} + 2\sqrt{a} = 5\sqrt{a}$	We can only add like surds.	$7\sqrt{5} + 3\sqrt{5} = 10\sqrt{5}$
$3\sqrt{a} - 2\sqrt{a} = \sqrt{a}$	We can only subtract like surds.	$9\sqrt{2} - 5\sqrt{2} = 4\sqrt{2}$
$\sqrt{a} + \sqrt{b} \neq \sqrt{a+b}$ and $\sqrt{a} - \sqrt{b} \neq \sqrt{a-b}$	Note: We **cannot** add or subtract unlike surds in this way. This is a very common mistake!	$\sqrt{2} + \sqrt{8} \neq \sqrt{2+8}$ $\sqrt{2} + \sqrt{8} \neq \sqrt{10}$ $\sqrt{8} - \sqrt{2} \neq \sqrt{8-2}$ $\sqrt{8} - \sqrt{2} \neq \sqrt{6}$

Example

Simplify each of the following surds:

(a) $\sqrt{90}$ **(b)** $\sqrt{27}+\sqrt{75}-\sqrt{48}$ **(c)** $\dfrac{15+\sqrt{72}}{3}$

Solution

(a) $\sqrt{90}$ Find factors such that one of the factors is a square number.

$=\sqrt{9\times 10}$ Simplify $\sqrt{9}$.

$=\sqrt{9}\times\sqrt{10}$

$=3\sqrt{10}$

(b) $\sqrt{27}+\sqrt{75}-\sqrt{48}$ Find factors such that one of the factors is a square number.

$=\sqrt{9\times 3}+\sqrt{25\times 3}-\sqrt{16\times 3}$ Simplify $\sqrt{9}$, $\sqrt{25}$ and $\sqrt{16}$.

$=3\sqrt{3}+5\sqrt{3}-4\sqrt{3}$

$=4\sqrt{3}$

(c) $\dfrac{15+\sqrt{72}}{3}$ Find factors such that one of the factors is a square number.

$=\dfrac{15+\sqrt{36\times 2}}{3}$ Simplify $\sqrt{36}$.

$=\dfrac{15+6\sqrt{2}}{3}$ Divide numerator and denominator by 3.

$=5+2\sqrt{2}$

Use of a calculator when dealing with surds

Points to note

On the calculator there are a number of buttons for surds:

1 Square root [$\sqrt{\ }$]

2 Cube root [$\sqrt[3]{\ }$]

3 Higher than cube roots [$\sqrt[x]{\ }$] or [$\sqrt[\square]{\ }$]

Calculate each of the following on your calculator.

Evaluate	Method	Answer
$\sqrt{81}$	Press [$\sqrt{\ }$] [8] [1] [=]	$\sqrt{81}=9$
$\sqrt[3]{64}$	Press [$\sqrt[3]{\ }$] [6] [4] [=]	$\sqrt[3]{64}=4$
$\sqrt[5]{7776}$	Press [$\sqrt[\square]{\ }$] Use the arrow button to input $\sqrt[5]{7776}$	$\sqrt[5]{7776}=6$

Real numbers

Points to note

The set of real numbers, $\mathbb{R}$

- $\mathbb{R}$ = the set of rational **and** irrational numbers.
- The sets of irrational numbers, rational numbers, integers and natural numbers are all subsets of the set of real numbers: $\mathbb{N} \subset \mathbb{Z} \subset \mathbb{Q} \subset \mathbb{R}$, and $\mathbb{R}/\mathbb{Q} \subset \mathbb{R}$

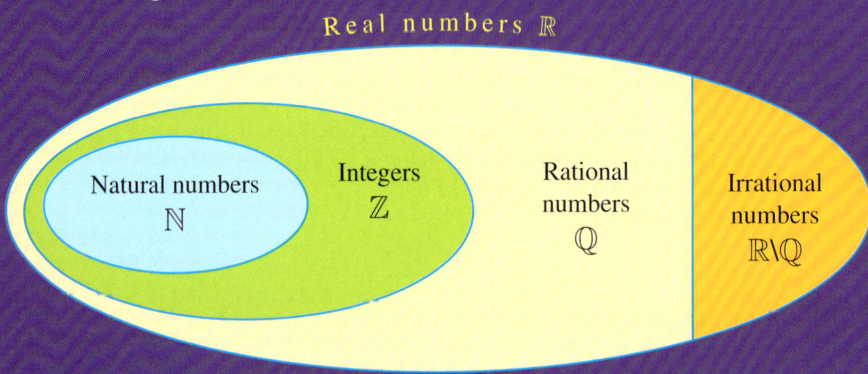

Example

Insert each of the following numbers in the correct place on the Venn diagram:

$\frac{3}{4}$, 5, 6·2, $\sqrt{5}$, 9, 3π and −4

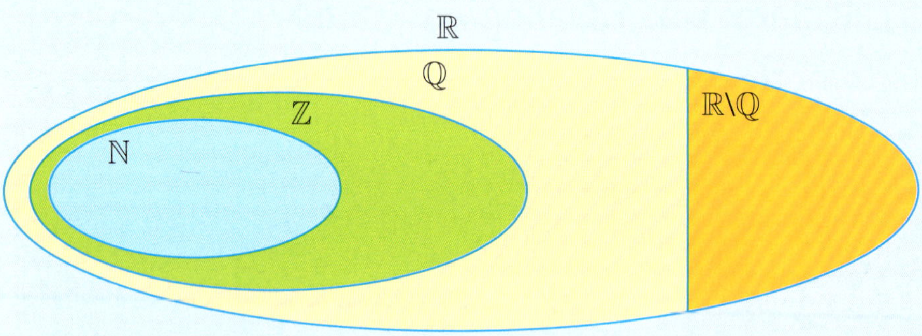

Solution

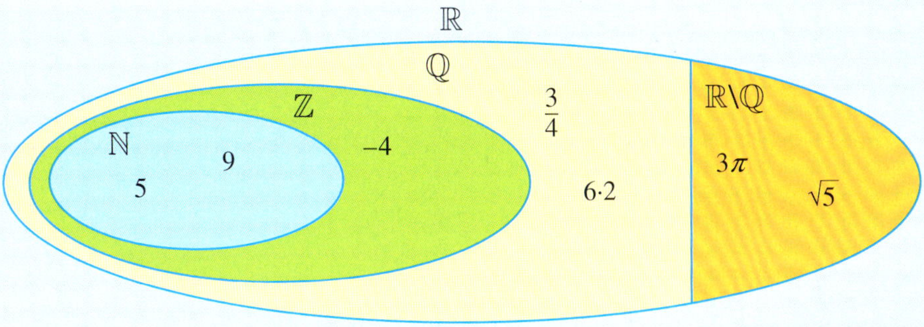

Example

Identify which sets each number belongs to by ticking (✓) the appropriate box(es).

Number/ Set	($\mathbb{N}$)	($\mathbb{Z}$)	($\mathbb{Q}$)	($\mathbb{R}\backslash\mathbb{Q}$)	($\mathbb{R}$)
-7					
$\frac{1}{4}$					
π					
$\sqrt{2}$					
10					

Solution

Number/ Set	($\mathbb{N}$)	($\mathbb{Z}$)	($\mathbb{Q}$)	($\mathbb{R}\backslash\mathbb{Q}$)	($\mathbb{R}$)
-7		✓	✓		✓
$\frac{1}{4}$			✓		✓
π				✓	✓
$\sqrt{2}$				✓	✓
10	✓	✓	✓		✓

Note: A number can never be both rational ($\mathbb{Q}$) and irrational ($\mathbb{R}\backslash\mathbb{Q}$).

Example

Place the following numbers in order, starting with the smallest: $\frac{9}{5}$, $\sqrt{3}$, $1\frac{3}{4}$, 1·7.

Solution

The easiest method is to convert all the numbers into decimal form and reorder them accordingly.

$\frac{9}{5} = 1{\cdot}8, \sqrt{3} = 1{\cdot}73..., 1\frac{3}{4} = 1{\cdot}75$ and 1·7

The numbers, in order, are: 1·7, $\sqrt{3}$, $1\frac{3}{4}$, $\frac{9}{5}$

Order of operations

Points to note

Order of operations applied to all the different number systems:
The **order of operations** is very important when we come across a sum that has multiple operations.
We must follow these steps:

1 Brackets
2 Indices (powers)
3 and 4 Multiplication and division (they hold equal importance)
5 and 6 Addition and subtraction (they hold equal importance).

There are many different acronyms for remembering the sequence.
Here are two which are commonly used.

1st	2nd	3rd and 4th		5th and 6th	
B	**I**	**M**	**D**	**A**	**S**
Brackets	Indices (powers)	Multiplication	Division	Addition	Subtraction

1st	2nd	3rd	4th and 5th		6th and 7th	
B	**I**	**R**	**D**	**M**	**A**	**S**
Brackets	Indices	Roots	Division	Multiplication	Addition	Subtraction

Example

Insert brackets into each of the following statements to make them true.
You may need more than one pair of brackets in some of the statements.

(a) $10 + 6 \div 2 + 2 = 10$ **(b)** $10 + 6 \div 2 + 2 = 4$ **(c)** $10 + 6 \div 2 + 2 = 15$

Solution

Using the acronym BIMDAS:

(a) $(10 + 6) \div 2 + 2 = 10$ **(b)** $(10 + 6) \div (2 + 2) = 4$ **(c)** $10 + (6 \div 2) + 2 = 15$

Example

Evaluate $7 \times 5 + (10 - 2)^2 - 9$, without using a calculator.

Solution

$7 \times 5 + (10 - 2)^2 - 9$	Step 1: Brackets.
$= 7 \times 5 + (8)^2 - 9$	Step 2: Indices (powers).
$= 7 \times 5 + 64 - 9$	Steps 3 and 4: Multiplication and division.
$= 35 + 64 - 9$	Steps 5 and 6: Addition and subtraction.
$= 99 - 9$	
$= 90$	

Example

Find the value of $\frac{3}{2} \times \frac{5}{6} - \left(\frac{2}{3} - \frac{1}{2}\right)^2$ without using a calculator.

Solution

$\frac{3}{2} \times \frac{5}{6} - \left(\frac{2}{3} - \frac{1}{2}\right)^2$ Step 1: Brackets first. The LCM is 6.

$= \frac{3}{2} \times \frac{5}{6} - \left(\frac{4}{6} - \frac{3}{6}\right)^2$

$= \frac{3}{2} \times \frac{5}{6} - \left(\frac{1}{6}\right)^2$ Step 2: Indices (powers).

$= \left(\frac{3}{2} \times \frac{5}{6}\right) - \frac{1}{36}$ Steps 3 and 4: Multiplication and division.

$= \left(\frac{3 \times 5}{2 \times 6}\right) - \frac{1}{36}$

$= \frac{15}{12} - \frac{1}{36}$ Steps 5 and 6: Addition and subtraction. The LCM is 36.

$= \frac{45}{36} - \frac{1}{36}$

$= \frac{44}{36} = \frac{11}{9} = 1\frac{2}{9}$

Exercise

Q1 Insert brackets into each of the following statements to make them true.

(a) $2 + 4 \div 2 - 1 = 6$ **(b)** $2 + 4 \div 2 - 1 = 2$ **(c)** $2 + 4 \div 2 - 1 = 3$

Q2 (a) Write each of the following numbers as a product of its prime factors:

(i) 340 **(ii)** 1950 **(iii)** 2100

(b) Find the HCF of each of the following:

(i) 34, 48 and 52 **(ii)** 70, 105 and 126 **(iii)** 248, 320 and 364

Q3 Classify each of the following numbers by placing a tick (✓) in the appropriate columns:

Number	Natural	Integer	Rational	Irrational	Real
$\frac{1}{6}$					
$\frac{\pi}{6}$					
6					
−6					
$\sqrt{6}$					

Q4 Thomas has a sheet of metal which is 234 cm by 156 cm. He wants to cut it up into squares as large as possible. What is the length of each side of the largest possible square that can be cut out, given that Thomas wants no waste?

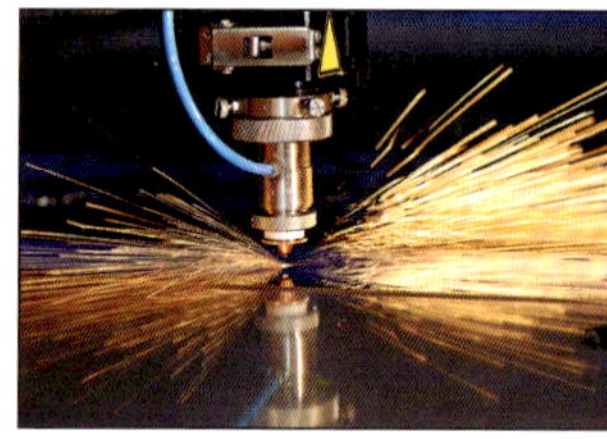

Q5 (a) Find the LCM for each of the following:

(i) 4, 6 and 8 **(ii)** 12, 18 and 24 **(iii)** 8, 7 and 21

(b) Ciara is organising a party and wants to buy plastic plates, cups and cutlery. She can buy the plates in packs of 12, the cups in packs of 8 and the cutlery in packs of 7. What is the lowest number of plates needed, such that she has the same number of each item with none left over?

Q6 Evaluate the following without the aid of a calculator.

(a) $3 + 2 \times 4 \div 2(5 - 3)^2 + (4 + 2 \times 3)$

(b) $\dfrac{3(1 + 4)^2 - 5}{9 - 4}$

(c) $\left(\dfrac{3}{2} \div \dfrac{2}{3}\right)^2 - \dfrac{3}{4} \times \dfrac{5}{2} + \dfrac{1}{8}$

Q7 (a) Copy the Venn diagram twice.

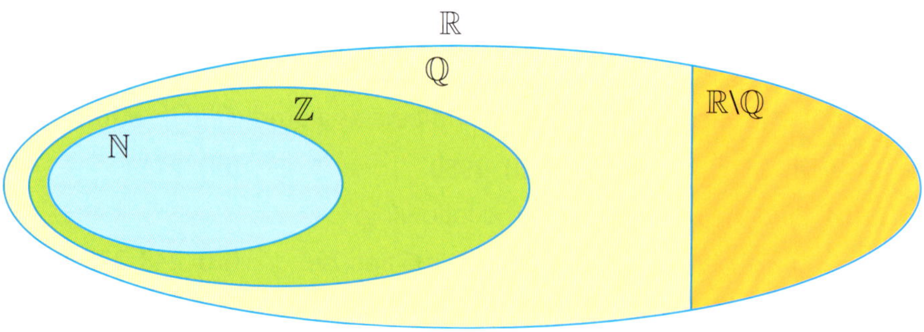

Insert each of the following numbers in the correct place on each diagram:

(i) $-\frac{4}{7}, 9, \sqrt{10}, \frac{\pi}{2}, 0, -20$ and 11 **(ii)** $-8{\cdot}2,\ 10, \frac{7}{1}, \frac{6}{7}, \pi^2, 5\sqrt{2}$ and 9^{-1}

(b) Simplify each of the following surds:

(i) $\sqrt{150}$ **(ii)** $\sqrt{112} - \sqrt{63} + \sqrt{28}$ **(iii)** $\sqrt{2}(4 + 2\sqrt{2})$

Q8 **(a)** Place each set of numbers in order, starting with the smallest:

(i) $3{\cdot}5, \frac{17}{5}, 2\sqrt{3}$ **(ii)** $2\pi, 3\sqrt{5}, \frac{20}{3}$

(b) Simplify each of the following:

(i) $\frac{9}{10} + \frac{5}{6}$ **(ii)** $\frac{9}{10} - \frac{5}{6}$ **(iii)** $\frac{9}{10} \times \frac{5}{6}$ **(iv)** $\frac{9}{10} \div \frac{5}{6}$

Solutions

Q1 **(a)** $2 + 4 \div (2 - 1) = 6$

(b) $(2 + 4) \div 2 - 1 = 2$

(c) $2 + (4 \div 2) - 1 = 3$

Q2 **(a)** **(i)** 340

$$\begin{array}{r|r} 2 & 340 \\ 2 & 170 \\ 5 & 85 \\ 17 & 17 \\ & 1 \end{array}$$

340 as a product of primes is: $2^2 \times 5 \times 17$

(ii) 1950

$$\begin{array}{r|r} 2 & 1950 \\ 3 & 975 \\ 5 & 325 \\ 5 & 65 \\ 13 & 13 \\ & 1 \end{array}$$

1950 as a product of primes is: $2 \times 3 \times 5^2 \times 13$

(iii) 2100

$$\begin{array}{r|r} 2 & 2100 \\ 2 & 1050 \\ 3 & 525 \\ 5 & 175 \\ 5 & 35 \\ 7 & 7 \\ & 1 \end{array}$$

2100 as a product of primes is: $2^2 \times 3 \times 5^2 \times 7$

(b) **(i)** 34, 48 and 52:

Factors of 34 are: 1, **2**, 17, 34.

Factors of 48 are: 1, **2**, 3, 4, 6, 8, 12, 16, 24, 48.

Factors of 52 are: 1, **2**, 4, 13, 26, 52.

Therefore the HCF is **2**.

(ii) 70, 105 and 126:

Factors of 70 are: 1, 2, 5, **7**, 10, 14, 35, 70.

Factors of 105 are: 1, 3, 5, **7**, 15, 21, 35, 105.

Factors of 126 are: 1, 2, 3, 6, **7**, 9, 14, 18, 21, 42, 63, 126.

Therefore the HCF is **7**.

(iii) 248, 320 and 364:

Factors of 248 are: 1, 2, **4**, 8, 31, 62, 124, 248.

Factors of 320 are: 1, 2, **4**, 5, 8, 10, 16, 20, 32, 40, 64, 80, 160, 320.

Factors of 364 are: 1, 2, **4**, 7, 13, 14, 26, 28, 52, 91, 182, 364.

Therefore the HCF is **4**.

Q3

Number	Natural	Integer	Rational	Irrational	Real
$\frac{1}{6}$			✓		✓
$\frac{\pi}{6}$				✓	✓
6	✓	✓	✓		✓
−6		✓	✓		✓
$\sqrt{6}$				✓	✓

Q4 • Find the prime factors of each number.

$$\begin{array}{r|r} 2 & 234 \\ 3 & 117 \\ 3 & 39 \\ 13 & 13 \\ & 1 \end{array} \qquad \begin{array}{r|r} 2 & 156 \\ 2 & 78 \\ 3 & 39 \\ 13 & 13 \\ & 1 \end{array}$$

• Write each number as a product of its prime factors.

$234 = 2 \times 3^2 \times 13$

$156 = 2^2 \times 3 \times 13$

• Choose the common prime factors with the lowest power.

$234 = \boxed{2} \times 3^2 \times \boxed{13}$

$156 = 2^2 \times \boxed{3} \times 13$

The common prime factors with the lowest powers are: 2, 3 and 13.

• To get the HCF, multiply the common prime factors with the lowest powers.

$\text{HCF} = 2 \times 3 \times 13 = 78$

This means that 78 cm is the length of one of the sides of the largest possible square that can be cut out.

Q5 (a) (i) 4, 6 and 8:

Multiples of 4 are 4, 8, 12, 16, 20, 24, 28, 32, …

Multiples of 6 are 6, 12, 18, 24, 30, 36, 42, …

Multiples of 8 are 8, 16, 24, …

The LCM of 4, 6 and 8 is 24.

(ii) 12, 18 and 24:

Multiples of 12 are 12, 24, 36, 48, 60, 72, 84, 96, …

Multiples of 18 are 18, 36, 54, 72, 90, 108, …

Multiples of 24 are 24, 48, 72, …

The LCM of 12, 18 and 24 is 72.

(iii) $8 = 2 \times 2 \times 2 = \boxed{2^3}$

$7 = 1 \times \boxed{7}$

$21 = \boxed{3} \times 7$

The common prime factors to their highest powers are: 2^3, 3 and 7.

The LCM of 8, 7 and 21 is $2^3 \times 3 \times 7 = 168$.

(b) • Write each number as a product of its prime factors.

$12 = 2 \times 2 \times 3 = 2^2 \times 3$

$8 = 2 \times 2 \times 2 = 2^3$

$7 = 7 \times 1$

• Write down each prime factor to its highest power as it appears as a prime factor of any of the numbers in the question.

$12 = 2 \times 2 \times 3 = 2^2 \times \boxed{3}$

$8 = 2 \times 2 \times 2 = \boxed{2^3}$

$7 = \boxed{7} \times 1$

The common prime factors to its highest power are: 2^3, 3 and 7.

• To get the LCM, multiply all these prime factors.
LCM is $2^3 \times 3 \times 7 = 168$.

This means that Ciara would have to buy 168 plates.

Q6 (a) $3 + 2 \times 4 \div 2(5 - 3)^2 + (4 + 2 \times 3)$ Step 1: Brackets.

$= 3 + 2 \times 4 \div 2(2)^2 + (4 + (2 \times 3))$

$= 3 + 2 \times 4 \div 2(2)^2 + (4 + 6)$ Step 2: Indices (powers).

$= 3 + 2 \times 4 \div 2(4) + (4 + 6)$ Steps 3 and 4: Multiplication and division.

$= 3 + 1 + 4 + 6$ Steps 5 and 6: Addition and subtraction.

$= 14$

(b) $\dfrac{3(1 + 4)^2 - 5}{9 - 4}$ Step 1: Brackets.

$= \dfrac{3(5)^2 - 5}{9 - 4}$ Step 2: Indices (powers).

$= \dfrac{3(25) - 5}{9 - 4}$

$= \dfrac{75 - 5}{9 - 4}$ Steps 3 and 4: Multiplication and division.

$= \dfrac{70}{5}$ Steps 5 and 6: Addition and subtraction.

$= 14$ Simplify.

(c) $\left(\frac{3}{2} \div \frac{2}{3}\right)^2 - \frac{3}{4} \times \frac{5}{2} + \frac{1}{8}$ Step 1: Brackets.

$= \left(\frac{3}{2} \times \frac{3}{2}\right)^2 - \frac{3}{4} \times \frac{5}{2} + \frac{1}{8}$ Step 2: Indices (powers).

$= \left(\frac{9}{4}\right)^2 - \frac{3}{4} \times \frac{5}{2} + \frac{1}{8}$

$= \frac{81}{16} - \frac{3}{4} \times \frac{5}{2} + \frac{1}{8}$ Steps 3 and 4: Multiplication and division.

$= \frac{81}{16} - \left(\frac{3}{4} \times \frac{5}{2}\right) + \frac{1}{8}$

$= \frac{81}{16} - \left(\frac{15}{8}\right) + \frac{1}{8}$ Steps 5 and 6: Addition and subtraction (LCM 16).

$= \frac{81}{16} - \frac{14}{8}$

$= \frac{53}{16} = 3\frac{5}{16}$

Q7 (a) (i)

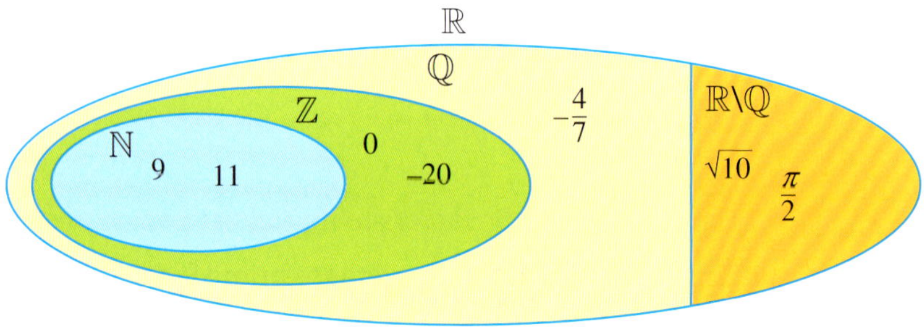

(ii)

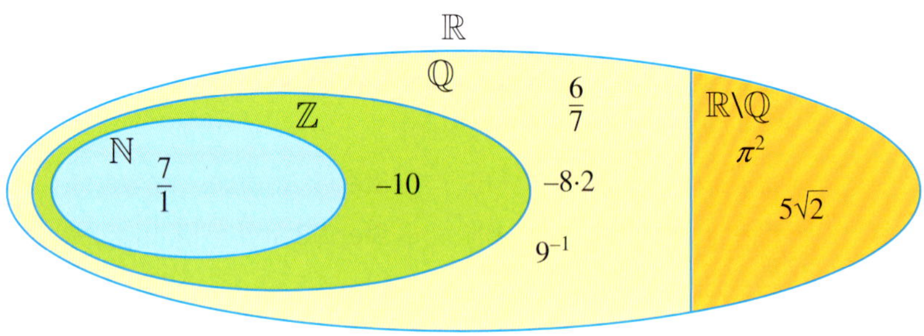

(b) (i) $\sqrt{150}$ Get factors such that one of the factors is a square number.

$= \sqrt{25 \times 6}$

$= \sqrt{25} \times \sqrt{6}$ Simplify $\sqrt{25}$.

$= 5\sqrt{6}$

(ii) $\sqrt{112} - \sqrt{63} + \sqrt{28}$ — Get factors such that one of the factors is a square number in each term.

$= \sqrt{16 \times 7} - \sqrt{9 \times 7} + \sqrt{4 \times 7}$ — Simplify $\sqrt{16}$, $\sqrt{9}$ and $\sqrt{4}$.

$= 4\sqrt{7} - 3\sqrt{7} + 2\sqrt{7}$ — Simplify again.

$= 3\sqrt{7}$

(iii) $\sqrt{2}(4 + 2\sqrt{2})$

$= \sqrt{2}(4) + \sqrt{2}\left(2\sqrt{2}\right)$ — Simplify using $\sqrt{2} \times \sqrt{2} = 2$.

$= 4\sqrt{2} + 4$

Q8 (a) (i) $3{\cdot}5$, $\frac{17}{5} = 3{\cdot}4\ldots$ and $2\sqrt{3} = 3{\cdot}4641$ — Write as decimals.

$\frac{17}{5}, 2\sqrt{3}, 3{\cdot}5$ — Reorder.

(ii) $2\pi = 6{\cdot}283\ldots$, $3\sqrt{5} = 6{\cdot}708\ldots$ and

$\frac{20}{3} = 6{\cdot}667$ — Write as decimals.

$2\pi, \frac{20}{3}, 3\sqrt{5}$ — Reorder.

(b) (i) $\frac{9}{10} + \frac{5}{6}$ (LCM = 30)

$= \frac{3(9)}{30} + \frac{5(5)}{30}$

$= \frac{27}{30} + \frac{25}{30}$

$= \frac{27 + 25}{30}$

$= \frac{52}{30} = 1\frac{22}{30} = 1\frac{11}{15}$

(ii) $\frac{9}{10} - \frac{5}{6}$ (LCM = 30)

$= \frac{3(9)}{30} - \frac{5(5)}{30}$

$= \frac{27}{30} - \frac{25}{30}$

$= \frac{27 - 25}{30}$

$= \frac{2}{30} = \frac{1}{15}$

(iii) $\frac{9}{10} \times \frac{5}{6} = \frac{9 \times 5}{10 \times 6} = \frac{45}{60} = \frac{3}{4}$

(iv) $\frac{9}{10} \div \frac{5}{6} = \frac{9}{10} \times \frac{6}{5} = \frac{54}{50} = \frac{27}{25}$

2 Applied Arithmetic 1

Learning objectives

In this chapter you will learn about:

- Working with percentages
- Decimals
- Estimation, rounding and significant figures
- Scientific notation
- Order of magnitude
- Ratios
- Speed.

Percentages

To find a **percentage** means to divide the whole into 100 equal parts; the whole can be a representation of anything, such as money, exam results, area, volume, weight, work, time, etc.

Working with percentages

Top Tip

To find a percentage of a given quantity, follow these steps:

1 Change the required percentage into a decimal or fraction.

2 Multiply the decimal or fraction by the given quantity.

Alternatively, you can use the % button on a calculator. The example below is for a Casio calculator.

To calculate 20% of 500 using the % button, press [2] [0] [SHIFT] [(] [×] [5] [0] [0] [=]

Answer: 100

	Examples	Solutions
1	Find 15% of €340.	15% × 340 = €51
2	Find 28% of 170 cm.	28% × 170 = 47·6 cm
3	Find 66% of 8·8 kg.	66% × 8·8 = 5·808 kg
4	Find 12·5% of 5000 people.	12·5% × 5000 = 625 people

Top Tip

To find one value as a percentage of another:

1 Write the value as a fraction (always make sure the units are the same).

2 Multiply the fraction by 100%.

Link

This section links directly with the compound interest formula in Chapter 11.

Example

Mark got 135 out of 250 marks in a maths test. What percentage did he get in the test?

Solution

1 Write the values as a fraction (always make sure the units are the same).

135 out of 250 marks as a fraction = $\frac{135}{250}$

2 Multiply the fraction by 100%.

$\frac{135}{250} \times 100\% = 54\%$.

Therefore, Mark got 54% in his maths test.

Percentage increase and decrease

Top Tip

To calculate the percentage increase or decrease, we can use either of the methods listed below.

Method 1: Formula method

1 Calculate the difference between the two values given (increase or decrease amount).

2 To calculate the % increase or % decrease, substitute all known values into the formula below:

$$\% \text{ increase/decrease} = \frac{\text{increase/decrease amount}}{\text{orignal amount}} \times 100\%$$

Method 2: Calculator method

To increase $2300 by 18%	To decrease $2300 by 18%
(100% + 18% = 118%)	(100% – 18% = 82%)
Press [1][1][8]	Press [8][2]
Press [SHIFT][(] to get the (%).	Press [SHIFT][(] to get the (%).
Press [×][2][3][0][0][=]	Press [×][2][3][0][0][=]
Answer: $2714	Answer: $1886

Example

An estate agent sold a house five years ago for €225 000. She is now selling the same house for €193 500. What is the percentage decrease in value of the house?

Solution

1 Calculate the difference between the two values given (increase or decrease amount).

Decrease amount = €225 000 – €193 500 = €31 500

2 Fill all information into the formula to find the % decrease.

$$\% \text{ decrease} = \frac{€31\,500}{€225\,000} \times 100\% = 14\%$$

Therefore, the house has decreased in value by 14%.

Decimals

Decimals are real numbers ($\mathbb{R}$). This means that natural numbers ($\mathbb{N}$), integers ($\mathbb{Z}$), rational numbers ($\mathbb{Q}$) and irrational numbers ($\mathbb{R}\backslash\mathbb{Q}$) can all be written as decimals.

$$34.6349 = 30 + 4 + \frac{6}{10} + \frac{3}{100} + \frac{4}{1000} + \frac{9}{10\,000}$$

Estimation or approximation

When we **estimate** or **approximate** a number, we are finding a number which is close to the original number within some degree of accuracy.

Rounding

Rounding is just another way of estimating. Rounding makes a number easier to work with, by keeping its value close to what its original value was, to some degree of accuracy.

Top Tip

Rules for rounding decimals

1 Identify the digit just to the right of the place value (the rounding digit).

2 Depending on the value of this digit, either:

- Round down. This means that if the digit is 0, 1, 2, 3, or 4 we do not change the value of the rounding digit, and we ignore all the digits to the right of it.

or

- Round up. This means that if the digit is 5, 6, 7, 8 or 9, we must add one to the rounding digit and ignore all digits to the right of it.

For example, for the number 3·245794:

Round to the nearest whole number	Round correct to 1 decimal place	Round correct to 2 decimal places	Round correct to 3 decimal places
3·245794	3·**24**5794	3·2**45**794	3·24**57**94
The rounding digit is **2**, so leave the place value digit (**3**) as it is, and ignore all numbers to the right of it. Thus 3·245794 rounded to the nearest whole number is 3.	The rounding digit is **4**, so leave the place value digit (**2**) as it is and ignore all numbers to the right of it. Thus 3·245794 rounded to 1 decimal place is 3·2.	The rounding digit is **5**, so increase the place value digit (**4**) by 1, and ignore all numbers to the right of it. Thus 3·245794 rounded to 2 decimal places is 3·25.	The rounding digit is **7**, so increase the place value digit (**5**) by 1, and ignore all numbers to the right of it. Thus 3·245794 rounded to 3 decimal places is 3·246.

Example

(a) By rounding each decimal to the nearest whole number, estimate the value of $(6{\cdot}05 - 1{\cdot}12)^2 + \frac{8{\cdot}23}{1{\cdot}92} - \sqrt{15{\cdot}89}\,(3{\cdot}12)$.

(b) Evaluate the value correct to two decimal places.

Solution

Top Tip!

We can find the answer by putting the entire sum directly into a calculator. Be careful to include all brackets and powers!

(a) Estimate:

$(6{\cdot}05 - 1{\cdot}12)^2 + \frac{8{\cdot}23}{1{\cdot}92} - \sqrt{15{\cdot}89}\,(3{\cdot}12)$

$\approx (6 - 1)^2 + \frac{8}{2} - \sqrt{16}\,(3)$ Round each decimal to the nearest whole number.

$= (5)^2 + \frac{8}{2} - (4)(3)$ Follow the rules of BIRDMAS.

$= 25 + 4 - 12$

$= 29 - 12 = 17$

(b) Evaluate correct to two decimal places:

$(6{\cdot}05 - 1{\cdot}12)^2 + \frac{8{\cdot}23}{1{\cdot}92} - \sqrt{15{\cdot}89}\,(3{\cdot}12)$ Follow the rules of BIRDMAS.

$\approx (4{\cdot}93)^2 + 4{\cdot}2865 - 12{\cdot}4370$

$= 24{\cdot}3049 + 4{\cdot}2865 - 12{\cdot}4370$ Round to four decimal places only, to ensure accuracy in the final result.

$= 28{\cdot}5914 - 12{\cdot}4370 = 16{\cdot}1544 = 16{\cdot}15$, correct to 2 d.p.

Note: If we put the entire sum directly into a calculator the answer is 16·15433232 which rounds to 16·15, correct to two decimal places.

Significant figures

Writing a value to a required number of **significant figures** is, again, just another way of estimating, which makes a number easier to work with by keeping its value close to the original value.

Top Tip

To round a number to a given number of significant figures:

1 Identify the digit just to the right of the place value (the rounding digit).

2 Depending on the value of this digit, we either:

- Round down. This means that if this digit is 0, 1, 2, 3 or 4, we do not change the value of the rounding digit and we change all the digits to the right of it to zero.

or

- Round up. This means that if this digit is 5, 6, 7, 8 or 9, we must add one to the rounding digit and change the digits to the right of it to zero.

Number	Round to 1 significant figure	Round to 2 significant figures	Round to 3 significant figures	Round to 4 significant figures
23 368	2(3)368 Round down to 20000	23(3)68 Round down to 23 000	233(6)8 Round up to 23 400	2336(8) Round up to 23 370
0·00345192	0·003(4)5192 Round down to 0·003	0·0034(5)192 Round up to 0·0035	0·00345(1)92 Round down to 0·00345	0·003451(9)2 Round up to 0·003452

Rules for working out if a digit in the number is a significant figure		
	Rule	**Examples**
1	All non-zero digits are significant.	473 has 3 significant figures 94·38 has 4 significant figures 12 341 has 5 significant figures
2	All leading zeros are not significant.	0·041 has 2 significant figures 0·343 has 3 significant figures 0·0000321 has 3 significant figures
3	All zeros between two significant digits are significant.	103 has 3 significant figures 40 034 has 5 significant figures 97·3023 has 6 significant figures
4	A final zero or trailing zeros are not significant.	1 000 000 has 1 significant figure 23 000 has 2 significant figures 1 345 000 has 4 significant figures

Scientific notation

Scientific notation or **index notation** is a way of making very large and very small numbers easier to work with.

Scientific notation is expressed in the form:

$$a \times 10^n$$

where $1 \le a < 10$, and n is an integer ($\mathbb{Z}$).

Number	Method Move the decimal point to get a, where $1 \le a < 10$	Scientific notation
0·000 000 005 6	Move the decimal point 9 spaces to the right to get 5·6.	$5{\cdot}6 \times 10^{-9}$
0·000 056	Move the decimal point 5 spaces to the right to get 5·6.	$5{\cdot}6 \times 10^{-5}$
0·056	Move the decimal point 2 spaces to the right to get 5·6.	$5{\cdot}6 \times 10^{-2}$
56	Move the decimal point 1 space to the left to get 5·6.	$5{\cdot}6 \times 10^{1}$
5600	Move the decimal point 3 spaces to the left to get 5·6.	$5{\cdot}6 \times 10^{3}$
5 600 000	Move the decimal point 6 spaces to the left to get 5·6.	$5{\cdot}6 \times 10^{6}$

Top Tip

When adding or subtracting numbers in scientific notation, we can use either of the two methods listed below:

Method 1

1 Write the number in decimal form, then add or subtract numbers.

2 Rewrite your answer in scientific notation.

Method 2: Calculator method (Casio)

This method is shown in the example on the next page.

Example

Evaluate $4{\cdot}56 \times 10^9 + 2{\cdot}34 \times 10^7$.

Give your answer in the form $a \times 10^n$ where $n \in \mathbb{Z}$, and $1 \leq a < 10$.

Solution

Method 1

1 Write each number in decimal form then add the numbers together.

$4{\cdot}56 \times 10^9 + 2{\cdot}34 \times 10^7$

$= 4\,560\,000\,000 + 23\,400\,000$

$= 4\,583\,400\,000$

2 Rewrite your answer in scientific notation.

$4\,583\,400\,000 = 4{\cdot}5834 \times 10^9$

Method 2: Calculator method (Casio)

Press [4] [·] [5] [6] [10^x] [9] [+]
[2] [·] [3] [4] [10^x] [7] [=]

Answer: $4\,583\,400\,000 = 4{\cdot}5834 \times 10^9$

Top Tip

When multiplying or dividing numbers in scientific notation, we can use either of the two methods below:

Method 1

1 Multiply or divide the decimal parts of each number and use the rules of indices to multiply or divide the index parts of each number.

2 Write your answer in scientific notation.

Method 2: Calculator method (Casio)

This method is shown in the example below.

Example

Evaluate each of the following:

(a) $9{\cdot}78 \times 10^8 \times 3{\cdot}12 \times 10^6$

(b) $\dfrac{4{\cdot}56 \times 10^9}{2{\cdot}34 \times 10^7}$

Give your answers correct to two decimal places in the form $a \times 10^n$, where $n \in \mathbb{Z}$, and $1 \leq a < 10$.

Solution

(a) Method 1

1 Multiply the decimal parts of each number and use the rules of indices to multiply the index parts of each number.

	Decimal part	**Index part**
$9{\cdot}78 \times 10^8$	$9{\cdot}78$	10^8
$3{\cdot}12 \times 10^6$	$3{\cdot}12$	10^6
Multiply	$9{\cdot}78 \times 3{\cdot}12 = 30{\cdot}5136$	$10^8 \times 10^6 = 10^{8+6} = 10^{14}$

2 Write your answer in scientific notation.

$$9{\cdot}78 \times 10^8 \times 3{\cdot}12 \times 10^6 = 30{\cdot}5136 \times 10^{14}$$
$$= 3{\cdot}05136 \times 10^{15}$$
$$= 3{\cdot}05 \times 10^{15}\text{, correct to two decimal places}$$

Method 2: Calculator method (Casio)

Press [9] [·] [7] [8] [10^x] [8] [3] [·] [1] [2] [×] [10^x] [6] [=]

Answer: $3{\cdot}05136 \times 10^{15} = 3{\cdot}05 \times 10^{15}$, correct to two decimal places

(b) Method 1

1 Divide the decimal parts of each number and use the rules of indices to divide the index parts of each number.

	Decimal part	**Index part**
$4{\cdot}56 \times 10^9$	$4{\cdot}56$	10^9
$2{\cdot}34 \times 10^7$	$2{\cdot}34$	10^7
Divide	$\frac{4{\cdot}56}{2{\cdot}34} = 1{\cdot}9487...$	$\frac{10^9}{10^7} = 10^{9-7} = 10^2$

2 Write your answer in scientific notation.

$$\frac{4{\cdot}56 \times 10^9}{2{\cdot}34 \times 10^7} = 1{\cdot}9487... \times 10^2$$
$$= 1{\cdot}95 \times 10^2\text{, correct to two decimal places}$$

Method 2: Calculator method (Casio)

Press [4] [·] [5] [6] [10^x] [9] [÷] [2] [·] [3] [4] [10^x] [7] [=]

Answer: $194{\cdot}8718... = 1{\cdot}9487 \times 10^2 = 1{\cdot}95 \times 10^2$, correct to two decimal places

Order of magnitude

The **order of magnitude** is an estimate of the size of a number, found by estimating the number as a power of 10.

Number	Scientific notation	Power of 10	Order of magnitude
0·000 000 000 003 4	$3{\cdot}4 \times 10^{-12}$	10^{-12}	−12
0·000 000 034	$3{\cdot}4 \times 10^{-8}$	10^{-8}	−8
0·0034	$3{\cdot}4 \times 10^{-3}$	10^{-3}	−3
3400	$3{\cdot}4 \times 10^{3}$	10^{3}	3
3 400 000	$3{\cdot}4 \times 10^{6}$	10^{6}	6
340 000 000 000 000	$3{\cdot}4 \times 10^{14}$	10^{14}	14

We can use the order of magnitude when comparing numbers of different size.

Example

Earth's mass is $5{\cdot}972 \times 10^{24}$ kg and the Sun's mass is $1{\cdot}989 \times 10^{30}$ kg.

Find the difference in the order of magnitude of the mass of the Sun and the mass of the Earth.

Solution

Round each number to the nearest power of 10.

Earth's mass is $5{\cdot}972 \times 10^{24}$ kg Round up.

$10^1 \times 10^{24}$ kg $= 10^{25}$ kg

Sun's mass is $1{\cdot}989 \times 10^{30}$ kg Round down.

$10^0 \times 10^{30}$ kg $= 10^{30}$ kg

Divide the larger number by the smaller number.

$$\frac{10^{30}}{10^{25}} = 10^{30-25} = 10^5$$

Therefore, the masses of the Earth and the Sun differ by 5 orders of magnitude.

Ratios

A **ratio** is a comparison of the size of one number in relation to the size of another number. When finding equivalent ratios, always multiply or divide the numbers by the same value.

Ratio	Equivalent ratio	
9 : 12	3 : 4	Divide each part by 3.
50 : 30	5 : 3	Divide each part by 10.
0·5 : 3	1 : 6	Multiply each part by 2.

Example

Divide 3445 g in the ratio $\frac{1}{2}:\frac{1}{3}:\frac{1}{4}$.

Solution

When dealing with fractions, the easiest method is to convert each fraction to a whole number. To do this we need to find the LCM and multiply it by each part.

$\frac{1}{2}:\frac{1}{3}:\frac{1}{4} = (12)\frac{1}{2} : (12)\frac{1}{3} : (12)\frac{1}{4}$ Multiply each fraction by the LCM of 2, 3 and 4, i.e. 12.

$= 6 : 4 : 3$ Simplify.

Total parts = 6 + 4 + 3 = 13 parts

Calculate each part of the ratio.

$\frac{6}{13} \times 3445\text{ g} = 1590\text{ g}$ $\frac{4}{13} \times 3445\text{ g} = 1060\text{ g}$ $\frac{3}{13} \times 3445\text{ g} = 795\text{ g}$

Hence, 3445 g divided in the ratio $\frac{1}{2}:\frac{1}{3}:\frac{1}{4}$ gives 1590 g, 1060 g and 795 g.

Example

Karl receives €4302 from an investment he made with his brother Paul.
The investment paid out Karl : Paul in the ratio 5 : 7, respectively.
How much did Paul receive from the investment?

Solution

The ratio Karl : Paul is equivalent to 5 : 7. Total number of parts = 5 + 7 = 12 parts.

Calculate how much Paul received from the investment.

Karl's part is $\frac{5}{12} = €4302$

To find the value of one part, divide by 5.

$\frac{1}{12} = \frac{€4302}{5} = €860·40$

Paul receives 7 parts:

$\frac{7}{12} = 7 \times €860·40 = €6022·80$

So Paul receives €6022·80.

Speed

Speed is the measurement of how fast an object moves from one place to another. Speed is measured in km per hour (km/h) or m/s.

Average speed

The average speed of an object is found by dividing the total distance travelled by the total time taken for the journey.

Top Tip

We can use the following triangle to help remember these formulae.

Speed = $\frac{\text{distance}}{\text{time}}$ $\left(S = \frac{D}{T}\right)$ Cover speed with your thumb to find the formula.

Time = $\frac{\text{distance}}{\text{speed}}$ $\left(T = \frac{D}{S}\right)$ Cover time with your thumb to find the formula.

Distance = speed × time ($D = S \times T$) Cover distance with your thumb to find the formula.

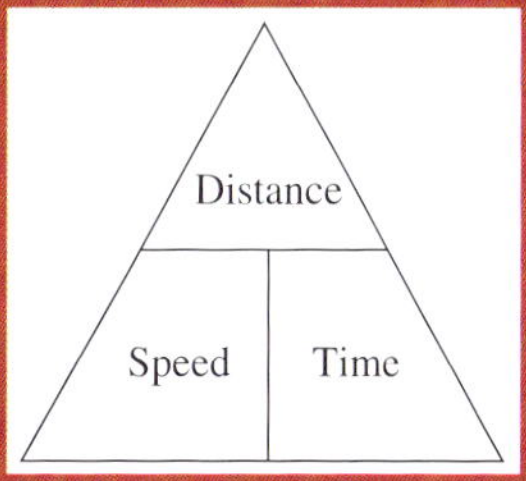

where:

S = speed (metres/second or kilometres per hour)

D = distance travelled (metres or kilometres)

T = time (seconds or hours).

Link

This section is related to speed–time graphs in Chapter 15.

Example

Pat left his house at 9:45 am to make a delivery to Cork and then to Limerick. He travelled at an average speed of 65 km/h for $1\frac{1}{2}$ hours to get to Cork. He then travelled for 125 km at an average speed of 60 km/h to get to Limerick.

(a) What is the distance travelled from Pat's house to Cork?

(b) How long did it take Pat to travel from Cork to Limerick?

(c) If Pat spent two hours in Cork before going to Limerick, at what time did he arrive in Limerick?

Solution

(a) Using the formula:

$$\text{Distance} = \text{speed} \times \text{time}$$
$$= 65 \times 1\tfrac{1}{2} = 97{\cdot}5 \text{ km}$$

(b) Using the formula:

$$\text{Time} = \frac{\text{distance}}{\text{speed}}$$
$$= \frac{125}{60} = 2\frac{1}{12} \text{ hr} = 2 \text{ h} + \left(60 \times \frac{1}{12}\right) \text{min} = 2 \text{ hours } 5 \text{ minutes}$$

(c) Taking into account the two hours Pat spent in Cork before going to Limerick:

Total time = 1·5 hours + 2 hours + 2 hours 5 minutes = 5 hour 35 minutes

Arrival time = 9:45 am + 5 hour 35 minutes = 15:20 = 3:20 pm

Example

The speed limit on a section of a motorway has been reduced to 60 km/h. Express this new speed limit in metres per second.

Solution

Note: 1 km = 1000 m, and 1 hour = 3600 seconds

Convert units:

60 km = 60 × 1000 = 60 000 m

1 hour = 60 × 60 seconds = 3600 seconds

$$\text{Speed} = \frac{\text{distance}}{\text{time}} = \frac{60\,000}{3600} = 16{\cdot}\dot{6}\dot{6} \text{ m/s} \approx 16{\cdot}67 \text{ m/s}$$

Exercise

Q1 Calculate each of the following, correct to the nearest whole number percentage:

(a) 38 cents as a percentage of €2·50

(b) 50 seconds as a percentage of 3 minutes

(c) 15 kg as a percentage of 75 kg.

Q2 (a) A company decides to increase its workforce from 1200 staff to 1450 staff over the coming year. What is the percentage increase in staff?

(b) A hairdresser offers '12% off' all haircuts for students. If the normal cost of a student's haircut is €22, what is the new price?

(c) Ciara sells 42 cupcakes in one day, which represents 21% of her stock. How many cupcakes did Ciara have at the start of the day?

Q3 (a) By rounding correct to the nearest whole number, estimate the value of $\frac{(10{\cdot}21)^2}{4{\cdot}91}(9{\cdot}98) - \sqrt{3{\cdot}81}(6{\cdot}13)^2$.

Then evaluate the value correct to one decimal place.

(b) By rounding correct to the nearest whole number, estimate the value of

$$\frac{\sqrt{35{\cdot}91}(6{\cdot}16) + 17{\cdot}94 - (4{\cdot}12)^2}{(3{\cdot}89)^3 - 7{\cdot}32}.$$

Then evaluate the value correct to two decimal places.

Q4 Given that $x = 1{\cdot}234 \times 10^5$, $y = 3{\cdot}241 \times 10^4$ and $z = 4{\cdot}641 \times 10^6$, evaluate each of the following:

(a) $z + 2y$

(b) $\frac{2z - x}{y}$.

Give your answers correct to two significant figures in the form $a \times 10^n$, where $n \in \mathbb{Z}$, $1 \leq a < 10$.

Q5 Answer the following questions based on the table given.

Give your answers correct to two significant figures in the form $a \times 10^n$, where $n \in \mathbb{Z}$ and $1 \leq a < 10$.

Object	Mass (kg)
Sun	$1{\cdot}9891 \times 10^{30}$
Jupiter	$1{\cdot}8986 \times 10^{27}$
Saturn	$5{\cdot}6846 \times 10^{26}$
Earth	$5{\cdot}9736 \times 10^{24}$
Mars	$6{\cdot}4185 \times 10^{23}$
Earth's moon	$7{\cdot}349 \times 10^{22}$
Pluto	$1{\cdot}25 \times 10^{22}$

(a) What are the combined masses of Jupiter, Mars and Pluto?

(b) Find the difference in the order of magnitude of the mass of Earth's moon and that of Saturn.

Q6 Divide each of the following amounts into the given ratio:

(a) €360 in the ratio 5 : 11

(b) 4494 cm in the ratio 3 : 5 : 13

(c) 3·120 kg in the ratio 3 : 6 : 11.

Q7 A prize fund pays out 1st, 2nd and 3rd prizes in the ratio 10 : 5 : 3.

The value of the 3rd prize was €1539. Calculate the value of the total prize fund.

Q8 Mark travelled a distance of 305 km from Wexford to Belfast in 3 hours and 15 minutes to collect a bedroom furniture set he bought online. He returned to Wexford with his goods using the same route, but he had to reduce his speed by 16 km/h due to the load.

(a) What was Mark's average speed when travelling from Wexford to Belfast?

(b) How much extra time did Mark take to return to Wexford?

(c) If he left Belfast at 10:40 am and travelled non-stop, what time did he arrive in Wexford?

Q9 Express 88 km/h in metres per second, correct to three decimal places.

Q10 (a) Peter and Anne share a lotto prize in the ratio $3\frac{1}{2}$ to $2\frac{1}{2}$. Peter's share is €35 000.

What is the value of the prize fund?

(b) The diameters of Venus and Saturn are $1{\cdot}21 \times 10^4$ km and $1{\cdot}21 \times 10^5$ km, respectively. What is the difference between the diameters of the two planets?

Give your answer in the form $a \times 10^n$, where $n \in \mathbb{Z}$ and $1 \leq a < 10$.

(c) By rounding to the nearest whole number, estimate the value of

$$\frac{\sqrt{(7{\cdot}17)^2 + 14{\cdot}59}}{8{\cdot}29 - 1{\cdot}64 \times 2{\cdot}23}.$$

Then find the value correct to one decimal place.

(SEC 2011)

Solutions

Q1 (a) Convert to the same unit:

38 cents

€2·50 = 250 cents

$\frac{38}{250} \times 100\% = 15{\cdot}2\% = 15\%$ to the nearest whole number

(b) Convert to the same unit:

50 seconds

3 minutes = 3 × 60 = 180 seconds

$\frac{50}{180} \times 100\% = 27{\cdot}\dot{7}\% = 28\%$ to the nearest whole number

(c) $\frac{15}{75} \times 100\% = 20\%$

Q2 (a) Increase in staff $= 1450 - 1200$ $= 250$ staff

$\% \text{ increase} = \frac{250}{1200} \times 100\%$

$= 20{\cdot}8\dot{3}\% = 20{\cdot}8\%$ to 1 d.p.

(b) '12% off' means a decrease of 12%.

$100\% - 12\% = 88\% = 0{\cdot}88$

€22 × 0·88 = €19·36

Therefore, the new price of a student's haircut is €19·36.

(c) 21% = 42 cupcakes

$1\% = \frac{42}{21} = 2$ cupcakes

100% = 2 × 100 = 200 cupcakes

Therefore, Ciara had 200 cupcakes at the start of the day.

Q3 (a) Estimate:

$$\frac{(10\cdot21)^2}{4\cdot91}(9\cdot98)-\sqrt{3\cdot81}(6\cdot13)^2$$

Round each decimal to the nearest whole number.

$$\approx\frac{(10)^2}{5}(10)-\sqrt{4}(6)^2$$

$$=\frac{100}{5}(10)-2(36)$$

Follow the rules of BIRDMAS.

$$=20(10)-72=200-72=128$$

Evaluate correct to one decimal place:

$$\frac{(10\cdot21)^2}{4\cdot91}(9\cdot98)-\sqrt{3\cdot81}(6\cdot13)^2$$

Follow the rules of BIRDMAS.

$$=\frac{104\cdot2441}{4\cdot91}(9\cdot98)-(1\cdot9519...)(37\cdot5769)$$

$$=21\cdot231(9\cdot98)-(73\cdot3472)$$

$$=211\cdot88538-73\cdot3472=138\cdot53818=138\cdot5 \text{ to 1 d.p.}$$

(b) Estimate:

$$\frac{\sqrt{35\cdot91}(6\cdot16)+17\cdot94-(4\cdot12)^2}{(3\cdot89)^3-7\cdot32}$$

Round each decimal to the nearest whole number.

$$\approx\frac{\sqrt{36}(6)+18-(4)^2}{(4)^3-7}$$

$$=\frac{6(6)+18-16}{64-7}$$

Follow the rules of BIRDMAS.

$$=\frac{36+18-16}{64-7}$$

$$=\frac{38}{57}=\frac{2}{3}=0\cdot\dot{6}\approx0\cdot7\approx1$$

Evaluate correct to two decimal places:

$$\frac{\sqrt{35\cdot91}(6\cdot16)+17\cdot94-(4\cdot12)^2}{(3\cdot89)^3-7\cdot32}$$

Follow the rules of BIRDMAS.

$$=\frac{5\cdot9925(6\cdot16)+17\cdot94-(16\cdot9744)}{58\cdot8639-7\cdot32}$$

$$=\frac{36\cdot9138+17\cdot94-16\cdot9744}{51\cdot5439}$$

$$=\frac{37\cdot8794}{51\cdot5439}=0\cdot73489...=0\cdot73 \text{ to 2 d.p.}$$

Q4 (a) $z + 2y = 4{\cdot}641 \times 10^6 + 2(3{\cdot}241 \times 10^4)$

$= 4{\cdot}641 \times 10^6 + 6{\cdot}482 \times 10^4$

- Write the number in decimal form, then add the numbers.

  $4{\cdot}641 \times 10^6 + 6{\cdot}482 \times 10^4 = 4\,641\,000 + 64\,820$

  $= 4\,705\,820$

- Rewrite your answer in scientific notation.
  $4\,705\,820 = 4{\cdot}7 \times 10^6$, correct to two significant figures

(b) $\frac{2z - x}{y} = \frac{2(4{\cdot}641 \times 10^6) - (1{\cdot}234 \times 10^5)}{3{\cdot}241 \times 10^4}$

$= \frac{(9{\cdot}282 \times 10^6) - (1{\cdot}234 \times 10^5)}{3{\cdot}241 \times 10^4}$

$= \frac{9\,282\,000 - 123\,400}{32\,410}$

$= \frac{9\,158\,600}{32\,410} = 282{\cdot}5856 = 2{\cdot}8 \times 10^2$

Q5 (a) Jupiter $= 1{\cdot}8986 \times 10^{27}$ kg

Mars $= 6{\cdot}4185 \times 10^{23}$ kg

Pluto $= 1{\cdot}25 \times 10^{22}$ kg

Combined mass $= 1{\cdot}8986 \times 10^{27} + 6{\cdot}4185 \times 10^{23} + 1{\cdot}25 \times 10^{22}$

$= 1{\cdot}8986 \times 10^{27} + 0{\cdot}000\,641\,85 \times 10^{27} + 0{\cdot}000\,012\,5 \times 10^{27}$

$= 1{\cdot}899 \times 10^{27} = 1{\cdot}9 \times 10^{27}$ kg, correct to two significant figures

(b) The moon's mass is $7{\cdot}349 \times 10^{22}$ kg and Saturn's mass is $5{\cdot}6846 \times 10^{26}$ kg.

Round each number to the nearest power of 10:

The moon's mass is $7{\cdot}349 \times 10^{22}$ kg Round up.

Mass $= 10^1 \times 10^{22}$ kg $= 10^{23}$ kg

Saturn's mass is $5{\cdot}6846 \times 10^{26}$ kg Round up.

Mass $= 10^1 \times 10^{26}$ kg $= 10^{27}$ kg

Divide the larger number by the smaller number:

$\frac{10^{27}}{10^{23}} = 10^{27-23} = 10^4$

The masses of the moon and Saturn differ by 4 orders of magnitude.

Q6 (a) €360 in the ratio 5 : 11

Total parts = 5 + 11 = 16 parts

Each portion of the ratio:

$\frac{5}{16} \times €360 = €112{\cdot}50$

$\frac{11}{16} \times €360 = €247{\cdot}50$

(b) 4494 cm in the ratio 3 : 5 : 13

Total parts = 3 + 5 + 13 = 21 parts

Each portion of the ratio:

$\frac{3}{21} \times 4494 = 642$ cm

$\frac{5}{21} \times 4494 = 1070$ cm

$\frac{13}{21} \times 4494 = 2782$ cm

(c) 3·120 kg = 3120 g

Total parts = 3 + 6 + 11 = 20 parts

Each portion of the ratio:

$\frac{3}{20} \times 3120 = 468$ g

$\frac{6}{20} \times 3120 = 936$ g

$\frac{11}{20} \times 3120 = 1716$ g

Q7 Ratio = 10 : 5 : 3

Total parts = 10 + 5 + 3 = 18 parts

Find the value of one part:

3rd prize is $\frac{3}{18} = €1539$

$\therefore \frac{1}{18} = \frac{€1539}{3} = €513$

Total prize fund is $\frac{18}{18} = €513 \times 18 = €9234$.

Q8 **(a)** Distance travelled = 305 km

Time taken = 3 hours 15 minutes = 3 hours and $\frac{15}{60}$ minutes = 3·25 h

Speed = $\frac{\text{distance}}{\text{time}} = \frac{305}{3{\cdot}25} = 93{\cdot}85 \approx 94$ km/h

(b) Distance travelled = 305 km

Reduced speed = 94 km/h − 16 km/h = 78 km/h

Time taken at this new speed:

Time = $\frac{\text{distance}}{\text{speed}} = \frac{305}{78} = 3{\cdot}9\dot{1}0256\dot{4}$

= 3·91 h = 3 hours and (0·91 × 60) minutes = 3 hours 54·6 minutes

≈ 3 hours 55 minutes

Extra time travelling on the return journey:

3 hours 55 minutes – 3 hours 15 minutes = 40 minutes

(c) 10:40 am + 3 h 55 mins = 14:35 = 2:35 pm

Q9 Convert units:

88 km = 88 × 1000 = 88 000 m

1 hour = 60 × 60 seconds = 3600 seconds

$$\text{Speed} = \frac{\text{distance}}{\text{time}} = \frac{88\,000}{3600} = 24{\cdot}\dot{4} \text{ m/s} \approx 24{\cdot}444 \text{ m/s}$$

Q10 (a) $\text{Ratio} = 3\frac{1}{2} : 2\frac{1}{2}$

$\text{Total parts} = 3\frac{1}{2} + 2\frac{1}{2} = 6$

Peter's share is €35 000, so $3\frac{1}{2}$ parts = €35 000

$$1 \text{ part} = \frac{35\,000}{3\frac{1}{2}} = €10\,000$$

Total prize fund = €10 000 × 6 = €60 000

(b) $(1{\cdot}21 \times 10^5) - (1{\cdot}21 \times 10^4) = 121\,000 - 12\,100 = 108\,900$

$= 1{\cdot}089 \times 10^5$ km

(c) Estimate:

$$\frac{\sqrt{(7{\cdot}17)^2 + 14{\cdot}59}}{8{\cdot}29 - 1{\cdot}64 \times 2{\cdot}23} = \frac{\sqrt{(7)^2 + 15}}{8 - 2 \times 2}$$

$$\approx \frac{\sqrt{64}}{4} = \frac{8}{4} = 2$$

Correct to one decimal place:

$$\frac{\sqrt{(7{\cdot}17)^2 + 14{\cdot}59}}{8{\cdot}29 - 1{\cdot}64 \times 2{\cdot}23} \approx \frac{\sqrt{51{\cdot}4089 + 14{\cdot}59}}{8{\cdot}29 - 3{\cdot}6572}$$

$$= \frac{\sqrt{65{\cdot}9989}}{4{\cdot}6328} = \frac{8{\cdot}123970704}{4{\cdot}6328} = 1{\cdot}7535... = 1{\cdot}8, \text{ correct to 1 d.p.}$$

Algebra 1: Algebraic Expressions

3

Learning objectives

In this chapter you will learn how to:

- Explain the terminology associated with algebraic expressions
- Evaluate an expression
- Explain the commutative, associative and distributive properties
- Multiply algebraic expressions
- Simplify algebraic expressions.

Key Terminology

Variable: The letters which stand for unknown numbers in algebra. For example: x, y, z.

Constant: A term whose value never changes. For example: +7, −31.

Term: When a constant and variable(s) are multiplied together. For example: $7x$, $6x^2$.

Coefficient: The constant multiplied by the variable in a term. For example: in the term $6x^2$, 6 is the coefficient of x^2.

Expression: A set of terms which are added or subtracted. For example: $13x + 7x^2 - 35 + 3y$.

Linear expression: $7x - 2$ is a linear expression, where the highest power (or degree) of x is 1.

Quadratic expression: $5x^2 - 3x + 4$ is a quadratic expression, where the highest power (or degree) of x is 2.

Cubic expression: $8x^3 - 3x^2 - 2x + 1$ is a cubic expression, where the highest power (or degree) of x is 3.

Example

(a) $17x - 3$ is a linear expression.

(i) Name the variable in the expression.

(ii) Write down the coefficient of x.

(iii) Write down the constant.

(b) $12x^2 - 23x + 10$ is a quadratic expression.

(i) Write down the coefficient of x^2.

(ii) Write down the coefficient of x.

(iii) Write down the constant.

Solution

(a) In the linear expression $17x - 3$:

(i) the variable in the expression is x

(ii) the coefficient of x is 17

(iii) the constant is −3.

(b) In the quadratic expression $12x^2 - 23x + 10$:

(i) the coefficient of x^2 is 12

(ii) the coefficient of x is −23

(iii) the constant is +10.

Evaluating expressions

Points to note

- **Evaluate an expression** means to find the value of the expression. We do this by replacing each variable in the expression with its value. Then we work out the final value of the expression, using the order of operations (BIRDMAS).

  For example: if $x = -2$ then the value of $7x - 2$ is $7(-2) - 2 = -14 - 2 = -16$.
- BIRDMAS: stands for Brackets, Indices and Roots, Division and Multiplication, Addition and Subtraction. This shows the order in which operations should be carried out when evaluating an expression. You might also hear it referred to as BOMDAS or BIMDAS.
- When there are two or more terms in a numerator and/or denominator, evaluate the numerator and denominator separately before dividing.

Top Tip

To evaluate an expression:

1 Substitute the correct number for each variable, using brackets.

2 Evaluate the expression, using:

- the order of operations (BIRDMAS) to work out the answer, or
- a scientific calculator, typing in the expression exactly as written in step 1.

Example

If $a = -3$ and $b = -7$, find the value of the following expressions:

(a) $3ab$ **(b)** $3a - b$ **(c)** $a^2 - ab + 3$ **(d)** $\frac{3a - b}{a^2 - ab + 3}$.

Solution

For each part, substitute −3 for a and −7 for b.

(a) $3ab = 3(-3)(-7) = 63$

(b) $3a - b = 3(-3) - (-7) = -9 + 7 = -2$

(c) $a^2 - ab + 3 = (-3)^2 - (-3)(-7) + 3 = 9 - 21 + 3 = -9$

(d) $\frac{3a - b}{a^2 - ab + 3} = \frac{-2}{-9} = \frac{2}{9}$ [$3a - b = -2$ from **(b)** and $a^2 - ab + 3 = -9$ from **(c)**]

Example

When $x = -7$ and $b = -25$, find the value of $\sqrt{3x - b}$.

Solution

$$\sqrt{3x - b} = \sqrt{3(-7) - (-25)}$$ Let $x = -7$ and $b = -25$.

$$= \sqrt{-21 + 25}$$

$$= \sqrt{4}$$

$$= \pm 2$$

Example

When $c = \frac{1}{3}$ and $d = -\frac{2}{3}$, find the value of $\frac{c^2 - 2d^2 - 3}{6c - 1}$.

Solution

$$\frac{c^2 - 2d^2 - 3}{6c - 1} = \frac{\left(\frac{1}{3}\right)^2 - 2\left(-\frac{2}{3}\right)^2 - 3}{6\left(\frac{1}{3}\right) - 1}$$

Let $c = \frac{1}{3}$ and $d = -\frac{2}{3}$.

Use the order of operations to simplify.

$$= \frac{\left(\frac{1}{9}\right) - 2\left(\frac{4}{9}\right) - 3}{6\left(\frac{1}{3}\right) - 1}$$

Remember when squaring $\left(-\frac{2}{3}\right)$ that (minus) × (minus) = (plus).

$$= \frac{\left(\frac{1}{9}\right) - \left(\frac{8}{9}\right) - 3}{\left(\frac{6}{3}\right) - 1} = \frac{-\left(\frac{7}{9}\right) - 3}{2 - 1} = \frac{-\frac{34}{9}}{1} = -\frac{34}{9}$$

Alternatively, type the formula into your calculator, including all brackets!

Simplifying and multiplying out expressions

Points to note

- **Monomial:** An expression with one term. For example: 3, x, $3x^3$.
- **Binomial:** An expression with two terms. For example: $x^2 - 6$.
- **Trinomial:** An expression with three terms. For example: $5x^2 - 3x + 4$.
- **Like terms:** Terms with the same variables and the same powers. For example: $2x$ and $-13x$.
- **Simplify an expression:** Reduce the expression to its simplest form. For example: $2x - 5x + 7x$ can be simplified to $4x$. This is also called **collecting like terms**.
- **Expand:** Multiply out/remove the brackets, by multiplying the terms within them. For example: $4(3x - 7)$ can be multiplied out/expanded to give $12x - 28$.
- **Product:** The answer when two or more terms are multiplied together.

Remember

Commutative, associative and distributive properties

You must be able to apply the commutative, associative and distributive properties when simplifying algebraic expressions.

Commutative property

The commutative property allows us to swap the order of terms when we add or multiply, without changing the result.

$a + b = b + a$

$a \times b = b \times a$

Associative property

The associative property states that it doesn't matter how we group terms when we add or multiply.

$(a + b) + c = a + (b + c)$

$(a \times b) \times c = a \times (b \times c)$

Distributive property

We only distribute multiplication over addition (or subtraction).

$a(b - c) = ab - ac$

$a(b + c) = ab + ac$

$(a + b)(c + d) = a(c + d) + b(c + d) = ac + ad + bc + bd$

$(a + b)(c + d + e) = a(c + d + e) + b(c + d + e) = ac + ad + ae + bc + bd + be$

In general, distribute the terms by multiplying each term in the first bracket by each term in the second bracket.

Example

Simplify the following expressions:

(a) $3x + 7y - 12x + 8y - 3$

(b) $(5a^2 - 4a + 3) - (7a^2 + 3a - 8)$

(c) $3(y^2 - 2y + 7) - (2y^2 + 7y - 9)$

(d) $2c(3c - 7) - 2(-2c + 5)$.

Solution

(a) $3x + 7y - 12x + 8y - 3 = 3x - 12x + 7y + 8y - 3$ Collect like terms.

$= -9x + 15y - 3$ Add/subtract like terms.

(b) $(5a^2 - 4a + 3) - (7a^2 + 3a - 8)$

$= 5a^2 - 4a + 3 - 7a^2 - 3a + 8$

$= 5a^2 - 7a^2 - 4a - 3a + 3 + 8$ Collect like terms.

$= -2a^2 - 7a + 11$ Add/subtract like terms.

(c) $3(y^2 - 2y + 7) - (2y^2 + 7y - 9)$

$= 3y^2 - 6y + 21 - 2y^2 - 7y + 9$

$= y^2 - 13y + 30$

(d) $2c(3c - 7) - 2(-2c + 5)$

$= 6c^2 - 14c + 4c - 10$

$= 6c^2 - 10c - 10$

Points to note

- **Perfect squares**

$(a + b)^2 = (a + b)(a + b)$

$= a(a + b) + b(a + b)$

$= a^2 + ab + ab + b^2$ The middle terms are the same.

$= a^2 + 2ab + b^2$

There is a clear pattern when we square a binomial:

$(\text{first} + \text{second})^2 = (\text{first})^2 + 2(\text{first})(\text{second}) + (\text{second})^2$.

- **Difference of two squares**

$(a + b)(a - b) = a(a - b) + b(a - b)$

$= a^2 - ab + ab - b^2$ The middle terms are the same but have different signs.

$= a^2 - b^2$

There is a clear pattern when we have the sum of two numbers multiplied by the difference of the same numbers:

$(\text{first} + \text{second})(\text{first} - \text{second}) = (\text{first})^2 - (\text{second})^2$

Example

Expand and simplify the following expressions:

(a) $(3x - y)(x + y)$

(b) $(ax - b)^2$

(c) $(5a + 3)^2$

(d) $(3x - 7)(3x + 7)$

(e) $(5x - 3)(2x + 4)$, using a multiplication array, or otherwise

(f) $(x - 4)(x^2 - 3x + 21)$.

Solution

(a) $(3x - y)(x + y) = 3x(x + y) - y(x + y)$

$= 3x^2 + 3xy - xy - y^2$

$= 3x^2 + 2xy - y^2$

(b) $(ax - b)^2 = (ax - b)(ax - b)$

This is a perfect square so we could use the rule above or the method below.

$= ax(ax - b) - b(ax - b)$

$= a^2x^2 - abx - abx + b^2$

$= a^2x^2 - 2abx + b^2$

(c) $(5a + 3)^2 = (5a)^2 + 2(5a)(3) + (3)^2$

Use $(\text{first} + \text{second})^2 = (\text{first})^2 + 2(\text{first})(\text{second}) + (\text{second})^2$.

$= 25a^2 + 30a + 9$

(d) $(3x - 7)(3x + 7) = (3x)^2 - (7)^2$

$= 9x^2 - 49$

This is a difference of two squares so use $(\text{first} + \text{second})(\text{first} - \text{second}) = (\text{first})^2 - (\text{second})^2$.

(e) **Method 1:** Expanding brackets.

$(5x - 3)(2x + 4) = 5x(2x + 4) - 3(2x + 4)$

$= 10x^2 + 20x - 6x - 12$

$= 10x^2 + 14x - 12$

Method 2: Array or box method.

×	$2x$	$+4$
$5x$	$10x^2$	$+20x$
-3	$-6x$	-12

$= 10x^2 - 6x + 20x - 12$

$= 10x^2 + 14x - 12$

(f) **Method 1:** Expanding brackets.

$(x - 4)(x^2 - 3x + 21) = x(x^2 - 3x + 21) - 4(x^2 - 3x + 21)$

$= x^3 - 3x^2 + 21x - 4x^2 + 12x - 84$

$= x^3 - 3x^2 - 4x^2 + 21x + 12x - 84$

$= x^3 - 7x^2 + 33x - 84$

Method 2: Array or box method.

×	x^2	$-3x$	$+21$
x	x^3	$-3x^2$	$+21x$
-4	$-4x^2$	$+12x$	-84

$= x^3 - 3x^2 + 21x - 4x^2 + 12x - 84$

$= x^3 - 7x^2 + 33x - 84$

Example

If $(2x + 5)(3x + a) = 6x^2 + 7x - 20$, find the value of a.

Solution

Point to note
Equate means 'put equal to'.

$(2x + 5)(3x + a) = 6x^2 + 7x - 20$

$\Rightarrow 2x(3x + a) + 5(3x + a) = 6x^2 + 7x - 20$

$\Rightarrow 6x^2 + 2ax + 15x + 5a = 6x^2 + 7x - 20$

Equating the constant terms gives:

$5a = -20$

$a = \dfrac{-20}{5} = -4$

We can check this by equating the x terms:

$2ax + 15x = 7x$ Divide across by x.

$\Rightarrow 2a + 15 = 7$

$\Rightarrow 2(-4) + 15 = 7$

$\Rightarrow -8 + 15 = 7$

$\Rightarrow 7 = 7$ ✓

Example

Simplify $(5x - 1)(x^2 + 3x - 1)$. Hence, find the value of the expression when $x = -3$.

Solution

'Hence' means that the second part of the question is dependent on the first part.

In this question it means that we must simplify the expression first, then evaluate the answer when $x = -3$.

$(5x - 1)(x^2 + 3x - 1) = 5x(x^2 + 3x - 1) - 1(x^2 + 3x - 1)$

$= 5x^3 + 15x^2 - 5x - x^2 - 3x + 1$

$= 5x^3 + 14x^2 - 8x + 1$

$= 5(-3)^3 + 14(-3)^2 - 8(-3) + 1$ Let $x = -3$ and evaluate using order of operations.

$= 5(-27) + 14(9) + 24 + 1$

$= -135 + 126 + 25$

$= 16$

Exercise

Q1 Explain the meaning of each of the following, with an example where possible:

(a) variable

(b) constant

(c) term

(d) coefficient

(e) expression

(f) linear expression

(g) quadratic expression

(h) cubic expression

Q2 Identify each type of expression (i.e. linear, quadratic or cubic):

(a) $5x^2 + 7x - 9$

(b) $x - 6$

(c) $x^2 - 7x + 3$

(d) $2a - 1$

(e) $3x^3 - x^2 - 2x - 3$

Q3 $x - 8$ is a linear expression.

(a) Name the variable in the expression.

(b) Write down the coefficient of x.

(c) Write down the constant.

Q4 $4x^2 + 12x + 9$ is a quadratic expression.

(a) Write down the coefficient of x^2.

(b) Write down the coefficient of x.

(c) Write down the constant.

Q5 (a) When $x = 7$ and $y = -1$, find the value of the following expressions:

(i) $x + y$

(ii) $x + 7y$

(iii) $2x - y^2$

(iv) $x^2 + y - 13$

(v) $\dfrac{x + 2y}{x^2 + y + 2}$

(b) When $a = 10$, $b = 4$ and $c = 2$ find the value of the following expressions:

(i) $a + b$

(ii) $(a + b)c$

(iii) $a + 2(b + c)$

(iv) $\dfrac{10b^2 + c^3}{a^2}$

Q6 Evaluate:

(a) $-4(3k + 5)$, when $k = 4$

(b) $\dfrac{d - 6}{7}$, when $d = 6$

(c) $-3(h - 7)^2$, when $h = 2$

(d) $-4(-7 - 6g + g^2)$, when $g = -1$

Q7 Evaluate:

(a) $z^2 + y + z$, when $y = -5$ and $z = -3$

(b) $k(h - j) + h$, when $h = 5$, $j = -4$ and $k = 2$

(c) $\dfrac{x}{y} + 6 + y^3$, when $x = 5$ and $y = 1$

(d) $y^2 + yz + z + y$, when $y = -2$ and $z = 6$

(e) $\sqrt{z^2 - x}$, when $x = -2$ and $z = -4$

(f) $\dfrac{(p - q)^2 - (q + 1)}{3p}$, when $p = 1$ and $q = -1$

Q8 Evaluate:

(a) $\dfrac{p^2 - (r - 2)}{6}$,

when $p = 5$ and $r = -3$

(b) $\dfrac{(a + b)^2 - 27b}{a - 3b + 20}$,

when $a = 7$ and $b = 11$

Q9 Explain the meaning of each of the following, with an example when possible:

(a) monomial

(b) binomial

(c) trinomial

(d) like terms

(e) simplify an expression

(f) product

(g) expand.

Q10 Explain the meaning of each of the properties below:

(a) commutative property

(b) associative property

(c) distributive property.

Q11 Simplify the expressions:

(a) $a + b - c + 2b + 7c - 5$

(b) $x^2 - 7x + 2x^2 - 11x + 13$

(c) $xy + y^2 - 2y - 7x - 17xy - 4y^2$

(d) $d^3 - 13 - 2d - 7d^2 + d + 7$

Q12 Simplify the expressions:

(a) $2(b - 3)$

(b) $x(x - 2) + 3(2x + 9)$

(c) $2n(n - 3) + 7m(5n - 7)$

(d) $x(x^2 + x - 2) + 3(x^2 - 7x + 1)$

(e) $(2a^2 - 7a - 2) - (5a^2 + 3a - 7)$

(f) $x(x^2 + 2xy + y^2) - 7(x^2 - 3xy)$

Q13 Simplify the expressions:

(a) $(2x + 3)^2$

(b) $(7a - 2)^2$

(c) $(6b + 7)^2$

(d) $(13d - 4)^2$

(e) $(7x + 8y)^2$

Q14 Simplify the expressions:

(a) $(x + y)(x - y)$

(b) $(4x - 3)(4x + 3)$

(c) $(2a - 7b)(2a + 7b)$

(d) $(3n - 15)(3n + 15)$

(e) $(2c - 7d)(2c + 7d)$

Q15 Expand and simplify the expressions:

(a) $(a - 2)(a + 5)$

(b) $(p - 5)(p + 3)$

(c) $(c - 4)(c + 3)$

(d) $(x - 5)(x + 9)$

(e) $(2x + 1)(x + 5)$

(f) $(6x - 3)(7 - 2x)$

(g) $(7x - 1)(3x - 2)$

Q16 Expand and simplify the expressions:

(a) $(x - 3)(1 - 2x + y)$

(b) $(a - b)(2a + b \quad 3)$

(c) $(3 + y)(y^2 + 5y - 36)$

(d) $(3a + 7b)(a^2 - 2ab + 4b^2)$

(e) $(2x - 3y)(-2x^2 + 9xy - 7y^2)$

Q17 Simplify $(x - 4)(x^2 - x + 2)$. Hence, evaluate the expression when $x = -3$.

Q18 If $(x + 2)(3x - a) = 3x^2 + 2x - 8$, find the value of a.

Solutions

Q1 (a) Variable: The letters which stand for unknown numbers in algebra. For example: x, y.

(b) Constant: A term whose value never changes. For example: +7, −31.

(c) Term: When a constant and variable(s) are multiplied together. For example: $7x$, $6x^2$.

(d) Coefficient: The constant multiplied by the variable in a term. For example: in the term $6x^2$, 6 is the coefficient of x^2.

(e) Expression: A set of terms which are added or subtracted. For example: $4x + 2$ and $2x^2 - x + 4$.

(f) Linear expression: $7x - 2$ is a linear expression, where the highest power (or degree) of x is 1.

(g) Quadratic expression: $5x^2 - 3x + 4$ is a quadratic expression, where the highest power (or degree) of x is 2.

(h) Cubic expression: $8x^3 - 3x^2 - 2x + 1$ is a cubic expression, where the highest power (or degree) of x is 3.

Q2 (a) Quadratic

(b) Linear

(c) Quadratic

(d) Linear

(e) Cubic

Q3 In the linear expression $x - 8$:

(a) the variable is x

(b) the coefficient of x is 1

(c) the constant is −8.

Q4 In the quadratic expression $4x^2 + 12x + 9$:

(a) the coefficient of x^2 is 4

(b) the coefficient of x is +12

(c) the constant is +9.

Q5 (a) When $x = 7$ and $y = -1$, then:

(i) $x + y = (7) + (-1) = 7 - 1 = 6$

(ii) $x + 7y = (7) + 7(-1) = 7 - 7 = 0$

(iii) $2x - y^2 = 2(7) - (-1)^2 = 14 - 1 = 13$

(iv) $x^2 + y - 13 = (7)^2 + (-1) - 13 = 49 - 1 - 13 = 35$

(v) $\dfrac{x + 2y}{x^2 + y + 2} = \dfrac{(7) + 2(-1)}{(7)^2 + (-1) + 2} = \dfrac{7 - 2}{49 - 1 + 2} = \dfrac{5}{50} = \dfrac{1}{10}$

(b) When $a = 10$, $b = 4$ and $c = 2$, then:

(i) $a + b = (10) + (4) = 10 + 4 = 14$

(ii) $(a + b)c = ((10) + (4))(2) = (14)(2) = 28$

(iii) $a + 2(b + c) = (10) + 2((4) + (2)) = 10 + 2(6) = 10 + 12 = 22$

(iv) $\dfrac{10b^2 + c^3}{a^2} = \dfrac{10(4)^2 + (2)^3}{(10)^2} = \dfrac{10(16) + (8)}{100} = \dfrac{160 + 8}{100} = \dfrac{168}{100} = \dfrac{84}{50} = \dfrac{42}{25}$

Q6 (a) When $k = 4$: $-4(3k + 5) = -4(3(4) + 5) = -4(12 + 5) = -4(17) = -68$.

(b) When $d = 6$: $\dfrac{d-6}{7} = \dfrac{(6)-6}{7} = \dfrac{0}{7} = 0$.

(c) When $h = 2$: $-3(h-7)^2 = -3((2)-7)^2 = -3(-5)^2 = -3(25) = -75$.

(d) When $g = -1$: $-4(-7 - 6g + g^2) = -4(-7 - 6(-1) + (-1)^2)$
$= -4(-7 + 6 + 1) = -4(0) = 0$.

Q7 (a) When $y = -5$ and $z = -3$: $z^2 + y + z = (-3)^2 + (-5) + (-3) = 9 - 5 - 3 = 1$.

(b) When $h = 5, j = -4$ and $k = 2$:
$k(h-j) + h = (2)((5) - (-4)) + (5) = 2(5 + 4) + 5 = 2(9) + 5 = 18 + 5 = 23$.

(c) When $x = 5$ and $y = 1$: $\dfrac{x}{y} + 6 + y^3 = \dfrac{(5)}{(1)} + 6 + (1)^3 = 5 + 6 + 1 = 12$.

(d) When $y = -2$ and $z = 6$: $y^2 + yz + z + y = (-2)^2 + (-2)(6) + (6) + (-2)$
$= 4 - 12 + 6 - 2 = -4$.

(e) When $x = -2$ and $z = -4$: $\sqrt{z^2 - x} = \sqrt{(-4)^2 - (-2)} = \sqrt{16 + 2} = \sqrt{18} = 3\sqrt{2}$.

(f) When $p = 1$ and $q = -1$: $\dfrac{(p-q)^2 - (q+1)}{3p} = \dfrac{((1)-(-1))^2 - ((-1)+1)}{3(1)}$
$= \dfrac{(1+1)^2 - 0}{3} = \dfrac{(2)^2 - 0}{3} = \dfrac{4}{3}$.

Q8 (a) When $p = 5$ and $r = -3$: $\dfrac{p^2 - (r-2)}{6} = \dfrac{(5)^2 - ((-3)-2)}{6} = \dfrac{25 - (-5)}{6}$
$= \dfrac{25 + 5}{6} = \dfrac{30}{6} = 5$.

(b) When $a = 7$ and $b = 11$: $\dfrac{(a+b)^2 - 27b}{a - 3b + 20} = \dfrac{((7)+(11))^2 - 27(11)}{(7) - 3(11) + 20}$
$= \dfrac{(18)^2 - 297}{7 - 33 + 20} = \dfrac{324 - 297}{-6} = \dfrac{27}{-6} = -\dfrac{9}{2}$.

Q9 (a) Monomial: An expression with one term. For example: $3, x, 5x^2$.

(b) Binomial: An expression with two terms. For example: $x^2 - 6$.

(c) Trinomial: An expression with three terms. For example: $5x^2 - 3x + 4$.

(d) Like terms: Terms with the same variables and the same powers.
For example: $2x$ and $-13x$.

(e) Simplify an expression: Reduce the expression to its simplest form.
For example: $2x - 5x + 7x$ can be simplified to $4x$. This is also called collecting like terms.

(f) Product: The answer when two or more terms are multiplied together.
For example: $(x + 3)(x - 2) = x(x - 2) + 3(x - 2) = x^2 - 2x + 3x - 6 = x^2 + x - 6$.

(g) Expand: Multiply out/remove the brackets, by multiplying the terms within them. For example: $4(3x - 7)$ can be multiplied out/expanded to give $12x - 28$.

Q10 (a) The commutative property allows us to swap the order of terms when we add or multiply, without changing the result.

- $a + b = b + a$
- $a \times b = b \times a$

(b) The associative property states that it doesn't matter how we group terms when we add or multiply.

- $(a + b) + c = a + (b + c)$
- $(a \times b) \times c = a \times (b \times c)$

(c) We only distribute multiplication over addition (or subtraction).

- $a(b - c) = ab - ac$
- $a(b + c) = ab + ac$
- $(a + b)(c + d) = a(c + d) + b(c + d) = ac + ad + bc + bd$
- $(a + b)(c + d + e) = a(c + d + e) + b(c + d + e) = ac + ad + ae + bc + bd + be$

In general, multiply each term in the first bracket by each term in the second bracket.

Q11 (a) $a + b - c + 2b + 7c - 5 = a + 3b + 6c - 5$

(b) $x^2 - 7x + 2x^2 - 11x + 13 = 3x^2 - 18x + 13$

(c) $xy + y^2 - 2y - 7x - 17xy - 4y^2 = -16xy - 3y^2 - 2y - 7x$

(d) $d^3 - 13 - 2d - 7d^2 + d + 7 = d^3 - 7d^2 - d - 6$

Q12 (a) $2(b - 3) = 2b - 6$

(b) $x(x - 2) + 3(2x + 9) = x^2 - 2x + 6x + 27 = x^2 + 4x + 27$

(c) $2n(n - 3) + 7m(5n - 7) = 2n^2 - 6n + 35mn - 49m$

(d) $x(x^2 + x - 2) + 3(x^2 - 7x + 1) = x^3 + x^2 - 2x + 3x^2 - 21x + 3 = x^3 + 4x^2 - 23x + 3$

(e) $(2a^2 - 7a - 2) - (5a^2 + 3a - 7) = 2a^2 - 7a - 2 - 5a^2 - 3a + 7 = -3a^2 - 10a + 5$

(f) $x(x^2 + 2xy + y^2) - 7(x^2 - 3xy) = x^3 + 2x^2y + xy^2 - 7x^2 + 21xy$

Q13 (a) $(2x + 3)^2 = (2x)^2 + 2(2x)(3) + (3)^2 = 4x^2 + 12x + 9$

Alternative method: $(2x + 3)(2x + 3) = 2x(2x + 3) + 3(2x + 3)$
$= 4x^2 + 6x + 6x + 9 = 4x^2 + 12x + 9$

(b) $(7a - 2)^2 = (7a)^2 + (2)(7a)(-2) + (-2)^2 = 49a^2 - 28a + 4$

(c) $(6b + 7)^2 = (6b)^2 + (2)(6b)(7) + (7)^2 = 36b^2 + 84b + 49$

(d) $(13d - 4)^2 = (13d)^2 + (2)(13d)(-4) + (-4)^2 = 169d^2 - 104d + 16$

(e) $(7x + 8y)^2 = (7x)^2 + (2)(7x)(8y) + (8y)^2 = 49x^2 + 112xy + 64y^2$

Q14 (a) $(x + y)(x - y) = x^2 - y^2$

(b) $(4x - 3)(4x + 3) = (4x)^2 - (3)^2 = 16x^2 - 9$

(c) $(2a - 7b)(2a + 7b) = (2a)^2 - (7b)^2 = 4a^2 - 49b^2$

(d) $(3n - 15)(3n + 15) = (3n)^2 - (15)^2 = 9n^2 - 225$

(e) $(2c - 7d)(2c + 7d) = (2c)^2 - (7d)^2 = 4c^2 - 49d^2$

Q15 (a) $(a-2)(a+5)=a(a+5)-2(a+5)=a^2+5a-2a-10=a^2+3a-10$

(b) $(p-5)(p+3)=p(p+3)-5(p+3)=p^2+3p-5p-15=p^2-2p-15$

(c) $(c-4)(c+3)=c(c+3)-4(c+3)=c^2+3c-4c-12=c^2-c-12$

(d) $(x-5)(x+9)=x(x+9)-5(x+9)=x^2+9x-5x-45=x^2+4x-45$

(e) $(2x+1)(x+5)=2x(x+5)+1(x+5)=2x^2+10x+x+5=2x^2+11x+5$

(f) $(6x-3)(7-2x)=6x(7-2x)-3(7-2x)=42x-12x^2-21+6x=-12x^2+48x-21$

(g) $(7x-1)(3x-2)=7x(3x-2)-1(3x-2)=21x^2-14x-3x+2=21x^2-17x+2$

Q16 (a) $(x-3)(1-2x+y)=x(1-2x+y)-3(1-2x+y)=x-2x^2+xy-3+6x-3y$

$=-2x^2+xy-3+7x-3y$

(b) $(a-b)(2a+b-3)=a(2a+b-3)-b(2a+b-3)$

$=2a^2+ab-3a-2ab-b^2+3b$

$=2a^2-ab-3a-b^2+3b$

(c) $(3+y)(y^2+5y-36)=3(y^2+5y-36)+y(y^2+5y-36)$

$=3y^2+15y-108+y^3+5y^2-36y$

$=y^3+8y^2-21y-108$

(d) $(3a+7b)(a^2-2ab+4b^2)=3a(a^2-2ab+4b^2)+7b(a^2-2ab+4b^2)$

$=3a^3-6a^2b+12ab^2+7a^2b-14ab^2+28b^3=3a^3+28b^3+a^2b-2ab^2$

(e) $(2x-3y)(-2x^2+9xy-7y^2)=2x(-2x^2+9xy-7y^2)-3y(-2x^2+9xy-7y^2)$

$=-4x^3+18x^2y-14xy^2+6x^2y-27xy^2+21y^3=-4x^3+21y^3+24x^2y-41xy^2$

Q17 $(x-4)(x^2-x+2)=x(x^2-x+2)-4(x^2-x+2)$

$=x^3-x^2+2x-4x^2+4x-8$

$=x^3-5x^2+6x-8$

'Hence' means that you use the previous answer and then follow on.

When $x=-3$, $x^3-5x^2+6x-8=(-3)^3-5(-3)^2+6(-3)-8$

$=-27-5(9)-18-8$

$=-27-45-18-8$

$=-98$

Q18 $(x+2)(3x-a)=3x^2+2x-8$

$\Rightarrow x(3x-a)+2(3x-a)=3x^2+2x-8$

$\Rightarrow 3x^2-ax+6x-2a=3x^2+2x-8$

Equating the constant terms gives:

$-2a=-8$

$\Rightarrow a=\dfrac{-8}{-2}=4$

We can check this by equating the x terms:

$-ax+6x=2x$

$\Rightarrow -(4)x+6x=2x$

$\Rightarrow -4x+6x=2x$

$\Rightarrow 2x=2x$ ✓

4 Algebra 2: Factorising

Learning objectives

In this chapter you will learn how to factorise expressions:

- With a common factor across all terms
- Where grouping is necessary
- With three terms (trinomials) – quadratic expressions
- Using the difference of two squares.

Factorising

Points to note

Factorising is the opposite/reverse of finding a product (multiplying).

- When we find a product, we multiply:

  $2(x - y) = 2x - 2y$

  $(a + b)(c - d) = ac - ad + bc - bd$

  $(x - 7)(x + 4) = x^2 - 3x - 28$

  $(x + 7)(x - 7) = x^2 - 49$

- When we do this process the other way round, i.e. convert terms to factors, we factorise (make factors).

  $2x - 2y = 2(x - y)$

  $ac - ad + bc - bd = (a + b)(c - d)$

  $x^2 - 3x - 28 = (x - 7)(x + 4)$

  $x^2 - 49 = (x + 7)(x - 7)$

  There are four factorisation methods we learn on the Junior Certificate course. They are:

  1 Taking out the highest common factor

  2 Grouping

  3 Quadratic trinomials

  4 Difference of two squares.

Factorising by taking out the highest common factor

Top Tip

When we have two or more terms in an expression with a common factor, we factorise by taking out the highest common factor (HCF).

To factorise by taking out the HCF, follow these steps:

1 Find the HCF of all the terms in the expression.

2 Put the HCF outside the brackets.

3 Divide each term by the HCF to find the factor inside the brackets.

4 Write down the factors.

5 Check the solution.

Remember

When 'taking out' a common factor, the number of terms in the brackets must be the same as the number of terms in the original expression.

Example

Factorise the following expressions:

(a) $3x - 6$

(b) $7x^2 - 63x$

(c) $5x^2 - x$

(d) $20xy^2 - 4xy$

(e) $3a^2 + 18a + 39ab$

(f) $2x^2yz - 10x^3yz^2 + 6x^2y^2z^3$.

Solution

(a) $3x - 6 = 3(x - 2)$ The HCF is 3.

(b) $7x^2 - 63x = 7x(x - 9)$ The HCF is $7x$.

(c) $5x^2 - x = x(5x - 1)$ Remember that $-x$ means $-1x$. The HCF is x.

(d) $20xy^2 - 4xy = 4xy(5y - 1)$ The HCF is $4xy$.

(e) $3a^2 + 18a + 39ab = 3a(a + 6 + 13b)$ The HCF is $3a$.

(f) $2x^2yz - 10x^3yz^2 + 6x^2y^2z^3 = 2x^2yz(1 - 5xz + 3yz^2)$ The HCF is $2x^2yz$.

Factorising by grouping

Top Tip

When we have four terms in an expression with no common factor, we factorise using grouping. To factorise by grouping, follow these steps:

1 Group the terms into pairs with a common factor.

2 Factorise each pair separately.

3 Make sure the factor inside the first and second brackets are the same.

4 Take out the new common factor.

5 Write down the factors.

6 Check the solution.

Example

Factorise the expression $3cd - 10c - 10e + 3ed$.

Solution

$3cd - 10c - 10e + 3ed$ Factorise each pair separately.

$= c(3d - 10) + e(-10 + 3d)$ Take out the common factor.

$= c(3d - 10) + e(3d - 10)$ Note that $-10 + 3d$ is the same as $3d - 10$.

$= (c + e)(3d - 10)$

Check solution:

$(c + e)(3d - 10)$

$= c(3d - 10) + e(3d - 10)$

$= 3cd - 10c + 3de - 10e$ ✓

Example

Factorise the expression $3x - 12yz + 4z - 9xy$.

Solution

$3x - 12yz + 4z - 9xy$ Group in pairs with a common factor.

$= 3x - 9xy - 12yz + 4z$ Factorise each pair separately.

$= 3x(1 - 3y) + 4z(-3y + 1)$ Make sure the factor inside the first and second brackets are the same.

$= 3x(1 - 3y) + 4z(1 - 3y)$ Take out the common factor. Note that $-3y + 1$ is the same as $1 - 3y$.

$= (3x + 4z)(1 - 3y)$

Factorising quadratic trinomials

Points to note

- A **trinomial** is a polynomial with three terms.
- A **quadratic trinomial** is an expression with three terms in the form $ax^2 + bx + c$, where $a, b, c \in \mathbb{R}$, $a \neq 0$ and the highest power of x is 2. For example: $5x^2 - 3x + 4$.
- When the sign of the constant is positive, then the signs inside the middle of the brackets will both be either plus (+, +) or minus (–, –). To work out which, look at the sign in front of the x term. The sign in both brackets will match the sign of this term.

$$x^2 + 5x + 6 = (x + 2)(x + 3)$$

$$x^2 - 5x + 6 = (x - 2)(x - 3)$$

- When the sign of the constant is negative, then the signs in the middle of the brackets will be different, i.e. one plus and one minus (+, –). The sign of the bigger constant in the brackets will be the same as the sign in front of the x term.

$$x^2 + 5x - 6 = (x + 6)(x - 1)$$

$$x^2 - 5x - 6 = (x - 6)(x + 1)$$

Point to note

We can factorise a quadratic trinomial using the following methods:

- guess and check method
- guide number method
- box/array method
- MAM method
- cross method

Top Tip

To factorise a quadratic trinomial using the **guess and check method**, follow these steps:

1 Remove common factors, if possible.

2 List all the factors of the coefficient of the x^2 term.

3 List all the factors of the constant term.

4 Test all possible binomials you can make from these factors.

5 Write down the factors.

6 Check the solution.

Example

Factorise the expression $x^2 + x - 2$ using the guess and check method.

Solution

$x^2 + x - 2 \Rightarrow (x \quad)(x \quad)$	The factors of x^2 are (x) and (x). Place both factors in the LHS of each bracket.
$\Rightarrow (x + \ )(x - \ )$	As the sign of the constant is minus, we must put a different sign in each bracket after the x term.
$\Rightarrow (x + 2)(x - 1)$	Find the factors of −2 which add to +1. These factors are (+2) and (−1).

Check: $(x + 2)(x - 1) = x(x - 1) + 2(x - 1) = x^2 - x + 2x - 2 = x^2 + x - 2$ ✓

Top Tip

To factorise a quadratic trinomial using the **box/array method**, follow these steps:

1 First draw a box and divide it into quarters, with spaces above and to the left as shown.

2 Place the term that contains x^2 in the top left hand side (LHS) of the box.

3 Place the constant in the bottom right hand side (RHS) of the box.

4 Multiply the term that contains x^2 by the constant.

5 List the factors of the number found in step 4.

6 Identify the factors that add to give the coefficient of the middle x term.

7 Place these factors in the remaining boxes with an x. It doesn't matter which box you place them in.

8 Take the common factors from the box and place them outside the shaded areas.

9 Use the sign of the constant to identify the signs.

10 Write down the factors.

11 Check the solution.

Example

Factorise the expression $2x^2 + x - 1$ using the box/array method.

Solution

Draw a box and divide into quarters, as shown below.

×		

Place the $2x^2$ term in the top LHS and −1 in the bottom RHS of the box.

×		
	$2x^2$	
		-1

Multiply the term that contains x^2 by the constant: $(2x^2)(-1) = -2x^2$.

List the factors of $-2x^2$:

$(-2x)(x)$

$(-x)(2x)$

Find the factors that add to give $+x$. They are $-x + 2x$. Place these factors in the box.

×		
	$2x^2$	$-x$
	$+2x$	-1

Take the common factors from inside the box and place them in the dark blue sections outside the box.

×	$2x$	-1
x	$2x^2$	$-x$
$+1$	$+2x$	-1

Write down the factors:

$2x^2 + x - 1 = (2x - 1)(x + 1)$

Check: $(2x - 1)(x + 1) = 2x(x + 1) - 1(x + 1) = 2x^2 + 2x - x - 1 = 2x^2 + x - 1$ ✓

Top Tip

To factorise a quadratic trinomial using the **cross method**, follow these steps:

1. Draw a St Andrew's cross:

2. Find two factors of the term that contains x^2.
3. Write these factors on the top left and bottom left of the cross.
4. Find two numbers which multiply to give the constant and write these on the top right and bottom right of the cross, so that the two products of the diagonals sum to give the middle x term value.
5. If this doesn't work for the chosen factors of the term that contains x^2, find new factors and repeat the steps until you find a pair that does work.
6. Write down the factors.
7. Check the solution.

Example

Factorise the expression $4x^2 - 4x - 3$ using the cross method.

Solution

Draw a St Andrew's cross.

Two factors of $4x^2$ are $4x$ and x.
Write these factors on the top left and bottom left of the cross.

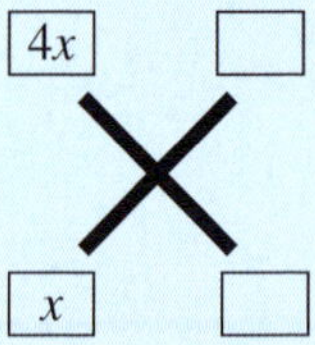

The factors of −3 are 1 and −3, or −1 and 3.

No matter which way we arrange these factors we cannot get the diagonals to sum to $(-4x)$.

$(4x)(1) + (x)(-3) = x$

$(4x)(-3) + (x)(1) = -11x$

$(4x)(-1) + (x)(3) = -x$

$(4x)(3) + (x)(-1) = 11x$

We must chose new factors for $4x^2$. These new factors are $2x$ and $2x$.
Place these factors on the top left and bottom left of the cross.

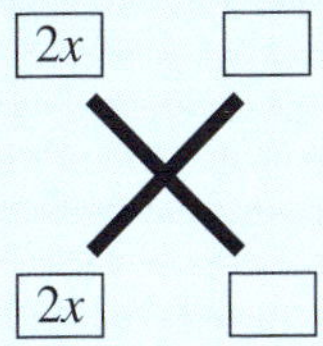

Repeating the factors for the RHS, we can now factorise as:

$(2x)(1) + (2x)(-3) = +2x - 6x = -4x$

Put +1 on the top RHS of the cross and −3 on the bottom RHS of the cross.

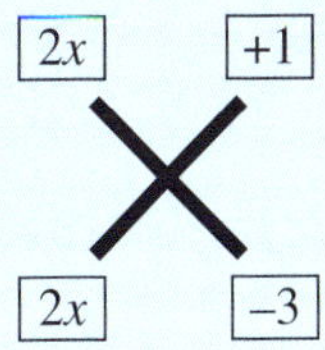

The factors are $(2x + 1)(2x - 3)$.

Check: $(2x + 1)(2x - 3) = 2x(2x - 3) + 1(2x - 3) = 4x^2 - 6x + 2x - 3 = 4x^2 - 4x - 3$ ✓

When quadratic trinomials become more difficult, the guess and check method, box/array method and cross method can take a long time to factorise, due to the number of combinations of factors. This is why the two methods listed below can be more useful.

Top Tip

To factorise a quadratic trinomial using the **guide number method**, follow these steps:

1. Remove common factors, if possible.
2. Find the guide number (GN) by multiplying the coefficient of the x^2 term by the constant.
3. Find the only pair of factors of the GN which add up to give the coefficient of the x term.
4. Break up the x term into two separate x terms with these factors as coefficients.
5. Use the grouping method to find the factors.
6. Write down the factors.

Example

Factorise the expression $x^2 + 9x + 20$ using the guide number method.

Solution

$x^2 + 9x + 20$ — Note: $x^2 = 1x^2$

The guide number is $(1)(+20) = +20$.
The plus sign tells us that the signs are the same.

Factors of $+20$ which add to $+9$ are $(+4)(+5)$.

$x^2 + 9x + 20 = x^2 + 5x + 4x + 20$ — Break up $+9x$ into $+5x + 4x$.

$= x(x + 5) + 4(x + 5)$ — Factorise using the grouping method.

$= (x + 4)(x + 5)$

Check: $(x + 4)(x + 5) = x(x + 5) + 4(x + 5) = x^2 + 5x + 4x + 20 = x^2 + 9x + 20$ ✓

Example

Factorise the expression $8x^2 + 14x - 15$ using the guide number method.

Solution

$8x^2 + 14x - 15$ — The guide number is $(+8)(-15) = -120$.
The minus sign tells us that the signs are different.

Factors of -120 which add to $+14$ are $(-6)(+20)$.

$= 8x^2 - 6x + 20x - 15$ — Break up $+14x$ into $-6x + 20x$.

$= 2x(4x - 3) + 5(4x - 3)$ — Factorise using the grouping method.

$= (2x + 5)(4x - 3)$

Check: $(2x + 5)(4x - 3) = 2x(4x - 3) + 5(4x - 3) = 8x^2 - 6x + 20x - 15 = 8x^2 + 14x - 15$ ✓

Top Tip

Note that the MAM method is very similar to the guide number method.

To factorise a quadratic trinomial using the **MAM method**, follow these steps:

1. Write **M** below both the coefficient of the x^2 term and the constant. This tells you that these terms should be **Multiplied**.
2. Write **A** below the coefficient of the x term. This tells you that you need to **Add** factors to get this term.

3 Multiply the coefficient of the x^2 term by the constant to find the guide number.
4 Find the factors of the number found in step 3 which add to give the coefficient of the x term.
5 Split the x term into two separate x terms with these factors as coefficients.
6 Factorise by grouping.
7 Write down the factors.

Example

Factorise the expression $6x^2 - x - 15$ using the MAM method.

Solution

$6x^2 - x - 15$

M **A** **M**

Multiply the two coefficients labelled **M** to find the guide number: $(+6)(-15) = -90$.
The minus sign tells us that the signs are different.

The coefficient labelled **A** is -1. The factors of -90 which add to -1 are $(+9)(-10)$.

$6x^2 - x - 15$

$= 6x^2 + 9x - 10x - 15$ Break up $-x$ into $+ 9x - 10x$.

$= 3x(2x + 3) - 5(2x + 3)$ Factorise using the grouping method.

$= (3x - 5)(2x + 3)$

Check: $(3x - 5)(2x + 3) = 3x(2x + 3) - 5(2x + 3) = 6x^2 + 9x - 10x - 15 = 6x^2 - x - 15$ ✓

Factorising using the difference of two squares

Remember

An expression of the form $a^2 - b^2$ is called the difference of two squares.

We can factorise an expression like this as:

$$a^2 - b^2 = (a - b)(a + b).$$

Note that this formula is **not** in the *Formulae and Tables* booklet.

Top Tip

To factorise an expression of the form $a^2 - b^2$, follow these steps:

1 Remove any common factor outside a bracket.

2 Write each term as a perfect square.

3 Use the rule $a^2 - b^2 = (a - b)(a + b)$ to completely factorise the expression.

Example

Factorise the following expressions:

(a) $x^2 - y^2$ **(b)** $64x^2 - 49$ **(c)** $9a^2 - 1$ **(d)** $8p^2 - 18q^2$.

Solution

(a) $x^2 - y^2$ — Write each term as a perfect square.

$= (x)^2 - (y)^2$ — Use the rule $a^2 - b^2 = (a - b)(a + b)$ to factorise the expression.

$= (x - y)(x + y)$

(b) $64x^2 - 49$ — Write each term as a perfect square: $\sqrt{64x^2} = 8x$ and $\sqrt{49} = 7$

$= (8x)^2 - (7)^2$ — Use the rule $a^2 - b^2 = (a - b)(a + b)$ to factorise the expression.

$= (8x - 7)(8x + 7)$

(c) $9a^2 - 1$ — Write each term as a perfect square: $\sqrt{9a^2} = 3a$ and $\sqrt{1} = 1$

$= (3a)^2 - (1)^2$ — Use the rule $a^2 - b^2 = (a - b)(a + b)$ to factorise the expression.

$= (3a - 1)(3a + 1)$

(d) $8p^2 - 18q^2$ — Remove the HCF of both terms outside the brackets. HCF = 2

$= 2(4p^2 - 9q^2)$ — Write each term as a perfect square: $\sqrt{4p^2} = 2p$ and $\sqrt{9q^2} = 3q$

$= 2[(2p)^2 - (3q)^2]$ — Use the rule $a^2 - b^2 = (a - b)(a + b)$ to factorise the expression.

$= 2(2p - 3q)(2p + 3q)$

Example

Use factors to evaluate:

(a) $(101)^2 - (99)^2$

(b) $(17{\cdot}1)^2 - (7{\cdot}1)^2$

Solution

Note: Use the difference of two squares rule $a^2 - b^2 = (a - b)(a + b)$ to evaluate.

(a) $(101)^2 - (99)^2 = (101 - 99)(101 + 99) = (2)(200) = 400$

(b) $(17{\cdot}1)^2 - (7{\cdot}1)^2 = (17{\cdot}1 - 7{\cdot}1)(17{\cdot}1 + 7{\cdot}1) = (10)(24{\cdot}2) = 242$

Exercise

Q1 Factorise fully each of the following expressions by taking out the HCF:

(a) $4a + 8b$

(b) $2xy + 18x$

(c) $a^2b - a^2b^2$

(d) $5x^2y^3 - 20xy^2$

(e) $4pq^2 - 8pq - 12p^2q$

(f) $4\pi r^2 - 8\pi r$.

Q2 Factorise fully each of the following expressions by grouping:

(a) $a - b - ax + bx$

(b) $c - d + cd - 1$

(c) $5x + ay + 5y + ax$

(d) $9a^2b + 3a^2 + 5b^2 + 15b^3$

(e) $10x^2 - 5x + 2xy - y$.

Q3 Factorise fully:

(a) $2p(a - b) - (a - b)$

(b) $3a(p - 3q) - 2b(p - 3q)$

(c) $7x(2y - 7z) + (7z - 2y)$

(d) $(3x - 7y) - 4p(3x - 7y)$.

Q4 Factorise fully each of the following expressions:

(a) $x^2 - y^2$

(b) $25c^2 - 49d^2$

(c) $36a^2 - 9b^2$

(d) $1 - 9a^2b^2$.

Q5 Factorise fully each of the following expressions:

(a) $2x^2 - 32$

(b) $12a^2y^2 - 27b^2y^2$

Evaluate each of the following:

(c) $43^2 - 13^2$

(d) $27^2 - 3^2$.

Q6 Factorise fully each of the following quadratic trinomials:

(a) $x^2 - 6x + 9$

(b) $c^2 - 2c + 1$

(c) $x^2 + 2xy + y^2$

(d) $x^2 - 6x - 16$

(e) $x^2 + 11x - 12$

(f) $x^2 - x - 2$.

Q7 Factorise fully each of the following quadratic trinomials:

(a) $2x^2 - 5x + 3$

(b) $22x^2 - 13x + 1$

(c) $7x^2 + 19x - 6$

(d) $6x^2 + 17x + 5$

Q8 Factorise fully:

(a) $6a^2b - 4ab^2$

(b) $36a^2 - 25b^2$

(c) $xy - 7a + xa - 7y$.

Solutions

Q1 (a) $4a + 8b = 4(a + 2b)$

(b) $2xy + 18x = 2x(y + 9)$

(c) $a^2b - a^2b^2 = a^2b(1 - b)$

(d) $5x^2y^3 - 20xy^2 = 5xy^2(xy - 4)$

(e) $4pq^2 - 8pq - 12p^2q = 4pq(q - 2 - 3p)$

(f) $4\pi r^2 - 8\pi r = 4\pi r(r - 2)$

Q2 (a) $a - b - ax + bx = 1(a - b) - x(a - b) = (1 - x)(a - b)$

(b) $c - d + cd - 1 = c + cd - 1 - d = c(1 + d) - 1(1 + d) = (c - 1)(1 + d)$

(c) $5x + ay + 5y + ax = 5x + ax + ay + 5y = x(5 + a) + y(a + 5) = (x + y)(a + 5)$
Note: $5 + a = a + 5$

(d) $9a^2b + 3a^2 + 5b^2 + 15b^3 = 3a^2(3b + 1) + 5b^2(1 + 3b) = (3a^2 + 5b^2)(1 + 3b)$
Note: $1 + 3b = 3b + 1$

(e) $10x^2 - 5x + 2xy - y = 5x(2x - 1) + y(2x - 1) = (5x + y)(2x - 1)$

Q3 (a) $2p(a - b) - 1(a - b) = (2p - 1)(a - b)$
Note: $-(a - b) = -1(a - b)$

(b) $3a(p - 3q) - 2b(p - 3q) = (3a - 2b)(p - 3q)$

(c) $7x(2y - 7z) + 1(7z - 2y) = 7x(2y - 7z) - 1(-7z + 2y) = (7x - 1)(2y - 7z)$
Note: $+1(7z - 2y) = -1(-7z + 2y)$

(d) $(3x - 7y) - 4p(3x - 7y) = 1(3x - 7y) - 4p(3x - 7y) = (1 - 4p)(3x - 7y)$

Q4 (a) $x^2 - y^2 = (x - y)(x + y)$

(b) $25c^2 - 49d^2 = (5c)^2 - (7d)^2 = (5c - 7d)(5c + 7d)$

(c) $36a^2 - 9b^2 = (6a)^2 - (3b)^2 = (6a - 3b)(6a + 3b)$

(d) $1 - 9a^2b^2 = (1)^2 - (3ab)^2 = (1 - 3ab)(1 + 3ab)$

Q5 (a) $2x^2 - 32 = 2(x^2 - 16) = 2[(x^2) - (4)^2] = 2(x - 4)(x + 4)$

(b) $12a^2y^2 - 27b^2y^2 = 3(4a^2y^2 - 9b^2y^2) = 3[(2ay)^2 - (3by)^2]$
$= 3(2ay - 3by)(2ay + 3by)$

(c) $43^2 - 13^2 = (43 - 13)(43 + 13) = (30)(56) = 1680$

(d) $27^2 - 3^2 = (27 - 3)(27 + 3) = (24)(30) = 720$

Any method can be used to factorise the quadratic trinomials in **Q6** and **Q7**. The solutions here use the guide number method.

Q6 (a) $x^2 - 6x + 9$ — The GN is (1)(+9) = +9.

Factors of +9 which add to −6 are (−3)(−3).

$= x^2 - 3x - 3x + 9$ — Break up $-6x$ into $-3x - 3x$.

$= x(x - 3) - 3(x - 3)$ — Factorise using the grouping method.

$= (x - 3)(x - 3)$

$= (x - 3)^2$

(b) $c^2 - 2c + 1$ — The GN is (1)(+1) = +1.

Factors of +1 which add to −2 are (−1)(−1).

$= c^2 - c - c + 1$ — Break up $-2c$ into $-c - c$.

$= c(c - 1) - 1(c - 1)$ — Factorise using the grouping method.

$= (c - 1)(c - 1)$

$= (c - 1)^2$

(c) $x^2 + 2xy + y^2$ — The GN is (1)(+1) = +1.

Factors of +1 which add to +2 are (+1)(+1).

$= x^2 + xy + xy + y^2$ — Break up $+2xy$ into $+xy + xy$.

$= x(x + y) + y(x + y)$ — Factorise using the grouping method.

$= (x + y)(x + y)$

$= (x + y)^2$

(d) $x^2 - 6x - 16$ — The GN is (1)(−16) = −16.

Factors of −16 which add to −6 are (−8)(+2).

$= x^2 + 2x - 8x - 16$ — Break up $-6x$ into $+2x - 8x$.

$= x(x + 2) - 8(x + 2)$ — Factorise using the grouping method.

$= (x - 8)(x + 2)$

(e) $x^2 + 11x - 12$ — The GN is (1)(−12) = −12.

Factors of −12 which add to +11 are (−1)(+12).

$= x^2 - x + 12x - 12$ — Break up $+11x$ into $-x + 12x$.

$= x(x - 1) + 12(x - 1)$ — Factorise using the grouping method.

$= (x + 12)(x - 1)$

(f) $x^2 - x - 2$ — The GN is $(1)(-2) = -2$.

Factors of -2 which add to -1 are $(+1)(-2)$.

$= x^2 + x - 2x - 2$ — Break up $-x$ into $+x - 2x$.

$= x(x + 1) - 2(x + 1)$ — Factorise using the grouping method.

$= (x - 2)(x + 1)$

Q7 (a) $2x^2 - 5x + 3$ — The GN is $(2)(-3) = -6$.

Factors of -6 which add to -5 are $(-2)(-3)$.

$= 2x^2 - 2x - 3x + 3$ — Break up $-5x$ into $-2x - 3x$.

$= 2x(x - 1) - 3(x - 1)$ — Factorise using the grouping method.

$= (2x - 3)(x - 1)$

(b) $22x^2 - 13x + 1$ — The GN is $(22)(+1) = +22$.

Factors of $+22$ which add to -13 are $(-11)(-2)$.

$= 22x^2 - 11x - 2x + 1$ — Break up $-13x$ into $-11x - 2x$.

$= 11x(2x - 1) - 1(2x - 1)$ — Factorise using the grouping method.

$= (11x - 1)(2x - 1)$

(c) $7x^2 + 19x - 6$ — The GN is $(7)(-6) = -42$.

Factors of -42 which add to $+19$ are $(+21)(-2)$.

$= 7x^2 + 21x - 2x - 6$ — Break up $+19x$ into $+21x - 2x$.

$= 7x(x + 3) - 2(x + 3)$ — Factorise using the grouping method.

$= (7x - 2)(x + 3)$

(d) $6x^2 + 17x + 5$ — The GN is $(6)(+5) = +30$.

Factors of $+30$ which add to $+17$ are $(+15)(+2)$.

$= 6x^2 + 2x + 15x + 5$ — Break up $+17x$ into $+2x + 15x$.

$= 2x(3x + 1) + 5(3x + 1)$ — Factorise using the grouping method.

$= (2x + 5)(3x + 1)$

Q8 (a) $6a^2b - 4ab^2 = 2ab(3a - 2b)$ — Factorise using the HCF method.

(b) $36a^2 - 25b^2$

$= (6a)^2 - (5b)^2$ — Factorise using the difference of two squares method.

$= (6a - 5b)(6a + 5b)$

(c) $xy - 7a + xa - 7y$

$= xy + xa - 7a - 7y$ — Factorise using the grouping method.

$= x(y + a) - 7(a + y)$ — Remember that $(y + a) = (a + y)$.

$= (x - 7)(a + y)$

Algebra 3: Algebraic Fractions and Long Division 5

Learning objectives

In this chapter you will learn how to:

- Add and subtract algebraic fractions
- Multiply algebraic fractions
- Divide algebraic fractions
- Divide algebraic expressions using long division.

Adding and subtracting algebraic fractions

Points to note

- The rules that apply for adding and subtracting **arithmetic** fractions also apply for adding and subtracting **algebraic** fractions.
- Equivalent fractions are fractions which can be written in a different form but which have the same value. For example: $\frac{2}{3} = \frac{4}{6} = \frac{6}{9}$
  Equivalent fractions are extremely useful when adding/subtracting fractions with different denominators.
- $\frac{0}{a} = 0, a \in \mathbb{R}$. A fraction can only be zero when the numerator is zero.
- $\frac{a}{0}$ is undefined for $a \in \mathbb{R}$. A scientific calculator will show 'math error' for this fraction.
- When we are asked to simplify an expression which contains algebraic fractions we must write the expression as a single fraction.

Top Tip

When adding/subtracting fractions, follow these steps:

1 Find the lowest common denominator (LCD).

2 Rewrite each fraction in terms of the LCD, using equivalent fractions.

3 Write the expression as a single fraction.

4 Simplify the numerator.

Example

Simplify $3 + \frac{x}{5}$.

Solution

$3 + \frac{x}{5}$ The LCD is 5.

$= \frac{5(3) + x}{5}$ Use brackets and expand.

$= \frac{15 + x}{5}$

Alternative method

Find equivalent fractions with an LCD of 5.

$\frac{3}{1} = \frac{3(5)}{5} = \frac{15}{5}$

$\frac{15}{5} + \frac{x}{5} = \frac{15 + x}{5}$

Example

Write the following expression as a single fraction: $\frac{3a-7}{3} - \frac{2a+1}{4} + 4a$.

Solution

$\frac{3a-7}{3} - \frac{2a+1}{4} + 4a$ The LCD is 12.

$= \frac{4(3a-7) - 3(2a+1) + 12(4a)}{12}$ Use brackets and expand for the numerator only.

$= \frac{12a - 28 - 6a - 3 + 48a}{12} = \frac{54a - 31}{12}$

Example

Write the following expression as a single fraction: $\frac{4}{7b-3} - \frac{1}{b-2}$.

Solution

$\frac{4}{7b-3} - \frac{1}{b-2}$ The LCD is $(7b-3)(b-2)$.

$= \frac{4(b-2) - 1(7b-3)}{(7b-3)(b-2)}$ Expand brackets for the numerator only.

$= \frac{4b - 8 - 7b + 3}{(7b-3)(b-2)}$ Simplify.

$= \frac{-3b-5}{(7b-3)(b-2)}$

Example

Write the following expression as a single fraction: $\frac{2}{x-3} - \frac{4}{2x-7} + \frac{2}{3}$.

Solution

$\frac{2}{x-3} - \frac{4}{2x-7} + \frac{2}{3}$ — The LCD is $(3)(x-3)(2x-7)$.

$= \frac{(2)(3)(2x-7) - (3)(4)(x-3) + (2)(x-3)(2x-7)}{(3)(x-3)(2x-7)}$

$= \frac{(6)(2x-7) - (12)(x-3) + (2x-6)(2x-7)}{(3)(x-3)(2x-7)}$ — Expand brackets for the numerator only.

$= \frac{12x - 42 - 12x + 36 + 2x(2x-7) - 6(2x-7)}{(3)(x-3)(2x-7)}$

$= \frac{-6 + 4x^2 - 14x - 12x + 42}{(3)(x-3)(2x-7)}$ — Simplify.

$= \frac{4x^2 - 26x + 36}{(3)(x-3)(2x-7)}$

$= \frac{2(2x^2 - 13x + 18)}{(3)(x-3)(2x-7)}$ — Factorise the numerator and simplify if possible.

$= \frac{2(2x-9)(x-2)}{3(x-3)(2x-7)}$

Multiplying algebraic fractions

Point to note

The rules that apply for multiplying **arithmetic** fractions also apply for multiplying **algebraic** fractions.

Top Tip

When multiplying algebraic fractions, follow these steps:

1. Factorise the algebraic expressions if possible.
2. Multiply the numerators by the numerators, and the denominators by the denominators.
3. Simplify.

Example

Simplify $\frac{6x^3}{5y^2} \times \frac{25y^3}{9x}$.

Solution

$\frac{6x^3}{5y^2} \times \frac{25y^3}{9x} = \frac{150x^3y^3}{45xy^2}$ Multiply top by top (numerators) and bottom by bottom (denominators). Divide by $15xy^2$.

$= \frac{10x^2y}{3}$

Alternatively we can cancel from the beginning.

Example

Simplify $\frac{(x-y)}{(x+y)} \times \frac{-(x+y)}{x}$.

Solution

$\frac{(x-y)}{(x+y)} \times \frac{-(x+y)}{x}$ Multiply top by top and bottom by bottom.

$= \frac{-(x-y)\cancel{(x+y)}}{x\cancel{(x+y)}}$ Simplify by cancelling factors where possible.

$= \frac{-(x-y)}{x}$ Multiply out the brackets.

$= \frac{-x+y}{x}$ Note: you cannot cancel the x terms here!

Example

Simplify $\frac{3x-2y+xy-6}{xy+3x} \times \frac{1}{x^2-4}$.

Solution

$\frac{3x-2y+xy-6}{xy+3x} \times \frac{1}{x^2-4}$ Factorise the numerator and denominator for both fractions.

$= \frac{3x+xy-2y-6}{xy+3x} \times \frac{1}{x^2-4}$

$= \frac{x(3+y)-2(y+3)}{x(y+3)} \times \frac{1}{(x-2)(x+2)}$

$= \frac{(x-2)(y+3)}{x(y+3)} \times \frac{1}{(x-2)(x+2)}$ Multiply top by top and bottom by bottom.

$= \frac{\cancel{(x-2)}\cancel{(y+3)}}{x\cancel{(y+3)}\cancel{(x-2)}(x+2)}$ Simplify by cancelling factors where possible.

$= \frac{1}{x(x+2)}$ Note: When all factors from the numerator are cancelled this is replaced by 1, not 0.

Example

Simplify: $\dfrac{6a^2 - 47a + 15}{27a^2 - 3}$.

Solution

First factorise the numerator and denominator.

Numerator: $6a^2 - 47a + 15 = (2a - 15)(3a - 1)$

Denominator:

$27a^2 - 3 = 3(9a^2 - 1)$ HCF is 3.

$= 3(3a - 1)(3a + 1)$ Factorise $(9a^2 - 1)$ using the difference of two squares formula.

$\Rightarrow \dfrac{6a^2 - 47a + 15}{27a^2 - 3}$

$= \dfrac{(2a - 15)\cancel{(3a - 1)}}{3\cancel{(3a - 1)}(3a + 1)}$ Cancel the common factor $(3a - 1)$ on the top and bottom.

$= \dfrac{2a - 15}{3(3a + 1)}$

Dividing algebraic fractions

Point to note

- The rules that apply for dividing **arithmetic** fractions also apply for dividing **algebraic** fractions.

Top Tip

When dividing algebraic fractions, follow these steps:

1 Factorise algebraic expressions where possible.

2 Turn the second fraction upside down.

3 Change the operation sign from division to multiplication.

4 Multiply the top by the top, and the bottom by the bottom.

5 Simplify.

Example

Simplify $\dfrac{5x}{3x-3y} \div \dfrac{10x^2}{3}$.

Solution

$\dfrac{5x}{3x-3y} \div \dfrac{10x^2}{3}$ — Factorise all parts.

$= \dfrac{5x}{3(x-y)} \div \dfrac{10x^2}{3}$ — Turn the second fraction upside down and change the sign to multiplication.

$= \dfrac{5x}{3(x-y)} \times \dfrac{3}{10x^2}$ — Multiply top by top and bottom by bottom.

$= \dfrac{15x}{30x^2(x-y)}$ — Divide like terms.

$= \dfrac{1}{2x(x-y)}$

Example

Simplify $\dfrac{4x^2-64y^2}{3x^2+7x-20} \div \dfrac{6x-24y}{3x-5}$.

Solution

$\dfrac{4x^2-64y^2}{3x^2+7x-20} \div \dfrac{6x-24y}{3x-5}$ — Factorise all parts.

$= \dfrac{(2x-8y)(2x+8y)}{(x+4)(3x-5)} \div \dfrac{3(2x-8y)}{(3x-5)}$ — Turn the second fraction upside down and multiply.

$= \dfrac{(2x-8y)(2x+8y)}{(x+4)(3x-5)} \times \dfrac{(3x-5)}{3(2x-8y)}$ — Multiply top by top and bottom by bottom.

$= \dfrac{\cancel{(2x-8y)}(2x+8y)\cancel{(3x-5)}}{3\cancel{(2x-8y)}(x+4)\cancel{(3x-5)}}$ — Cancel like factors.

$= \dfrac{(2x+8y)}{3(x+4)}$ — Factorise the numerator (top).

$= \dfrac{2(x+4y)}{3(x+4)}$

Applications of algebraic expressions

We use algebraic fractions on occasions to solve practical applications.

Example

(a) Find the perimeter of the rectangle.

(b) Express your answer as a single fraction.

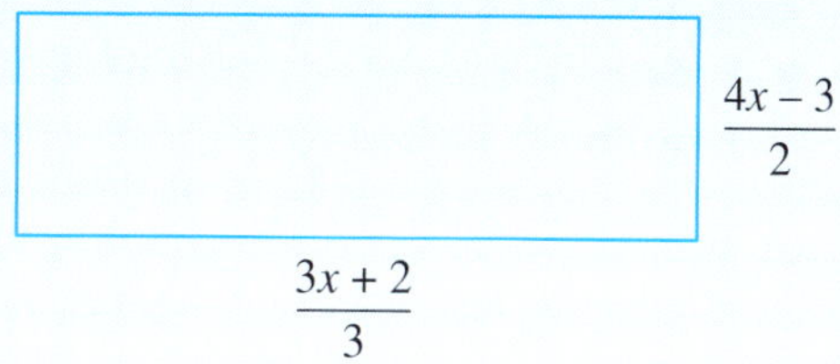

Solution

(a) Perimeter = 2(length) + 2(width)

$$= 2\left(\frac{4x-3}{2}\right) + 2\left(\frac{3x+2}{3}\right) \text{ units}$$

(b) As a single fraction:

$$\text{Perimeter} = 2\left(\frac{4x-3}{2}\right) + 2\left(\frac{3x+2}{3}\right)$$

$$= \frac{\cancel{2}(4x-3)}{\cancel{2}} + \frac{2(3x+2)}{3}$$

$$= \frac{(4x-3)}{1} + \frac{2(3x+2)}{3}$$ The LCD is 3.

$$= \frac{3(4x-3)+2(3x+2)}{3}$$ Expand brackets and simplify.

$$= \frac{12x-9+6x+4}{3}$$

$$= \frac{18x-5}{3} \text{ units}$$

Long division of algebraic expressions

Points to note

1. The rules that apply for **traditional** long division also apply for **algebraic** long division.
2. If an algebraic expression is a factor of another expression then there must be no remainder when it is divided.
3. If the expression that you are dividing has a term missing, add this term and place a zero in front of it. For example: before dividing the expression $3x^3 + 2x - 3$, we will rewrite it as $3x^3 + 0x^2 + 2x - 3$.

Example

Divide $2x^2 - 9x - 5$ by $x - 5$.

Solution

Method 1

Divide $2x^2 - 9x - 5$ by $x - 5$ using long division.

$$
\begin{array}{r}
2x + 1 \\
x - 5\,\overline{)\,2x^2 - 9x - 5} \\
\underline{-2x^2 + 10x \quad} \\
+x - 5 \\
\underline{-x + 5} \\
0
\end{array}
$$

Divide x into $2x^2 \Rightarrow 2x$ on top line.

Multiply $2x$ by $(x - 5) \Rightarrow 2x^2 - 10x$.

Subtract $(2x^2 - 10x)$ from $(2x^2 - 9x)$. Result $= +x$.

Note: $-(2x^2 - 10x) = -2x^2 + 10x$. Bring down -5.

Divide x into $+x \Rightarrow +1$ on top line.

Multiply $+1$ by $(x - 5) \Rightarrow x - 5$.

Subtract $(x - 5)$ from $x - 5$. Note: $-(x - 5) = -x + 5$.

Answer = $2x + 1$

Method 2

Divide $2x^2 - 9x - 5$ by $x - 5$ using the box method/array model.

×	?	?
x	$2x^2$	
-5		-5

To get the term $2x^2$ we must multiply x by $2x$.
So the first ? $= 2x$.

×	$2x$	?
x	$2x^2$	
-5		-5

To get the constant -5 we must multiply -5 by $+1$.
So the second ? $= +1$.

So the factor is $(2x + 1)$.

×	$2x$	$+1$
x	$2x^2$	
-5		-5

Fill in the remainder of the box/array model and check that your solution is correct.

×	$2x$	$+1$
x	$2x^2$	$+x$
-5	$-10x$	-5

Check:

$2x^2 + x - 10x - 5 = 2x^2 - 9x - 5$ ✓

$(x - 5)(2x + 1) = x(2x + 1) - 5(2x + 1) = 2x^2 + x - 10x - 5 = x^2 - 9x - 5$ ✓

Example

Divide $3x^3 - 5x + 2$ by $x - 1$.

Solution

$$
\begin{array}{r|l}
 & 3x^2 + 3x \quad - 2 \\
\hline
x - 1 & 3x^3 + 0x^2 - 5x + 2 \\
 & -3x^3 + 3x^2 \\
\hline
 & \quad +3x^2 - 5x \\
 & \quad -3x^2 + 3x \\
\hline
 & \qquad -2x + 2 \\
 & \qquad +2x - 2 \\
\hline
 & \qquad\qquad 0
\end{array}
$$

Include $0x^2$. Divide x into $3x^3 \Rightarrow 3x^2$ on top line.
Multiply $3x^2$ by $(x - 1) \Rightarrow 3x^3 - 3x^2$.
Subtract $(3x^3 - 3x^2)$ from $3x^3 + 0x^2$. Bring down $-5x$.
Divide x into $3x^2 \Rightarrow +3x$ on top line.
Multiply $+3x$ by $(x - 1) \Rightarrow 3x^2 - 3x$.
Subtract $(3x^2 - 3x)$ from $3x^2 - 5x$. Bring down $+2$.
Divide x into $-2x \Rightarrow -2$ on top line.
Multiply -2 by $(x - 1) \Rightarrow -2x + 2$.
Subtract $(-2x + 2)$ from $-2x + 2$.

Answer = $3x^2 + 3x - 2$

Long division of algebraic expressions can be used to solve practical problems.

Example

The area of a rectangle is $x^3 + x^2 - 12x + 10$.
If one of the sides is $x - 1$, find the other side.

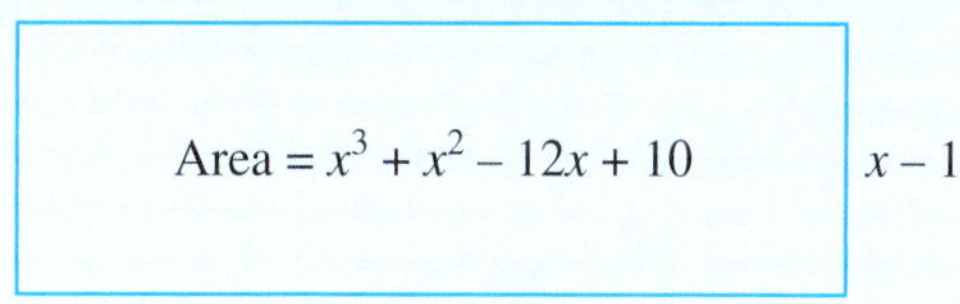

Solution

$$
\begin{array}{r|l}
 & x^2 + 2x - 10 \\
\hline
x - 1 & x^3 + x^2 - 12x + 10 \\
 & -x^3 + x^2 \\
\hline
 & \quad +2x^2 - 12x \\
 & \quad -2x^2 + \ \ 2x \\
\hline
 & \qquad -10x + 10 \\
 & \qquad +10x - 10 \\
\hline
 & \qquad\qquad 0
\end{array}
$$

Divide x into $x^3 \Rightarrow x^2$ on top line.
Multiply x^2 by $(x - 1) \Rightarrow x^3 - x^2$.
Subtract $(x^3 - x^2)$ from $x^3 + x^2$. Bring down $-12x$.
Divide x into $2x^2 \Rightarrow +2x$ on top line.
Multiply $+2x$ by $(x - 1) \Rightarrow 2x^2 - 2x$.
Subtract $(2x^2 - 2x)$ from $2x^2 - 12x$. Bring down $+10$.
Divide x into $-10x \Rightarrow -10$ on top line.
Multiply -10 by $(x - 1) \Rightarrow -10x + 10$.
Subtract $(-10x + 10)$ from $-10x + 10$.

Answer = $x^2 + 2x - 10$

Exercise

Q1 (a) Complete: $\frac{1}{2} = \frac{\ }{4} = \frac{\ }{6} = \frac{\ }{24}$.

(b) Simplify the following:

(i) $\frac{16}{30}$

(ii) $22 \div \frac{1}{2}$

(iii) $\frac{2}{3} \times \frac{12}{8}$

(iv) $\frac{23x}{x}$

(v) $\frac{-xyz}{-2yz}$

(vi) $\frac{12a^3b^5c^2}{3ab^6c^2}$

(vii) $\frac{3a-3b}{a-b}$

(viii) $\frac{(c-d)}{-(c-d)}$.

Q2 Simplify the following:

(a) $\frac{(x+2)(x-2)}{x^2-4x+4}$

(b) $\frac{y-5}{y^2-25}\times\frac{y+5}{3}$

(c) $\frac{(x+y^2)}{(x+y)}\times\frac{(x^2-y^2)}{x}$

(d) $\frac{x^2+ax-bx-ab}{bx+ab}\times\frac{ax^2+a^2x}{ax}$

(e) $\frac{4x^2+4x-3}{2}\times\frac{6x}{4x^2-9}$

(f) $\frac{a^4-1}{6a^2+6}\times\frac{1}{a^2-2a+1}$.

Q3 Simplify the following:

(a) $\frac{a}{3b}\div\frac{a^2}{6abc}$

(b) $\frac{9a^5}{x^4}\div\frac{3a^3}{3x^5}$

(c) $\frac{x^2-x}{2}\div\frac{x}{8}$

(d) $\frac{x+y}{8}\div\frac{x^2-y^2}{12}$

(e) $\frac{3x-9y}{2x-5}\div\frac{3}{8x-20}$

(f) $\frac{x^2+x}{x^2+2x+1}\div\frac{x}{x+1}$.

Q4 Simplify the following:

(a) $\frac{1}{2}+\frac{5}{6}$

(b) $\frac{1}{5}+\frac{3}{10}$

(c) $\frac{2}{13}-\frac{1}{39}$

(d) $\frac{9}{10}-\frac{2}{5}$.

Q5 Write each of the following expressions as a single fraction:

(a) $\frac{1}{x}+\frac{3}{y}$

(b) $2+\frac{1}{x}$

(c) $\frac{x}{y}-\frac{y}{x}$

(d) $\frac{3c}{2}+\frac{5c}{6}$

(e) $\frac{14d}{3}-3d$

(f) $\frac{4x-1}{2}+\frac{3x-2}{5}$

(g) $\frac{7x-4}{3}+\frac{2-3x}{5}$

(h) $\frac{3x-1}{5}-\frac{5x-3}{2}$

(i) $\frac{2a-7}{2}-\frac{3-5a}{5}$

(j) $\frac{1}{3}(2b-1)+\frac{2}{5}(5b-3)$

(k) $\frac{x}{2}-\frac{2x-1}{5}+\frac{x+1}{10}$

(l) $\frac{f+1}{2}-\frac{f-1}{3}+f$

(m) $\frac{x-1}{5}+\frac{3x-4}{3}-\frac{5x+3}{15}$

(n) $\frac{2x-1}{4}-\frac{x+1}{7}-\frac{5x-1}{28}$.

Q6 Use long division for the following questions.

(a) If $x-1$ is factor of x^2+3x-4, find the second factor.

(b) If $x+1$ is factor of x^2-x-2, find the second factor.

(c) If $x+6$ is factor of $x^2+2x-24$, find the second factor.

(d) If $x-5$ is factor of $2x^2-7x-15$, find the second factor.

Q7 (a) Divide $x^3-5x^2-2x+24$ by $x-4$.

(b) Divide $x^3+6x^2+5x-12$ by $x+3$.

(c) Divide $2x^3-3x+1$ by $x-1$.

(d) Divide x^3-8 by $x-2$.

Q8 (a) Find the perimeter of the rectangle below in terms of x.

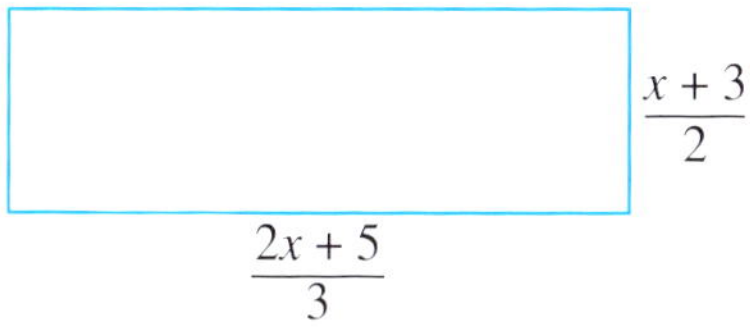

(b) Express your answer as a single fraction.

(c) If $x = 2$, find the perimeter of the rectangle.

Q9 Find the width of the rectangle below in terms of x, if the area of the rectangle is $x^2 - 6x - 27$ and the length is $x + 3$.

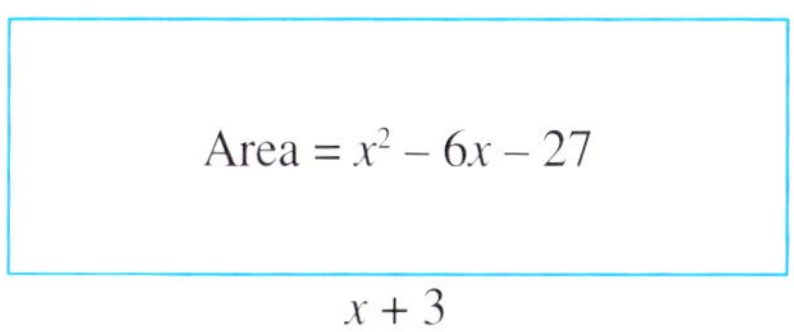

Q10 (a) Find the perimeter of this triangle:

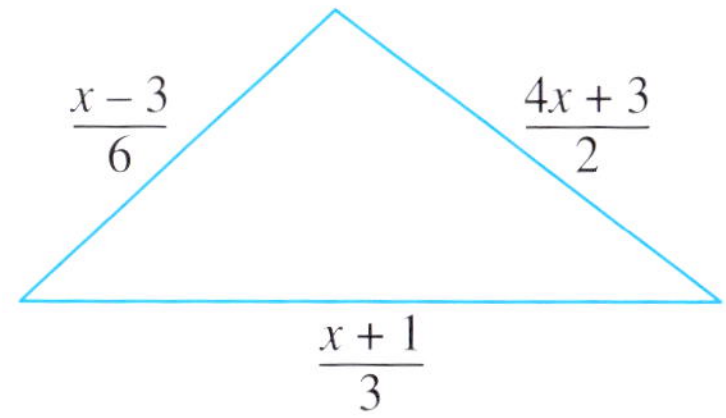

(b) Express your answer as a single fraction.

Q11 (a) Express $\frac{3}{x+1} - \frac{2}{x+4}$ in its simplest form.

(b) Divide $3x^2 - 19x - 14$ by $x - 7$, by factorisation.

(SEC 2010)

Solutions

Q1 (a) $\frac{1}{2} = \frac{2}{4} = \frac{3}{6} = \frac{12}{24}$

(b) (i) $\frac{16}{30} = \frac{8}{15}$

(ii) $22 \div \frac{1}{2} = \frac{22}{1} \times \frac{2}{1} = \frac{44}{1} = 44$

(iii) $\frac{2}{3} \times \frac{12}{8} = \frac{24}{24} = 1$

(iv) $\frac{23x}{x} = 23$

(v) $\frac{-xyz}{-2yz} = \frac{x}{2}$

(vi) $\frac{12a^3b^5c^2}{3ab^6c^2} = \frac{4a^2}{b}$

(vii) $\frac{3a - 3b}{a - b} = \frac{3\cancel{(a-b)}}{\cancel{(a-b)}} = 3$

(viii) $\frac{(c-d)}{-(c-d)} = -1$

Q2 (a) $\frac{(x+2)(x-2)}{x^2 - 4x + 4} = \frac{(x+2)\cancel{(x-2)}}{(x-2)\cancel{(x-2)}} = \frac{(x+2)}{(x-2)}$

(b) $\frac{y-5}{y^2-25} \times \frac{y+5}{3} = \frac{\cancel{(y-5)}\cancel{(y+5)}}{3\cancel{(y-5)}\cancel{(y+5)}} = \frac{1}{3}$

(c) $\frac{(x+y^2)}{(x+y)} \times \frac{(x^2-y^2)}{x} = \frac{(x+y^2)(x-y)\cancel{(x+y)}}{x\cancel{(x+y)}} = \frac{(x+y^2)(x-y)}{x}$

(d) $$\frac{x^2+ax-bx-ab}{bx+ab}\times\frac{ax^2+a^2x}{ax}=\frac{(x-b)\cancel{(x+a)}}{b\cancel{(x+a)}}\times\frac{\cancel{ax}(x+a)}{\cancel{ax}}$$
$$=\frac{(x-b)}{b}\times\frac{(x+a)}{1}=\frac{(x-b)(x+a)}{b}$$

Note: $x^2+ax-bx-ab$
$=x(x+a)-b(x+a)$
$=(x-b)(x+a)$

(e) $$\frac{4x^2+4x-3}{2}\times\frac{6x}{4x^2-9}=\frac{(2x-1)(2x+3)}{2}\times\frac{6x}{(2x-3)(2x+3)}$$
$$=\frac{6x(2x-1)\cancel{(2x+3)}}{2(2x-3)\cancel{(2x+3)}}=\frac{3x(2x-1)}{(2x-3)}$$

(f) $$\frac{a^4-1}{6a^2+6}\times\frac{1}{a^2-2a+1}=\frac{(a^2-1)\cancel{(a^2+1)}}{6\cancel{(a^2+1)}}\times\frac{1}{(a-1)(a-1)}$$
$$=\frac{\cancel{(a-1)}(a+1)}{6\cancel{(a-1)}(a-1)}=\frac{(a+1)}{6(a-1)}$$

Note:
$a^4-1=(a^2)^2-(1)^2$
$=(a^2-1)(a^2+1)$

Q3 (a) $$\frac{a}{3b}\div\frac{a^2}{6abc}=\frac{a}{3b}\times\frac{6abc}{a^2}=\frac{6a^2bc}{3a^2b}=2c$$

(b) $$\frac{9a^5}{x^4}\div\frac{3a^3}{3x^5}=\frac{9a^5}{x^4}\times\frac{3x^5}{3a^3}=\frac{27a^5x^5}{3a^3x^4}=9a^2x$$

(c) $$\frac{x^2-x}{2}\div\frac{x}{8}=\frac{x(x-1)}{2}\times\frac{8}{x}=\frac{8x(x-1)}{2x}=4(x-1)=4x-4$$

(d) $$\frac{x+y}{8}\div\frac{x^2-y^2}{12}=\frac{x+y}{8}\div\frac{(x-y)(x+y)}{12}$$
$$=\frac{(x+y)}{8}\times\frac{12}{(x-y)(x+y)}=\frac{12\cancel{(x+y)}}{8(x-y)\cancel{(x+y)}}=\frac{3}{2(x-y)}$$

(e) $$\frac{3x-9y}{2x-5}\div\frac{3}{8x-20}=\frac{3(x-3y)}{2x-5}\times\frac{4(2x-5)}{3}=\frac{12(x-3y)\cancel{(2x-5)}}{3\cancel{(2x-5)}}$$
$$=4(x-3y)=4x-12y$$

(f) $$\frac{x^2+x}{x^2+2x+1}\div\frac{x}{x+1}=\frac{x(x+1)}{(x+1)(x+1)}\times\frac{(x+1)}{x}=\frac{\cancel{x(x+1)(x+1)}}{\cancel{x(x+1)(x+1)}}=1$$

Q4 (a) $$\frac{1}{2}+\frac{5}{6}=\frac{3(1)+1(5)}{6}=\frac{3+5}{6}=\frac{8}{6}=\frac{4}{3}$$

(b) $$\frac{1}{5}+\frac{3}{10}=\frac{2(1)+1(3)}{10}=\frac{2+3}{10}=\frac{5}{10}=\frac{1}{2}$$

(c) $$\frac{2}{13}-\frac{1}{39}=\frac{3(2)-1(1)}{39}=\frac{6-1}{39}=\frac{5}{39}$$

(d) $$\frac{9}{10}-\frac{2}{5}=\frac{1(9)-2(2)}{10}=\frac{9-4}{10}=\frac{5}{10}=\frac{1}{2}$$

Q5 (a) $$\frac{1}{x}+\frac{3}{y}=\frac{y(1)+x(3)}{xy}=\frac{y+3x}{xy}$$

(b) $$2+\frac{1}{x}=\frac{x(2)+1(1)}{x}=\frac{2x+1}{x}$$

(c) $\dfrac{x}{y}-\dfrac{y}{x}=\dfrac{x(x)-y(y)}{xy}=\dfrac{x^2-y^2}{xy}=\dfrac{(x-y)(x+y)}{xy}$

(d) $\dfrac{3c}{2}+\dfrac{5c}{6}=\dfrac{3(3c)+1(5c)}{6}=\dfrac{9c+5c}{6}=\dfrac{14c}{6}=\dfrac{7c}{3}$

(e) $\dfrac{14d}{3}-3d=\dfrac{14d-3(3d)}{3}=\dfrac{14d-9d}{3}=\dfrac{5d}{3}$

(f) $\dfrac{4x-1}{2}+\dfrac{3x-2}{5}=\dfrac{5(4x-1)+2(3x-2)}{10}=\dfrac{20x-5+6x-4}{10}=\dfrac{26x-9}{10}$

(g) $\dfrac{7x-4}{3}+\dfrac{2-3x}{5}=\dfrac{5(7x-4)+3(2-3x)}{15}=\dfrac{35x-20+6-9x}{15}=\dfrac{26x-14}{15}$

(h) $\dfrac{3x-1}{5}-\dfrac{5x-3}{2}=\dfrac{2(3x-1)-5(5x-3)}{10}=\dfrac{6x-2-25x+15}{10}=\dfrac{-19x+13}{10}$

(i) $\dfrac{2a-7}{2}-\dfrac{3-5a}{5}=\dfrac{5(2a-7)-2(3-5a)}{10}=\dfrac{10a-35-6+10a}{10}=\dfrac{20a-41}{10}$

(j) $\dfrac{1}{3}(2b-1)+\dfrac{2}{5}(5b-3)=\dfrac{5(2b-1)+3(2)(5b-3)}{15}$

$=\dfrac{10b-5+6(5b-3)}{15}=\dfrac{10b-5+30b-18}{15}$

$=\dfrac{40b-23}{15}$

Note: $\dfrac{1}{3}(2b-1)=\dfrac{2b-1}{3}$

and $\dfrac{2}{5}(5b-3)=\dfrac{2(5b-3)}{5}$

(k) $\dfrac{x}{2}-\dfrac{2x-1}{5}+\dfrac{x+1}{10}=\dfrac{5(x)-2(2x-1)+(x+1)}{10}$

$=\dfrac{5x-4x+2+x+1}{10}=\dfrac{2x+3}{10}$

(l) $\dfrac{f+1}{2}-\dfrac{f-1}{3}+f=\dfrac{3(f+1)-2(f-1)+6(f)}{6}=\dfrac{3f+3-2f+2+6f}{6}=\dfrac{7f+5}{6}$

(m) $\dfrac{x-1}{5}+\dfrac{3x-4}{3}-\dfrac{5x+3}{15}=\dfrac{3(x-1)+5(3x-4)-1(5x+3)}{15}$

$=\dfrac{3x-3+15x-20-5x-3}{15}=\dfrac{13x-26}{15}$

(n) $\dfrac{2x-1}{4}-\dfrac{x+1}{7}-\dfrac{5x-1}{28}=\dfrac{7(2x-1)-4(x+1)-1(5x-1)}{28}$

$=\dfrac{14x-7-4x-4-5x+1}{28}=\dfrac{5x-10}{28}$

Q6 (a)

$$\begin{array}{r|l} & x+4 \\ \hline x-1 & x^2+3x-4 \\ & -x^2+x \\ \hline & +4x-4 \\ & -4x+4 \\ \hline & 0 \end{array}$$

Answer $= x+4$

(b)

$$\begin{array}{r|l} & x-2 \\ \hline x+1 & x^2-x-2 \\ & -x^2-x \\ \hline & -2x-2 \\ & +2x+2 \\ \hline & 0 \end{array}$$

Answer $= x-2$

(c)

$$\begin{array}{r} x-4 \\ x+6\,\overline{\smash{)}\,x^2+2x-24} \\ \underline{-x^2-6x} \\ -4x-24 \\ \underline{+4x+24} \\ 0 \end{array}$$

Answer $= x-4$

(d)

$$\begin{array}{r} 2x+3 \\ x-5\,\overline{\smash{)}\,2x^2-7x-15} \\ \underline{-2x^2+10x} \\ +3x-15 \\ \underline{-3x+15} \\ 0 \end{array}$$

Answer $= 2x+3$

Q7 (a)

$$\begin{array}{r} x^2-x-6 \\ x-4\,\overline{\smash{)}\,x^3-5x^2-2x+24} \\ \underline{-x^3+4x^2} \\ -\ x^2-2x \\ \underline{+\ x^2-4x} \\ -6x+24 \\ \underline{+6x-24} \\ 0 \end{array}$$

Answer $= x^2-x-6$

(b)

$$\begin{array}{r} x^2+3x-4 \\ x+3\,\overline{\smash{)}\,x^3+6x^2+5x-12} \\ \underline{-x^3-3x^2} \\ +3x^2+5x \\ \underline{-3x^2-9x} \\ -4x-12 \\ \underline{+4x+12} \\ 0 \end{array}$$

Answer $= x^2+3x-4$

(c)

$$\begin{array}{r} 2x^2+2x-1 \\ x-1\,\overline{\smash{)}\,2x^3+0x^2-3x+1} \\ \underline{-2x^3+2x^2} \\ +2x^2-3x \\ \underline{-2x^2+2x} \\ -x+1 \\ \underline{+x-1} \\ 0 \end{array}$$

Answer $= 2x^2+2x-1$

(d)

$$\begin{array}{r} x^2+2x+4 \\ x-2\,\overline{\smash{)}\,x^3+0x^2+0x-8} \\ \underline{-x^3+2x^2} \\ +2x^2+0x \\ \underline{-2x^2+4x} \\ +4x-8 \\ \underline{-4x+8} \\ 0 \end{array}$$

Answer $= x^2+2x+4$

Q8 (a) Perimeter $= 2\left(\dfrac{x+3}{2}\right)+2\left(\dfrac{2x+5}{3}\right)$ units

(b) Perimeter $= (x+3)+\dfrac{(4x+10)}{3}$

$$= \frac{3(x+3)+4x+10}{3} = \frac{3x+9+4x+10}{3}$$

$$= \frac{7x+19}{3} \text{ units}$$

(c) Perimeter $= \dfrac{7x+19}{3} = \dfrac{7(2)+19}{3} = \dfrac{14+19}{3} = \dfrac{33}{3} = 11$ units

Q9

$$\begin{array}{r} x-9 \\ x+3\overline{)x^2-6x-27} \\ \underline{-x^2-3x\quad\;\;} \\ -9x-27 \\ \underline{+9x+27} \\ 0 \end{array}$$

Width = $x - 9$ units

Q10 (a) Perimeter of the triangle = $\frac{x-3}{6} + \frac{x+1}{3} + \frac{4x+3}{2}$ units

(b) Perimeter of the triangle = $\frac{x-3}{6} + \frac{x+1}{3} + \frac{4x+3}{2} = \frac{x-3+2(x+1)+3(4x+3)}{6}$

$= \frac{x-3+2x+2+12x+9}{6} = \frac{15x+8}{6}$ units

Q11 (a) $\frac{3}{x+1} - \frac{2}{x+4}$

$= \frac{3(x+4)-2(x+1)}{(x+1)(x+4)}$

$= \frac{3x+12-2x-2}{(x+1)(x+4)}$

$= \frac{x+10}{(x+1)(x+4)}$

Top Tip

There are two methods which can be used to divide a linear expression into a quadratic expression.

Method 1: Long division.

Method 2: Factorisation.

For the factorisation method:

1. Put the quadratic expression over the linear expression.
2. Factorise the quadratic expression.
3. Cancel any common factors on the top and bottom.

(b) $\frac{3x^2-19x-14}{x-7} = \frac{3x^2-21x+2x-14}{(x-7)}$ Factorise the numerator.

$= \frac{3x(x-7)+2(x-7)}{(x-7)}$

$= \frac{(3x+2)\cancel{(x-7)}}{\cancel{(x-7)}}$

$= 3x + 2$

6 Algebra 4: Linear Equations

Learning objectives

In this chapter you will learn about:

- The key terminology and information associated with linear equations
- Different methods used to solve linear equations
- How to solve different types of linear equations
- Applications of linear equations.

Key Terminology

Word	Meaning
Expression	An **expression** is a set of terms which are added or subtracted. An expression does not have an equals sign. For example: $7x - 2$, $5x^2 - 3x + 4$, $8x^3 - 3x^2 - 2x + 1$.
Term	A **term** is an individual part of an expression or an equation. For example: $5x^2$, $-3x$, $+4$.
Constant	A **constant** is a term whose value never changes. For example: +7, −31.
Variable	**Variables** are the letters which stand for unknown numbers in algebra. For example: x, y, z.
Equation	An **equation** is an expression equal to another expression, term or constant. An equation can be solved to find the value(s) of unknown variable(s), but only certain values will work to make the equation true. For example: $2x - 7 = 1$.

Word	Meaning
Linear equation in one variable	An equation of the form $ax + b = 0$, where $a, b, x \in \mathbb{R}$. Here, x is the unknown variable. The equation is **linear** because the highest power of x is 1 $(x = x^1)$.
Solve	Find the value of the unknown variable(s). For example: $2x = 4 \Rightarrow x = \frac{4}{2} \Rightarrow x = 2$.
Substitute	Replace the unknown variable with the value of the solution found.
Inverse operation	The **inverse operation** is the opposite operation. For example: • the inverse of addition is subtraction and vice versa • the inverse of multiplication is division and vice versa. We use inverse operations to help solve linear equations.
LHS	Left hand side
RHS	Right hand side
Solution/ root	The **solution** or **root** is the value of the unknown variable which makes an equation true.
Verify/ check	Replace the unknown with the value of the solution/root and show that the left hand side of the equation is equal to the right hand side.

Points to note

To solve a linear equation, we must:

- find a value for the unknown variable that makes the linear equation true
- perform the same 'inverse operation' to both sides of the equation so that the equation remains balanced, i.e. LHS = RHS
- verify that the solution/root is true by substituting the value for the unknown variable into the original equation and showing that both sides are equal.

The two important pairs of 'inverse operations' that we use in this chapter are:

- + and −
- × and ÷

Different methods used to solve linear equations

Linear equations can be solved using the methods listed below:

- trial and improvement
- the balance method.

Example

(a) Solve the linear equation $x - 5 = 4$, using the methods listed above.

(b) Hence, verify your solution.

Solution

(a) Method 1: Trial and improvement

To solve a linear equation using the trial and improvement method, we substitute the unknown variable with different values until the linear equation is balanced.

Try x	Substitute the value for x into $x - 5 = 4$	Is the solution correct? Does LHS = RHS?
1	$x - 5 = 1 - 5 = -4$	No: $-4 \neq 4$ ✗
2	$x - 5 = 2 - 5 = -3$	No: $-3 \neq 4$ ✗
3	$x - 5 = 3 - 5 = -2$	No: $-2 \neq 4$ ✗
4	$x - 5 = 4 - 5 = -1$	No: $-1 \neq 4$ ✗
5	$x - 5 = 5 - 5 = 0$	No: $0 \neq 4$ ✗
6	$x - 5 = 6 - 5 = 1$	No: $1 \neq 4$ ✗
7	$x - 5 = 7 - 5 = 2$	No: $2 \neq 4$ ✗
8	$x - 5 = 8 - 5 = 3$	No: $3 \neq 4$ ✗
9	$x - 5 = 9 - 5 = 4$	Yes: $4 = 4$ ✓

Alternatively, we can use the table function on a calculator to find the solution for x.

Using a Casio calculator:

1. Press [ON].
2. Press [MODE] [3] to choose the table option.
3. At the prompt '$f(x)$ =' press [ALPHA] [)] [−5] [=].
4. At the prompt 'Start?' choose an appropriate value for x. In this case choose 1. Press [=].
5. At the prompt 'End?' choose an appropriate value for x. In this case choose 9. Press [=].

6 At the prompt 'Step?' choose an appropriate value. In this case choose 1, so that the values for x are 1, 2, 3, 4, 5, 6, 7, etc. Press [=].

7 From the table shown on the calculator read off the value of x which makes $f(x) = 4$.

8 From the table we can see that the equation is true when $x = 9$.

Method 2: The balance method

To find the value for x, we put the x's on the left and the constants on the right.

$x - 5 = 4$ — Add 5 to both sides (as the 'inverse operation' of − 5 is + 5).

$\Rightarrow x - \cancel{5} + \cancel{5} = 4 + 5$ — Note: when we add 5 to the LHS we are left with x terms only.

$\Rightarrow x = 4 + 5$

$\Rightarrow x = 9$

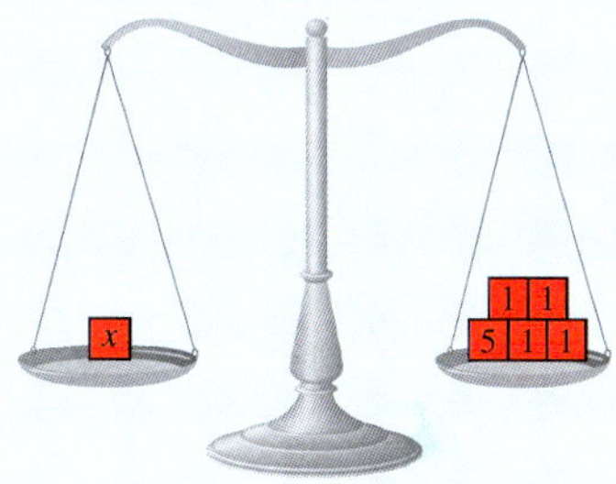

(b) Verify/check the solution is true:

$x - 5 = 4$

$(9) - 5 = 4$

$4 = 4$ ✓

As shown in the example above, the balance method can take less time than the trial and improvement method.

From this point on we will use the balance method to solve all problems.

Solving different types of linear equations

Points to note

To solve a linear equation containing an unknown variable and constants, follow these steps:

1 If the linear equation contains fractions, multiply both sides of the equation by the lowest common denominator (LCD).

2 Expand/multiply out any brackets.

3 Rearrange the formula so that the terms with unknown variables are on one side and the constants are on the other.

4 Collect all like terms.

5 Divide both sides by the coefficient of the unknown variable to find the solution/root.

6 Verify (check) the solution is true by substituting the solution into the original equation.

Example

Solve the linear equations:

(a) $x + 3 = 8$ **(b)** $a - 11 = -2$ **(c)** $2y = 7$ **(d)** $\frac{b}{7} = -4.$

Solution

(a) $x + 3 = 8$

$\Rightarrow x + \cancel{3} - \cancel{3} = 8 - 3$

$\Rightarrow x = 5$

Subtract 3 from both sides, as the opposite operation to + 3 is – 3.

(b) $a - 11 = -2$

$\Rightarrow a - \cancel{11} + \cancel{11} = -2 + 11$

$\Rightarrow a = 9$

Add 11 to both sides, as the opposite operation to – 11 is + 11.

(c) $2y = 7$

$\Rightarrow \frac{\cancel{2}y}{\cancel{2}} = \frac{7}{2}$

$\Rightarrow y = 3{\cdot}5$

To find the value of y, divide both sides by 2. This is because the inverse/opposite operation to multiplication is division.

(d) $\frac{b}{7} = -4$

$\Rightarrow \frac{\cancel{7}b}{\cancel{7}} = 7(-4)$

$\Rightarrow b = -28$

To find the value of b, multiply both sides by 7. This is because the inverse/opposite operation to division is multiplication.

Example

Solve the linear equation $2(x - 4) + 7 = x - 3$ and verify your answer.

Solution

$2(x - 4) + 7 = x - 3$	Expand brackets.	Verify:
$\Rightarrow 2x - 8 + 7 = x - 3$	Simplify.	$2(x - 4) + 7 = x - 3$
$\Rightarrow 2x - 1 = x - 3$	Add 1 to both sides.	$2(-2 - 4) + 7 = -2 - 3$
$\Rightarrow 2x = x - 3 + 1$	Subtract x from both sides.	$2(-6) + 7 = -5$
$\Rightarrow 2x - x = -2$	Simplify.	$-12 + 7 = -5$
$\Rightarrow x = -2$		$-5 = -5$ ✓

Example

Solve the linear equation $5(3 - a) + 4 = a + 7$ and verify your answer.

Solution

$5(3 - a) + 4 = a + 7$	Expand brackets.	Verify:
$\Rightarrow 15 - 5a + 4 = a + 7$	Add like terms on both sides.	$5(3 - a) + 4 = a + 7$
$\Rightarrow -5a + 19 = a + 7$	Subtract 19 from both sides.	$5(3 - 2) + 4 = 2 + 7$
$\Rightarrow -5a = a + 7 - 19$	Subtract a from both sides.	$5(1) + 4 = 9$
$\Rightarrow -5a - a = -12$		$5 + 4 = 9$
$\Rightarrow -6a = -12$	Divide both sides by −6.	$9 = 9$ ✓
$\Rightarrow a = \frac{-12}{-6}$		
$\Rightarrow a = 2$		

Example

Solve the linear equation $\frac{5t}{4} - 2 = \frac{t}{4} + 15$ and verify your answer.

Solution

$\frac{5t}{4} - 2 = \frac{t}{4} + 15$	Multiply all terms by 4 (the LCD).
$\Rightarrow 4\left(\frac{5t}{4}\right) - 4(2) = 4\left(\frac{t}{4}\right) + 4(15)$	Multiply out brackets.
$\Rightarrow 5t - 8 = t + 60$	Add 8 to both sides.
$\Rightarrow 5t = t + 60 + 8$	Subtract t from both sides.
$\Rightarrow 5t - t = 68$	
$\Rightarrow 4t = 68$	Divide both sides by 4.
$\Rightarrow t = \frac{68}{4}$	
$\Rightarrow t = 17$	

Verify:

$$\frac{5(17)}{4} - 2 = \frac{(17)}{4} + 15$$

$19{\cdot}25 = 19{\cdot}25$ ✓

Example

Solve the linear equation $\frac{1}{7}(2m+3) - \frac{7m-4}{2} = \frac{-11}{14}$ and verify your answer.

Solution

$\frac{1}{7}(2m+3) - \frac{7m-4}{2} = \frac{-11}{14}$ — Multiply all terms by 14 (the LCD).

$\Rightarrow \frac{14}{7}(2m+3) - 14\left(\frac{7m-4}{2}\right) = 14\left(\frac{-11}{14}\right)$ — Simplify.

$\Rightarrow 2(2m+3) - 7(7m-4) = 1(-11)$ — Expand the brackets.

$\Rightarrow 4m + 6 - 49m + 28 = -11$ — Simplify.

$\Rightarrow -45m + 34 = -11$ — Subtract 34 from both sides.

$\Rightarrow -45m = -11 - 34$

$\Rightarrow -45m = -45$ — Divide each side by −45.

$\Rightarrow m = \frac{-45}{-45}$

$\Rightarrow m = 1$

Verify:

$\frac{1}{7}(2(1)+3) - \frac{7(1)-4}{2} = \frac{-11}{14}$

$\frac{1}{7}(2+3) - \frac{7-4}{2} = \frac{-11}{14}$

$\frac{1}{7}(5) - \frac{3}{2} = \frac{-11}{14}$

$\frac{5}{7} - \frac{3}{2} = \frac{-11}{14}$

$\frac{-11}{14} = \frac{-11}{14}$ ✓

Applications of linear equations

Linear equations can be used to solve problems in many areas of mathematics. On the JCHL course, the use of linear equations can be linked directly with other topics such as geometry, statistics, functions, sets, trigonometry, and distance, speed and time, to mention a few.

Example

A number is doubled and divided by 5. This has the same answer as the sum of the number and 3, divided by 8. What is the number?

Solution

We know:

A number doubled and divided by 5 = sum of the number and 3, divided by 8.

Let x = number.

A number doubled and divided by 5 can be written as $\frac{2x}{5}$.

The sum of the number and 3, divided by 8 can be written as $\frac{x+3}{8}$.

Hence:

$$\frac{2x}{5} = \frac{x+3}{8}$$

Solve:

$\Rightarrow \frac{2x}{5} = \frac{x+3}{8}$	Multiply both sides by 40 (the LCD).
$\Rightarrow 40\left(\frac{2x}{5}\right) = 40\left(\frac{x+3}{8}\right)$	Simplify.
$\Rightarrow 8(2x) = 5(x+3)$	Expand the brackets.
$\Rightarrow 16x = 5x + 15$	Subtract $5x$ from both sides.
$\Rightarrow 16x - 5x = 15$	
$\Rightarrow 11x = 15$	Divide both sides by 11.
$\Rightarrow x = \frac{15}{11}$	

Verify:

$$\frac{2\left(\frac{15}{11}\right)}{5} = \frac{\left(\frac{15}{11}\right) + 3}{8}$$

$$\frac{\left(\frac{30}{11}\right)}{5} = \frac{\left(\frac{48}{11}\right)}{8}$$

$$\frac{6}{11} = \frac{6}{11} \quad \checkmark$$

Example

The base of a box is 12 cm longer than it is wide, and the perimeter of the base of the box is 56 cm. Allow w to represent the width of the base of the box. Write an equation for the information given and solve to find both the width and the length of the base of the box.

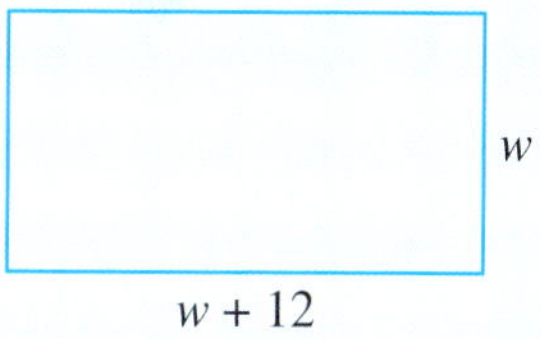

Solution

Let:

w = width of the base of the box

$w + 12$ = length of the base of the box

We know that the perimeter of the base = 2(length) + 2(width) = 56.

$\therefore 2(w + 12) + 2(w) = 56$	Expand the brackets.
$\Rightarrow 2w + 24 + 2w = 56$	Simplify.
$\Rightarrow 24 + 4w = 56$	Subtract 24 from both sides.
$\Rightarrow 4w = 56 - 24$	
$\Rightarrow 4w = 32$	Divide both sides by 4.
$\Rightarrow w = \frac{32}{4}$	
$\Rightarrow w = 8$	

Width = 8 cm

Length = $w + 12 = 8 + 12 = 20$ cm

Exercise

Q1 Explain the meaning of the following words, or give an example:

(a) expression
(b) term
(c) constant
(d) variable
(e) equation
(f) linear equation
(g) solve
(h) substitute
(i) inverse operation
(j) solution/root
(k) verify/check.

Q2 Solve the following linear equations for each unknown variable:

(a) $-3 + x = 7$
(b) $a + 9 = 17$
(c) $6 = -b + 3$
(d) $-2 = k - 1$
(e) $14f = 182$
(f) $7h = -56$
(g) $\frac{2y}{-3} = 4$
(h) $\frac{3d}{-7} = -9$.

Q3 Solve the following linear equations for the unknown variable:

(a) $12 + 5x = 47$
(b) $2a - 7 = -9$
(c) $-3 - 8c = -11$
(d) $-22 = 3y - 1$.

Q4 Solve the following linear equations for the unknown variable:

(a) $-2a - 14 = 5 - 3a$
(b) $7b - 11 = 13b + 25$
(c) $3x - 7 = -4 + 5x$
(d) $5 + 6d - 8 = 2d - 3 - 5d$.

Q5 Solve the following linear equations for the unknown variable:

(a) $6y - 3(y + 2) = 3 - 6y$
(b) $3(w - 2) - 4(w - 1) = 2(4 - w) - 7$
(c) $2(c + 1) - (3 - 2c) = 2c - 7(1 - 2c)$
(d) $5(1 - 3z) - 2(10 - z) = -10 + z$.

Q6 Solve the following linear equations for the unknown variable:

(a) $3 - \frac{y - 2}{4} = -4$
(b) $\frac{x}{3} - \frac{1}{5} = 2$
(c) $\frac{b}{5} - \frac{b}{2} = 3$
(d) $\frac{d - 1}{3} - 5 = -d$
(e) $\frac{2}{3}(3x - 5) + 2 = \frac{1}{2}(x - 1)$.

Q7 Solve the following linear equations for the unknown variable:

(a) $\frac{x + 3}{4} - \frac{x - 4}{2} = 7$
(b) $\frac{2n - 3}{2} + \frac{n + 1}{3} = \frac{3n - 1}{3}$
(c) $\frac{x}{3} + \frac{x + 2}{4} = \frac{3}{4} + \frac{x}{2}$
(d) $\frac{3y + 2}{8} = \frac{2y + 1}{4} + \frac{1}{3}$.

Q8 Write each statement below as a linear equation and solve to find the unknown number.

(a) If a number is tripled and 4 is subtracted from the result, then the answer is 17. Find the number.
(b) The sum of three consecutive natural numbers is 99. Find the three numbers.
(c) Jack thinks of a number, divides it by 4 and subtracts 6, and the answer is 15. Find the number.

Q9 Katie has €438 in her credit union account and saves €12 per week. Conor has €620 in his credit union account and withdraws €14 each week. They wish to know when they will have the same amount of money in their credit union accounts.

(a) Write an equation to represent this information. Let x equal the number of weeks.

(b) After how many weeks will they have the same amount in their accounts?

(c) Verify your answer.

Solutions

Q1 (a) An expression is a set of terms which are added or subtracted. For example: $7x - 2$, $5x^2 - 3x + 4$, $8x^3 - 3x^2 - 2x + 1$.

(b) A term is an individual part of an expression or an equation. For example: $5x^2$, $-3x$, $+4$.

(c) A constant is a term whose value never changes. For example: +7, −31.

(d) Variables are the letters which stand for unknown numbers in algebra. For example: x, y, z.

(e) An equation is an expression equal to another expression, term or constant. For example: $2x - 7 = 1$.

(f) A linear equation in one variable is an equation of the form $ax + b = 0$, where $a, b, x \in \mathbb{R}$. Here x is the unknown variable and the equation is linear because the highest power of x equals 1 ($x = x^1$).

(g) Solve means to find the value of the unknown variable(s). For example: $2x = 4 \Rightarrow x = \frac{4}{2} \Rightarrow x = 2$.

(h) Substitute means to replace the unknown variable with the value of the solution found.

(i) The inverse operation is the opposite operation. For example:

- the inverse of addition is subtraction and vice versa
- the inverse of multiplication is division and vice versa.

We use inverse operations to help solve linear equations.

(j) The solution or root is the value of the unknown variable which makes the equation true.

(k) Verify/check means to replace the unknown with the value of the solution/root and show that the left hand side of the equation is equal to the right hand side.

Q2 (a) $-3 + x = 7$ Add 3 to both sides.

$\Rightarrow x = 7 + 3$

$\Rightarrow x = 10$

(b) $a + 9 = 17$ Subtract 9 from both sides.

$\Rightarrow a = 17 - 9$

$\Rightarrow a = 8$

(c) $6 = -b + 3$ Add b to both sides.

$\Rightarrow b + 6 = 3$ Subtract 6 from both sides.

$\Rightarrow b = 3 - 6$

$\Rightarrow b = -3$

(d) $-2 = k - 1$ Add 1 to both sides.

$\Rightarrow -2 + 1 = k$

$\Rightarrow -1 = k$ Note: writing $-1 = k$ is the same as writing $k = -1$.

$\Rightarrow k = -1$

(e) $14f = 182$ Divide both sides by 14.

$\Rightarrow f = \frac{182}{14}$

$\Rightarrow f = 13$

(f) $7h = -56$ Divide both sides by 7.

$\Rightarrow h = \frac{-56}{7}$

$\Rightarrow h = -8$

(g) $\frac{2y}{-3} = 4$ Multiply both sides by −3.

$\Rightarrow 2y = 4(-3)$

$\Rightarrow 2y = -12$ Divide both sides by 2.

$\Rightarrow y = \frac{-12}{2}$

$\Rightarrow y = -6$

(h) $\frac{3d}{-7} = -9$ Multiply both sides by −7.

$\Rightarrow 3d = -7(-9)$

$\Rightarrow 3d = 63$ Divide both sides by 3.

$\Rightarrow d = \frac{63}{3}$

$\Rightarrow d = 21$

Q3 (a) $12 + 5x = 47$ Subtract 12 from both sides.

$\Rightarrow 5x = 47 - 12$

$\Rightarrow 5x = 35$ Divide both sides by 5.

$\Rightarrow x = \frac{35}{5}$

$\Rightarrow x = 7$

(b) $2a - 7 = -9$ Add 7 to both sides.

$\Rightarrow 2a = -9 + 7$

$\Rightarrow 2a = -2$ Divide both sides by 2.

$\Rightarrow a = \frac{-2}{2}$

$\Rightarrow a = -1$

(c) $-3 - 8c = -11$ Add 3 to both sides.

$\Rightarrow -8c = -11 + 3$

$\Rightarrow -8c = -8$ Divide both sides by −8.

$\Rightarrow c = \frac{-8}{-8}$

$\Rightarrow c = 1$

(d) $-22 = 3y - 1$ Add 1 to both sides.

$\Rightarrow -22 + 1 = 3y$

$\Rightarrow -21 = 3y$ Divide both sides by 3.

$\Rightarrow \frac{-21}{3} = y$

$\Rightarrow -7 = y$

$\Rightarrow y = -7$

Q4 (a)	$-2a - 14 = 5 - 3a$	Add $3a$ to both sides.
	$\Rightarrow -2a - 14 + 3a = 5$	
	$\Rightarrow a - 14 = 5$	Add 14 to both sides.
	$\Rightarrow a = 5 + 14$	
	$\Rightarrow a = 19$	
(b)	$7b - 11 = 13b + 25$	Subtract $13b$ from both sides.
	$\Rightarrow 7b - 13b - 11 = 25$	
	$\Rightarrow -6b - 11 = 25$	Add 11 to both sides.
	$\Rightarrow -6b = 25 + 11$	
	$\Rightarrow -6b = 36$	Divide both sides by −6.
	$\Rightarrow b = \frac{36}{-6}$	
	$\Rightarrow b = -6$	
(c)	$3x - 7 = -4 + 5x$	Subtract $5x$ from both sides.
	$\Rightarrow 3x - 7 - 5x = -4$	
	$\Rightarrow -2x - 7 = -4$	Add 7 to both sides.
	$\Rightarrow -2x = -4 + 7$	
	$\Rightarrow -2x = 3$	Divide both sides by −2.
	$\Rightarrow x = \frac{3}{-2}$	
	$\Rightarrow x = -\frac{3}{2}$	
(d)	$5 + 6d - 8 = 2d - 3 - 5d$	Collect like terms on both sides.
	$\Rightarrow 6d - 3 = -3d - 3$	Add $3d$ to both sides.
	$\Rightarrow 6d + 3d - 3 = -3$	Simplify and add 3 to both sides.
	$\Rightarrow 9d = -3 + 3$	
	$\Rightarrow 9d - 0$	Divide by 9.
	$\Rightarrow d = \frac{0}{9}$	Note: $\frac{0}{\text{any number}} = 0$.
	$\Rightarrow d = 0$	
Q5 (a)	$6y - 3(y + 2) = 3 - 6y$	Expand the brackets.
	$\Rightarrow 6y - 3y - 6 = 3 - 6y$	Collect like terms on both sides.
	$\Rightarrow 3y - 6 = 3 - 6y$	Add $6y$ to both sides.
	$\Rightarrow 3y + 6y - 6 = 3$	Add 6 to both sides.
	$\Rightarrow 9y = 3 + 6$	
	$\Rightarrow 9y = 9$	Divide both sides by 9.
	$\Rightarrow y = 1$	

(b) $3(w-2)-4(w-1)=2(4-w)-7$	Expand the brackets.
$\Rightarrow 3w-6-4w+4=8-2w-7$	Collect like terms on both sides.
$\Rightarrow -w-2=1-2w$	Add $2w$ to both sides.
$\Rightarrow -w+2w-2=1$	Add 2 to both sides.
$\Rightarrow w=1+2$	
$\Rightarrow w=3$	
(c) $2(c+1)-(3-2c)=2c-7(1-2c)$	Expand the brackets.
$\Rightarrow 2c+2-3+2c=2c-7+14c$	Collect like terms on both sides.
$\Rightarrow 4c-1=16c-7$	Subtract $16c$ from both sides.
$\Rightarrow 4c-1-16c=-7$	Add 1 to both sides.
$\Rightarrow -12c=-7+1$	Simplify and divide by −12.
$\Rightarrow c=\frac{-6}{-12}$	
$\Rightarrow c=\frac{1}{2}$	
(d) $5(1\quad 3z)\quad 2(10-z)=-10+z$	Expand the brackets.
$\Rightarrow 5-15z-20+2z=-10+z$	Collect like terms on both sides.
$\Rightarrow -13z-15=-10+z$	Subtract z from both sides.
$\Rightarrow -13z-15-z=-10$	Add 15 to both sides.
$\Rightarrow -14z=-10+15$	
$\Rightarrow -14z=5$	Divide both sides by −14.
$\Rightarrow z=-\frac{5}{14}$	
Q6 (a) $3-\frac{y-2}{4}=-4$	Multiply by 4 (the LCD). Put brackets around $y-2$.
$\Rightarrow 12-(y-2)=-16$	Expand the brackets.
$\Rightarrow 12-y+2=-16$	
$\Rightarrow 14-y=-16$	Subtract 14 from both sides.
$\Rightarrow -y=-16-14$	Remember that $-y=-1y$.
$\Rightarrow -y=-30$	Divide both sides by −1.
$\Rightarrow y=\frac{-30}{-1}$	
$\Rightarrow y=30$	
(b) $\frac{x}{3}-\frac{1}{5}=2$	Multiply by 15 (the LCD of 3 and 5).
$\Rightarrow 5x-3=15(2)$	Add 3 to both sides.
$\Rightarrow 5x=30+3$	Divide both sides by 5.
$\Rightarrow x=\frac{33}{5}$	

(c) $\frac{b}{5}-\frac{b}{2}=3$ — Multiply both sides by 10 (the LCD of 2 and 5).

$\Rightarrow 2b-5b=30$

$\Rightarrow -3b=30$ — Divide both sides by −3.

$\Rightarrow b=\frac{30}{-3}$

$\Rightarrow b=-10$

(d) $\frac{d-1}{3}-5=-d$ — Multiply both sides by 3 (the LCD).

$\Rightarrow d-1-15=-3d$ — Add 16 to both sides.

$\Rightarrow d=-3d+16$ — Add $3d$ to both sides.

$\Rightarrow d+3d=16$

$\Rightarrow 4d=16$ — Divide both sides by 4.

$\Rightarrow d=\frac{16}{4}$

$\Rightarrow d=4$

(e) $\frac{2}{3}(3x-5)+2=\frac{1}{2}(x-1)$ — Multiply both sides by 6 (the LCD of 3 and 2).

$\Rightarrow 4(3x-5)+6(2)=3(x-1)$ — Expand the brackets.

$\Rightarrow 12x-20+12=3x-3$ — Simplify.

$\Rightarrow 12x-8=3x-3$ — Subtract $3x$ from both sides.

$\Rightarrow 12x-3x-8=-3$ — Simplify.

$\Rightarrow 9x-8=-3$ — Add 8 to both sides.

$\Rightarrow 9x=-3+8$

$\Rightarrow 9x=5$ — Divide both sides by 9.

$\Rightarrow x=\frac{5}{9}$

Q7 (a) $\frac{x+3}{4}-\frac{x-4}{2}=7$ — Multiply both sides by 4 (the LCD of 2 and 4). Put brackets around $x+3$ and $x-4$.

$\Rightarrow (x+3)-2(x-4)=4(7)$ — Expand the brackets.

$\Rightarrow x+3-2x+8=28$

$\Rightarrow -x+11=28$

$\Rightarrow -x=28-11$ — Subtract 11 from both sides.

$\Rightarrow -x=17$ — Remember that $-x=-1x$.

$\Rightarrow x=-17$ — Divide both sides by −1.

(b) $\frac{2n-3}{2}+\frac{n+1}{3}=\frac{3n-1}{3}$	Multiply both sides by 6 (the LCD of 2 and 3). Put brackets around each numerator.
$\Rightarrow 3(2n-3)+2(n+1)=2(3n-1)$	Expand the brackets.
$\Rightarrow 6n-9+2n+2=6n-2$	
$\Rightarrow 8n-7=6n-2$	Subtract $6n$ from both sides.
$\Rightarrow 8n-6n-7=-2$	Add 7 to both sides.
$\Rightarrow 2n=-2+7$	Divide both sides by 2.
$\Rightarrow n=\frac{5}{2}$	
(c) $\frac{x}{3}+\frac{x+2}{4}=\frac{3}{4}+\frac{x}{2}$	Multiply both sides by 12 (the LCD of 2, 3 and 4). Put brackets around each numerator.
$\Rightarrow 4x+3(x+2)=3(3)+6(x)$	Expand the brackets.
$\Rightarrow 4x+3x+6=9+6x$	Collect like terms on each side.
$\Rightarrow 7x+6=9+6x$	Subtract $6x$ from each side.
$\Rightarrow 7x-6x+6=9$	Subtract 6 from each side.
$\Rightarrow x=9-6$	
$\Rightarrow x=3$	
(d) $\frac{3y+2}{8}=\frac{2y+1}{4}+\frac{1}{3}$	Multiply both sides by 24 (the LCD of 3, 4 and 8).
$\Rightarrow 3(3y+2)=6(2y+1)+8(1)$	Expand the brackets.
$\Rightarrow 9y+6=12y+6+8$	Subtract $12y$ from both sides.
$\Rightarrow 9y-12y+6=14$	Simplify and subtract 6 from both sides.
$\Rightarrow -3y=14-6$	
$\Rightarrow -3y=8$	
$\Rightarrow y=\frac{8}{-3}$	
$\Rightarrow y=-\frac{8}{3}$	

Q8 (a) Let x = number.

$3x - 4 = 17$ — Add 4 to both sides.

$\Rightarrow 3x = 17 + 4$ — Simplify and divide by 3.

$\Rightarrow x = \frac{21}{3}$

$\Rightarrow x = 7$

The number is 7.

(b) We know:

Consecutive natural numbers are natural numbers which are next to each other (one after the other).

Let:

x = first natural number

$x + 1$ = second natural number

$x + 2$ = third natural number

First natural number + second natural number + third natural number = 99

$x + (x + 1) + (x + 2) = 99$ — Expand the brackets and simplify.

$\Rightarrow 3x + 3 = 99$ — Subtract 3 from both sides.

$\Rightarrow 3x = 99 - 3$

$\Rightarrow 3x = 96$ — Divide both sides by 3.

$\Rightarrow x = \frac{96}{3}$

$\Rightarrow x = 32$

$x = 32$ is the first natural number.

$x + 1 = 32 + 1 = 33$ is the second natural number.

$x + 2 = 32 + 2 = 34$ is the third natural number.

Verify:

$x + (x + 1) + (x + 2) = 99$

$32 + 33 + 34 = 99$

$99 = 99$ ✓

(c) Let x = number.

$\frac{x}{4} - 6 = 15$ — Add 6 to both sides.

$\Rightarrow \frac{x}{4} = 15 + 6$ — Simplify.

$\Rightarrow \frac{x}{4} = 21$ — Multiply both sides by 4.

$\Rightarrow x = 4(21)$

$\Rightarrow x = 84$

The number is 84.

Q9 (a) Let x = the number of weeks it will take for both Katie and Conor to have the same amount in their accounts.

$438 + 12x = 620 - 14x$

(b) $438 + 12x = 620 - 14x$ — Add $14x$ to both sides.

$\Rightarrow 438 + 12x + 14x = 620$ — Subtract 438 from both sides.

$\Rightarrow 26x = 620 - 438$

$\Rightarrow 26x = 182$ — Divide both sides by 26.

$\Rightarrow x = \frac{182}{26}$

$\Rightarrow x = 7$

It will be 7 weeks before Katie and Conor have the same amount in their accounts.

(c) Verify:

$438 + 12x = 620 - 14x$

$438 + 12(7) = 620 - 14(7)$

$438 + 84 = 620 - 98$

$522 = 522$ ✓

Algebra 5: Solving Linear Inequalities

7

Learning objectives

In this chapter you will learn about:

- Linear inequalities
- Compound inequalities
- Word problems using linear inequalities.

Linear inequalities

Key Terminology

Word/ Symbol	Meaning
Linear inequality	A linear inequality involves a linear function and contains one of the symbols of inequality: $<$, $>$, $\leq$, or $\geq$, and may have an infinite number of solutions, or a range of values as the solution. For example: $3 < x, x \in \mathbb{R}$, is a linear inequality whose solution set has an infinite number of elements, whereas $3 < x < 7, x \in \mathbb{Z}$ is a linear inequality whose solution set has three elements: {4, 5, 6}.
Solution	The values of the unknown variable which make the inequality true.
LCD	Lowest common denominator
$<$	Less than
$\leq$	Less than or equal to
$>$	Greater than
$\geq$	Greater than or equal to
$\in$	An element of the set
$\mathbb{N}$	The set of natural numbers: $\{1, 2, 3, 4, 5, \ldots\}$

Word/ Symbol	Meaning
$\mathbb{Z}$	Integers: $\{\ldots, -3, -2, -1, 0, 1, 2, 3, \ldots\}$
$\mathbb{Q}$	Rational numbers are the set of numbers which **can** be written in the form $\frac{p}{q}$, where p and $q \in \mathbb{Z}$, and $q \neq 0$.
$\mathbb{R}\backslash\mathbb{Q}$	Irrational numbers are the set of numbers which **cannot** be written in the form $\frac{p}{q}$, where p and $q \in \mathbb{Z}$, and $q \neq 0$.
$\mathbb{R}$	Real numbers: all the rational and irrational numbers. The set of real numbers includes the sets $\mathbb{N}$, $\mathbb{Z}$, $\mathbb{Q}$ and $\mathbb{R}\backslash\mathbb{Q}$.

Note: The number systems $\mathbb{N}$, $\mathbb{Z}$, $\mathbb{Q}$ and $\mathbb{R}$ are described in the *Formulae and Tables* booklet.

Points to note

To represent the solution set of an inequality on the number line:

- For < and > we use an unshaded circle ○ to indicate that an endpoint is not part of the solution set.
- For ≤ and ≥ we use a shaded circle ● to indicate that an endpoint is part of the solution set.
- For the $\mathbb{N}$, $\mathbb{Z}$, $\mathbb{Q}$ and $\mathbb{R}\backslash\mathbb{Q}$ sets, the data is discrete, and is represented by shaded circles on the number line.

  For example: when $x \leq 3, x \in \mathbb{N}$, the data is discrete it is represented by shaded circles on the number line, as shown:

- For the real numbers $\mathbb{R}$, the data is continuous, and is represented by a thick line with a shaded circle or unshaded circle at either end.

  For example: when $x > -3, x \in \mathbb{R}$, as the data is continuous it is represented on the number line by a thick line with an unshaded circle, as shown:

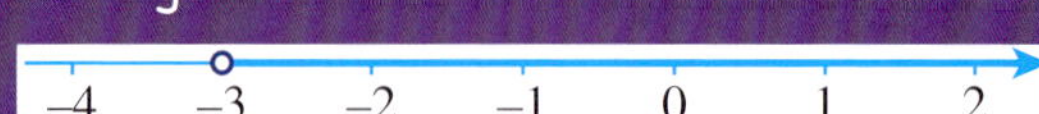

- To multiply or divide a linear inequality by a negative number we must divide across by the negative number and reverse the inequality sign. This means that:
  - < changes to >
  - ≤ changes to ≥
  - > changes to <
  - ≥ changes to ≤

Solving inequalities

Top Tip

To solve a linear inequality:

1. Expand/multiply out any brackets and collect like terms.
2. Rearrange the inequality so that terms containing the unknown variable are on one side of the inequality sign and the constants are on the other.
3. Divide both sides by the coefficient of the unknown variable to find the solution set. If we divide across by a negative number, we must remember to reverse the direction of the inequality.
4. List the elements of the solution set or represent the solution set on a number line, as requested.

Example

(a) Solve the inequality $3x - 8 \leq 4$.

(b) Hence, graph the following solution sets on the number line:

(i) $x \in \mathbb{N}$ **(ii)** $x \in \mathbb{Z}$ **(iii)** $x \in \mathbb{R}$

(c) List the elements of the solution set A, for $x \in \mathbb{N}$.

Solution

(a) $3x - 8 \leq 4$ — Add 8 to both sides.

$\Rightarrow 3x - 8 + 8 \leq 4 + 8$

$\Rightarrow 3x \leq 12$ — Divide both sides by 3.

$\Rightarrow \frac{3x}{3} \leq \frac{12}{3}$

$\Rightarrow x \leq 4$

(b) (i) $x \leq 4, x \in \mathbb{N}$ — For the natural numbers, $\mathbb{N}$, the data is discrete, so use shaded circles on the number line.

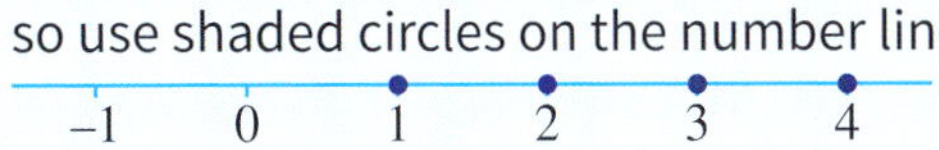

(ii) $x \leq 4, x \in \mathbb{Z}$ — For the integers, $\mathbb{Z}$, the data is discrete, so use shaded circles on the number line. The inequality sign points left, so the arrow on the number line should point left.

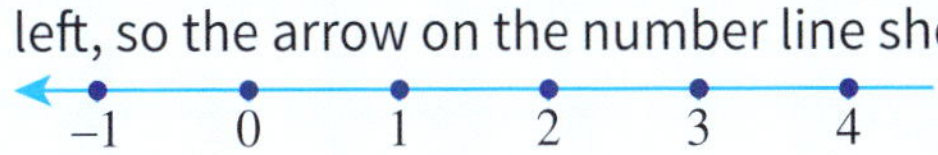

(iii) $x \leq 4, x \in \mathbb{R}$ — For the real numbers, $\mathbb{R}$, the data is continuous, and is represented by a thick line. The inequality sign points left, so the arrow on the number line should point left.

(c) $A = \{1, 2, 3, 4\}$

Example

(a) Solve the inequality $3(x-2)-7(3x+1) \leq 2-3x, x \in \mathbb{N}$.

(b) Graph the solution set on the number line.

Solution

(a) $3(x-2)-7(3x+1) \leq 2-3x$

$\Rightarrow 3x-6-21x-7 \leq 2-3x$ Expand the brackets.

$\Rightarrow -18x-13 \leq 2-3x$ Collect like terms.

$\Rightarrow -18x+3x \leq 2+13$ Put x terms on the left and constants on the right.

$\Rightarrow -15x \leq 15$

$\Rightarrow \frac{-15x}{-15} \geq \frac{15}{-15}$ Divide by −15 and change the direction of the inequality sign.

$\Rightarrow x \geq -1$

(b) $x \geq -1, x \in \mathbb{N}$ As the solution to this inequality is for natural numbers, we start at 1 and include all natural numbers to the right.

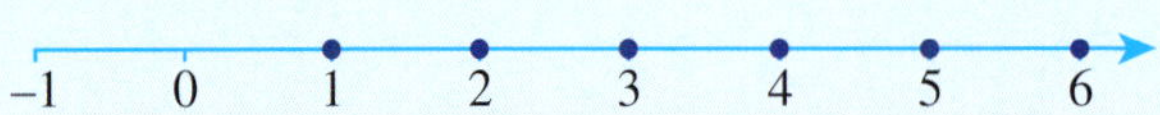

Top Tip

To solve a double/compound linear inequality, use either of the two methods listed below:

Method 1

- Separate the double inequality into two separate inequalities and solve each one as normal.

Method 2

- Rearrange the inequality so only the unknown variable is in the middle of the inequality, and the constants are on either side. Continue as normal.

Example

(a) Solve the inequality $-6 < 4x + 2 \leq 14, x \in \mathbb{R}$.

(b) Graph the solution set on the number line.

Solution

(a) **Method 1:** Solving the inequalities separately.

$-6 < 4x + 2 \leq 14$	Separate the double inequality into two separate inequalities.
$\Rightarrow -6 < 4x + 2$ and $\Rightarrow 4x + 2 \leq 14$	Put x terms on the left and constants on the right.
$\Rightarrow -4x < 2 + 6$ $\quad \Rightarrow 4x \leq 14 - 2$	
$\Rightarrow -4x < 8$ $\quad \Rightarrow 4x \leq 12$	
$\Rightarrow \frac{-4x}{-4} > \frac{8}{-4}$ $\quad \Rightarrow \frac{4x}{4} \leq \frac{12}{4}$	
$\Rightarrow x > -2$ $\quad \Rightarrow x \leq 3$	

Method 2: Solving the inequalities simultaneously (at the same time).

$-6 < 4x + 2 \leq 14$	Subtract 2 from each part of the inequality.
$\Rightarrow -6 - 2 < 4x + 2 - 2 \leq 14 - 2$	
$\Rightarrow -8 < 4x \leq 12$	Divide each part of the inequality by 4.
$\Rightarrow \frac{-8}{4} < \frac{4x}{4} \leq \frac{12}{4}$	
$\Rightarrow -2 < x \leq 3, x \in \mathbb{R}$	

Points to note

It is important to note that we read the inequality from the:

- centre to the left for the inequality $x > -2$
- centre to the right for the inequality $x \leq 3$.

(b) $-2 < x \leq 3, x \in \mathbb{R}$

The unshaded circle at -2 shows that the number is not included.

The shaded circle at 3 shows that the number is included.

For the real numbers, $\mathbb{R}$, the data is continuous, and is represented by a thick line.

Applications of linear inequalities

Example

(a) Find the solution set of A: $1 - 4x \leq 21, x \in \mathbb{R}$.

(b) Find the solution set of B: $5x + 2 \leq 22, x \in \mathbb{R}$.

(c) Graph the solution set of $A \cap B$ on the number line.

Solution

(a) $1 - 4x \leq 21$ — Subtract 1.

$\Rightarrow 1 - 4x - 1 \leq 21 - 1$

$\Rightarrow -4x \leq 20$ — Divide by −4 and change the direction of the inequality sign.

$\Rightarrow \frac{-4x}{-4} \geq \frac{20}{-4}$

$\Rightarrow x \geq -5$

(b) $5x + 2 \leq 22$ — Subtract 2.

$\Rightarrow 5x \leq 22 - 2$

$\Rightarrow 5x \leq 20$ — Divide by 5.

$\Rightarrow \frac{5x}{5} \leq \frac{20}{5}$

$\Rightarrow x \leq 4$

(c) $-5 \leq x \leq 4, x \in \mathbb{R}$

The shaded circles at −5 and 4 show that both numbers are included.

For the real numbers, $\mathbb{R}$, the data is continuous, and is represented by a thick line.

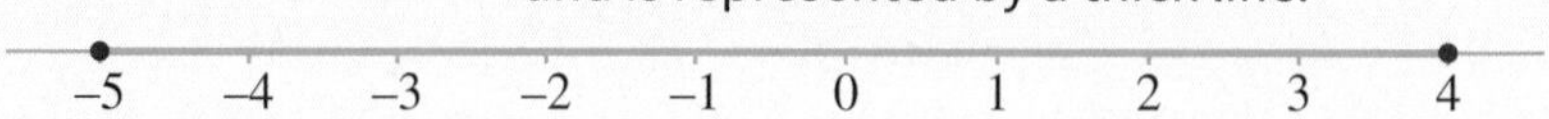

Example

The relationship between Fahrenheit temperature and Celsius temperature is given by the formula: $C = \frac{5}{9}(F - 32)$. If the temperature in the Sahara Desert ranges from 10 °C to 45 °C in a 24-hour period, what is the temperature range in degrees Fahrenheit?

Solution

The temperature is between 10 °C and 45 °C, so C must be greater than or equal to 10 °C and less than or equal to 45 °C.

$10 \leq C \leq 45$

$\Rightarrow 10 \leq \frac{5}{9}(F - 32) \leq 45$ — Let $C = \frac{5}{9}(F - 32)$.

$\Rightarrow \left(\frac{9}{5}\right)10 \leq \left(\frac{9}{5}\right)\frac{5}{9}(F - 32) \leq \left(\frac{9}{5}\right)45$ Multiply all parts by $\left(\frac{9}{5}\right)$, the reciprocal of $\left(\frac{5}{9}\right)$.

$\Rightarrow 18 \leq F - 32 \leq 81$ Add 32 to all parts of the inequality.

$\Rightarrow 18 + 32 \leq F - 32 + 32 \leq 81 + 32$

$\Rightarrow 50 \leq F \leq 113$

The temperature range in the Sahara Desert is from 50 °F to 113 °F.

Exercise

Q1 Write an inequality which is represented by the following graphs:

(a) 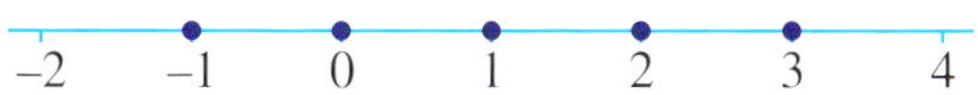

(b) 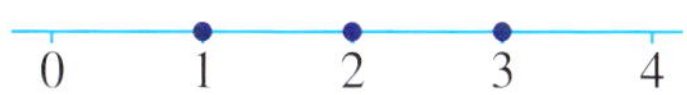

(c) 

(d) 

Q2 Graph on the number line the solution sets of:

(a) $9 - 4x > -3, x \in \mathbb{N}$ **(b)** $\frac{1 - 3x}{2} < 5, x \in \mathbb{R}$

Q3 List the elements of the solution sets of:

(a) $-1 \leq -3x + 5 < 8, x \in \mathbb{Z}$ **(b)** $2x - 1 < x - 2 \leq 2x + 10, x \in \mathbb{Z}$

Q4 Graph on the number line the solution sets of:

(a) $14x + 1 > 2(6x - 3) - 5, x \in \mathbb{R}$ **(b)** $6x - 3 > 2(4x - 3) - 6, x \in \mathbb{R}$

Q5 Graph on the number line the solution sets of:

(a) $5x - 3(2x - 1) \geq 2(x - 3), x \in \mathbb{N}$ **(b)** $2(x - 2) \leq 2(2x - 1) < 2x + 6, x \in \mathbb{Z}$

Q6 (a) Write out a compound inequality which represents the set of values of c for which $c^2 \leq 9, c \in \mathbb{R}$.

(b) Graph the solution set on a number line.

Q7 (a) Solve the inequality $7x - 3 > 18$, where $x \in \mathbb{N}$.

(b) Write down the smallest value of x for which the inequality is true.

Q8 (a) Graph on a number line the solution set of A where $A = \{x | x \in 3x - 8 < 7, x \in \mathbb{Z}\}$.

(b) Graph on a number line the solution set of B where $B = \{x | x \in 5 - 2x < 9, x \in \mathbb{Z}\}$.

(c) List all the elements of $A \cap B$.

Q9 Passenger trains in Ireland have a minimum speed limit of 10 km/h and a maximum speed limit of 160 km/h.

(a) Represent this information as a compound inequality, where s represents speed.

(b) Graph this information on a number line.

Q10 A gymnast scores 7·5, 8·5, 8·2 and 9 in four events out of five. In order to get a minimum overall average score of 8·5, what score must she get in the fifth event?

Q11 Niamh is in a clothes shop and has a voucher which she must use. The voucher gives a €10 reduction when more than €35 is spent. She also has €50 cash.

(a) Write down an inequality in x to show the range of money she could spend in the shop.

(b) Write an inequality in y to show the price range of articles she could buy.

(SEC 2015)

Q12 Josephine hopes to go to college. She has saved €3000. She will attend college for 32 weeks in her first year. She plans to have at least €800 left at the end of the year.

(a) If she spends €x each week, write an inequality to represent her spending during the year.

(b) Hence, or otherwise, find the maximum amount Josephine can spend each week.

(SEC 2013)

Solutions

Q1 (a) $-2 < x < 4, x \in \mathbb{Z}$; or $-1 \leq x \leq 3, x \in \mathbb{Z}$.

(b) $0 < x < 4, x \in \mathbb{Z}$; $1 \leq x \leq 3, x \in \mathbb{N}$; or $x < 4, x \in \mathbb{N}$.

(c) $-4 \leq x < 5, x \in \mathbb{R}$.

(d) $x > -9, x \in \mathbb{R}$.

Q2 (a) $9 - 4x > -3, x \in \mathbb{N}$ Subtract 9 from each side.

$\Rightarrow 9 - 4x - 9 > -3 - 9$

$\Rightarrow \quad -4x > -12$ Divide by −4 and change the direction of the inequality sign.

$\Rightarrow \quad \frac{-4x}{-4} < \frac{-12}{-4}$

$\Rightarrow \quad x < 3, x \in \mathbb{N}$

(b) $\frac{1-3x}{2} < 5, x \in \mathbb{R}$ — Multiply both sides of the inequality by 2.

$\Rightarrow 2\left(\frac{1-3x}{2}\right) < 2(5)$

$\Rightarrow \quad 1 - 3x < 10$ — Subtract 1 from each side of the inequality.

$\Rightarrow 1 - 3x - 1 < 10 - 1$ — Divide by −3 and change the direction of the inequality sign.

$\Rightarrow \quad \frac{-3x}{-3} > \frac{9}{-3}$

$\Rightarrow \quad x > -3, x \in \mathbb{R}$

Q3 (a) $-1 \le -3x + 5 < 8, x \in \mathbb{Z}$ — Subtract 5 from all parts.

$\Rightarrow -1 - 5 \le -3x + 5 - 5 < 8 - 5$

$\Rightarrow -6 \le -3x < 3$ — Divide by −3 and change the direction of the inequality signs.

$\Rightarrow \frac{-6}{-3} \ge \frac{-3x}{-3} > \frac{3}{-3}$

$\Rightarrow 2 \ge x > -1$

$\Rightarrow -1 < x \le 2$

$\therefore x = \{0, 1, 2\}$

(b) $2x - 1 < x - 2 \le 2x + 10, x \in \mathbb{Z}$ — Add 2 to all parts.

$\Rightarrow 2x - 1 + 2 < x - 2 + 2 \le 2x + 10 + 2$

$\Rightarrow 2x + 1 < x \le 2x + 12$ — Subtract $2x$ from all parts.

$\Rightarrow 2x + 1 - 2x < x - 2x \le 2x + 12 - 2x$

$\Rightarrow 1 < -x \le 12$ — Divide by −1 and change the direction of the inequality signs.

$\Rightarrow \frac{1}{-1} > \frac{-x}{-1} \ge \frac{12}{-1}$

$\Rightarrow -1 > x \ge -12$

$\Rightarrow -12 \le x < -1$

$\therefore x = \{-2, -3, -4, -5, -6, -7, -8, -9, -10, -11, -12\}$

Q4 (a) $14x + 1 > 2(6x - 3) - 5, x \in \mathbb{R}$ — Expand the brackets.

$\Rightarrow 14x + 1 > 12x - 6 - 5$ — Subtract $12x$ from both sides.

$\Rightarrow 14x - 12x + 1 > 12x - 11 - 12x$

$\Rightarrow \quad 2x + 1 > -11$ Subtract 1 from both sides.

$\Rightarrow 2x + 1 - 1 > -11 - 1$ Divide both sides by 2.

$\Rightarrow \quad \dfrac{2x}{2} > \dfrac{-12}{2}$

$\Rightarrow \quad x > -6, x \in \mathbb{R}$

(b) $6x - 3 > 2(4x - 3) - 6, x \in \mathbb{R}$ Expand the brackets.

$\Rightarrow 6x - 3 > 8x - 6 - 6$ Subtract $8x$ from both sides.

$\Rightarrow 6x - 8x - 3 > 8x - 12 - 8x$

$\Rightarrow -2x - 3 > -12$ Add 3 to both sides.

$\Rightarrow -2x - 3 + 3 > -12 + 3$ Divide by −2 and change the direction of the inequality sign.

$\Rightarrow \dfrac{-2x}{-2} < \dfrac{-9}{-2}$

$\Rightarrow x < 4{\cdot}5, x \in \mathbb{R}$

Q5 (a) $5x - 3(2x - 1) \geq 2(x - 3), x \in \mathbb{N}$ Expand the brackets.

$\Rightarrow 5x - 6x + 3 \geq 2x - 6$

$\Rightarrow \quad -x + 3 \geq 2x - 6$ Subtract $2x$ from both sides.

$\Rightarrow -x + 3 - 2x \geq 2x - 6 - 2x$

$\Rightarrow \quad -3x + 3 \geq -6$ Subtract 3 from both sides.

$\Rightarrow -3x + 3 - 3 \geq -6 - 3$ Divide by −3 and change the direction of the inequality sign.

$\Rightarrow \quad \dfrac{-3x}{-3} \leq \dfrac{-9}{-3}$

$\Rightarrow \quad x \leq 3, x \in \mathbb{N}$

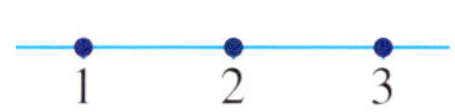

(b) $2(x - 2) \leq 2(2x - 1) < 2x + 6, x \subset \mathbb{Z}$ Expand the brackets.

$\Rightarrow 2x - 4 \leq 4x - 2 < 2x + 6$ Add 2 to all parts.

$\Rightarrow 2x - 4 + 2 \leq 4x - 2 + 2 < 2x + 6 + 2$

$\Rightarrow 2x - 2 \leq 4x < 2x + 8$ Subtract $2x$ from all parts.

$\Rightarrow 2x - 2 - 2x \leq 4x - 2x < 2x + 8 - 2x$

$\Rightarrow -2 \leq 2x < 8$ Divide all parts by 2.

$\Rightarrow \frac{-2}{2} \leq \frac{2x}{2} < \frac{8}{2}$

$\Rightarrow -1 \leq x < 4, x \in \mathbb{Z}$

Q6 (a) $-3 \leq c \leq 3$

(b)

Q7 (a) $7x - 3 > 18, x \in \mathbb{N}$ Add 3 to both sides.

$\Rightarrow 7x - 3 + 3 > 18 + 3$

$\Rightarrow 7x > 21$ Divide both sides by 7.

$\Rightarrow \frac{7x}{7} > \frac{21}{7}$

$\Rightarrow x > 3, x \in \mathbb{N}$

(b) $x = 4$

Q8 (a) $3x - 8 < 7, x \in \mathbb{Z}$ Add 8 to both sides.

$\Rightarrow 3x - 8 + 8 < 7 + 8$

$\Rightarrow 3x < 15$ Divide both sides by 3.

$\Rightarrow \frac{3x}{3} < \frac{15}{3}$

$\Rightarrow x < 5, x \in \mathbb{Z}$

$A = \{x | x < 5, x \in \mathbb{Z}\}$

(b) $5 - 2x < 9, x \in \mathbb{Z}$ Subtract 5 from both sides.

$\Rightarrow 5 - 2x - 5 < 9 - 5$

$\Rightarrow -2x < 4$ Divide by −2 and change the direction of the inequality signs.

$\Rightarrow \frac{-2x}{-2} > \frac{4}{-2}$

$\Rightarrow x > -2, x \in \mathbb{Z}$

$B = \{x | x > -2, x \in \mathbb{Z}\}$

(c) $A \cap B = \{-1, 0, 1, 2, 3, 4\}$

Q9 (a) $10 \le s \le 160$

(b)

Q10 Let x = score of fifth event that gives an average $\ge 8{\cdot}5$

$$\Rightarrow \frac{7{\cdot}5 + 8{\cdot}5 + 8{\cdot}2 + 9 + x}{5} \ge 8{\cdot}5$$

$$\Rightarrow \frac{33{\cdot}2 + x}{5} \ge 8{\cdot}5$$ Multiply both sides by 5.

$$\Rightarrow 5\left(\frac{33{\cdot}2 + x}{5}\right) \ge 5(8{\cdot}5)$$

$$\Rightarrow 33{\cdot}2 + x \ge 42{\cdot}5$$ Subtract 33·2 from both sides.

$$\Rightarrow 33{\cdot}2 + x - 33{\cdot}2 \ge 42{\cdot}5 - 33{\cdot}2$$

$$\Rightarrow x \ge 9{\cdot}3$$

The gymnast must get a minimum score of 9·3 in the fifth event to get an average of at least 8·5 overall.

Q11 (a) The voucher requires a minimum of €35 to be spent. Since Niamh must use her voucher, she must spend a minimum of €35. If she spends this amount, she gets a €10 discount, meaning the minimum she can spend is €25. The maximum amount of cash she can spend is €50, so the range will be $25 \le x \le 50$.

(b) As before, the minimum value Niamh can spend is €35. The maximum amount of cash she can spend is €50, and including the discount, the item of clothing could cost up to €60. Thus the range will be $35 \le y \le 60$.

Q12 (a) $3000 - 32x \ge 800$

(b) $3000 - 32x \ge 800$ Subtract 3000 from both sides.

$$\Rightarrow -32x \ge 800 - 3000$$

$$\Rightarrow -32x \ge -2200$$ Divide across by −32 and change the direction of the inequality sign.

$$\Rightarrow \frac{-32x}{-32} \le \frac{-2200}{-32}$$

$$\Rightarrow x \le 68{\cdot}75$$

Hence, the maximum amount Josephine can spend each week is €68·75.

Algebra 6: Solving Simultaneous Equations

8

Learning objectives

In this chapter you will learn about:

- Linear equations in two variables (simultaneous equations)
- Word problems using simultaneous equations.

Simultaneous equations

Key Terminology

Word	Meaning
Variable	The letters which stand for unknown numbers in algebra. For example: x, y, z.
Linear equation	An equation of the form $ax + by = c$, where $a, b, c \in \mathbb{R}$.
Simultaneous equations	Can be two linear equations with two unknown variables, which are both true at the same time. The equations must be solved, either algebraically or graphically, to find the values of the unknown variables. For example: $x + y = 9$ and $x - y = 3$.
Solution	The values of the unknown variables which make the equation true.
Verify/check	Replace the unknowns with the values of the variables found and show that the left hand side (LHS) of the equation equals the right hand side (RHS).
Point of intersection	Graphically, the point where two lines cross is called the point of intersection. The point of intersection is the solution to the simultaneous equations that describe the two lines.

Solving simultaneous equations

Points to note

- In order to solve two linear equations in two variables (say x and y), we need two equations to be true at the same time. These are known as **simultaneous equations**.
- We can solve simultaneous equations in two unknowns either algebraically or graphically. These methods are:

  1 trial and improvement
  2 elimination
  3 substitution
  4 graphing.

Top Tip

To solve simultaneous equations in two unknowns, using the 'trial and improvement' method:

1 Label the linear equations (1) and (2).

2 Rearrange both equations in the form 'y ='.

3 'Guess and check' for values of x until you find the correct solution.

Note: The correct solution is found when the value of y is the same for both equations when the correct value for x is substituted in.

Example

Solve the two simultaneous equations using the 'trial and improvement' method:

$x + y = 9$

$x - y = 3$

Solution

1 Label the linear equations (1) and (2).

$x + y = 9 \quad (1)$

$x - y = 3 \quad (2)$

2 Rearrange both equations in the form '$y =$':

$y = 9 - x \quad (3)$

$y = x - 3 \quad (4)$

3 'Guess and check' for values of x until you find the correct solution.

Try x	Substitute the guessed value of x into equation (3): $y = 9 - x$	Check solutions by substituting the values of x and y into equation (4): $y = x - 3$	Are the solutions correct?
$x = 1$	$y = 9 - x = 9 - (1)$ $= 9 - 1 = 8$	$y = x - 3 = (1) - 3$ $= 1 - 3 = -2$	✗ wrong solution
$x = 2$	$y = 9 - x = 9 - (2)$ $= 9 - 2 = 7$	$y = x - 3 = (2) - 3$ $= 2 - 3 = -1$	✗ wrong solution
$x = 3$	$y = 9 - x = 9 - (3)$ $= 9 - 3 = 6$	$y = x - 3 = (3) - 3$ $= 3 - 3 = 0$	✗ wrong solution
$x = 4$	$y = 9 - x = 9 - (4)$ $= 9 - 4 = 5$	$y = x - 3 = (4) - 3$ $= 4 - 3 = 1$	✗ wrong solution
$x = 5$	$y = 9 - x = 9 - (5)$ $= 9 - 5 = 4$	$y = x - 3 = (5) - 3$ $= 5 - 3 = 2$	✗ wrong solution
$x = 6$	$y = 9 - x = 9 - (6)$ $= 9 - 6 = 3$	$y = x - 3 = (6) - 3$ $= 6 - 3 = 3$	✓ $x = 6$ and $y = 3$

The correct solution is: $x = 6$ and $y = 3$.

Top Tip

To solve simultaneous equations in two unknowns using the 'substitution' method:

1 Label the linear equations (1) and (2).

2 Rearrange one equation in the form '$y =$' (or '$x =$').

3 Substitute this expression into the other equation.

4 Find the value of the x variable (or the y variable).

5 Find the value of the second variable by substituting the value of the x variable (or the y variable) into the equation, found in step 2.

6 Check the values of both variables by substitution into the other linear equation.

Example

Solve the following simultaneous equations using the 'substitution' method:

$$5a - b = 15$$
$$a + b = -3$$

Solution

$5a - b = 15 \quad (1)$ — Label the linear equations (1) and (2).

$a + b = -3 \quad (2)$

$5a - b = 15 \quad (1)$ — Rearrange equation (1) in the form '$b =$'.

$\Rightarrow b = 5a - 15$

$a + b = -3 \quad (2)$ — Substitute $5a - 15$ into equation (2) for b and find the value of a.

$\Rightarrow a + (5a - 15) = -3$

$\Rightarrow a + 5a - 15 = -3$ — Add 15 to both sides.

$\Rightarrow 6a = -3 + 15$

$\Rightarrow 6a = 12$ — Divide across by 6 to find a.

$\Rightarrow a = \frac{12}{6} = 2$

Find the value of b by substituting the value of a into the equation: $b = 5a - 15$.

$\Rightarrow b = 5(2) - 15$

$\Rightarrow b = 10 - 15$

$\Rightarrow b = -5$

Check the values of both variables by substitution into either linear equation.

$a + b = -3$

$\Rightarrow 2 - 5 = -3$

$\Rightarrow -3 = -3$ ✓

Top Tip

To solve simultaneous equations in two unknowns using the 'elimination' method:

1 Label the linear equations (1) and (2).

2 Rearrange both equations in the form $ax + by = c$.

3 Eliminate one variable and find the value of the other variable.

4 Find the value of the second variable by substitution into either original linear equation.

5 Check the values of both variables by substitution into the other linear equation.

Example

Solve the following simultaneous equations using the 'elimination' method:

$2x - 6 = -y$

$-2y = 16 - 3x$

Solution

- Label the linear equations (1) and (2).

$2x - 6 = -y \qquad (1)$

$-2y = 16 - 3x \qquad (2)$

- Rearrange both equations in the form $ax + by = c$.

$2x + y = 6 \qquad (3)$

$3x - 2y = 16 \qquad (4)$

- To eliminate y, multiply equation (3) by 2 and add equation (4).

$4x + 2y = 12$ — Equation (3) multiplied by 2.

$+ \; 3x - 2y = 16$ — Equation (4).

$7x = 28$

$\Rightarrow \quad x = \frac{28}{7}$ — Divide across by 7 to find x.

$\Rightarrow \quad x = 4$

- Find the value of y by substituting $x = 4$ into equation (3).

$2x + y = 6 \qquad (3)$

$\Rightarrow \quad 2(4) + y = 6$

$\Rightarrow \quad 8 + y = 6$

$\Rightarrow \quad y = 6 - 8$

$\Rightarrow \quad y = -2$

- Check the values of both variables by substitution into equation (4).

$3x - 2y = 16 \qquad (4)$

$\Rightarrow \quad 3(4) - 2(-2) = 16$

$\Rightarrow \quad 12 + 4 = 16$

$\Rightarrow \quad 16 = 16$ ✓

Top Tip

To solve simultaneous equations in two unknowns, using the 'graphical' method:

1. Label the linear equations (1) and (2).
2. Find a minimum of two coordinates for each linear equation.
3. Plot the points and draw a graph for each linear equation, labelling each line.
4. Find the point where the two lines cross (called the point of intersection).
5. Check the solution/values of both variables by substitution into either linear equation.

Example

Solve the following simultaneous equations 'graphically':

$x + y = 5$

$2x - 3y = -30$

Solution

- Label the equations (1) and (2).

$x + y = 5 \qquad (1)$

$2x - 3y = -30 \qquad (2)$

- Find two points for each linear equation.

Equation 1:	$x + y = 5$	(1)	
When $x = 0$, find y:	$0 + y = 5$	$\Rightarrow y = 5$	Point 1 is (0, 5).
When $y = 0$, find x:	$x + 0 = 5$	$\Rightarrow x = 5$	Point 2 is (5, 0).
Equation 2:	$2x - 3y = -30$	(2)	
When $x = 0$ find y:	$2(0) - 3y = -30$	$\Rightarrow -3y = -30$	
		$\Rightarrow y = \frac{-30}{-3} = 10$	Point 3 is (0, 10).
When $y = 0$ find x:	$2x - 3(0) = -30$	$\Rightarrow 2x = -30$	
		$\Rightarrow y = \frac{-30}{2} = -15$	Point 4 is (−15, 0).

- Plot the points and draw a graph for each linear equation, labelling each line.

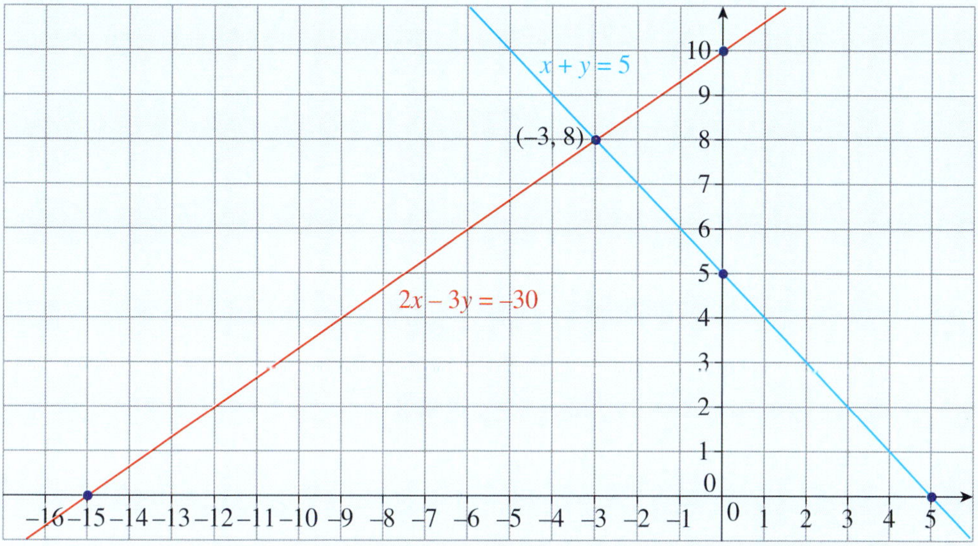

- The point where the two lines cross is (−3, 8). This is the solution ($x = -3$ and $y = 8$), and shows that by solving simultaneous equations we are finding the point of intersection.
- Check the values of both variables by substitution into either linear equation.

$x + y = 5 \Rightarrow -3 + 8 = 5 \Rightarrow 5 = 5$ ✓

Top Tip

To solve simultaneous equations containing fractions:

1. Rearrange both equations in the form $ax + by = c$, where $a, b, c \in \mathbb{Z}$.
2. Multiply all terms by the LCD.
3. Label the linear equations (1) and (2).
4. Solve using one of the previously described methods.

Example

Solve the simultaneous equations:

$3x - y = 7$

$\frac{x-1}{3} - \frac{y+4}{2} = 0$

Solution

$$\frac{x-1}{3}-\frac{y+4}{2}=0$$ Multiply each term by the LCD = 6.

$$\Rightarrow \quad 6\left(\frac{x-1}{3}\right)-6\left(\frac{y+4}{2}\right)=0$$ Simplify.

$$\Rightarrow \quad 2(x-1)-3(y+4)=0$$ Expand brackets.

$$\Rightarrow \quad 2x-2-3y-12=0$$

$$\Rightarrow \quad 2x-3y=14$$

- Label the equations (1) and (2):

$$3x-y=7 \qquad (1)$$

$$2x-3y=14 \qquad (2)$$

- Eliminate the y variable:

$$-9x+3y=-21 \qquad (1)\times -3$$

$$+\quad 2x-3y=14 \qquad (2)$$

$$-7x=-7$$

$$\Rightarrow \quad x=\frac{-7}{-7}$$

$$\Rightarrow \quad x=1$$

- Substitute $x=1$ into (1) to find y:

$$3x-y=7$$

$$\Rightarrow \quad 3(1)-y=7$$

$$\Rightarrow \quad -y=7-3$$

$$\Rightarrow \quad -y=4$$

$$\Rightarrow \quad y=-4$$

- Check your solution by substituting both values into equation (2):

$2x-3y=14 \Rightarrow 2(1)-3(-4)=14 \Rightarrow 2+12=14 \Rightarrow 14=14$ ✓

Answer: $x=1$ and $y=-4$

Top Tip

To solve word problems using simultaneous equations:

1 Select/set two variables to represent the two unknowns.

2 Write two linear equations to represent the information provided.

3 Label the linear equations (1) and (2).

4 Solve using one of the previously described methods.

Example

Marie has €25 made up of 20-cent coins and 50-cent coins. She has 104 coins in total.

(a) Taking x to be the number of 20-cent coins and y to be the number of 50-cent coins, write down two equations in x and y to represent this information.

(b) Solve the equations to find the number of each type of coin Marie has.

(SEC 2004)

Solution

(a) Write two linear equations to represent the information given and label them (1) and (2):

Let x = number of 20-cent coins

Let y = number of 50-cent coins

$x + y = 104$ (1)

$20x + 50y = 2500$ (2)

Note: €25 has been converted into cents i.e. €25 = 2500 cents.

(b)
- Eliminate the y variable to find x:

$$\begin{array}{rl} -50x - 50y = -5200 & (1) \times -50 \\ + \quad 20x + 50y = 2500 & (2) \\ \hline -30x = -2700 & \end{array}$$

$$\Rightarrow \quad x = \frac{-2700}{-30}$$

$$\Rightarrow \quad x = 90$$

- Substitute $x = 90$ into (1) to find y.

$$x + y = 104$$

$$\Rightarrow \quad 90 + y = 104$$

$$\Rightarrow \quad y = 104 - 90$$

$$\Rightarrow \quad y = 14$$

- Check your solution by substituting both values into equation (2):

$20x + 50y = 2500 \Rightarrow 20(90) + 50(14) = 2500$

$\Rightarrow 1800 + 700 = 2500 \Rightarrow 2500 = 2500$ ✓

Answer: There are ninety 20-cent coins and fourteen 50-cent coins.

Exercise

Q1 Solve the following simultaneous equations using the elimination method:

(a) $x + 2y = 20$
$9x - 2y = 80$

(b) $4x - 3y = 3$
$2x + 6y = -1$

(c) $3x + 4y = -1$
$2x + 9 = -6y$

Q2 Solve the following simultaneous equations using the substitution method:

(a) $x - 2y = 5$
$x + 5y = -9$

(b) $3x + 4y = 1$
$x = -3 + 2y$

(c) $a - 2b = -3$
$a + 2b = 1$

Q3 Solve the following simultaneous equations graphically:

(a) $x + y = 3$
$2x - 3y = 6$

(b) $y = x + 1$
$y = -2x + 4$

(c) $x - 2y = 5$
$x + 5y = -9$

Q4 Solve the following simultaneous equations:

(a) $\frac{x}{3} - y = -1$
$4x - y = 10$

(b) $\frac{1}{2}x - y = -5$
$\frac{5}{2}x + y = -1$

(c) $\frac{2x}{5} - \frac{2y}{3} = \frac{12}{5}$
$\frac{x-3}{4} - \frac{y-1}{3} = \frac{5}{6}$

Q5 The Henry family of two adults and three children plan to visit Dublin Zoo. The total cost of admission for the whole family is €68.40. On the same day they meet the Clarke family of three adults and four children who pay €96.70 to visit the zoo.

(a) Write down two equations to represent the above information.

(b) Find the cost of admission to Dublin Zoo for an adult, and for a child.

(c) Verify your answer.

Q6 Jack saves 1-cent and 2-cent coins in a money box. After counting his money, he finds he has 250 coins in total which add up to €4.10.

(a) Taking x to be the number of 1-cent coins and y to be the number of 2-cent coins, write down two equations in x and y to represent this information.

(b) Solve these equations to find the number of each type of coin Jack has saved.

(c) Verify your answer.

Solutions

Q1 (a)

$$x + 2y = 20 \qquad (1)$$
$$+\ 9x - 2y = 80 \qquad (2)$$
$$10x = 100$$ Add equation (1) and equation (2).

$$\Rightarrow \quad x = \frac{100}{10}$$
$$\Rightarrow \quad x = 10$$

Substitute $x = 10$ into (1) to find y.

$$x + 2y = 20 \qquad (1)$$
$$\Rightarrow 10 + 2y = 20$$
$$\Rightarrow \quad 2y = 10$$
$$\Rightarrow \quad y = \frac{10}{2}$$
$$\Rightarrow \quad y = 5$$

Check solution with equation (2):

$$9x - 2y = 80 \Rightarrow 9(10) - 2(5) = 80$$
$$\Rightarrow 90 - 10 = 80 \Rightarrow 80 = 80 \quad ✓$$

(b)

$$4x - 3y = 3 \qquad (1)$$ Label the equations (1) and (2).

$$2x + 6y = -1 \qquad (2)$$
$$8x - 6y = 6 \qquad (1) \times 2$$ Eliminate the y variable.

$$+\ 2x + 6y = -1 \qquad (2)$$
$$10x = 5$$
$$\Rightarrow \quad x = \frac{5}{10}$$
$$\Rightarrow \quad x = \frac{1}{2}$$

Substitute $x = \frac{1}{2}$ into (1) to find y:

$$4x - 3y = 3 \qquad (1)$$
$$\Rightarrow 4\left(\frac{1}{2}\right) - 3y = 3$$
$$\Rightarrow \quad -3y = 3 - 2$$
$$\Rightarrow \quad y = -\frac{1}{3}$$

Check solution with equation (2):

$$2x + 6y = -1 \Rightarrow 2\left(\frac{1}{2}\right) + 6\left(-\frac{1}{3}\right) = -1$$
$$\Rightarrow 1 - 2 = -1 \Rightarrow -1 = -1 \quad ✓$$

(c) $3x + 4y = -1$

$2x + 9 = -6y$

Rearrange both equations in the form $ax + by = c$ and label them (1) and (2):

$3x + 4y = -1 \qquad (1)$

$2x + 6y = -9 \qquad (2)$

Eliminate the x variable:

$$\begin{array}{rll} & -6x - 8y = 2 & (1) \times -2 \\ + & 6x + 18y = -27 & (2) \times 3 \\ \hline & 10y = -25 & \end{array}$$

$\Rightarrow \quad y = \dfrac{-25}{10}$

$\Rightarrow \quad y = -2{\cdot}5$

Substitute $y = -2{\cdot}5$ into (1) to find x:

$3x + 4y = -1 \qquad (1)$

$\Rightarrow \quad 3x + 4(-2{\cdot}5) = -1$

$\Rightarrow \quad 3x = -1 + 10$

$\Rightarrow \quad x = \dfrac{9}{3}$

$\Rightarrow \quad x = 3$

Check solution with equation (2): $2x + 6y = -9 \Rightarrow 2(3) + 6(-2{\cdot}5) = -9$
$\Rightarrow 6 - 15 = -9 \Rightarrow -9 = -9$ ✓

Q2 (a) Label the linear equations (1) and (2):

$x - 2y = 5 \qquad (1)$

$x + 5y = -9 \qquad (2)$

Rearrange equation (2) in the form '$x =$ ':

$x = -5y - 9$

Substitute $x = -5y - 9$ into equation (1) to find y:

$x - 2y = 5 \qquad (1)$

$\Rightarrow \quad (-5y - 9) - 2y = 5$

$\Rightarrow \quad -7y = 14$

$\Rightarrow \quad y = \dfrac{14}{-7}$

$\Rightarrow \quad y = -2$

Substitute $y = -2$ into $x = -5y - 9$:

$x = -5(-2) - 9$

$\Rightarrow x = 10 - 9$

$\Rightarrow x = 1$

Check solution with equation (2): $x + 5y = -9 \Rightarrow (1) + 5(-2) = -9$

$\Rightarrow 1 - 10 = -9 \Rightarrow -9 = -9$ ✓

(b) Label the linear equations as (1) and (2):

$3x + 4y = 1$ (1)

$x = -3 + 2y$ (2)

Substitute $-3 + 2y$ into equation (1) for x:

$3x + 4y = 1$ (1)

$\Rightarrow 3(-3 + 2y) + 4y = 1$

$\Rightarrow -9 + 6y + 4y = 1$

$\Rightarrow 10y = 1 + 9$

$\Rightarrow y = \frac{10}{10}$

$\Rightarrow y = 1$

Substitute $y = 1$ into $x = -3 + 2y$ to find x:

$x = -3 + 2(1)$

$\Rightarrow x = -3 + 2$

$\Rightarrow x = -1$

Check solution: $3x + 4y = 1 \Rightarrow 3(-1) + 4(1) = 1$

$\Rightarrow -3 + 4 = 1 \Rightarrow 1 = 1$ ✓

(c) Label the linear equations as (1) and (2):

$a - 2b = -3$ (1)

$a + 2b = 1$ (2)

Rearrange equation (2) in the form '$a =$ ':

$a = -2b + 1$

Substitute $-2b + 1$ into equation (1) for a:

$a - 2b = -3$ (1)

$\Rightarrow (-2b + 1) - 2b = -3$

$\Rightarrow -2b + 1 - 2b = -3$

$\Rightarrow -4b = -4$

$\Rightarrow b = \frac{-4}{-4}$

$\Rightarrow b = 1$

Substitute $b = 1$ into $a = -2b + 1$ to find a:

$a = -2b + 1$

$\Rightarrow \ a = -2(1) + 1$

$\Rightarrow \ a = -2 + 1$

$\Rightarrow \ a = -1$

Check solution: $a - 2b = -3 \Rightarrow -1 - 2(1) = -3$

$\Rightarrow -1 - 2 = -3 \Rightarrow -3 = -3$ ✓

Q3 (a) Label the equations (1) and (2).

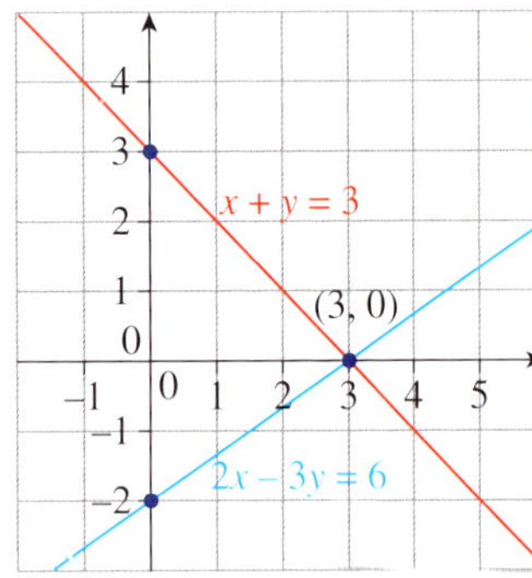

$x + y = 3$ (1)

$2x - 3y = 6$ (2)

Find two points for each linear equation.

Equation (1):

$x + y = 3$ (1)

When $x = 0$, find y:

$0 + y = 3 \Rightarrow y = 3$ Point 1 is (0, 3).

When $y = 0$, find x:

$x + 0 = 3 \Rightarrow x = 3$ Point 2 is (3, 0).

Equation (2):

$2x - 3y = 6$ (2)

When $x = 0$, find y:

$0 - 3y = 6 \Rightarrow y = \frac{6}{-3} = -2$ Point 3 is (0, −2).

When $y = 0$, find x:

$2x - 0 = 6 \Rightarrow x = \frac{6}{2} = 3$ Point 4 is (3, 0).

From the graph the point of intersection is (3, 0).

Solution: $x = 3$ and $y = 0$

(b) Label the equations (1) and (2).

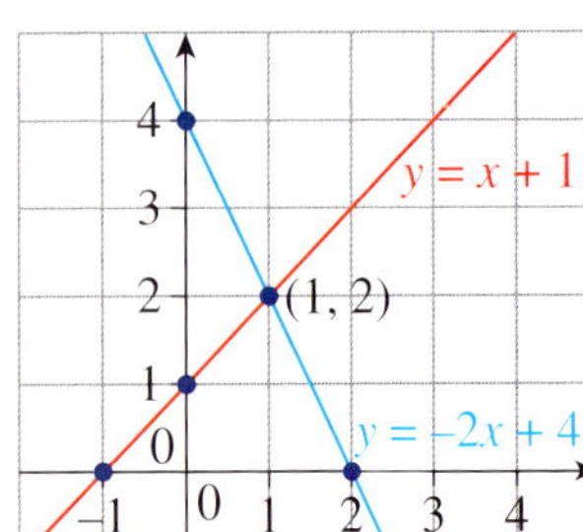

$y = x + 1$ (1)

$y = -2x + 4$ (2)

Find two points for each linear equation.

Equation (1):

$y = x + 1$ (1)

When $x = 0$, find y:

$y = 0 + 1 \Rightarrow y = 1$ Point 1 is (0, 1).

When $y = 0$, find x:

$0 = x + 1 \Rightarrow x = -1$ Point 2 is $(-1, 0)$.

Equation (2):

$y = -2x + 4$ (2)

When $x = 0$, find y:

$y = 0 + 4 \Rightarrow y = 4$ Point 3 is $(0, 4)$.

When $y = 0$, find x:

$0 = -2x + 4 \Rightarrow 2x = 4 \Rightarrow x = 2$ Point 4 is $(2, 0)$.

From the graph, the point where the two lines cross/the point of intersection is $(1, 2)$.

Solution: $x = 1$ and $y = 2$.

(c) Label the equations (1) and (2).

$x - 2y = 5$ (1)

$x + 5y = -9$ (2)

Find two points for each linear equation.

Equation (1):

$x - 2y = 5$ (1)

When $x = 0$, find y:

$0 - 2y = 5 \Rightarrow y = -2{\cdot}5$ Point 1 is $(0, -2{\cdot}5)$.

When $y = 0$, find x:

$x + 0 = 5 \Rightarrow x = 5$ Point 2 is $(5, 0)$.

Equation (2):

$x + 5y = -9$ (2)

When $x = 0$, find y:

$0 + 5y = -9$

$\Rightarrow 5y = -9 \Rightarrow y = -1{\cdot}8$ Point 3 is $(0, -1.8)$.

When $y = 0$, find x:

$x + 5(0) = -9 \Rightarrow x = -9$ Point 4 is $(-9, 0)$.

From the graph, the point where the two lines cross/the point of intersection is $(1, -2)$.

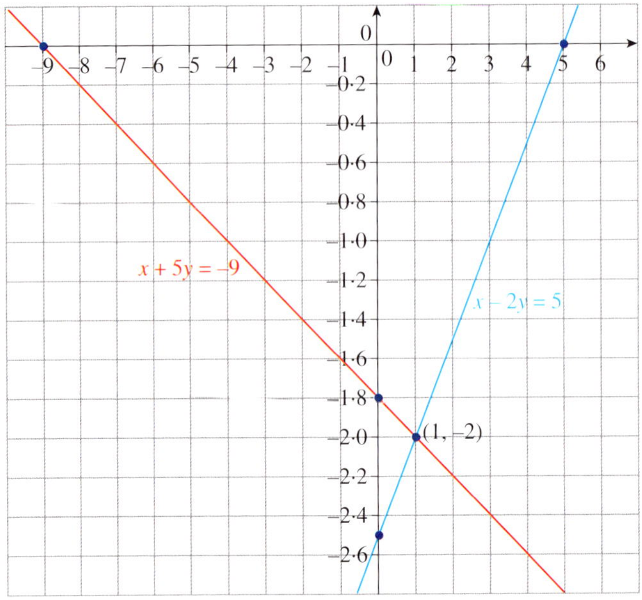

Solution: $x = 1$ and $y = -2$.

Q4 (a) Rearrange $\frac{x}{3} - y = -1$ in the form $ax + by = c$, where $a, b, c \in \mathbb{Z}$:

$$\frac{x}{3} - y = -1 \qquad \text{Multiply by 3.}$$

$$\Rightarrow \quad x - 3y = -3$$

Label the equations (1) and (2):

$x - 3y = -3 \qquad (1)$

$4x - y = 10 \qquad (2)$

Eliminate the y variable:

$$x - 3y = -3 \qquad (1)$$

$$+ \quad -12x + 3y = -30 \qquad (2) \times -3$$

$$-11x = -33$$

$$\Rightarrow \quad x = \frac{-33}{-11}$$

$$\Rightarrow \quad x = 3$$

Substitute $x = 3$ into (2) to find y:

$$4x - y = 10$$

$$\Rightarrow \quad 4(3) - 10 = y$$

$$\Rightarrow \quad y = 12 - 10$$

$$\Rightarrow \quad y = 2$$

Check your solution by substituting both values into equation (1):

$x - 3y = -3 \Rightarrow 3 - 3(2) = -3$

$\Rightarrow 3 - 6 = -3 \Rightarrow -3 = -3$ ✓

(b) Rearrange both equations in the form $ax + by = c$, where $a, b, c \in \mathbb{Z}$:

$\frac{1}{2}x - y = -5$ Multiply by 2.

$\Rightarrow x - 2y = -10$

$\frac{5}{2}x + y = -1$ Multiply by 2.

$\Rightarrow 5x + 2y = -2$

Label the equations (1) and (2) and eliminate the y variable:

$$\begin{array}{rll} & x - 2y = -10 & (1) \\ + & \underline{5x + 2y = -2} & (2) \\ & 6x = -12 & \end{array}$$

$\Rightarrow x = \frac{-12}{6}$

$\Rightarrow x = -2$

Substitute $x = -2$ into (1) to find y:

$x - 2y = -10$

$\Rightarrow -2 - 2y = -10$

$\Rightarrow -2y = -10 + 2$

$\Rightarrow y = \frac{-8}{-2}$

$\Rightarrow y = 4$

Check your solution by substituting both values into equation (2):

$5x + 2y = -2 \Rightarrow 5(-2) + 2(4) = -2$

$\Rightarrow -10 + 8 = -2 \Rightarrow -2 = -2$ ✓

(c) Rearrange both equations in the form $ax + by = c$, where $a, b, c \in \mathbb{Z}$:

$\frac{2x}{5} - \frac{2y}{3} = \frac{12}{5}$ Multiply by the LCD, 15.

$\Rightarrow 15\left(\frac{2x}{5}\right) - 15\left(\frac{2y}{3}\right) = 15\left(\frac{12}{5}\right)$

$\Rightarrow 3(2x) - 5(2y) = 3(12)$

$\Rightarrow 6x - 10y = 36$

$\frac{x-3}{4} - \frac{y-1}{3} = \frac{5}{6}$ Multiply by the LCD, 12.

$\Rightarrow 12\left(\frac{x-3}{4}\right) - 12\left(\frac{y-1}{3}\right) = 12\left(\frac{5}{6}\right)$

$\Rightarrow 3(x-3) - 4(y-1) = 2(5)$

$\Rightarrow 3x - 9 - 4y + 4 = 10$

$\Rightarrow 3x - 4y = 15$

Label the equations (1) and (2):

$6x - 10y = 36$ (1)

$3x - 4y = 15$ (2)

Eliminate the x variable:

$6x - 10y = 36$ (1)

$+ \quad -6x + 8y = -30$ (2) × −2

$-2y = 6$

$\Rightarrow \quad y = \frac{6}{-2}$

$\Rightarrow \quad y = -3$

Substitute $y = -3$ into (2) to find x:

$3x - 4y = 15$ (2)

$\Rightarrow \quad 3x - 4(-3) = 15$

$\Rightarrow \quad 3x = 15 - 12$

$\Rightarrow \quad x = \frac{3}{3}$

$\Rightarrow \quad x = 1$

Check your solution by substituting both values into equation (1):

$6x - 10y = 36 \Rightarrow 6(1) - 10(-3) = 36$

$\Rightarrow 6 + 30 = 36 \Rightarrow 36 = 36$ ✓

Q5 (a) Write two linear equations to represent the information provided and label them (1) and (2):

Let x = admission price for an adult to Dublin Zoo.

Let y = admission price for a child to Dublin Zoo.

Henry family: $2x + 3y = 68{\cdot}40$ (1)

Clarke family: $3x + 4y = 96{\cdot}70$ (2)

(b) Eliminate the x variable:

$6x + 9y = 205{\cdot}20$ (1) × 3

$+ \quad -6x - 8y - -193{\cdot}40$ (2) × −2

$y = 11{\cdot}80$

Substitute $y = 11{\cdot}80$ into (1) to find x.

$2x + 3y = 68{\cdot}40$

$\Rightarrow \quad 2x + 3(11{\cdot}80) = 68{\cdot}40$

$\Rightarrow \quad 2x + 35{\cdot}40 = 68{\cdot}40$

$$\Rightarrow \quad 2x = 68{\cdot}40 - 35{\cdot}40$$

$$\Rightarrow \quad 2x = 33$$

$$\Rightarrow \quad x = \frac{33}{2}$$

$$\Rightarrow \quad x = 16{\cdot}5$$

An adult ticket costs €16·50.

A child ticket costs €11·80.

(c) Verify the solution by substituting $x = 16{\cdot}50$ and $y = 11{\cdot}80$ into (2).

$3x + 4y = 96{\cdot}70 \Rightarrow 3(16{\cdot}5) + 4(11{\cdot}80) = 96{\cdot}70$

$\Rightarrow 49{\cdot}50 + 47{\cdot}20 = 96{\cdot}70 \Rightarrow 96{\cdot}70 = 96{\cdot}70$ ✓

Q6 (a) Write two linear equations to represent the information provided and label them (1) and (2):

Let x = number of 1-cent coins

Let y = number of 2-cent coins

$x + y = 250$ (1)

$x + 2y = 410$ (2) €4·10 equals 410 cents

(b) Eliminate the x variable:

$$\begin{array}{rrl} & x + y = 250 & (1) \\ + & -x - 2y = -410 & (2) \times -1 \\ \hline & -y = -160 & \end{array}$$

$$\Rightarrow \quad y = \frac{-160}{-1}$$

$$\Rightarrow \quad y = 160$$

Substitute $y = 160$ into (1) to find x.

$$x + y = 250$$

$$\Rightarrow x + 160 = 250$$

$$\Rightarrow \quad x = 250 - 160$$

$$\Rightarrow \quad x = 90$$

There are ninety 1-cent coins

There are one hundred and sixty 2-cent coins.

(c) Verify the solution by substituting $x = 90$ and $y = 160$ into (2).

$x + 2y = 410 \Rightarrow 90 + 2(160) = 410 \Rightarrow 90 + 320 = 410 \Rightarrow 410 = 410$ ✓

9 Algebra 7: Solving Quadratic Equations

Learning objectives

In this chapter you will learn:

- How to solve quadratic equations using factors
- How to solve quadratic equations using the quadratic formula
- How to solve quadratic equations with algebraic fractions
- How to form quadratic equations given the roots
- How to solve problems using quadratic equations.

Quadratic equations

Key Terminology

Word	Meaning
Quadratic equation	An equation of the form $ax^2 + bx + c = 0$, where $a \neq 0$ and $a, b, c \in \mathbb{R}$.
Zero rule	When we factorise a quadratic equation we get two factors: i.e. $(a)(b) = 0$ This is called the **zero rule**, which means that either $a = 0$ or $b = 0$. The zero rule is used when solving quadratic equations.
Roots	When we **solve** a quadratic equation we can get two values for x, as the highest power of a quadratic equation is 2. The values of x are called the **solution** or the **roots** of the quadratic equation. Graphically, the roots of a quadratic equation are found where the graph cuts the x-axis, i.e. when $y = 0$.

Points to note

The roots of a quadratic equation are found where the graph cuts the x-axis, i.e. when $y = 0$.

When a quadratic equation is graphed, its shape is commonly called a parabola.

If the coefficient of the x^2 term is a positive number, then the graph will be '∪-shaped'.	If the coefficient of the x^2 term is a negative number, then the graph will be '∩-shaped'.
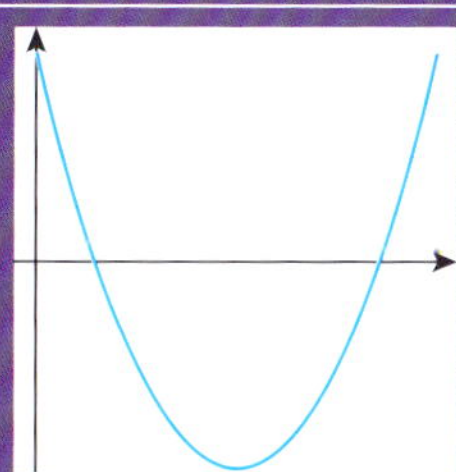	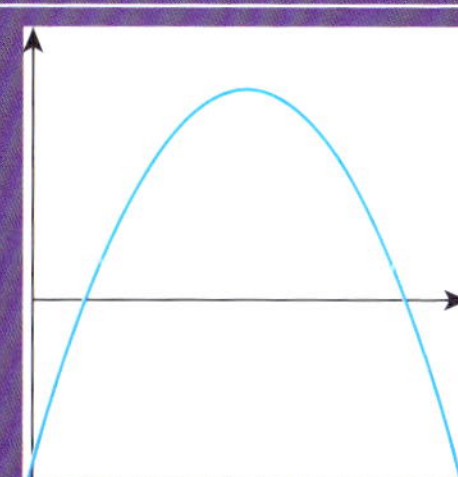

This is covered in further detail in Chapter 14.

Solving quadratic equations using factors

We can solve quadratic equations using the factorisation methods we met in Chapter 4. They are:

1. Taking out the highest common factor. For example: $7x^2 - 63x = 7x(x - 9)$.
2. The difference of two squares.
   For example: $64x^2 - 49 = (8x)^2 - (7)^2 = (8x - 7)(8x + 7)$.
3. Quadratic trinomials. For example: $x^2 + 5x + 6 = (x + 2)(x + 3)$.

Please review these methods at this point.

Top Tip

To solve a quadratic equation of the form $ax^2 + bx + c = 0$, where $a \neq 0$, and $a, b, c \in \mathbb{R}$:

1. Ensure that the quadratic equation is written in the form $ax^2 + bx + c = 0$.
2. Factorise the left hand side (LHS) of the equation.
3. Set each factor equal to zero, from the 'zero rule'.
4. Find the value(s) of x.

Example

Solve the quadratic equation $5x^2 - x = 0$.

Solution

$5x^2 - x = 0$	Take out the HCF = x.
$\Rightarrow x(5x - 1) = 0$	Factorise the LHS.
$\Rightarrow x = 0 \quad \text{or} \quad 5x - 1 = 0$	Let each factor = 0.
$\Rightarrow x = 0 \quad \text{or} \quad 5x = 1$	
$\Rightarrow x = 0 \quad \text{or} \quad x = \frac{1}{5}$	These values for x are the roots.

Graphically, we see that the roots are found where the graph cuts the x-axis, i.e. when $y = 0$.

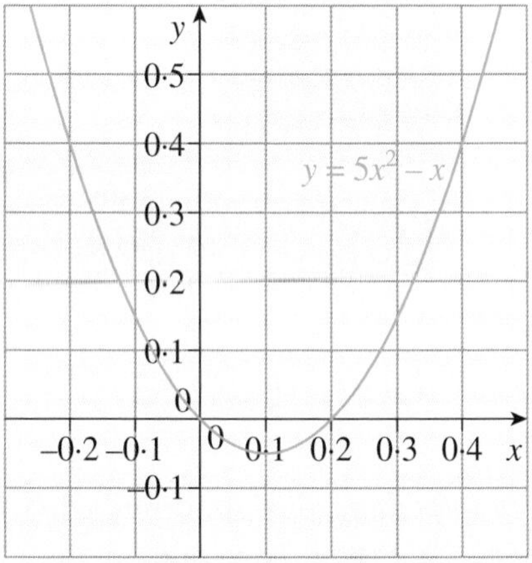

Algebraically, check the roots by substituting $x = 0$ and $x = \frac{1}{5}$ into the original equation:

When $x = 0$: $5x^2 - x = 0 \Rightarrow 5(0)^2 - (0) = 0 \Rightarrow 0 = 0$ ✓

When $x = \frac{1}{5}$: $5x^2 - x = 0 \Rightarrow 5\left(\frac{1}{5}\right)^2 - \left(\frac{1}{5}\right) = 0$

$\Rightarrow 5\left(\frac{1}{25}\right) - \left(\frac{1}{5}\right) = 0$

$\Rightarrow \left(\frac{1}{5}\right) - \left(\frac{1}{5}\right) = 0 \Rightarrow 0 = 0$ ✓

Example

Solve the quadratic equation $110x^2 - 11x = 0$.

Solution

$110x^2 - 11x = 0$	Take out the HCF = $11x$.
$\Rightarrow 11x(10x - 1) = 0$	Factorise the LHS. Let each factor = 0.
$\Rightarrow x = \frac{0}{11} \quad \text{or} \quad 10x = 1$	
$\Rightarrow x = 0 \quad \text{or} \quad x = \frac{1}{10}$	These values for x are the roots.

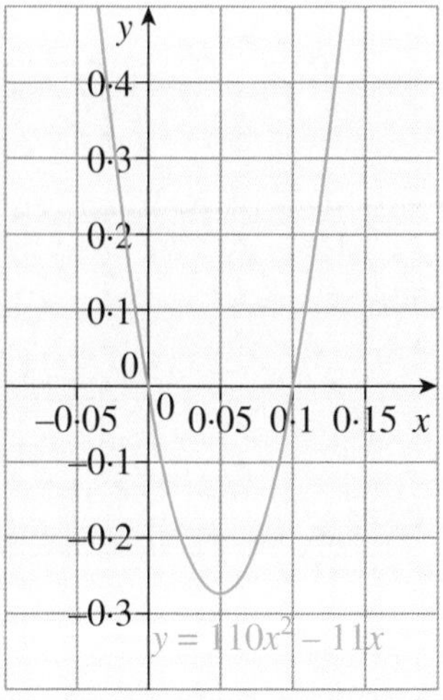

Graphically, we see that the roots are found where the graph cuts the x-axis, i.e. when $y = 0$.

Check the roots algebraically by substituting $x = 0$ and $x = \frac{1}{10}$ into the original equation.

Example

Solve the quadratic equation $x^2 + x - 2 = 0$.

Solution

$x^2 + x - 2 = 0$	Factorise the LHS using the guide number method.
	Guide number = (coefficient of x^2 term) × (constant). Here $x^2 = 1x^2$, so the coefficient of x^2 is 1 and the constant is −2.
	The guide number is $(1)(-2) = -2$.
$\Rightarrow x^2 - x + 2x - 2 = 0$	The factors which add to $+x$ are $-x + 2x$.
$\Rightarrow x(x-1) + 2(x-1) = 0$	Factorise using grouping.
$\Rightarrow (x+2)(x-1) = 0$	
$\Rightarrow x + 2 = 0$ or $x - 1 = 0$	Let each factor = 0.
$\Rightarrow x = -2$ or $x = 1$	These values for x are the roots.

Graphically, we see that the roots are found when $y = 0$.

Check the roots by substituting $x = -2$ and $x = 1$ into the original equation.

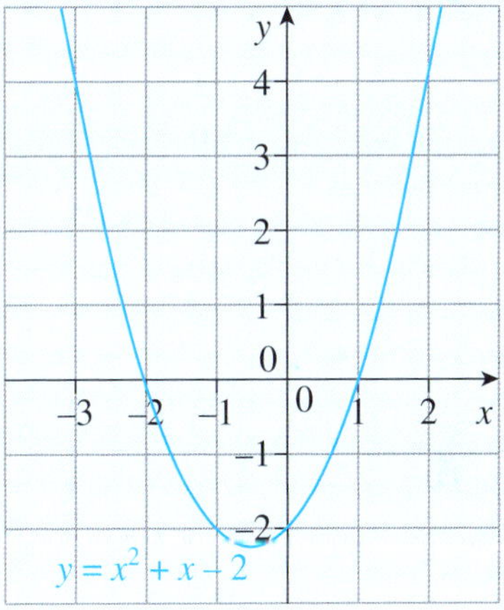

Example

Solve the quadratic equation $4x^2 - 4x - 3 = 0$.

Solution

$4x^2 - 4x - 3 = 0$	Factorise the LHS using the guide number method. Guide number = $(4)(-3) = -12$.
$\Rightarrow 4x^2 + 2x - 6x - 3 = 0$	The factors which add to $-4x$ are $+2x - 6x$.
$\Rightarrow 2x(2x+1) - 3(2x+1) = 0$	Factorise using grouping.

$\Rightarrow (2x - 3)(2x + 1) = 0$

$\Rightarrow 2x - 3 = 0$ or $2x + 1 = 0$ — Let each factor = 0.

$\Rightarrow 2x = 3$ or $2x = -1$

$\Rightarrow x = \frac{3}{2}$ or $x = -\frac{1}{2}$ — These values for x are the roots.

Graphically, we see that the roots are found where the graph cuts the x-axis, i.e. when $y = 0$.

Algebraically, check the roots by substituting $x = -\frac{1}{2}$ and $x = \frac{3}{2}$ into the original equation.

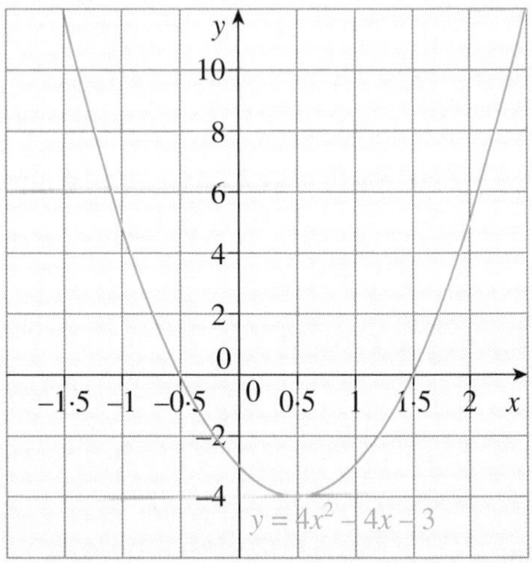

Example

(a) Solve the equation $x^2 - 4x - 12 = 0$.

(b) Hence, solve the equation $(y - 1)^2 - 4(y - 1) - 12 = 0$.

Solution

(a) $x^2 - 4x - 12 = 0$ — Factorise the LHS.

Guide Number = $(1)(-12) = -12$

Factors which add to $-4x$ are $-6x + 2x$.

$\Rightarrow x^2 + 2x - 6x - 12 = 0$

$\Rightarrow x(x + 2) - 6(x + 2) = 0$ — Factorise.

$\Rightarrow (x - 6)(x + 2) = 0$

$\Rightarrow x - 6 = 0$ or $x + 2 = 0$

$\Rightarrow x = 6$ or $x = -2$

(b) The equation $(y - 1)^2 - 4(y - 1) - 12 = 0$ is of the same form as $x^2 - 4x - 12 = 0$, except that x has been replaced with $(y - 1)$. We can therefore replace x by $(y - 1)$ in the answers.

$y - 1 = x$

$\therefore y - 1 = 6$ or $y - 1 = -2$

$\therefore y = 6 + 1$ or $y = -2 + 1$

$\therefore y = 7$ or $y = -1$

Solving quadratic equations using the quadratic formula

There are occasions when it is not possible to find integer values for the factors of a quadratic equation. For example, when factorising the quadratic formula $x^2 + x - 1 = 0$, it is not possible to find integer factors of the guide number $= -1$, where the factors sum to give the middle term $+1x$.

In such cases, mathematicians use the quadratic formula, also known as the '$-b$ formula': $x = \frac{-b \pm \sqrt{b^2 - 4ac}}{2a}$, given in the *Formulae and Tables* booklet, to find the roots/solution of the quadratic equation $ax^2 + bx + c = 0$.

We always use this formula when we are asked to find the values of the roots to a given number of decimal places, or a number of significant figures, or the nearest integer or in surd form.

Top Tip

To solve a quadratic equation using the quadratic formula:

1. Ensure that the quadratic equation is written in the form $ax^2 + bx + c = 0$.
2. Identify the values of a, b and c, including the sign of each.
3. Substitute the values of a, b and c into the quadratic formula: $x = \frac{-b \pm \sqrt{b^2 - 4ac}}{2a}$.
4. Calculate both values for x.

Example

Solve the quadratic equation $3x^2 - 2x - 3 = 0$, giving your answer in surd form, correct to two decimal places.

Solution

$3x^2 - 2x - 3 = 0$

We know that: $a = 3, b = -2$ and $c = -3$.

$$x = \frac{-b \pm \sqrt{b^2 - 4ac}}{2a}$$

Substitute $a = 3$, $b = -2$ and $c = -3$ into the quadratic formula.

$$\Rightarrow x = \frac{-(-2) \pm \sqrt{(-2)^2 - 4(3)(-3)}}{2(3)} \Rightarrow x = \frac{2 \pm \sqrt{4 + 36}}{6}$$

$$\Rightarrow x = \frac{2 + \sqrt{40}}{6} \quad \text{or} \quad x = \frac{2 - \sqrt{40}}{6}$$

Simplify $\sqrt{40} = 2\sqrt{10}$ using a calculator.

$\Rightarrow x = \dfrac{2 + 2\sqrt{10}}{6}$ or $x = \dfrac{2 - 2\sqrt{10}}{6}$ Leave the roots in surd form.

$\Rightarrow x = \dfrac{1}{3} + \dfrac{\sqrt{10}}{3}$ or $x = \dfrac{1}{3} - \dfrac{\sqrt{10}}{3}$

$\Rightarrow x = 1{\cdot}39$ or $x = -0{\cdot}72$

Check the roots by substituting them into the original equation.

Example

Verify that $1 - \sqrt{15}$ is one root of the quadratic equation $x^2 - 2x - 14 = 0$.

Solution

Solve the quadratic equation $x^2 - 2x - 14 = 0$ to verify that one of the roots is $1 - \sqrt{15}$.

We know that: $a = 1$, $b = -2$ and $c = -14$.

$x = \dfrac{-b \pm \sqrt{b^2 - 4ac}}{2a}$ Substitute $a = 1$, $b = -2$ and $c = -14$ into the quadratic formula.

$\Rightarrow x = \dfrac{-(-2) \pm \sqrt{(-2)^2 - 4(1)(-14)}}{2(1)}$

$\Rightarrow x = \dfrac{2 \pm \sqrt{4 + 56}}{2}$

$\Rightarrow x = \dfrac{2 + \sqrt{60}}{2}$ or $x = \dfrac{2 - \sqrt{60}}{2}$ Simplify $\sqrt{60} = 2\sqrt{15}$ using a calculator.

$\Rightarrow x = \dfrac{2 + 2\sqrt{15}}{2}$ or $x = \dfrac{2 - 2\sqrt{15}}{2}$ Leave the roots in surd form.

$\Rightarrow x = 1 + \sqrt{15}$ or $x = 1 - \sqrt{15}$

We have verified that $1 - \sqrt{15}$ is a root of the equation $x^2 - 2x - 14 = 0$.

Solving quadratic equations with algebraic fractions

Top Tip

To solve a quadratic equation with algebraic fractions:

1. Find the lowest common denominator (LCD) for the fractions in the equation.
2. Multiply each term in the equation by the LCD.
3. Ensure that the quadratic equation is written in the form $ax^2 + bx + c = 0$ and solve.

Example

Solve the equation $\frac{x^2}{3} - \frac{1}{2} = \frac{3x-1}{6}$.

Solution

$\frac{x^2}{3} - \frac{1}{2} = \frac{3x-1}{6}$ Multiply all terms by the LCD = 6.

$\Rightarrow 2x^2 - 3 = 3x - 1$

$\Rightarrow 2x^2 - 3x - 3 + 1 = 0$

$\Rightarrow 2x^2 - 3x - 2 = 0$ Factorise the LHS.

$\Rightarrow (2x + 1)(x - 2) = 0$

$\Rightarrow 2x + 1 = 0$ or $x - 2 = 0$

$\Rightarrow 2x = -1$ or $x = 2$

$\Rightarrow x = -0{\cdot}5$ or $x = 2$

Forming quadratic equations given the roots

Top Tip

To form a quadratic equation given the roots, we can use either of the methods below.

Method 1: Working back from the roots

1. Assume that a and b are the roots.
2. Let x equal the value of each root: $x = a$ and $x = b$.
3. Form both factors: $(x - a) = 0$ and $(x - b) = 0$.

4 Set the factors equal to zero: $(x - a)(x - b) = 0$, using the zero rule.

5 Expand the brackets:

$x(x - b) - a(x - b) = 0 \quad \Rightarrow x^2 - bx - ax + ab = 0$

$\Rightarrow x^2 - (a + b)x + ab = 0$

Method 2: Using the formula x^2 – (sum of the roots)x + (product of the roots) = 0

1 Assume that a and b are the roots.

2 Add both roots together: **sum of the roots** = $a + b$.

3 Multiply both roots together: **product of the roots** = ab.

4 Substitute the value for the sum and the product into the quadratic formula below:

x^2 – (sum of the roots)x + (product of the roots) = 0

$\Rightarrow x^2 - (a + b)x + ab = 0$ (This is the same formula used in Method 1.)

Note: This formula is **not** in the *Formulae and Tables* booklet.

Example

Form the quadratic equation for the roots $x = -4$ and $x = 5$.

Solution

Method 1: The roots are $x = -4$ and $x = 5$

$\Rightarrow x + 4 = 0$ and $x - 5 = 0$ The factors.

$\Rightarrow (x + 4)(x - 5) = 0$

$\Rightarrow x(x - 5) + 4(x - 5) = 0$ Expand the brackets.

$\Rightarrow x^2 - 5x + 4x - 20 = 0$ Simplify.

$\Rightarrow x^2 - x - 20 = 0$

Method 2: The roots are $x = -4$ and $x = 5$

The sum of the roots $= -4 + 5 = 1$

The product of the roots $= (-4)(5) = -20$

Substitute into the quadratic formula:

x^2 – (sum of the roots)x + (product of the roots) = 0

$\Rightarrow x^2 - (1)x + (-20) = 0$

$\Rightarrow x^2 - x - 20 = 0$

Example

Form the quadratic equation for the graph shown.

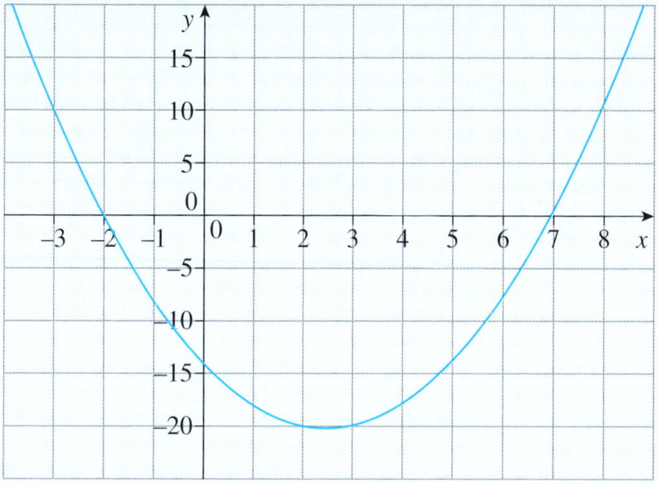

Solution

The roots of the quadratic equation are found from the graph where $y = 0$.

From the graph we see that the roots are $x = -2$ and $x = 7$.

Using Method 1:

The roots of this quadratic equation are $x = -2$ and $x = 7$.

$\Rightarrow x + 2 = 0$ and $x - 7 = 0$ $\quad$ $(x + 2)$ and $(x - 7)$ are the factors.

$\Rightarrow (x + 2)(x - 7) = 0$

$\Rightarrow x(x - 7) + 2(x - 7) = 0$ $\quad$ Expand the brackets.

$\Rightarrow x^2 - 7x + 2x - 14 = 0$ $\quad$ Simplify.

$\Rightarrow x^2 - 5x - 14 = 0$

Using Method 2:

The roots of this quadratic equation are $x = -2$ and $x = 7$.

The sum of the roots $= -2 + 7 = 5$.

The product of the roots $= (-2)(7) = -14$.

Substitute the value for the sum and the product of the roots into the quadratic formula below:

$x^2 - (\text{sum of the roots})x + (\text{product of the roots}) = 0$

$\Rightarrow x^2 - (5)x + (-14) = 0$

$\Rightarrow x^2 - 5x - 14 = 0$

Solving problems using quadratic equations

Example

In a right-angled triangle ABC, the hypotenuse AB is 18 cm longer than AC, and BC is 17 cm longer than AC.

(a) Draw a sketch to represent this information.

(b) Using Pythagoras' Theorem, write a formula that represents this information and simplify to a quadratic equation.

(c) Solve the quadratic equation.

(d) Find the lengths of the three sides.

(e) Verify that the triangle is right-angled.

Solution

(a)

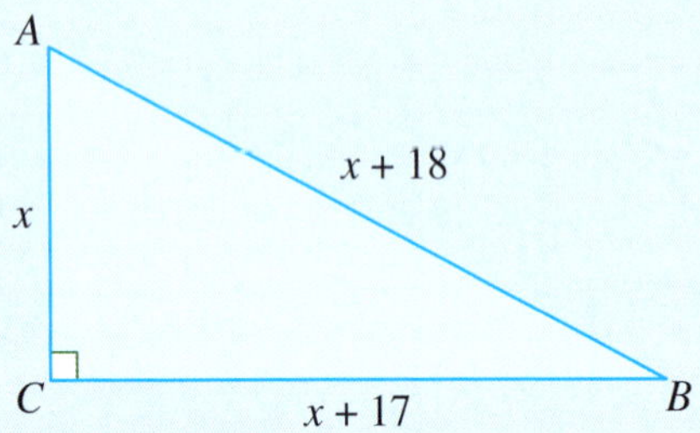

(b) $x^2 + (x + 17)^2 = (x + 18)^2$

$\Rightarrow x^2 + x^2 + 34x + 289 = x^2 + 36x + 324$

$\Rightarrow x^2 - 2x - 35 = 0$

(c) $x^2 - 2x - 35 = 0$

$\Rightarrow (x - 7)(x + 5) = 0$

$\Rightarrow x = 7 \quad \text{or} \quad x = -5$

(d) $x = 7$ cm as we cannot have a negative length.

$|AB| = x + 17 = 24$ cm

$|CB| = x + 18 = 25$ cm

(e) If the triangle is right-angled then:

$(24)^2 + (7)^2 = (25)^2$

$\Rightarrow 576 + 49 = 625$

$\Rightarrow 625 = 625$ ✓

Example

A parachutist descends at a speed of 10 m/s. At an altitude (height) of 50 m above the ground she drops her locker key. The quadratic equation $h = -4{\cdot}9t^2 + 10t + 50$ describes the height h (in m) of the locker key above the ground, t seconds after being dropped. After how many seconds does the locker key hit the ground? Write your answer correct to two decimal places.

Solution

When the key hits the ground, the height is 0 m. So we need to find t when $h = 0$.

$h = -4{\cdot}9t^2 + 10t + 50$

$\Rightarrow 0 = -4{\cdot}9t^2 + 10t + 50$

We know that: $a = -4{\cdot}9$, $b = 10$ and $c = 50$.

$$t = \frac{-b \pm \sqrt{b^2 - 4ac}}{2a}$$

Substitute $a = -4{\cdot}9$, $b = 10$ and $c = 50$ into the quadratic formula.

$$\Rightarrow t = \frac{-(10) \pm \sqrt{(10)^2 - 4(-4{\cdot}9)(50)}}{2(-4{\cdot}9)}$$

$$\Rightarrow t = \frac{-10 \pm \sqrt{100 + 980}}{-9{\cdot}8}$$

$$\Rightarrow t = \frac{-10 + \sqrt{1080}}{-9{\cdot}8} \quad \text{or} \quad t = \frac{-10 - \sqrt{1080}}{-9{\cdot}8}$$

Find the roots using a calculator.

$\Rightarrow t = -2{\cdot}33$ or $t = 4{\cdot}37$

Note: Time can't be negative so we disregard the $t = -2{\cdot}33$ option.

The locker key reached the ground after 4·37 seconds.

Exercise

Q1 Solve the following quadratic equations using a suitable factorisation method:

(a) $36x^2 = 9$

(b) $2x^2 - 32 = 0$

(c) $c^2 - 2c + 1 = 0$

(d) $x^2 + 11x - 12 = 0$

Q2 Solve each of the following quadratic equations:

(a) $2x^2 - 5x - 3 = 0$

(b) $22x^2 - 13x + 1 = 0$

(c) $7x^2 + 19x - 6 = 0$

(d) $-4x^2 - 7x + 2 = 0$

Q3 Solve each of the following quadratic equations, giving your answers in surd form:

(a) $x^2 - 7x + 2 = 0$

(b) $3x^2 - 4x - 5 = 0$

Q4 Solve each of these quadratic equations, correct to two decimal places:

(a) $2x^2 + 9x - 13 = 0$ **(b)** $8x^2 + 7x - 8 = 0$ **(c)** $5x^2 - 3x - 4 = 0$ **(d)** $6x^2 + 5x - 7 = 0$

Q5 Solve the following equations:

(a) $\frac{x^2}{4} + 2x - \frac{9}{4} = 0$ **(c)** $\frac{x^2}{5} - \frac{x}{2} = \frac{3}{10}$

(b) $\frac{x^2 - 3x}{2} = 5$ **(d)** $\frac{2x^2}{3} = \frac{5x}{6} + \frac{7}{2}$

Q6 **(a)** Verify that $2 - \sqrt{5}$ is one root of the quadratic equation $x^2 - 4x - 1 = 0$.

(b) Verify that $4 + \sqrt{11}$ is one root of the quadratic equation $x^2 - 8x + 5 = 0$.

Q7 Form the quadratic equations given the roots below, algebraically in parts **(a)** and **(b)**, and graphically in parts **(c)** and **(d)**:

(a) $x = 3$ and $x = -1$ **(b)** $x = -5$ and $x = -4$

(c)

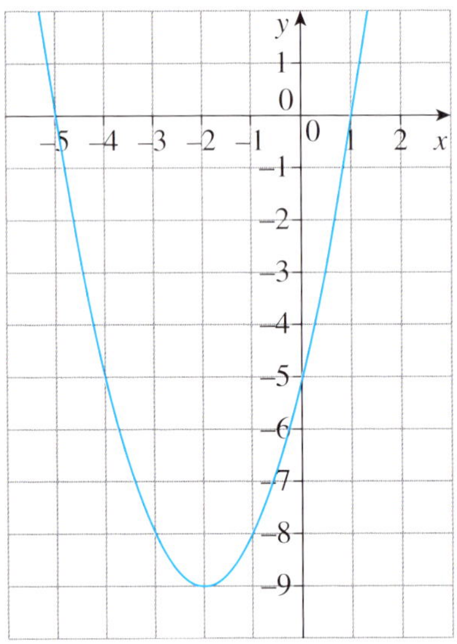

(d)

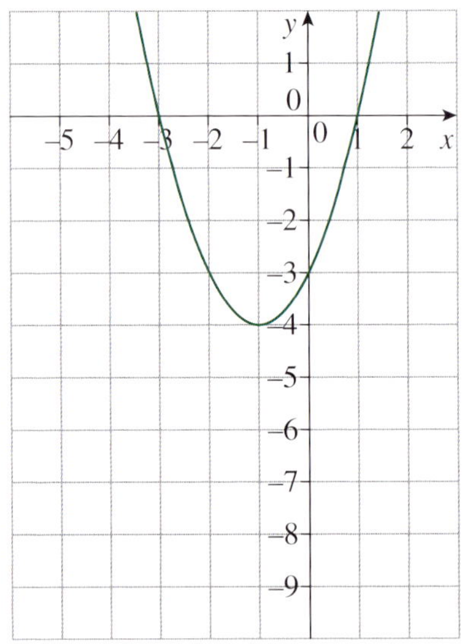

Q8 The roots of the quadratic equation $x^2 + bx + c = 0$ are 7 and −6. Find the values of b and c.

Q9 **(a)** Solve the equation $2x^2 - 5x - 3 = 0$.

(b) Hence, solve the equation $2(y - 3)^2 - 5(y - 3) - 3 = 0$.

Q10 The number x is a real number. Number A is equal to 1 less than x. Number B is equal to 2 greater than seven times x.

(a) Write down the numbers A and B, in terms of x.

(b) The product of A and B is 2. Use this information to write an equation in x.

(c) Solve this equation to find the two possible values of x. Give each of your answers correct to two decimal places.

Q11 A feather is dropped vertically downwards from the shorter side of the Leaning Tower of Pisa, a height of 55 m. The quadratic equation $h = -4{\cdot}9t^2 + 55$ describes the height h (m) of the feather above the ground, t seconds after being dropped.

How long will it take the feather to reach the ground? Write your solution correct to two decimal places.

Q12 In a right-angled triangle ABC, the hypotenuse AB is 8 cm longer than AC, and BC is 4 cm longer than AC.

(a) Draw a sketch to represent this information.

(b) Using Pythagoras' Theorem, write a formula that represents this information and simplify it to a quadratic equation.

(c) Solve the quadratic equation.

(d) Find the lengths of the three sides.

(e) Verify that the triangle is right-angled.

Q13 A teacher checks out the cost of calculators for her students on two websites, C and D. On website C, for €480, she can get a class set of calculators, one for each student. On website D, for the same price, she can get four extra calculators.

(a) If x represents the number of students in her class, write an expression in x for the cost per calculator on website C and an expression in x for the cost per calculator on website D.

The cost per calculator on website D is €6 cheaper than the cost per calculator on website C.

(b) Use this information to form an equation in x and solve it to find the number of students in the class.

(SEC 2013)

Solutions

Q1 (a) Rewrite $36x^2 = 9$ as $ax^2 + bx + c = 0$

$\Rightarrow 36x^2 - 9 = 0$ — Difference of two squares.

$\Rightarrow (6x)^2 - (3)^2 = 0$ — Factorise.

$\Rightarrow (6x - 3)(6x + 3) = 0$

$\Rightarrow 6x = 3 \quad \text{or} \quad 6x = -3$

$\Rightarrow x = \frac{1}{2} \quad \text{or} \quad x = -\frac{1}{2}$

(b) $2x^2 - 32 = 0$ — Take out HCF = 2.

$\Rightarrow 2(x^2 - 16) = 0$ — Difference of two squares.

$\Rightarrow 2((x)^2 - (4)^2) = 0$ — Factorise.

$\Rightarrow 2(x - 4)(x + 4) = 0$ — Divide by 2.

$\Rightarrow (x - 4)(x + 4) = 0$

$\Rightarrow x - 4 = 0$ or $x + 4 = 0$

$\Rightarrow x = 4$ or $x = -4$

(c) $c^2 - 2c + 1 = 0$ — Factorise the LHS.

$\Rightarrow (c - 1)(c - 1) = 0$

$\Rightarrow c - 1 = 0$

$\Rightarrow c = 1$ — Only one root means the curve touches the x-axis only once.

(d) $x^2 + 11x - 12 = 0$ — Factorise the LHS.

$\Rightarrow (x - 1)(x + 12) = 0$

$\Rightarrow x - 1 = 0$ or $x + 12 = 0$

$\Rightarrow x = 1$ or $x = -12$

Q2 (a) $2x^2 - 5x - 3 = 0$ — Guide number = −6. Factors which add to $-5x$ are $+x - 6x$.

$\Rightarrow 2x^2 + x - 6x - 3 = 0$ — Factorise.

$\Rightarrow x(2x + 1) - 3(2x + 1) = 0$

$\Rightarrow (x - 3)(2x + 1) = 0$

$\Rightarrow x - 3 = 0$ or $2x + 1 = 0$

$\Rightarrow x = 3$ or $x = -\frac{1}{2}$

(b) $22x^2 - 13x + 1 = 0$ — Guide number = +22. Factors which add to $-13x$ are $-11x - 2x$.

$\Rightarrow 22x^2 - 11x - 2x + 1 = 0$ — Factorise.

$\Rightarrow 11x(2x - 1) - 1(2x - 1) = 0$

$\Rightarrow (11x - 1)(2x - 1) = 0$

$\Rightarrow 11x - 1 = 0$ or $2x - 1 = 0$

$\Rightarrow x = \frac{1}{11}$ or $x = \frac{1}{2}$

(c) $7x^2 + 19x - 6 = 0$ — Guide number = −42. Factors which add to $19x$ are $21x - 2x$.

$\Rightarrow 7x^2 + 21x - 2x - 6 = 0$ — Factorise.

$\Rightarrow 7x(x+3) - 2(x+3) = 0$

$\Rightarrow (7x-2)(x+3) = 0$

$\Rightarrow 7x - 2 = 0 \quad \text{or} \quad x + 3 = 0$

$\Rightarrow x = \frac{2}{7} \qquad \text{or} \quad x = -3$

(d) $-4x^2 - 7x + 2 = 0$

Guide number = −8. Factors which add to $-7x$ are $-8x + 1x$.

$\Rightarrow -4x^2 - 8x + 1x + 2 = 0$

Factorise.

$\Rightarrow -4x(x+2) + 1(x+2) = 0$

$\Rightarrow (-4x+1)(x+2) = 0$

$\Rightarrow -4x + 1 = 0 \quad \text{or} \quad x + 2 = 0$

$\Rightarrow x = \frac{1}{4} \qquad \text{or} \quad x = -2$

Q3 (a) $x^2 - 7x + 2 = 0$

We know that: $a = 1$, $b = -7$ and $c = 2$.

$$x = \frac{-b \pm \sqrt{b^2 - 4ac}}{2a}$$

Substitute $a = 1$, $b = -7$ and $c = 2$ into the quadratic formula.

$$\Rightarrow x = \frac{-(-7) \pm \sqrt{(-7)^2 - 4(1)(2)}}{2(1)}$$

$$\Rightarrow x = \frac{7 \pm \sqrt{49 - 8}}{2}$$

$$\Rightarrow x = \frac{7 + \sqrt{41}}{2} \quad \text{or} \quad x = \frac{7 - \sqrt{41}}{2}$$

These are the roots in surd form.

(b) $3x^2 - 4x - 5 = 0$

We know that: $a = 3$, $b = -4$ and $c = -5$.

$$x = \frac{-b + \sqrt{b^2 - 4ac}}{2a}$$

Substitute $a = 3$, $b = -4$ and $c = -5$ into the quadratic formula.

$$\Rightarrow x = \frac{-(-4) \pm \sqrt{(-4)^2 - 4(3)(-5)}}{2(3)}$$

$$\Rightarrow x = \frac{4 \pm \sqrt{16 + 60}}{6}$$

$$\Rightarrow x = \frac{4 \pm \sqrt{76}}{6}$$

$$\Rightarrow x = \frac{4 \pm 2\sqrt{19}}{6}$$

$$\Rightarrow x = \frac{2 + \sqrt{19}}{3} \quad \text{or} \quad x = \frac{2 - \sqrt{19}}{3}$$

These are the roots in surd form.

Q4 (a) $2x^2 + 9x - 13 = 0$

We know that: $a = 2$, $b = 9$ and $c = -13$.

$$x = \frac{-b \pm \sqrt{b^2 - 4ac}}{2a}$$

Substitute $a = 2$, $b = 9$ and $c = -13$ into the quadratic formula.

$$\Rightarrow x = \frac{-(9) \pm \sqrt{(9)^2 - 4(2)(-13)}}{2(2)}$$

$$\Rightarrow x = \frac{-9 \pm \sqrt{81 + 104}}{4}$$

$$\Rightarrow x = \frac{-9 \pm \sqrt{185}}{4}$$

$$\Rightarrow x = \frac{-9 + \sqrt{185}}{4} \quad \text{or} \quad x = \frac{-9 - \sqrt{185}}{4}$$

Use a calculator to solve correct to two decimal places.

$$\Rightarrow x = 1{\cdot}15 \quad \text{or} \quad x = -5{\cdot}65$$

(b) $8x^2 + 7x - 8 = 0$

We know that: $a = 8$, $b = 7$ and $c = -8$.

$$x = \frac{-b \pm \sqrt{b^2 - 4ac}}{2a}$$

Substitute $a = 8$, $b = 7$ and $c = -8$ into the quadratic formula.

$$\Rightarrow x = \frac{-(7) \pm \sqrt{(7)^2 - 4(8)(-8)}}{2(8)}$$

$$\Rightarrow x = \frac{-7 \pm \sqrt{49 + 256}}{16}$$

$$\Rightarrow x = \frac{-7 \pm \sqrt{305}}{16}$$

$$\Rightarrow x = \frac{-7 + \sqrt{305}}{16} \quad \text{or} \quad x = \frac{-7 - \sqrt{305}}{16}$$

Use a calculator to solve correct to two decimal places.

$$\Rightarrow x = 0{\cdot}65 \quad \text{or} \quad x = -1{\cdot}53$$

(c) $5x^2 - 3x - 4 = 0$

We know that: $a = 5$, $b = -3$ and $c = -4$.

$$x = \frac{-b \pm \sqrt{b^2 - 4ac}}{2a}$$

Substitute $a = 5$, $b = -3$ and $c = -4$ into the quadratic formula.

$$\Rightarrow x = \frac{-(-3) \pm \sqrt{(-3)^2 - 4(5)(-4)}}{2(5)}$$

$$\Rightarrow x = \frac{3 \pm \sqrt{9 + 80}}{10}$$

$$\Rightarrow x = \frac{3 \pm \sqrt{89}}{10}$$

$$\Rightarrow x = \frac{3 + \sqrt{89}}{10} \quad \text{or} \quad x = \frac{3 - \sqrt{89}}{10}$$

Use a calculator to solve correct to two decimal places.

$$\Rightarrow x = 1{\cdot}24 \quad \text{or} \quad x = -0{\cdot}64$$

(d) $6x^2 + 5x - 7 = 0$

We know that: $a = 6$, $b = 5$ and $c = -7$.

$$x = \frac{-b \pm \sqrt{b^2 - 4ac}}{2a}$$

Substitute $a = 6$, $b = 5$ and $c = -7$ into the quadratic formula.

$$\Rightarrow x = \frac{-(5) \pm \sqrt{(5)^2 - 4(6)(-7)}}{2(6)}$$

$$\Rightarrow x = \frac{-5 \pm \sqrt{25 + 168}}{12}$$

$$\Rightarrow x = \frac{-5 \pm \sqrt{193}}{12}$$

$$\Rightarrow x = \frac{-5 + \sqrt{193}}{12} \quad \text{or} \quad x = \frac{-5 - \sqrt{193}}{12}$$

Use a calculator to solve correct to two decimal places.

$$\Rightarrow x = 0{\cdot}74 \quad \text{or} \quad x = -1{\cdot}57$$

Q5 (a) $\frac{x^2}{4} + 2x - \frac{9}{4} = 0$

Multiply by the LCD = 4.

$\Rightarrow x^2 + 8x - 9 = 0$

$\Rightarrow x^2 + 9x - x - 9 = 0$

$\Rightarrow x(x + 9) - 1(x + 9) = 0$

Factorise.

$\Rightarrow (x - 1)(x + 9) = 0$

$\Rightarrow x - 1 = 0 \quad \text{or} \quad x + 9 = 0$

$\Rightarrow x = 1 \quad \text{or} \quad x = -9$

(b) $\frac{x^2 - 3x}{2} = 5$

Multiply by the LCD = 2.

$\Rightarrow x^2 - 3x - 10 = 0$

$\Rightarrow x^2 - 5x + 2x - 10 = 0$

$\Rightarrow x(x - 5) + 2(x - 5) = 0$

Factorise.

$\Rightarrow (x + 2)(x - 5) = 0$

$\Rightarrow x + 2 = 0 \quad \text{or} \quad x - 5 = 0$

$\Rightarrow x = -2 \quad \text{or} \quad x = 5$

(c) $\frac{x^2}{5} - \frac{x}{2} = \frac{3}{10}$ — Multiply by the LCD = 10.

$\Rightarrow 2x^2 - 5x - 3 = 0$

$\Rightarrow 2x^2 - 6x + x - 3 = 0$

$\Rightarrow 2x(x - 3) + 1(x - 3) = 0$ — Factorise.

$\Rightarrow (2x + 1)(x - 3) = 0$

$\Rightarrow 2x + 1 = 0 \quad \text{or} \quad x - 3 = 0$

$\Rightarrow x = -\frac{1}{2} \quad \text{or} \quad x = 3$

(d) $\frac{2x^2}{3} = \frac{5x}{6} + \frac{7}{2}$ — Multiply by the LCD = 6.

$\Rightarrow 4x^2 - 5x - 21 = 0.$

$\Rightarrow 4x^2 - 12x + 7x - 21 = 0$

$\Rightarrow 4x(x - 3) + 7(x - 3) = 0$ — Factorise.

$\Rightarrow (4x + 7)(x - 3) = 0$

$\Rightarrow 4x + 7 = 0 \quad \text{or} \quad x - 3 = 0$

$\Rightarrow x = -\frac{7}{4} \quad \text{or} \quad x = 3$

Q6 (a) Verify that one of the roots is $2 - \sqrt{5}$.

$x^2 - 4x - 1 = 0$ — We know that: $a = 1$, $b = -4$ and $c = -1$.

$x = \frac{-b \pm \sqrt{b^2 - 4ac}}{2a}$ — Substitute $a = 1$, $b = -4$ and $c = -1$ into the quadratic formula.

$\Rightarrow x = \frac{-(-4) \pm \sqrt{(-4)^2 - 4(1)(-1)}}{2(1)}$

$\Rightarrow x = \frac{4 \pm \sqrt{16 + 4}}{2}$

$\Rightarrow x = \frac{4 + \sqrt{20}}{2} \quad \text{or} \quad x = \frac{4 - \sqrt{20}}{2}$ — Simplify $\sqrt{20} = 2\sqrt{5}$ using a calculator.

$\Rightarrow x = \frac{4 + 2\sqrt{5}}{2} \quad \text{or} \quad x = \frac{4 - 2\sqrt{5}}{2}$ — Leave the roots in surd form.

$\Rightarrow x = 2 + \sqrt{5} \quad \text{or} \quad x = 2 - \sqrt{5}$

We have verified that $2 - \sqrt{5}$ is a root of the equation $x^2 - 4x - 1 = 0$.

(b) Verify that one of the roots is $4 + \sqrt{11}$.

$x^2 - 8x + 5 = 0$	We know that: $a = 1$, $b = -8$ and $c = 5$.
$x = \dfrac{-b \pm \sqrt{b^2 - 4ac}}{2a}$	Substitute $a = 1$, $b = -8$ and $c = 5$ into the quadratic formula.
$\Rightarrow x = \dfrac{-(-8) \pm \sqrt{(-8)^2 - 4(1)(5)}}{2(1)}$	
$\Rightarrow x = \dfrac{8 \pm \sqrt{64 - 20}}{2}$	
$\Rightarrow x = \dfrac{8 + \sqrt{44}}{2}$ or $x = \dfrac{8 - \sqrt{44}}{2}$	Simplify $\sqrt{44} = 2\sqrt{11}$ using a calculator.
$\Rightarrow x = \dfrac{8 + 2\sqrt{11}}{2}$ or $x = \dfrac{8 - 2\sqrt{11}}{2}$	Leave the roots in surd form.
$\Rightarrow x = 4 + \sqrt{11}$ or $x = 4 - \sqrt{11}$	

We have verified that $4 + \sqrt{11}$ is a root of the equation $x^2 - 8x + 5 = 0$.

Q7 (a) Method 1:

The roots are $x = 3$ and $x = -1$

$\therefore (x - 3)$ and $(x + 1)$ are the factors.

$\Rightarrow (x - 3)(x + 1) = 0$	Multiply out the brackets.
$\Rightarrow x(x + 1) - 3(x + 1) = 0$	
$\Rightarrow x^2 + x - 3x - 3 = 0$	Collect like terms and simplify.
$\Rightarrow x^2 - 2x - 3 = 0$	

Method 2:

The roots are $x = 3$ and $x = -1$

The sum of the roots = $3 - 1 = 2$

The product of the roots = $(3)(-1) = -3$

Substitute the value for the sum and the product into the quadratic formula below:

x^2 − (sum of the roots)x + (product of the roots) = 0

$\Rightarrow x^2 - (2)x + (-3) = 0$

$\Rightarrow x^2 - 2x - 3 = 0$

From this point onwards only Method 2 will be shown, but either method could be used.

(b) The roots are $x = -5$ and $x = -4$

The sum of the roots $= -5 - 4 = -9$

The product of the roots $= (-5)(-4) = 20$

Substitute the values into the quadratic formula below:

$x^2 - (\text{sum of the roots})x + (\text{product of the roots}) = 0$

$\Rightarrow x^2 - (-9)x + (20) = 0$

$\Rightarrow x^2 + 9x + 20 = 0$

(c) The roots are $x = 1$ and $x = -5$

The sum of the roots $= 1 - 5 = -4$

The product of the roots $= (1)(-5) = -5$

Substitute the values into the quadratic formula below:

$x^2 - (\text{sum of the roots})x + (\text{product of the roots}) = 0$

$\Rightarrow x^2 - (-4)x + (-5) = 0$

$\Rightarrow x^2 + 4x - 5 = 0$

(d) The roots are $x = -3$ and $x = 1$

The sum of the roots $= -3 + 1 = -2$

The product of the roots $= (-3)(1) = -3$

Substitute the values into the quadratic formula below:

$x^2 - (\text{sum of the roots})x + (\text{product of the roots}) = 0$

$\Rightarrow x^2 - (-2)x + (-3) = 0$

$\Rightarrow x^2 + 2x - 3 = 0$

Q8 The roots are $x = 7$ and $x = -6$

The sum of the roots $= 7 - 6 = 1$

The product of the roots $= (7)(-6) = -42$

Substitute the value for the sum and the product into the quadratic formula:

$x^2 - (\text{sum of the roots})x + (\text{product of the roots}) = 0$

$\Rightarrow x^2 - (1)x + (-42) = 0$

$\Rightarrow x^2 - x - 42 = 0$

Hence, $b = -1$ and $c = -42$.

Q9 (a) $2x^2 - 5x - 3 = 0$ Factorise the LHS.

$\Rightarrow 2x^2 - 6x + x - 3 = 0$

$\Rightarrow 2x(x - 3) + 1(x - 3) = 0$

$\Rightarrow (2x + 1)(x - 3) = 0$

$\Rightarrow 2x + 1 = 0$ or $x - 3 = 0$

$\Rightarrow x = -\frac{1}{2}$ or $x = 3$ These values for x are the roots.

(b) The equation $2(y - 3)^2 - 5(y - 3) - 3 = 0$ is of the same form as $2x^2 - 5x - 3 = 0$ except that x has been replaced with $(y - 3)$.

We can therefore replace x by $(y - 3)$ in the answers.

$y - 3 = x$

$\therefore y - 3 = -\frac{1}{2}$ or $y - 3 = 3$

$\therefore y = -\frac{1}{2} + 3$ or $y = 3 + 3$

$\therefore y = 2{\cdot}5$ or $y = 6$

Q10 (a) $A = x - 1,\ B = 7x + 2$

(b) $(x - 1)(7x + 2) = 2$

$\Rightarrow x(7x + 2) - 1(7x + 2) = 2$

$\Rightarrow 7x^2 + 2x - 7x - 2 = 2$

$\Rightarrow 7x^2 - 5x - 4 = 0$

(c) $7x^2 - 5x - 4 = 0$

We know that: $a = 7$, $b = -5$ and $c = -4$.

$$x = \frac{b \pm \sqrt{b^2 - 4ac}}{2a}$$

Substitute $a = 7$, $b = -5$ and $c = -4$ into the quadratic formula.

$$\Rightarrow x = \frac{-(-5) \pm \sqrt{(-5)^2 - 4(7)(-4)}}{2(7)}$$

$$\Rightarrow x = \frac{5 \pm \sqrt{25 + 112}}{14}$$

$$\Rightarrow x = \frac{5 \pm \sqrt{137}}{14}$$

$$\Rightarrow x = \frac{5 + \sqrt{137}}{14} \quad \text{or} \quad x = \frac{5 - \sqrt{137}}{14}$$

Use a calculator to solve correct to two decimal places.

$\Rightarrow x = 1{\cdot}19$ or $x = -0{\cdot}48$

Q11 When the feather hits the ground, the height is 0 m.
So we need to find t when $h = 0$.

$h = -4{\cdot}9t^2 + 55$

$\Rightarrow 0 = -4{\cdot}9t^2 + 55$

We know that: $a = -4{\cdot}9$, $b = 0$ and $c = 55$.

$t = \dfrac{-b \pm \sqrt{b^2 - 4ac}}{2a}$

Substitute $a = -4{\cdot}9$, $b = 0$ and $c = 55$ into the quadratic formula.

$\Rightarrow t = \dfrac{-(0) \pm \sqrt{(0)^2 - 4(-4{\cdot}9)(55)}}{2(-4{\cdot}9)}$

$\Rightarrow t = \dfrac{\pm\sqrt{1078}}{-9{\cdot}8}$

$\Rightarrow t = \dfrac{+\sqrt{1078}}{-9{\cdot}8}$ or $t = \dfrac{-\sqrt{1078}}{-9{\cdot}8}$

Find the roots using a calculator.

$\Rightarrow t = -3{\cdot}35$ or $t = 3{\cdot}35$

The answer cannot be a negative value for time, so the feather hits the ground after 3·35 s.

Q12 (a)

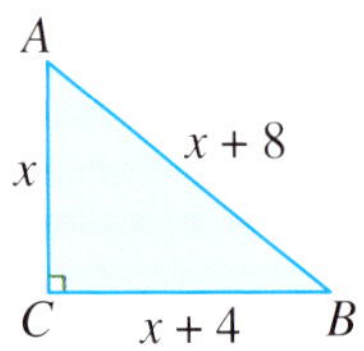

(b) $x^2 + (x + 4)^2 = (x + 8)^2$

$\Rightarrow x^2 + x^2 + 8x + 16 = x^2 + 16x + 64$

$\Rightarrow x^2 - 8x - 48 = 0$

(c) $x^2 - 8x - 48 = 0$

$\Rightarrow x^2 + 4x - 12x - 48 = 0$

$\Rightarrow x(x + 4) - 12(x + 4) = 0$

$\Rightarrow (x - 12)(x + 4) = 0$

$\Rightarrow x = 12$ or $x = -4$

(d) $x = 12$ cm as we cannot have a negative length.

$x + 4 = 12 + 4 = 16$ cm

$x + 8 = 12 + 8 = 20$ cm

(e) If the triangle is right-angled then:

$(12)^2 + (16)^2 = (20)^2$

$\Rightarrow 144 + 256 = 400$

$\Rightarrow 400 = 400$ ✓

Q13 (a) Let x represent the number of students in her class.

Cost per calculator on website $C = \frac{480}{x}$.

Cost per calculator on website $D = \frac{480}{x+4}$.

(b) $\frac{480}{x} - \frac{480}{x+4} = 6$ Multiply across by the LCD $= x(x+4)$.

$\Rightarrow x(x+4)\frac{480}{x} - x(x+4)\frac{480}{x+4} = 6x(x+4)$

$\Rightarrow (x+4)480 - x(480) = 6x^2 + 24x$

$\Rightarrow 480x + 1920 - 480x - 6x^2 - 24x = 0$

$\Rightarrow 6x^2 + 24x - 1920 = 0$ Divide by 6.

$\Rightarrow x^2 + 4x - 320 = 0$

$\Rightarrow (x-16)(x+20) = 0$

$\Rightarrow x - 16 = 0$ or $x + 20 = 0$

$\Rightarrow x = 16$ or $x = -20$

Answer: $x = 16$, as you cannot have a negative number of calculators.

10 Algebra 8: Surds, Indices, Exponential Equations and Manipulating Formulae

Learning objectives

In this chapter you will learn about:

- Simplifying surds and solving problems using surds
- Using exponential notation and rules of indices
- Solving exponential equations
- Manipulating formulae.

Key Terminology

Word	Meaning
Index notation	The expression a^n is written in index form, where a = base number, and n = index or power or exponent. a^n is read as 'a to the power of n'.
Exponential equation	An equation in which the variable is contained in the index. For example: $4 = 2^{x-1}$
Numerator	The top part of a rational number. For example: the numerator of $\frac{3}{4}$ is 3.
Denominator	The lower part of a rational number. For example: the denominator of $\frac{3}{4}$ is 4.
Surd	A surd is an irrational number which can be written in the form $a\sqrt{b}$, where $a \in \mathbb{Q}$ and $b \in \mathbb{N}$.
Manipulate a formula	Rearrange the formula (equation) to make the requested variable the subject.

Simplifying surds and solving problems using surds

Points to note

A **surd** is an irrational number written in the form $a\sqrt{b}$, where $a \in \mathbb{Q}$ and $b \in \mathbb{N}$.

Surd rules

Rule	Example, using $a = 2$ and $b = 5$
$\sqrt{a}\sqrt{a} = a^{\frac{1}{2}} \times a^{\frac{1}{2}} = a^{\frac{1}{2}+\frac{1}{2}} = a^1 = a$	$\sqrt{2}\sqrt{2} = 2$
$\sqrt{a}\sqrt{b} = a^{\frac{1}{2}} \times b^{\frac{1}{2}} = (ab)^{\frac{1}{2}} = \sqrt{ab}$	$\sqrt{2}\sqrt{5} = \sqrt{(2)(5)} = \sqrt{10}$
$\frac{\sqrt{a}}{\sqrt{b}} = \frac{a^{\frac{1}{2}}}{b^{\frac{1}{2}}} = \left(\frac{a}{b}\right)^{\frac{1}{2}} = \sqrt{\frac{a}{b}}$	$\frac{\sqrt{2}}{\sqrt{5}} = \frac{2^{\frac{1}{2}}}{5^{\frac{1}{2}}} = \left(\frac{2}{5}\right)^{\frac{1}{2}} = \sqrt{\frac{2}{5}}$
Like terms can be added.	$b\sqrt{a} + c\sqrt{a}$ and $b\sqrt{a} - c\sqrt{a}$ can be simplified by taking out $\sqrt{a}$ as a common factor.
Unlike terms **cannot** be added.	$\sqrt{a} + \sqrt{b}$ and $\sqrt{a} - \sqrt{b}$ cannot be simplified.

Link

Chapters 1, 2, 12 and RW Book 2, Chapter 13: Applied Measure

Example

Simplify $(2\sqrt{3}) \times (3\sqrt{10})$.

Solution

$(2\sqrt{3}) \times (3\sqrt{10})$ — Use the associative law for multiplication.

$= (2)(3) \times (\sqrt{3})(\sqrt{10})$ — Simplify using the rule $\sqrt{a}\sqrt{b} = \sqrt{ab}$.

$= 6\sqrt{30}$

Top Tip

To check the solution, put the entire sum directly into your calculator. Please be careful to include all brackets and square roots.

Example

The rectangle shown has sides of length $5 - \sqrt{7}$ and $5 + \sqrt{7}$.

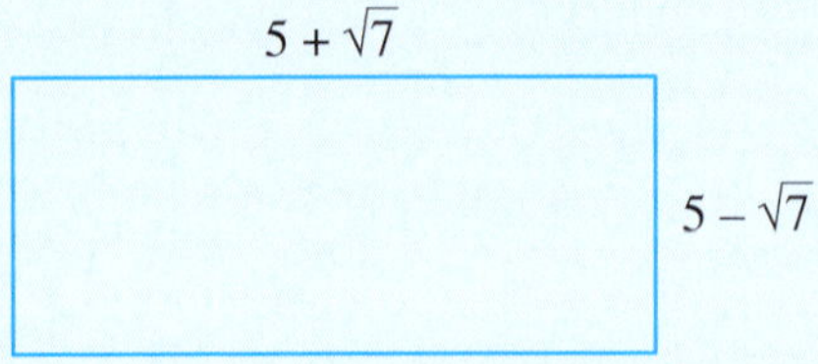

(a) Show that the area of the rectangle is a natural number.

(b) Show that the perimeter of the rectangle is also a natural number.

Solution

(a) Area = length × width

$\Rightarrow \text{Area} = (5 + \sqrt{7})(5 - \sqrt{7})$ — Expand brackets.

$= 5(5 - \sqrt{7}) + \sqrt{7}(5 - \sqrt{7})$

$= 25 - 5\sqrt{7} + 5\sqrt{7} - \sqrt{7}\sqrt{7}$ — Use the rule $\sqrt{a}\sqrt{a} = a$ to simplify.

$= 25 - 7$

$= 18 \text{ units}^2$

(b) Perimeter = 2(length + width)

$\Rightarrow \text{Perimeter} = 2(5 + \sqrt{7} + 5 - \sqrt{7})$

$= 2(10)$

$= 20 \text{ units}$

Exponential notation and rules of indices

Points to note

Exponential notation is a shorter way of writing repeated multiplication. For example: $7^3 = 7 \times 7 \times 7$. The exponent (index or power) shows how many times the base is multiplied by itself. In general, for any natural number a^n, a = base number, n = power/exponent/index and a^n is pronounced as 'a to the power of n'.

Rules for indices

Rule	Example, using $a = 2$, $b = 5$, $p = 3$ and $q = 7$
$a^p a^q = a^{p+q}$	$2^3 2^7 = 2^{3+7} = 2^{10}$
$\dfrac{a^p}{a^q} = a^{p-q}$	$\dfrac{2^3}{2^7} = 2^{3-7} = 2^{-4}$
$(a^p)^q = a^{pq}$	$(2^3)^7 = 2^{(3)(7)} = 2^{21}$
$a^0 = 1$	$2^0 = 1$
$a^{-p} = \dfrac{1}{a^p}$	$2^{-3} = \dfrac{1}{2^3}$
$a^{\frac{1}{q}} = \sqrt[q]{a}$	$2^{\frac{1}{7}} = \sqrt[7]{2}$
$a^{\frac{p}{q}} = \sqrt[q]{a^p}$	$2^{\frac{3}{7}} = \sqrt[7]{2^3}$
$(ab)^p = a^p b^p$	$(2 \times 5)^3 = 2^3 5^3 = (8)(125) = 1000$
$\left(\dfrac{a}{b}\right)^p = \dfrac{a^p}{b^p}$	$\left(\dfrac{2}{5}\right)^3 = \dfrac{2^3}{5^3} = \dfrac{8}{125}$

All of the rules for indices above are listed in the *Formulae and Tables* booklet.

Example

Write in expanded form:

(a) 2^3 **(b)** 5^6 **(c)** a^3b^2

Solution

(a) $2^3 = 2 \times 2 \times 2$ Note: the base number is 2 and the power/index is 3.

(b) $5^6 = 5 \times 5 \times 5 \times 5 \times 5 \times 5$

(c) $a^3b^2 = a \times a \times a \times b \times b$

Example

Evaluate the following using the rules for indices.

(a) $3^2 3^3$ **(d)** $(2^3)^2$ **(g)** 9^{-1} **(j)** $\left(\dfrac{1}{144}\right)^{\frac{1}{2}}$ **(m)** $(7 \times 9)^2$

(b) $5^1 5^{-2}$ **(e)** $\left(5^{\frac{1}{2}}\right)^2$ **(h)** $\left(\dfrac{1}{7}\right)^{-1}$ **(k)** $(4)^{\frac{2}{3}}$ **(n)** $\left(\dfrac{4}{5}\right)^3$

(c) $\dfrac{2^5}{2^3}$ **(f)** 89^0 **(i)** $(25)^{\frac{1}{2}}$ **(l)** $\left(\dfrac{36}{100}\right)^{\frac{3}{2}}$

Solution

		Rule
(a)	$3^2 3^3 = 3^{2+3} = 3^5 = 243$	$a^p a^q = a^{p+q}$
(b)	$5^1 5^{-2}$	
	$= 5^{1-2}$	$a^p a^q = a^{p+q}$
	$= 5^{-1} = \frac{1}{5}$	$a^{-p} = \frac{1}{a^p}$
(c)	$\frac{2^5}{2^3} = 2^{5-3} = 2^2 = 4$	$\frac{a^p}{a^q} = a^{p-q}$
(d)	$(2^3)^2 = 2^{3\times 2} = 2^6 = 64$	$(a^p)^q = a^{pq}$
(e)	$\left(5^{\frac{1}{2}}\right)^2 = 5^{\frac{1}{2}\times 2} = 5^1 = 5$	$(a^p)^q = a^{pq}$
(f)	$89^0 = 1$	$a^0 = 1$
(g)	$9^{-1} = \frac{1}{9}$	$a^{-p} = \frac{1}{a^p}$

		Rule
(h)	$\left(\frac{1}{7}\right)^{-1} = \frac{7}{1} = 7$	$a^{-p} = \frac{1}{a^p}$
(i)	$(25)^{\frac{1}{2}} = \sqrt[2]{25} = \sqrt{25} = \pm 5$	$a^{\frac{1}{q}} = \sqrt[q]{a}$ $\sqrt[2]{a} = \sqrt{a}$
(j)	$\left(\frac{1}{144}\right)^{\frac{1}{2}} = \sqrt{\frac{1}{144}} = \pm\frac{1}{12}$	$a^{\frac{1}{q}} = \sqrt[q]{a}$
(k)	$(4)^{\frac{2}{3}} = \sqrt[3]{4^2} = \sqrt[3]{16}$	$a^{\frac{p}{q}} = \sqrt[q]{a^p}$
(l)	$\left(\frac{36}{100}\right)^{\frac{3}{2}} = \left(\sqrt{\frac{36}{100}}\right)^3$	
	$= \left(\frac{6}{10}\right)^3 = \frac{216}{1000}$	$a^{\frac{p}{q}} = \sqrt[q]{a^p}$
(m)	$(7 \times 9)^2 = (7)^2 (9)^2$	
(n)	$\left(\frac{4}{5}\right)^3 = \frac{4^3}{5^3} = \frac{64}{125}$	$\left(\frac{a}{b}\right)^p = \frac{a^p}{b^p}$

Solving exponential equations

Points to note

- An exponential equation is of the form $a^x = b$, $a \neq 1$, $a > 0$.

  Note: If $a^x = a^y$, where $a \neq 1$, $a > 0$, then $x = y$.

  Note: a is the base number and both x and y are powers.

Top Tip

To solve exponential equations:

1. Write all numbers as powers of the same prime number.
2. Use the rules for indices to write each side of the equation as a power with the same base number.
3. Set both powers equal to one another (equate the powers/indices).
4. Solve for x (or the variable).

Example

Solve the equation $5^x = 125$ for x.

Solution

The base number is 5.

$5^x = 125$ Write 125 as a power of 5.

$\Rightarrow 5^x = 5^3$ Equate the indices.

$\Rightarrow x = 3$

Example

Solve the equation $16^{x-1} = 32^{1+x}$ for x.

Solution

The base number is 2, as this is the lowest common prime factor of 16 and 32.

$16^{x-1} = 32^{1+x}$

$\Rightarrow (2^4)^{x-1} = (2^5)^{1+x}$ Rule $(a^p)^q = a^{pq}$.

$\Rightarrow 2^{4x-4} = 2^{5x+5}$ Equate the powers.

$\Rightarrow 4x - 4 = 5x + 5$

$\Rightarrow 4x - 5x = 5 + 4$

$\Rightarrow -x = 9$

$\Rightarrow x = -9$

Example

If $\dfrac{3^2 \times 81^{\frac{1}{4}}}{27^{\frac{1}{2}} \times 3^5} = 3^n$, find n, where $n \in \mathbb{Q}$.

Solution

$\dfrac{3^2 \times 81^{\frac{1}{4}}}{27^{\frac{1}{2}} \times 3^5} = 3^n$ Write as powers of 3.

$\Rightarrow \dfrac{3^2 \times (3^4)^{\frac{1}{4}}}{(3^3)^{\frac{1}{2}} \times 3^5} = 3^n$ Rule $(a^p)^q = a^{pq}$.

$\Rightarrow \dfrac{3^2 \times 3^1}{3^{\frac{3}{2}} \times 3^5} = 3^n$ Rule $a^p a^q = a^{p+q}$.

$$\Rightarrow \frac{3^{2+1}}{3^{\frac{3}{2}+5}} = 3^n$$

$$\Rightarrow \frac{3^3}{3^{6\cdot5}} = 3^n$$ Rule $\frac{a^p}{a^q} = a^{p-q}$.

$$\Rightarrow 3^{3-6\cdot5} = 3^n$$

$$\Rightarrow 3^{-3\cdot5} = 3^n$$ Equate the powers.

$$\Rightarrow -3\cdot5 = n$$

$$\Rightarrow n = -3\cdot5$$

Example

Solve the simultaneous equations:

$2^x = 8^{y+1}$

$3^{x-9} = 9^y$

Solution

$2^x = 8^{y+1}$	Write as powers of 2.
$\Rightarrow 2^x = (2^3)^{y+1}$	Rule $(a^p)^q = a^{pq}$.
$\Rightarrow 2^x = 2^{3y+3}$	Equate the powers.
$\Rightarrow x = 3y + 3$	
$\Rightarrow x - 3y = 3$	(1)
$3^{x-9} = 9^y$	Write as powers of 3.
$\Rightarrow 3^{x-9} = (3^2)^y$	Rule $(a^p)^q = a^{pq}$.
$\Rightarrow 3^{x-9} = 3^{2y}$	Equate the powers.
$\Rightarrow x - 9 = 2y$	
$\Rightarrow x - 2y = 9$	(2)

Solve the equations:

$x - 3y = 3$ (1)

$x - 2y = 9$ (2) Eliminate x by (1) + −1(2).

$x - 3y = 3$	(1)
$+ \quad -x + 2y = -9$	(2) × −1
$-y = -6$	Divide by −1.
$\Rightarrow y = 6$	

Calculate the value of x by substituting $y = 6$ into $x = 3y + 3$:

$x = 3y + 3 \Rightarrow x = 3(6) + 3 \Rightarrow x = 18 + 3 \Rightarrow x = 21$

Check the solution for $x = 21$ and $y = 6$:

$3^{x-9} = 9^y$

$\Rightarrow 3^{21-9} = 9^6 \quad \Rightarrow 3^{12} = 9^6 \Rightarrow 531\,441 = 531\,441$ ✓

Solution: $x = 21$ and $y = 6$

Manipulating formulae

Top Tip

To manipulate/rearrange formulae:

1 Identify the variable that needs to be isolated.

2 Use SADMIB, the opposite operations to BIMDAS to make this variable the subject of the formula.

We can use the acronym **SADMIB** to help remember the sequence:

1st and 2nd		3rd and 4th		5th	6th
S	A	D	M	I	B
Subtraction	Addition	Division	Multiplication	Indices (Powers)	Brackets

Note: Other acronyms are used such as BIRDMAS, etc. When reversed this becomes SAMDRIB.

Example

Make T the subject of the formula $K = \sqrt{\frac{R^2T}{V}}$.

Solution

$K = \sqrt{\frac{R^2T}{V}}$ The inverse operation to square rooting is squaring, so square both sides of the equation.

$K^2 = \frac{R^2T}{V}$ The inverse operation to division is multiplication, so multiply by V.

$\Rightarrow VK^2 = R^2T$ The inverse operation to multiplication is division, so divide by R^2.

$\Rightarrow \frac{VK^2}{R^2} = T \qquad \Rightarrow T = \frac{VK^2}{R^2}$

Example

(a) Make a the subject of the formula $s = ut + \frac{1}{2}at^2$.

(b) Hence, find the value of a in m/s^2 if $s = 40$ m, $u = 10$ m/s and $t = 3$ s.

Solution

(a) $s = ut + \frac{1}{2}at^2$ The opposite operation to addition is subtraction, so subtract ut.

$\Rightarrow s - ut = \frac{1}{2}at^2$ The opposite operation to division is multiplication, so multiply by 2.

$\Rightarrow 2s - 2ut = at^2$ The opposite operation to multiplication is division, so divide by t^2.

$\Rightarrow \frac{2s - 2ut}{t^2} = a$

$\Rightarrow a = \frac{2s - 2ut}{t^2}$

(b) $a = \frac{2s - 2ut}{t^2} = \frac{2(40) - 2(10)(3)}{(3)^2} = \frac{80 - 60}{9} = \frac{20}{9}$ m/s^2

Example

The stopping distance of a car (d) in metres depends on the road surface and the speed (v) in km/h that the car is travelling. The speed and the stopping distance for a wet road surface is given by the formula $v = \sqrt{88{\cdot}9d}$.

(a) Rearrange the formula $v = \sqrt{88{\cdot}9d}$ to find the equation for the stopping distance (d).

(b) Complete the table below for the general speed limits in Ireland and calculate the stopping distance using the formula in part **(a)**, correct to two decimal places.

Speed (km/h)	Stopping distance (m)
30	
40	
50	
60	
80	
100	
120	

Solution

(a) We need to make d the subject of the formula:

$v = \sqrt{88{\cdot}9d}$ Square both sides of the equation.

$\Rightarrow v^2 = 88{\cdot}9d$ Divide both sides by 88·9.

$\Rightarrow d = \dfrac{v^2}{88{\cdot}9}$

(b)

Speed (km/h)	Stopping distance (m)
30	$d = \dfrac{v^2}{88{\cdot}9} = \dfrac{(30)^2}{88{\cdot}9} = \dfrac{900}{88{\cdot}9} = 10{\cdot}12$ m
40	$d = \dfrac{v^2}{88{\cdot}9} = \dfrac{(40)^2}{88{\cdot}9} = \dfrac{1600}{88{\cdot}9} = 18{\cdot}00$ m
50	$d = \dfrac{v^2}{88{\cdot}9} = \dfrac{(50)^2}{88{\cdot}9} = \dfrac{2500}{88{\cdot}9} = 28{\cdot}12$ m
60	$d = \dfrac{v^2}{88{\cdot}9} = \dfrac{(60)^2}{88{\cdot}9} = \dfrac{3600}{88{\cdot}9} = 40{\cdot}49$ m
80	$d = \dfrac{v^2}{88{\cdot}9} = \dfrac{(80)^2}{88{\cdot}9} = \dfrac{6400}{88{\cdot}9} = 71{\cdot}99$ m
100	$d = \dfrac{v^2}{88{\cdot}9} = \dfrac{(100)^2}{88{\cdot}9} = \dfrac{10\,000}{88{\cdot}9} = 112{\cdot}49$ m
120	$d = \dfrac{v^2}{88{\cdot}9} = \dfrac{(120)^2}{88{\cdot}9} = \dfrac{14\,400}{88{\cdot}9} = 161{\cdot}98$ m

Exercise

Q1 Simplify:

(a) $(3\sqrt{11} - \sqrt{2})(3\sqrt{11} + \sqrt{2})$ **(b)** $\sqrt{3}(\sqrt{2} + \sqrt{3}) + \sqrt{2}(\sqrt{2} - \sqrt{3})$

Q2 The rectangle and square below have the same area. The dimensions of both are in cm. The diagrams are not drawn to scale.

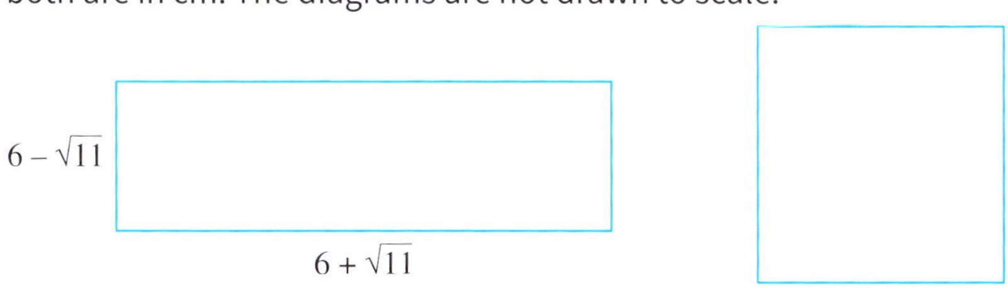

(a) Find the area of the rectangle.

(b) Find the length of one side of the square.

(SEC 2012)

Q3 Evaluate the following:

(a) $2^2 2^3$ **(b)** $\frac{5^8}{5^3}$ **(c)** $\frac{11^4}{11^4}$ **(d)** $(3)^{-2}$ **(e)** $\left(\frac{1}{2}\right)^{-1}$ **(f)** $(49)^{\frac{1}{2}}$ **(g)** $\left(\frac{1}{144}\right)^{\frac{1}{2}}$ **(h)** $(32)^{\frac{4}{5}}$ **(i)** $(2^3)^2$ **(j)** $\left(\frac{5}{2}\right)^2$

Q4 Simplify $\frac{(x^5)(x^2)\left(\sqrt[3]{x^2}\right)}{(x^3)\left(x^{\frac{4}{3}}\right)}$, giving your answer in the form x^n.

Q5 Solve for each unknown variable:

(a) $2^{3x+12} = 16^x$ **(b)** $25^n = 5^{2+n}$ **(c)** $\frac{8}{2^{y+1}} = 64$ **(d)** $\frac{\sqrt{8}}{16} = \left(\frac{1}{4}\right)^{2x-1}$

Q6 Solve the simultaneous equations:

(a) $3^{2x+y} = 3^7$
$7^{x-2y} = 7$

(b) $7^{x+2y} = \frac{1}{7}$
$4^x = \frac{1}{8^y}$

Q7 **(a)** Express $\sqrt{32}$ as a power of 2.

(b) Hence, solve the equation $\frac{2^5}{2^x} = \sqrt{32}$.

(c) Verify your answer to part **(b)**.

(d) Use the properties of surds to show that $\frac{\sqrt{128} - \sqrt{50}}{\sqrt{8}}$ simplifies to a constant.

Q8 **(a)** If $A = \pi(R^2 - r^2)$, make r the subject of the formula.

(b) If $\frac{1}{u} + \frac{1}{v} = \frac{1}{f}$, make f the subject of the formula.

Q9 The area of a parallelogram is 20 cm^2.
The perpendicular height is h.

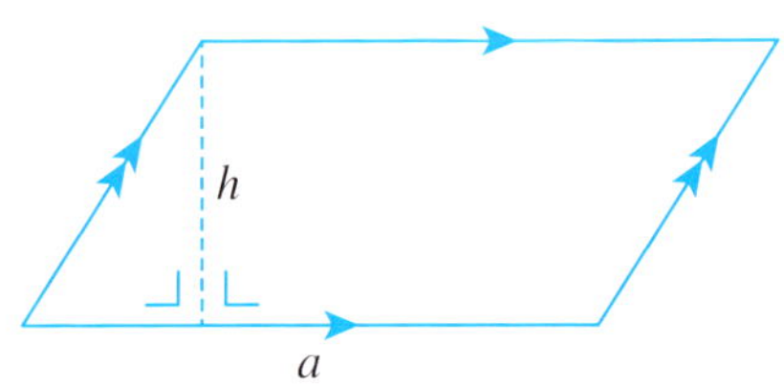

(a) Rearrange the formula $A = ah$ to make h the subject.

(b) Find the perpendicular height h if the base length a is 4 cm.

Q10 The height a ball can be thrown, h, is given by the formula $h = \frac{u^2}{2g}$, where u = initial speed and g = acceleration due to gravity.

(a) Rearrange the formula to make u the subject.

(b) If the ball is thrown to a height of 82·45 m and $g = 9{\cdot}8$ m/s², find the initial speed In m/s.

Q11 The formula for the volume of a sphere is $V = \frac{4}{3}\pi r^3$, where V = volume of the sphere and r = radius of the sphere.

(a) Rearrange the formula $V = \frac{4}{3}\pi r^3$, to make r the subject.

The volume of the Earth is $108{\cdot}21 \times 10^{10}$ km³.

Take $\pi = 3{\cdot}14$.

(b) Assuming the Earth to be a perfect sphere, find the radius of the Earth, correct to two decimal places.

Solutions

Q1 (a) $\left(3\sqrt{11} - \sqrt{2}\right)\left(3\sqrt{11} + \sqrt{2}\right)$ — Expand the brackets.

$= 3\sqrt{11}\left(3\sqrt{11} + \sqrt{2}\right) - \sqrt{2}\left(3\sqrt{11} + \sqrt{2}\right)$ — Rule $\sqrt{a}\sqrt{b} = \sqrt{ab}$.

$= 9\sqrt{11}\sqrt{11} + 3\sqrt{11}\sqrt{2} - 3\sqrt{11}\sqrt{2} - \sqrt{2}\sqrt{2}$ — Rule $\sqrt{a}\sqrt{a} = a$.

$= 9(11) - 2 = 99 - 2 = 97$

Note: We can also use the difference of two squares method here.

(b) $\sqrt{3}\left(\sqrt{2} + \sqrt{3}\right) + \sqrt{2}\left(\sqrt{2} - \sqrt{3}\right)$ — Expand the brackets.

$= \sqrt{3}\sqrt{2} + \sqrt{3}\sqrt{3} + \sqrt{2}\sqrt{2} - \sqrt{2}\sqrt{3}$ — Rules $\sqrt{a}\sqrt{b} = \sqrt{ab}$ and $\sqrt{a}\sqrt{a} = a$.

$= 3 + 2 = 5$

Q2 (a) Area of rectangle = length × width

$\Rightarrow$ Area $= \left(6 + \sqrt{11}\right)\left(6 - \sqrt{11}\right)$ — Expand the brackets.

$= 6\left(6 - \sqrt{11}\right) + \sqrt{11}\left(6 - \sqrt{11}\right)$

$= 36 - 6\sqrt{11} + 6\sqrt{11} - \sqrt{11}\sqrt{11}$ — Rule $\sqrt{a}\sqrt{a} = a$ to simplify.

$= 36 - 11 = 25$ cm²

Note: We can also use the difference of two squares method here.

(b) We know that the area of the rectangle = the area of the square = 25 cm^2

Area of square = length^2 — Let the length of the square = x.

Area of square $\Rightarrow x^2 = 25\ cm^2$

$\Rightarrow x = \sqrt{25}$ cm

$\Rightarrow x = \pm 5$ cm

The length of one side of the square is 5 cm, as length cannot be a negative value.

Q3 (a) $2^2 2^3 = 2^{2+3} = 2^5 = 32$ — $a^p a^q = a^{p+q}$.

(b) $\frac{5^8}{5^3} = 5^{8-3} = 5^5 = 3125$ — $\frac{a^p}{a^q} = a^{p-q}$.

(c) $\frac{11^4}{11^4} = 11^{4-4} = 11^0 = 1$ — $\frac{a^p}{a^q} = a^{p-q}$ and $a^0 = 1$.

(d) $(3)^{-2} = \frac{1}{3^2} = \frac{1}{9}$ — Use the rule $a^{-p} = \frac{1}{a^p}$.

(e) $\left(\frac{1}{2}\right)^{-1} = \frac{2}{1} = 2$ — Use the rule $a^{-p} = \frac{1}{a^p}$.

(f) $(49)^{\frac{1}{2}} = \sqrt{49} = \pm 7$ — Rule $a^{\frac{1}{q}} = \sqrt[q]{a}$.

(g) $\left(\frac{1}{144}\right)^{\frac{1}{2}} = \sqrt{\left(\frac{1}{144}\right)} = \frac{\sqrt{1}}{\sqrt{144}} = \pm\frac{1}{12}$ — Use the rules $a^{\frac{1}{q}} = \sqrt[q]{a}$ and $\sqrt{\frac{a}{b}} = \frac{\sqrt{a}}{\sqrt{b}}$.

(h) $(32)^{\frac{4}{5}} = \sqrt[5]{(32)^4} = \sqrt[5]{1\,048\,576} = 16$ — Use the rule $a^{\frac{p}{q}} = \sqrt[q]{a^p}$.

or $(32)^{\frac{4}{5}} = (2^5)^{\frac{4}{5}} = 2^{5 \times \frac{4}{5}} = 2^4 = 16$ — Use the rule $(a^p)^q = a^{pq}$.

(i) $(2^3)^2 = 2^{3 \times 2} = 2^6 = 64$ — Use the rule $(a^p)^q = a^{pq}$.

(j) $\left(\frac{5}{2}\right)^2 = \frac{5^2}{2^2} = \frac{25}{4}$ — Use the rule $\left(\frac{a}{b}\right)^p = \frac{a^p}{b^p}$.

Q4 $\frac{(x^5)(x^2)\left(\sqrt[3]{x^2}\right)}{(x^3)\left(x^{\frac{4}{3}}\right)}$ — Use the rule $a^{\frac{p}{q}} = \sqrt[q]{a^p}$ to simplify $\sqrt[3]{x^2}$.

$= \frac{(x^5)(x^2)\left(x^{\frac{2}{3}}\right)}{(x^3)\left(x^{\frac{4}{3}}\right)}$ — Use the rule $a^p a^q = a^{p+q}$ to simplify the numerator and the denominator.

$= \frac{x^{5+2+\frac{2}{3}}}{x^{3+\frac{4}{3}}} = \frac{x^{7\frac{2}{3}}}{x^{4\frac{1}{3}}}$ — Use the rule $\frac{a^p}{a^q} = a^{p-q}$.

$= x^{7\frac{2}{3} - 4\frac{1}{3}} = x^{\frac{10}{3}}$

Q5 (a) $2^{3x+12} = 16^x$ Write 16 as a power of 2.

$\Rightarrow 2^{3x+12} = (2^4)^x$ Rule $(a^p)^q = a^{pq}$.

$\Rightarrow 2^{3x+12} = 2^{4x}$ Equate the indices.

$\Rightarrow 3x + 12 = 4x$

$\Rightarrow 12 = 4x - 3x$

$\Rightarrow x = 12$

(b) $25^n = 5^{2+n}$ Write 25 as a power of 5.

$\Rightarrow (5^2)^n = (5)^{2+n}$ Rule $(a^p)^q = a^{pq}$.

$\Rightarrow 5^{2n} = 5^{2+n}$ Equate the indices.

$\Rightarrow 2n = 2 + n$

$\Rightarrow 2n - n = 2$

$\Rightarrow n = 2$

(c) $\frac{8}{2^{y+1}} = 64$ Write all base numbers as powers of 2.

$\Rightarrow \frac{2^3}{2^{y+1}} = 2^6$ Rule $\frac{a^p}{a^q} = a^{p-q}$.

$\Rightarrow 2^{3-y-1} = 2^6$

$\Rightarrow 2^{2-y} = 2^6$ Equate the indices.

$\Rightarrow 2 - y = 6$

$\Rightarrow 2 - 6 = y$

$\Rightarrow y = -4$

(d) $\frac{\sqrt{8}}{16} = \left(\frac{1}{4}\right)^{2x-1}$ Write 8, 16 and 4 as powers of 2.

$\Rightarrow \frac{\sqrt{2^3}}{2^4} = \left(\frac{1}{2^2}\right)^{2x-1}$ Simplify $\sqrt{2^3}$ and $\frac{1}{2^2}$ using $a^{\frac{p}{q}} = \sqrt[q]{a^p}$ and $a^{-p} = \frac{1}{a^p}$ rules.

$\Rightarrow \frac{2^{\frac{3}{2}}}{2^4} = (2^{-2})^{2x-1}$ Use $\frac{a^p}{a^q} = a^{p-q}$ and $(a^p)^q = a^{pq}$ to simplify the LHS and RHS.

$\Rightarrow 2^{\frac{3}{2}-4} = 2^{-4x+2}$

$\Rightarrow 2^{-2\cdot5} = 2^{-4x+2}$ Equate indices.

$\Rightarrow -2\cdot5 = -4x + 2$

$\Rightarrow 4x = 2\cdot5 + 2$

$\Rightarrow x = \frac{4\cdot5}{4} = \frac{9}{8}$

Q6 (a) $3^{2x+y} = 3^7$ Equate the powers.

$\Rightarrow 2x + y = 7$ (1)

$7^{x-2y} = 7^1$ Equate the powers.

$\Rightarrow x - 2y = 1$ (2)

Solve the equations:

$2x + y = 7$ (1)

$x - 2y = 1$ (2) Eliminate y.

$4x + 2y = 14$ (1) × 2

$+\quad x - 2y = 1$ (2)

$5x = 15$ Divide by 5.

$x = \frac{15}{5} \Rightarrow x = 3$

Calculate the value of y by substituting $x = 3$ into $2x + y = 7$.

$2x + y = 7 \Rightarrow 2(3) + y = 7 \Rightarrow 6 + y = 7 \Rightarrow y = 7 - 6 \Rightarrow y = 1$

Check the solution for $x = 3$ and $y = 1$:

$3^{2x+y} = 3^7 \quad \Rightarrow 3^{2(3)+(1)} = 3^7 \Rightarrow 3^{6+1} = 3^7 \Rightarrow 3^7 = 3^7$ ✓

Solution: $x = 3$ and $y = 1$.

(b) $7^{x+2y} = \frac{1}{7}$ Write $\frac{1}{7}$ as a power of 7.

$\Rightarrow 7^{x+2y} = 7^{-1}$ Equate the powers.

$\Rightarrow x + 2y = -1$ (1)

$4^x = \frac{1}{8y}$ Write as powers of 2.

$\Rightarrow (2^2)^x = \frac{1}{(2^3)^y}$

$\Rightarrow 2^{2x} = 2^{-3y}$ Equate the powers.

$\Rightarrow 2x = -3y$

$\Rightarrow 2x + 3y = 0$ (2)

Solve the equations:

$x + 2y = -1$ (1)

$2x + 3y = 0$ (2) Eliminate x (1) × −2 + (2).

$-2x - 4y = 2$ (1) × −2

$+\quad 2x + 3y = 0$ (2)

$-y = 2 \quad \Rightarrow y = -2$

Calculate the value of x by substituting $y = -2$ into $x + 2y = -1$.

$x + 2y = -1 \Rightarrow x = -2y - 1 \Rightarrow x = -2(-2) - 1 = 3$

Solution: $x = 3$ and $y = -2$

Q7 (a) $\sqrt{32}$	Use the rule $a^{\frac{1}{q}} = \sqrt[q]{a}$.
$= (32)^{\frac{1}{2}}$	Write 32 as a power of 2.
$= (2^5)^{\frac{1}{2}}$	Use the rule $(a^p)^q = a^{pq}$.
$= 2^{\frac{5}{2}}$	
(b) $\dfrac{2^5}{2^x} = \sqrt{32}$	Write 32 as a power of 2.
$\dfrac{2^5}{2^x} = \sqrt{2^5}$	Rules $a^{\frac{p}{q}} = \sqrt[q]{a^p}$ and $\dfrac{a^p}{a^q} = a^{p-q}$.
$\Rightarrow 2^{5-x} = 2^{\frac{5}{2}}$	Equate indices.
$\Rightarrow 5 - x = 2{\cdot}5$	
$\Rightarrow x - 2{\cdot}5$	

(c) Verify the solution: $\dfrac{2^5}{2^{2\cdot5}} = \sqrt{32} \Rightarrow 2^{5-2\cdot5} = 2^{2\cdot5} \Rightarrow 2^{2\cdot5} = 2^{2\cdot5}$ ✓

(d) $\dfrac{\sqrt{128} - \sqrt{50}}{\sqrt{8}}$	Get factors of 128, 50 and 8 so that one factor is a square number.
$= \dfrac{\sqrt{64 \times 2} - \sqrt{25 \times 2}}{\sqrt{4 \times 2}}$	Rule: $\sqrt{a}\sqrt{b} = \sqrt{ab}$.
$= \dfrac{\sqrt{64}\sqrt{2} - \sqrt{25}\sqrt{2}}{\sqrt{4}\sqrt{2}}$	
$= \dfrac{8\sqrt{2} - 5\sqrt{2}}{2\sqrt{2}}$	Simplify.
$= \dfrac{3\sqrt{2}}{2\sqrt{2}} = \dfrac{3}{2}$	
Q8 (a) $A = \pi(R^2 - r^2)$	Divide both sides by π.
$\Rightarrow \dfrac{A}{\pi} = (R^2 - r^2)$	Subtract R^2.
$\Rightarrow \dfrac{A}{\pi} - R^2 = -r^2$	Divide both sides by -1.
$\Rightarrow -\dfrac{A}{\pi} + R^2 = r^2$	Square root both sides.
$\Rightarrow r = \sqrt{R^2 - \dfrac{A}{\pi}}$	
(b) $\dfrac{1}{u} + \dfrac{1}{v} = \dfrac{1}{f}$	Multiply by LCD $= uvf$.
$\Rightarrow vf + uf = uv$	Take out f.
$\Rightarrow f(v + u) = uv$	Divide by $v + u$.
$\Rightarrow f = \dfrac{uv}{v + u}$	

Q9 (a) $A = ah$

$\Rightarrow h = \frac{A}{a}$

(b) $h = \frac{A}{a} = \frac{20}{5} = 4$ cm

Q10 (a) $h = \frac{u^2}{2g}$ Multiply both sides by $2g$.

$\Rightarrow 2gh = u^2$ Take the square root of both sides.

$\Rightarrow u = \sqrt{2gh}$

(b) $h = 82{\cdot}45$ m and $g = 9{\cdot}8$ m/s^2.

$u = \sqrt{2gh} = \sqrt{2(9{\cdot}8)(82{\cdot}45)} = \sqrt{1616{\cdot}02} \approx 40{\cdot}2$ m/s

Q11 (a) $V = \frac{4}{3}\pi r^3$ Multiply both sides by $\frac{3}{4\pi}$.

$\Rightarrow \frac{3}{4\pi}V = r^3$ Take the third root of both sides.

$\Rightarrow r = \sqrt[3]{\frac{3}{4\pi}V}$

(b) Assuming the Earth to be a perfect sphere, the radius of the Earth, correct to two decimal places is:

$r = \sqrt[3]{\frac{3}{4\pi}V} = \sqrt[3]{\frac{3}{4(3{\cdot}14)}(108{\cdot}21 \times 10^{10})} \approx 6369{\cdot}91$ km

Applied Arithmetic 2 11

Learning objectives

In this chapter you will learn about:

- Currency exchange
- Percentage profit and loss
- Value added tax
- Discounts
- Value-for-money calculations and judgements
- Household bills and meter readings
- Income tax and net pay
- Compound interest.

Currency exchange

Key Terminology

Currency exchange rates are given as direct proportions, such as the conversion rate of €1 = $1·15.

This means that 1 Euro buys $1·15, or $1·15 will buy 1 Euro.

Top Tip

There are a number of methods used when converting currency.
Two of these methods are shown below:

Method 1: The unitary method

1. Always put the currency you require on the **right hand side (RHS)** of the equation, equal to a unit of 1 of the other currency in the question.
2. Then multiply both sides of the equation by the amount to be converted.

For example: if given €1 = $1·15

Convert €1000 to $	Convert $1000 to €

Always put the currency you require on the **right hand side** of the equation, equal to a unit of 1 of the other currency.

Convert €1000 to $	Convert $1000 to €
€1 = $1·15	$1·15 = €1
	$\$\frac{1{\cdot}15}{1{\cdot}15} = €\frac{1}{1{\cdot}15}$
	$\$1 = €\frac{1}{1{\cdot}15}$

Multiply both sides of the equation by the amount to be converted.

Convert €1000 to $	Convert $1000 to €
1000 × €1 = 1000 × $1·15	$1000 \times \$1 = 1000 \times €\frac{1}{1{\cdot}15}$
€1000 = $1150	$1000 = €869·565
	$1000 = €869·57, correct to 2 d.p.

Method 2: The array method

1 Draw a 2 × 3 grid.

2 Place the symbols for the given exchange rate into the first row of the grid.

3 Then, place the given exchange rate value in the next row of the grid.

4 Now, complete the grid by placing the currency amount to be exchanged under its given currency symbol and place an X in the last box in the grid.

5 To solve for X, you simply multiply diagonally the values in the grid and rearrange if needed.

For example: if given €1 = $1·15

Convert €1000 to $	Convert $1000 to €

1 Draw a 2 × 3 grid as shown.

2 Place the symbols for the given exchange rate into the first row of the grid.

3 Then, place the given exchange rate value in the next row of the grid.

4 Now, complete the grid by placing the currency amount to be exchanged under its given currency symbol and place an X in the last box in the grid.

€	$
1	1·15
1000	X

€	$
1	1·15
X	1000

5 To solve for X, you simply multiply diagonally the values on the grid and rearrange if needed.

€	\$
1	1·15
1000	X

$1 \times X = 1 \cdot 15 \times 1000$

$X = 1150$

Therefore €1000 = \$1150

€	\$
1	1·15
X	1000

$X \times 1 \cdot 15 = 1 \times 1000$

$X = \frac{1000}{1 \cdot 15} = 869 \cdot 565...$

Therefore \$1000 = €869·57

Example

Nathan wants to exchange €1589 for US Dollars (\$). There is a 4% commission on the transaction charged by the bank. If Nathan receives \$1800, what is the exchange rate that Nathan received, correct to two decimal places?

Solution

Amount received less commission:

$100\% - 4\% = 96\% = \$1800$ Divide by 96.

$1\% = \frac{1800}{96} = \$18 \cdot 75$ Multiply by 100.

$100\% = \frac{1800}{96} \times 100 = \$1875$

€1589 × (Exchange rate) = \$1875

$\text{Exchange rate} = \frac{1875}{1589} = 1 \cdot 17998... \approx 1 \cdot 18$

Exchange rate: €1 = \$1·18

Percentage profit and loss

Key Terminology

Definition	Formula
The **percentage profit**	$\% \text{ profit} = \dfrac{\text{profit amount}}{\text{cost price}} \times 100\%$
The **percentage loss**	$\% \text{ loss} = \dfrac{\text{loss amount}}{\text{cost price}} \times 100\%$
Percentage mark-up This is the profit as a percentage (%) of the **cost price**.	$\% \text{ mark-up} = \dfrac{\text{selling price} - \text{cost price}}{\text{cost price}} \times 100\%$ $\Rightarrow \% \text{ mark-up} = \dfrac{\text{profit}}{\text{cost price}} \times 100\%$
Percentage margin This is the profit as a percentage (%) of the **selling price**.	$\% \text{ margin} = \dfrac{\text{selling price} - \text{cost price}}{\text{selling price}} \times 100\%$ $\Rightarrow \% \text{ margin} = \dfrac{\text{profit}}{\text{selling price}} \times 100\%$

% Margin versus % mark-up

Points to note

% Margin	% Mark-up
$\dfrac{\text{profit}}{\text{selling price}} \times 100\%$	$\dfrac{\text{profit}}{\text{cost price}} \times 100\%$

Note: Both numerators are the same.

$$\frac{\text{profit}}{\text{selling price}} < \frac{\text{profit}}{\text{cost price}}$$

$$\% \text{ margin} < \% \text{ mark-up}$$

The cost price is **smaller** than the selling price if a profit is made. Therefore, the fraction with the **smaller denominator is the larger value**.

Example

A company sells computers for €675, which gives them a profit margin of 30%.

(a) Calculate the profit made on one computer, to the nearest cent.

(b) What is the cost price of one computer?

The company decides to reduce the selling price of the computer in a sale.
They want the new selling price to include a profit mark-up of 26%.

(c) Find the selling price of each computer in the sale.

Solution

(a) Information given: Selling price = €675, % margin = 30%

Substitute the information into the required formula.

$$\% \text{ margin} = \frac{\text{profit}}{\text{selling price}} \times 100\%$$

$$30\% = \frac{\text{profit}}{675} \times 100\%$$

Let x = profit — Divide both sides by 100.

$$\frac{30}{100} = \frac{x}{675}$$ Multiply both sides by 675.

$$(0{\cdot}3) \times 675 = x$$

$$€202{\cdot}50 = \text{profit}$$

(b) Cost price = selling price − profit

$$= €675 - €202{\cdot}50$$

$$= €472{\cdot}50$$

(c) Information given: Cost price = €472·50, % mark-up = 26%

Substitute information into the required formula.

Let x = profit.

$$\% \text{ mark-up} = \frac{\text{profit}}{\text{cost price}} \times 100\%$$

$$26 = \frac{x}{472{\cdot}50} \times 100\%$$ Multiply both sides by 472·50.

$$26(472{\cdot}50) = x(100)$$ Divide both sides by 100.

$$\frac{26(472{\cdot}50)}{100} = x$$

$$€122{\cdot}85 = x = \text{profit}$$

Therefore, new selling price = cost price + profit

New selling price = €472·50 + €122·85 = €595·35

Value added tax (VAT)

Value added tax (VAT) is a tax on consumer spending which is charged on the sale of most products and services. VAT is charged at every stage of the sale of an item or product.

Points to note

Different VAT rates are applied to various products and services. These VAT rates include:

23% = the standard rate of VAT on all goods and services that do not fall into the reduced rate category.

13·5% = the reduced rate of VAT applied to items including fuel, electricity, building and building services, etc.

9% = a special reduced rate of VAT applied to tourism-related goods and services including restaurants, hotels, cinemas, hairdressers, etc.

Top Tip

- **VAT inclusive** means that the price shown includes VAT.
- **VAT exclusive** means that the price shown does **not** include VAT.

Example

A shop sells a particular sofa for €899 + VAT @ 23%.

(a) What is the total selling price of a sofa?

In a sale, the shop sells a sofa for €950 VAT inclusive.

(b) What is the selling price of the sofa before VAT @ 23% was added?

(c) Calculate the saving as a percentage of the original price of the sofa, correct to the nearest percent.

Solution

(a) Method 1

Find the VAT @ 23% of €899. Multiply by 0·23 (23% written as a decimal).

VAT = €899 × 0·23 = €206·77

Find the total price of the sofa.

Total price = €899 + VAT @ 23%

= €899 + €206·77 = €1105·77

Method 2

Total price including VAT = cost price + VAT @ 23%

= 100% + 23% = 123%

= €899 × 1·23 = €1105·77

(b) Total price including VAT = cost price + VAT @ 23%

= 100% + 23% = 123%

= €950

€950 = 123%

$\frac{€950}{123} = 1\%$

Price excluding VAT:

$\frac{€950}{123} \times 100 = 100\%$

€772·357 =100%

Selling price excluding VAT is €772·36

(c) Savings made: original selling price − sales price

Savings made: €1105·77 − €950 = €155·77

$\% \text{ Savings} = \frac{\text{savings}}{\text{original selling price}} \times 100\%$

$= \frac{155{\cdot}77}{1105{\cdot}77} \times 100\% = 14{\cdot}087\% = 14\%$, correct to the nearest percent

Bills

Top Tip

When working with bills, always:

- include the standing charge for the goods or service if given
- know the units you are working in
- calculate the total units used in the given time frame
- calculate the total cost of the units used in the given time frame
- note if VAT is inclusive or exclusive in the question.

Example

A gas bill shows the following information for the month of September:

	Unit price	Present reading	Previous reading
Night rate	€0·083 45	38 465	37 253
Day rate	€0·153 86	21 082	20 192

(a) Calculate the cost for the units used.

A service charge of €18 per month, and VAT at 13·5% is included on the bill.

(b) Calculate the total gas bill inclusive of VAT.

Solution

(a) Night rate

Units used = present reading – previous reading

= 38 465 – 37 253 = 1212

Cost @ €0·083 45 per unit = 1212 × €0·083 45 = €101·14

Day rate

Units used = present reading – previous reading

= 21 082 – 20 192 = 890

Cost @ €0·153 86 per unit = 890 × €0·153 86 = €136·94

Total cost = €101·14 + €136·94 = €238·08

(b) Total bill = service charge + cost of units used + VAT @13·5%

= €18 + €238·08 + (€238·08 × 0·135)

= €290·65

Example

The conditions of Susannah's mobile phone contract are given below:

Standing charge = €23

200 minutes of free calls and 150 free text messages per month.

Additional calls are charged at 12c per minute.

Additional texts are charged at 9c per text.

During the month of February, Susannah made 3 hours and 34 minutes of calls and she sent 173 text messages.

Calculate Susannah's total bill for the month of February, if VAT is charged at 23%.

Solution

	Calculation	Amount
Standing charge: including 200 minutes of free calls and 150 free text messages		€23
Additional call minutes over 200 minutes are charged at 12c per minute.	3 hours and 34 minutes = 214 minutes 214 − 200 = 14 minutes 14 × 0·12 = €1·68	€1·68
Additional texts over 150 texts are charged at 9c per text.	173 − 150 = 23 text messages 23 × 0·09 = €2·07	€2·07
Subtotal (excluding VAT)		€26·75
VAT @ 23% (0·23 × €26·75 = €6·1525)		€6·15
Total bill		€32·90

Discounts

Discounts are a reduction in the original price of goods or services. Generally, discounts are offered to encourage people to buy or pay for services quickly, for example, in a sale.

Top Tip

Formula for calculating % discount:

$$\% \text{ Discount} = \frac{\text{discount amount}}{\text{original selling price}} \times 100\%$$

Example

In the January sales, an electrical shop sells all smart TVs for 12% off the retail recommended price. John bought a smart TV for €836 in the sale. Calculate the original price of the smart TV before the sale.

Solution

Sale price = 100% − 12% = 88%

88% = €836

$1\% = \frac{€836}{88} = €9{\cdot}5$

100% = €9·5 × 100 = €950

The original price of the smart TV was €950.

Example

In a sale, a hardware shop offers €70 back when you spend over €350.

What is the percentage discount offered by the hardware shop?

Solution

$$\% \text{ Discount} = \frac{\text{discount amount}}{\text{original selling price}} \times 100\%$$

$$= \frac{70}{350} \times 100\% = 20\%$$

'Value for money' deals

Top Tip

Many companies offer their products in different size containers or as multi-packs. When deciding on the best value-for-money deal on offer, we generally find the lowest common unit price and compare.

Example

Ciara sees two different offers on packs of crisps in her local shop. Option A is a 12-pack of crisps for €4·80 and option B is a 15-pack of crisps for €5·25.

Which option offers the better 'value for money'?

Solution

- Option A: a 12-pack of crisps costing €4·80

12-pack = €4·80 Divide by 12.

$$1 \text{ pack} = \frac{4{\cdot}80}{12} = 0{\cdot}4$$

$$= 40 \text{ cents}$$

- Option B: a 15-pack of crisps costing €5·25

15-pack = €5·25 Divide by 15.

$$1 \text{ pack} = \frac{5{\cdot}25}{15} = 0{\cdot}35$$

$$= 35 \text{ cents}$$

As the unit cost for option B is less than that for option A, the 15-pack of crisps for €5·25 is the better deal.

Wages

Key Terminology

Key words	Definitions
Gross salary/ gross pay	Income before deductions is called **gross salary** or **gross pay**.
Standard rate of tax	The **standard rate of tax** is 20%, for 2016.
Higher rate of tax	The **higher rate of tax** is 40%, for 2016.
Standard rate cut-off point (SRCOP)	The **SRCOP** is the amount of the gross salary/pay that we pay the standard rate of tax on.
Gross tax	**Gross tax** is the total tax owed to the government before any deductions are made. It is calculated using the formula: Gross tax = (SRCOP × standard rate of tax) + (all income above SRCOP × higher rate of tax)
Tax credits	**Tax credits** are the amount the state allows each person to earn before paying tax. Tax credits are deducted from gross tax.
Tax payable	**Tax payable** is also called tax due. It is calculated using the formula: Tax payable = gross tax − tax credits
Net income	**Net income** is also called **net pay** or **take-home pay**. It is calculated using the formula: Net income/take-home pay = gross salary − all deductions

Point to note

The **standard rate of tax**, **higher rate of tax**, **standard rate cut-off point (SRCOP)** and **tax credits** can change yearly depending on the government's yearly budget.

Example

Fergus has a gross income of €42 500 for the year. He has an annual tax credit of €1650. The standard rate cut-off point is €33 800. The standard rate of income tax is 20% and the higher rate is 40%.

(a) Calculate Fergus' net income for the year.

Fergus receives a pay rise and thus his net income for the year increases to €45 500.

(b) Find Fergus's new gross income for the year.

Solution

(a)

Steps to calculating net income	Calculation
1 Standard rate of tax @ 20%	0·2 × 33 800 = €6760
2 Higher rate of tax @ 40% on balance	Balance = €42 500 − €33 800 = €8700
	0·4 × 8700 = €3480
3 Gross tax due = standard rate of tax + higher rate of tax	
	€6760 + €3480 = €10 240
4 Tax payable = gross tax – tax credits	€10 240 − €1650 = €8590
5 Net income/take-home pay = gross salary – tax payable	
	€42 500 − €8590 = €33 910

Fergus's net income for the year is €33 910.

(b) His net income increase = €45 500 − €42 500 = €3000

Note: As the higher rate of tax @ 40% on the balance has been paid, we can state that:

€3000 = 60% of increase in gross income

Solve to find 100%: Divide by 60.

$$\frac{€3000}{60} = 1\%$$

€50 = 1% Multiply by 100.

€50 × 100 = 100%

€5000 = 100%

New gross income = €42 500 + €5000 = €47 500.

Fergus's new gross income for the year is €47 500.

Deductions

There are two main types of deductions we will focus on:

	Statutory deductions	Non-statutory deductions
Meaning	These are deductions which must be paid to the state from each person's gross income.	These are voluntary deductions that each person has a choice of paying.
Examples	• PAYE – income tax • PRSI – pay related social insurance • USC – universal social charge	• Health insurance • Pension deductions • Gym membership • Union fees

Statutory deductions in more detail

PAYE

PAYE (pay as you earn) is money all employees pay for public services such as healthcare, education, gardaí, etc.

Deduction	PAYE (Pay as you earn)
Single person	Tax credits of €1650 **Income tax rates:** €33 800 @ 20%, balance @ 40%
Married couple or couple in a civil partnership with two incomes	Tax credits of €3300 **Income tax rates:** €42 800 @ 20% (with an increase of €24 800 max), balance @ 40%

All tax rates are accurate for 2016. These tax rates can vary on a yearly basis.

PRSI

PRSI stands for **pay related social insurance**. Both the employer and the employee must pay a PRSI contribution which goes towards services such as social welfare benefits.

USC

USC stands for **universal social charge**.

Note: All PAYE workers pay USC if their total income is more than €13 000 a year.

For people with incomes of €13 000 or more, the following USC rates apply:

USC (universal service charge)	
2016	**Rate**
On the first €12 012	1%
On the next €6656	3%
On the next €51 376	5·5%
On the balance	8%

All tax rates are accurate for 2016. These tax rates can vary on a yearly basis.

Example

Karen has a gross income of €50 800.

She has to pay universal social charge (USC) and income tax on her gross income.

Use the USC rates given in the table above.

(a) Calculate the amount of USC that Karen must pay.

Karen has an annual tax credit of €3300. The standard rate cut-off point is €33 800. The standard rate of income tax is 20% and the higher rate is 40%. Karen also pays private health insurance of €45 per month and union fees of €28 per month.

(b) Calculate Karen's net income for the year.

Solution

(a)

USC (universal service charge)		
2016	**Rate**	**Calculation**
On the first €12 012	1%	0·01 × 12 012 = €120·12
On the next €6656	3%	0·03 × 6656 = €199·68
On the next €51 376	5·5%	0·055 × (50 800 − 12 012 − 6656)
		= 0·055 × 32 132 = €1767·26

Total USC to be deducted = €120·12 + €199·68 + €1767·26 = €2087·06

The total USC that Karen must pay is €2087·06.

(b) Steps to calculating net income	**Calculation**
1 Standard rate of tax @ 20%	$0{\cdot}2 \times 33\,800 = €6760$
2 Higher rate of tax @ 40% on balance	Balance $= €50\,800 - €33\,800 = €17\,000$ $0{\cdot}4 \times €17\,000 = €6800$
3 Gross tax due	$€6760 + €6800 = €13\,560$
4 Tax payable = gross tax − tax credits	$€13\,560 - €3300 = €10\,260$
5 Other deductions per month: private health insurance of €45, union fees of €28	Per year: $€45 \times 12 = €540$ $€28 \times 12 = €336$
6 Net income/take-home pay = gross salary − all deductions	$€50\,800 - (€2087{\cdot}06 + €10\,260 + €540 + €336)$ $= €37\,576{\cdot}94$

Karen's net income for the year is €37 576·94.

Compound interest

Compound interest is the interest which is added to the principal of an investment or loan each year, which in turn becomes the principal for the next year and so on.

Method 1: Using the compound interest formula

$F = P(1 + i)^t$ is given in the *Formulae and Tables* booklet, where:

- F = final amount including interest (also called the future value)
- P = principal invested (also called the present value)
- i = annual interest rate (as a decimal)
- t = time in years.

Note: This formula assumes that compounding happens once a year.

Method 2: Compounding the interest one year at a time

- Final amount for year 1 = multiply the principal for year 1 by $(1 + i)$
- Final amount for year 2 = multiply the principal for year 2 by $(1 + i)$, and so on.

Note: Generally used when the interest rate varies from year to year.

Top Tip

Always convert the annual interest rate given into a decimal.

For example:

- $i = 6\% = 0{\cdot}06$
- $i = 11\% = 0{\cdot}11$
- $i = 15{\cdot}5\% = 0{\cdot}155$

Points to note

Annual percentage rate (APR) and annual equivalent rate (AER)

- We use the **annual percentage rate (APR)** when dealing with loan and credit agreement calculations. The APR is the interest rate paid to the financial institution.
- When dealing with savings and investments we use the **annual equivalent rate (AER)**. The AER is the interest rate paid by the financial institution.
- To calculate the interest rate for a given year we need to know both the principal and interest for that year.
- Interest rate (%) = $\dfrac{\text{interest amount}}{\text{principal}} \times 100\%$
- When asked for the value of an investment when it 'matures', we mean the amount the investment is worth at the end of the given time period.

Example

Jack invests €2500 for two years in an investment which offers a compound interest rate of 8%.

(a) How much will Jack's investment be worth when it matures?

(b) What is the total interest earned on this investment?

At the end of the third year the amount of the investment was €3207·60.

(c) Calculate the rate of interest for the third year.

Solution

(a) Method 1: Using the compound interest formula

$F = P(1 + i)^t$, as shown in the *Formula and Tables* booklet.

Information given:

F = final amount = ?

P = principal (investment) = €2500

i = interest rate 8% = 0·08

t = time = 2 years

Substitute all known values into the compound interest formula to find F:

$F = 2500(1 + 0{\cdot}08)^2$

$= 2500(1{\cdot}08)^2$

$= €2916$

Method 2: Compounding the interest one year at a time

Investment at the start of year 1 = €2500

Final amount at the end of year 1 = €2500 × 1·08 = €2700

Investment at the start of year 2 = €2700

Final amount at the end of year 2 = €2700 × 1·08 = €2916

Jack's investment will be worth €2916 when it matures.

(b) Total interest earned = final amount − investment

= €2916 − €2500

= €416

(c) At the end of the third year the total investment was €3207·60.

Interest earned = final amount − investment

= €3207·60 − €2916

= €291·60

$$\text{Interest rate (\%)} = \frac{\text{interest}}{\text{principal}} \times 100\%$$

$$= \frac{291{\cdot}60}{2916} \times 100\% = 10\%$$

The rate of interest for the third year was 10%.

Example

Mark decides to invest money for three years at an annual interest rate of 12·5%. He wants the investment to return €5400 at the end of the three years.

How much money does Mark need to invest?

Solution

Method 1

Information given:

F = final amount = €5400

P = principal (investment) = P

i = interest rate of 12·5% = 0·125

t = time = 3 years

Using the formula:

$F = P(1 + i)^t$

Substitute all known values into the compound interest formula. Rearrange the formula to make P the subject and solve for the principal.

$5400 = P(1 + 0{\cdot}125)^3$

$$\frac{5400}{(1{\cdot}125)^3} = P$$

$3792{\cdot}5925... = P$

Mark needs to invest €3793.

Depreciation

In real-life situations the value of certain items/investments may reduce (**depreciate**) in value as times goes by.

The depreciation formula

$$F = P(1 - i)^t$$

where:

- F = final amount including interest
- P = principal invested
- i = annual depreciation rate (as a decimal)
- t = time in years.

Example

Eva buys a new car for €28 000. If it depreciates in value at a rate of 11% per annum, calculate the value of the car in three years, to the nearest Euro.

Solution

Use the depreciation formula: $F = P(1 - i)^t$

Information given:

F = final amount

P = €28 000

$i = 11\% = 0{\cdot}11$

$t = 3$

Substitute all known values into the depreciation formula. Hence, solve to find the value of the car after three years.

$$F = P(1 - i)^t$$
$$= 28\,000(1 - 0{\cdot}11)^3$$
$$= 19\,739{\cdot}132$$

The value of the car in three years will be €19 739.

Exercise

Q1 (a) The table at the right shows the value of one Euro against other currencies on a particular day at a bank.

The bank charges 3% on all currency transactions.

Currency	Rate (€)
US Dollar ($)	1·12
Chinese Yuan (¥)	7·26
Mexican Peso ($)	20·91
Swedish Krona (kr)	9·46

Based on the information given, calculate the value of each of the following transactions:

(i) \$510 to Euro

(ii) €2100 to Chinese Yuan

(iii) kr1750 to Euro

(iv) €2500 to Mexican Pesos

(b) A man buys the following items on a shopping website:

A DVD boxset for £32

A book for £9·40

A set of pens for £12·99

(i) Based on the exchange rate of €1 = £0·81, calculate the total cost of the items in Euros.

VAT is charged at 23% on all goods and a shipping charge of £7·50 is applied.

(ii) What is the total cost for all items to be shipped?

Q2 (a) Mark sells a bike and treadmill for €530 online, making a profit of 18%.

(i) What was the total original cost of both items?

Mark paid €115 for the bike and sold it for €140.

(ii) Calculate the percentage mark-up on the bike, correct to 1 d.p.

(iii) Calculate the percentage margin on the treadmill, correct to 2 d.p.

(b) A jeweller buys watches for €170 each. The jeweller sells the watches with a percentage mark-up of 28%.

(i) For how much does the jeweller sell each watch?

(ii) What is the percentage profit margin, to the nearest percent?

Q3 (a) In a sale, a store offers 25% discount on all products. If a coffee maker is €160 in the sale, what was the original price of the coffee maker before the sale?

(b) In a sale, a clothing store offers a 30% discount on all marked prices.

(i) What was the marked price of a pair of shoes if the sales price is €85?

(ii) What is the sale price of a pair of jeans if the marked price is €70?

(c) A supermarket sells two types of printer:

Printer Type	Price	% Profit
A	€190	24%
B	€400	22%

(i) What is the cost price of each of the printers?

In a sale, the supermarket reduced the price of each printer to the prices listed below:

Printer Type	Sale Price
A	€165
B	€360

(ii) What is the percentage mark-up on each of the printers in the sale, correct to one decimal place?

(iii) What is the percentage discount given on each of the printers in the sale, to the nearest percent?

Q4 (a) David wishes to get some chocolate bars for a party. A packet of 12 bars costs €4·08 in shop A. A packet of 7 bars costs €2·17 in shop B.

(i) Find the cost of one bar in each shop.

(ii) If David buys 84 bars, how much will he save by buying the bars in the shop offering the better value?

(b) A supermarket has a special offer on three different brands of baby food. The following table gives details of the offer:

Brand	No. of tins per packet	Weight of each tin	Price per packet
A	2	130 g	€2·10
B	3	130 g	€4·00
C	3	240 g	€8·00

Which brand has the cheapest price per gram?

Q5 (a) A gas bill has the following information for the month of June:

	Unit price	Present reading	Previous reading
Night rate	€0·083 45	41 323	40 451
Day rate	€0·153 86	32 912	32 198

(i) Calculate the cost for the units used.

(ii) A service charge per month of €23 is added to the bill, plus VAT at 13·5%. Calculate the gas bill, VAT inclusive.

(b) The terms and conditions of Matt's mobile phone contract are listed below:

- Standing charge of €28, which includes 250 free minutes of calls and 250 free text messages.
- Exceeding limits:
  - Calls are charged at 12 cents per minute
  - Texts are charged at 9 cents per text.

During the month of May, the duration of Matt's calls were 4 hours and 51 minutes and he sent 310 text messages. VAT on this bill is charged at 23%.

Calculate his total bill for the month of May.

Q6 (a) Jack has a gross income of €57 000. His total income tax payable adds up to €12 740. The standard rate cut-off point is €33 800. The standard rate of tax is 20% and the higher rate is 40%. What are Jack's tax credits for the year?

(b) Aoife has a gross income of €43 500. She pays universal social charge (USC) and income tax on her gross income. The rates and bands for USC are shown in the table below:

USC	
2016	**Rate**
On the first €12 012	1%
On the next €6656	3%
On the next €51 376	5·5%
On the balance	8%

(i) Calculate the amount of USC that Aoife must pay.

The standard rate of income tax is 20% and the higher rate is 40%. Aoife has tax credits of €2700 for the year and the standard rate cut-off point is €33 800.

(ii) Calculate the total tax payable by Aoife for the year.

Michael pays tax at the same rates as Aoife. Michael has tax credits of €3500 for the year and has the same standard rate cut-off point as Aoife. His total tax payable amounts to €13 680 for the year.

(iii) Calculate Michael's gross income for the year.

(c) Fiona has tax credits of €1790 for the year and a standard rate cut-off point of €33 800. She has a gross income of €39 700 for the year. The standard rate of income tax is 20% and the higher rate is 40%.

(i) After tax is paid, what is Fiona's income for the year?

(ii) What would Fiona's gross income for the year need to be in order for her to have an after-tax income of €38 450?

Q7 (a) €7600 was invested in an account offering compound interest. The rate for the first year was 6% per annum.

(i) Calculate the total investment at the end of the first year.

(ii) At the end of the second year the investment amounted to €8660·20. Calculate the rate per annum for the second year.

(b) Denis has €6800 and decides to invest it for three years. The bank offers him a special savings account which has an interest rate of 4·5% for the first two years and a higher rate for the third year, if the money is retained in the account. Tax of 24% will be deducted each year from the interest earned.

(i) How much will the investment be worth at the end of second year, after tax is deducted?

(ii) At the end of the third year the investment will be worth €7577·10. Calculate the rate of interest for the third year. Give your answer as a percentage, correct to one decimal place.

(c) Thomas decides to invest money for three years at an annual interest rate of 9·5%. He wants the investment to return €7500 at the end of the three years. How much money does Thomas need to invest, to the nearest Euro?

Q8 (a) A car was bought for €23 540. At the end of the first year the car was worth €20 400. What was the rate of depreciation for the car, to the nearest percent?

(b) A type of machine depreciates in value by 16% per year.

(i) If one machine is bought for €4500, find its value at the end of four years, to the nearest Euro.

(ii) If the value of another machine is €2300 after three years, find the value when new, to the nearest cent.

Solutions

Q1 (a) (i) Convert \$510 to Euro:

Commission charged 3%: $0{\cdot}03 \times \$510 = \$15{\cdot}30$

Amount to be exchanged: $\$510 - \$15{\cdot}30 = \$494{\cdot}70$

\$494·70 to Euro:

Exchange rate: $€1 = \$1{\cdot}12$

$$\$1{\cdot}12 = €1$$

$$\$\frac{1{\cdot}12}{1{\cdot}12} = €\frac{1}{1{\cdot}12}$$

$$\$1 = €\frac{1}{1{\cdot}12}$$

Multiply both sides of the equation by the amount to be converted.

$$\$1 \times 494{\cdot}70 = €\frac{1}{1{\cdot}12} \times 494{\cdot}70$$

$$\$494{\cdot}70 = €441{\cdot}6964\ldots$$

$$= €441{\cdot}70$$

(ii) Convert €2100 to Chinese Yuan:

Commission charged 3% : $0{\cdot}03 \times €2100 = €63$

Amount to be exchanged: $€2100 - €63 = €2037$

€2037 to Chinese Yuan:

Exchange rate: $€1 = ¥7{\cdot}26$

Multiply both sides of the equation by the amount to be converted.

$€1 = ¥7{\cdot}26$

$€1 \times 2037 = ¥7{\cdot}26 \times 2037$

$€2037 = ¥14\,788{\cdot}62$

(iii) Convert 1750 Swedish Krona to Euro:

Commission charged 3% : $0{\cdot}03 \times \text{kr}1750 = \text{kr}52{\cdot}50$

Amount to be exchanged: $\text{kr}1750 - \text{kr}52{\cdot}50 = \text{kr}1697{\cdot}50$

kr1697·50 to Euro:

Exchange rate: $€1 = \text{kr}9{\cdot}46$

$\text{kr}9{\cdot}46 = €1$

$\text{kr}\frac{9{\cdot}46}{9{\cdot}46} = €\frac{1}{9{\cdot}46}$

$\text{kr}1 = €\frac{1}{9{\cdot}46}$

Multiply both sides of the equation by the amount to be converted.

$\text{kr}1 \times 1697{\cdot}50 = €\frac{1}{9{\cdot}46} \times 1697{\cdot}50$

$\text{kr}1697{\cdot}50 = €179{\cdot}4397...$

$= €179{\cdot}44$

Therefore, kr1697·50 is equal to €179·44.

(iv) Convert €2500 to Mexican Pesos:

Commission charged 3% : $0{\cdot}03 \times €2500 = €75$

Amount to be exchanged: $€2500 - €75 = €2425$

€2425 to Mexican Pesos

Exchange rate: $€1 = \$20{\cdot}91$

Multiply both sides of the equation by the amount to be converted.

$€1 \times 2425 = \$20{\cdot}91 \times 2425$

$€2425 = \$50\,706{\cdot}75$

Therefore, €2425 is equal to $50 706·75.

(b) (i) The exchange rate is €1 = £0·81.

Total cost of items = £32 + £9·40 + £12·99 = £54·39

£0·81 = €1

$£\frac{0·81}{0·81} = €\frac{1}{0·81}$

$£1 = €\frac{1}{0·81}$

$£1 \times 54·39 = €\frac{1}{0·81} \times 54·39$

£54·39 = €67·1481...

= €67·15

(ii) Cost of items = €67·15

VAT @23% : 0·23 × €67·15 = €15·4445 = €15·44

Convert shipping charge of £7·50 to Euros:

The exchange rate is €1 = £0·81.

£0·81 = €1

$£\frac{0·81}{0·81} = €\frac{1}{0·81}$

$£1 = €\frac{1}{0·81}$

$£1 \times 7·50 = €\frac{1}{0·81} \times 7·50$

£7·50 = €9·2592... = €9·26

Total cost: €67·15 + €15·44 + €9·26 = €91·85

Q2 (a) (i) Original cost:

118% = €530

$1\% = €\frac{530}{118} = €4·491\,525$

$\simeq €4·4915$

100% = €449·15

Original cost price was €449·15.

(ii) Profit made on the bike:

Selling price – cost price = €140 – €115 = €25

$\%\text{ mark-up} = \frac{\text{profit}}{\text{cost price}} \times 100\%$

$= \frac{25}{115} \times 100\% = 21·7391\% = 21·7\%$ to 1 d.p.

(iii) Cost of the treadmill:

Total cost – cost of the bike = €449·15 – €115 = €334·15

Selling price of the treadmill: €530 – €140 = €390

Profit on the treadmill:
Selling price – cost price = €390 – €334·15 = €55·85

$$\% \text{ margin} = \frac{\text{profit}}{\text{selling price}} \times 100\%$$

$$= \frac{55{\cdot}85}{390} \times 100\% = 14{\cdot}3205\% = 14{\cdot}32\%, \text{ correct to 2 d.p.}$$

(b) **(i)** Information given:

Cost price = €170

% mark-up = 28%

Substitute information into the formula:

$$\% \text{ mark-up} = \frac{\text{profit}}{\text{cost price}} \times 100\%$$

$$28\% = \frac{\text{profit}}{170} \times 100\%$$

$$\Rightarrow \frac{\text{profit}}{170} = \frac{28}{100}$$

$$\Rightarrow \text{profit} = \frac{28}{100} \times 170$$

$$= €47{\cdot}60$$

Selling price = cost price + profit
= €170 + €47·60
= €217·60

(ii) Selling price = €217·60

Profit = €47·60

$$\% \text{ margin} = \frac{\text{profit}}{\text{selling price}} \times 100\%$$

$$= \frac{47{\cdot}60}{217{\cdot}60} \times 100\%$$

$$= 21{\cdot}875\%$$

$$\simeq 22\%$$

Q3 (a) Sale price = 100% – 25% = 75%

75% = €160

$$1\% = €\frac{160}{75} = €2{\cdot}1333...$$

100% = €2·1333 × 100 = €213·33

The original price of the coffee maker was €213·33.

(b) **(i)** Sale price = 100% – 30% = 70%

70% = €85

$$1\% = €\frac{85}{70} = €1{\cdot}2143...$$

100% = €1·2143 × 100
= €121·43

The original price of the shoes was €121·43.

(ii) Marked price = 100% = €70

$1\% = €\frac{70}{100} = €0{\cdot}7$

$70\% = 0{\cdot}7 \times 70 = €49$

The sales price of the pair of jeans is €49.

(c) **(i)** **Printer A:**

Original cost price:

$124\% = €190$

$1\% = €\frac{190}{124} = €1{\cdot}5322...$

$1\% = €1{\cdot}5322$

$100\% = €153{\cdot}22$

Original cost price was €153·22

Printer B:

Original cost price:

$122\% = €400$

$1\% = €\frac{400}{122} = €3{\cdot}27868...$

$1\% = €3{\cdot}2787$

$100\% = €327{\cdot}87$

Original cost price was €327·87

(ii) **Printer A:**

New selling price: €165

Cost price: €153

Profit: €165 − €153 = €12

$$\% \text{ mark-up} = \frac{\text{profit}}{\text{cost price}} \times 100\%$$

$$= \frac{12}{153} \times 100\% = 7{\cdot}8431...\% \simeq 7{\cdot}8\%$$

Printer B:

New selling price: €360

Cost price: €328

Profit: €360 − €328 = €32

$$\% \text{ mark-up} = \frac{\text{profit}}{\text{cost price}} \times 100\%$$

$$= \frac{32}{328} \times 100\% = 9{\cdot}7560...\% \simeq 9{\cdot}8\%$$

(iii) **Printer A:**

Discount = original selling price – new selling price

$= €190 - €165 = €25$

$$\% \text{ Discount} = \frac{\text{discount}}{\text{original selling price}} \times 100\%$$

$$= \frac{25}{190} \times 100\% = 13{\cdot}1578...\% \simeq 13\%$$

Printer B:

Discount: original selling price – new selling price

Discount: $€400 - €360 = €40$

$$\% \text{ Discount} = \frac{\text{discount}}{\text{original selling price}} \times 100\%$$

$$= \frac{40}{400} \times 100\% = 10\%$$

Q4 (a) **(i)** **Shop A:**

1 bar : $€4{\cdot}08 \div 12 = €0{\cdot}34$

Shop B:

1 bar : $€2{\cdot}17 \div 7 = €0{\cdot}31$

(ii) Number of packets of bars required in Shop A: $84 \div 12 = 7$ packets needed.

Cost of 7 packets of bars: $€4{\cdot}08 \times 7 = €28{\cdot}56$

Number of packets of bars required in Shop B: $84 \div 7 = 12$ packets needed.

Cost of 12 packets of bars: $€2{\cdot}17 \times 12 = €26{\cdot}04$

Savings made by buying the bars in shop B: $€28{\cdot}56 - €26{\cdot}04 = €2{\cdot}52$

(b)

Brand	Total grams per packet	Price per gram to the nearest cent
A	$2 \times 130 = 260$ g	$\frac{210}{260} = 0{\cdot}81 = 81$ cents
B	$3 \times 130 = 390$ g	$\frac{400}{390} = 1{\cdot}0256 \simeq 103$ cents
C	$3 \times 240 = 720$ g	$\frac{800}{720} = 1{\cdot}1112 \simeq 111$ cents

Therefore, brand A is the cheapest.

Q5 (a) (i) Night rate

Units used = present reading – previous reading

= 41 323 − 40 451 = 872

Cost @ €0·083 45 per unit = 872 × €0·083 45 = €72·7684 ≃ €72·77

Day rate

Units used = present reading – previous reading

= 32 912 – 32 198 = 714

Cost @ €0·153 86 per unit = 714 × €0·153 86 = €109·856 04 ≃ €109·86

Total cost = €72·77 + €109·86 = €182·63

(ii) Total bill = Service charge + cost of units used + VAT @13·5%

= €23 + €182·63 + (€182·63 × 0·135)

= €230·28505 = €230·29

(b)

	Calculation	Amount
Standing charge:		€28
Includes 250 minutes of calls and 250 text messages		
Exceeding limits 250: Calls are charged at 12c per minute.	4 hours and 51 minutes = 291 minutes 291 – 250 = 41 minutes 41 × 0·12 = €4·92	€4·92
Exceeding limits 250: Texts are charged at 9c per text.	310 – 250 = 60 text messages 60 × 0·09 = €5·40	€5·40
Subtotal (excluding VAT)		€38·32
VAT @ 23% (0·23 × €38·32 = €8·8136)		€8·81
Total bill		€47·13

Q6 (a) Steps to calculating net income	**Calculation**
1 Standard rate of tax @ 20%	0·2 × €33 800 = €6760
2 Higher rate of tax @ 40% on balance	Balance = €57 000 − €33 800 = €23 200 Higher rate of tax: 0·4 × €23 200 = €9280
3 Gross tax due	€6760 + €9280 = €16 040
4 Tax credits = gross tax – tax paid	€16 040 − €12 740 = €3300

(b) **(i)**

	Rate	Calculation
On the first €12 012	1%	0·01 × €12 012 = €120·12
On the next €6656	3%	0·03 × €6656 = €199·68
On the next €51 376	5·5%	0·055 × (€43 500 − €12 012 − €6656)
		= 0·055 × €24 832 = €1365·76

Total USC to pay = €120·12 + €199·68 + €1365·76 = €1685·56

(ii)

Steps to calculating tax payable	Calculation
1 Standard rate of tax @ 20%	0·2 × €33 800 = €6760
2 Higher rate of tax @ 40% on balance	Balance = €43 500 − €33 800 = €9700 Higher tax = 0·4 × €9700 = €3880
3 Gross tax due	€6760 + €3880 = €10 640
4 Tax payable = gross tax – tax credits	€10 640 − €2700 = €7940

(iii) Total tax payable: €13 680

Tax credits: €3500

Gross tax = tax payable + tax credits

Gross tax = €13 680 + €3500 = €17 180

Tax @ 20%: 0·2 × €33 800 = €6760

Tax @ 40%: €17 180 − €6760 = €10 420

Income over €33 800:

40% = €10 420

$1\% = \frac{€10\,420}{40} = €260{\cdot}50$

100% = €260·50 × 100 = €26 050

Michael's gross income:

€26 050 + €33 800 = €59 850

(c) **(i)**

Steps to calculating net income	Calculation
1 Standard rate of tax @ 20%	0·2 × €33 800 = €6760
2 Higher rate of tax @ 40% on balance	Balance = €39 700 − €33 800 = €5900 Higher tax = 0·4 × €5900 = €2360
3 Gross tax due	€6760 + €2360 = €9120

4 Tax payable = gross tax – tax credits €9120 − €1790 = €7330

5 Net income/take-home pay = gross salary – deductions €39 700 − €7330 = €32 370

(ii) New take-home pay: €38 450

Increase in take-home pay: €38 450 − €32 370 = €6080

As the higher rate of tax @ 40% on balance has been paid, we can state €6080 = 60% of increase in gross income.

Solve to find 100%:

$\frac{€6080}{60} = 1\%$ Divide by 60.

€101·33 = 1%

€101·33 × 100 = 100% Multiply by 100.

€10 133 = 100%

New gross income = €39 700 + €10 133 = €49 833.

Q7 (a) (i) Investment at the start of year 1 = €7600.

Final amount at end of year 1 = €7600 × 1·06 = €8056

(ii) Interest earned = final amount − investment

= €8660·20 − €8056

= €604·20

$$\text{Interest rate (\%)} = \frac{\text{interest}}{\text{principal}} \times 100\%$$

$$= \frac{604{\cdot}20}{8056} \times 100\% = 7{\cdot}5\%$$

(b) (i) Investment at the start of year 1 = €6800.

Interest earned: 0·045 × €6800 = €306

Tax @ 24% on interest: 0·24 × €306 = €73·44

Final amount at end of year 1 = €6800 + €306 − €73·44 = €7032·56

Investment at the start of year 2 = €7032·56.

Interest earned: 0·045 × €7032·56 = €316·465 = €316·47

Tax @ 24% on interest: 0·24 × €316·47 = €75·95

Final amount at end of year 2 = €7032·56 + €316·47 − €75·95
= €7273·08

(ii) Investment at the start of year 3 = €7273·08.

Investment at the end of year 3 = €7577·10.

Interest earned after tax @ 24%: = €7577·10 − €7273·08
= €304·02

To calculate the interest:

$76\% = €304{\cdot}02$

$1\% = \frac{€304{\cdot}02}{76} = €4{\cdot}0003$

$100\% = €4{\cdot}0003 \times 100 = €400{\cdot}03$

$$\text{Interest rate (\%)} = \frac{\text{interest}}{\text{principal}} \times 100\%$$

$$= \frac{400{\cdot}03}{7273{\cdot}08} \times 100\% = 5{\cdot}5\%$$

(c) Information given:

F = final amount = €7500

P = principal (investment) = P

i = interest rate of 9·5% = 0·095

t = time = 4 years

Using the formula:

$F = P(1 + i)^t$

Rearrange and solve for the principal:

$7500 = P(1 + 0{\cdot}095)^4$

$\frac{7500}{(1{\cdot}095)^4} = P$

$5216{\cdot}8072\ldots = P$

€5217 = principal to be invested, to the nearest Euro.

Q8 (a) Depreciated amount = €23 540 − €20 400
= €3140

$$\text{Depreciation rate (\%)} = \frac{3140}{23\,540} \times 100\% = 13{\cdot}3389\% \simeq 13\%$$

(b) (i) Information given:

F = final amount

P = €4500

$i = 16\% = 0{\cdot}16$

t = 4 years

Using the formula:

$F = P(1 - i)^t$

$= 4500(1 - 0{\cdot}16)^4$

$= 2240{\cdot}42112$

$\simeq 2240$

The value of the machine in three years will be €2240, to the nearest Euro.

(ii) Information given:

F = final amount = €2300

P = principal investment

$i = 16\% = 0{\cdot}16$

t = 3 years

Using the formula:

$F = P(1 - i)^t$

Rearrange and solve for the principal:

$2300 = P(1 - 0{\cdot}16)^3$

$\frac{2300}{(0{\cdot}84)^3} = P$

$3880{\cdot}5204\ldots = P$

Price of the machine new = €3880·52.

12 Sets

Learning objectives

In this chapter you will learn about:

- Revision of set notation
- Venn diagrams
- How to solve (word) problems using two-set Venn diagrams
- Venn diagrams with three sets
- Set operations
- How to solve (word) problems using three-set Venn diagrams.

Revision of set notation

What is the definition of a set?

A **set** is a collection of well-defined things, objects or symbols. Each object in the set is called a **member** or **element**. Sets are named by capital letters: A, B, C, etc.

Key Terminology

Symbol	Description	Examples
$\in$	'is an element of'	$5 \in \{5, 10, 15\}$
		$3 \in \{x \mid x < 6, x \in \mathbb{N}\}$
$\notin$	'is **not** an element of'	$a \notin \{h, o, u, s, e\}$
		$7.5 \notin \{x \mid x > 1, x \in \mathbb{Z}\}$

Cardinal number (#)

The **cardinal number** of a given set is the number of elements in the set.

Key Terminology

Symbol	Description	Examples
#	'the number of elements of a set'	If $A = \{h, a, t\}$, then $\#A = 3$. If $B = \{x \mid x < 12, x \in \mathbb{N}\}$, then $\#B = 11$.

Null set

The **null set** or **empty set** is the set that contains no elements.

Key Terminology

Symbol	Description	Examples
Ø or { }	'the null set or empty set'	Set A is the set of months of the year that begin with the letter P, therefore $A = \{\ \}$. Set B is the set of all multiples of 8 that are odd numbers.

Subsets

A is a **subset** of B if every element of set A is also in set B.

Key Terminology

Symbol	Description	Examples
$\subset$	'is a subset of the set' The Ø or { } set is a subset of every set.	$\{a, t\} \subset \{h, a, t\}$ $\{5, 7, 9\} \subset \{1, 3, 5, 7, 9, 11\}$
$\not\subset$	'is **not** a subset of the set'	$\{c\} \not\subset \{h, a, t\}$ $\{5, 7, 9\} \not\subset \{1, 3, 5, 7\}$

Example

(a) List all the subsets of the set $A = \{2, 4, 6\}$.

(b) How many subsets are there in total for set A?

Solution

(a) 3-element subset: $\{2, 4, 6\}$

2-element subsets: $\{2, 4\}, \{2, 6\}, \{4, 6\}$

1-element subsets: $\{2\}, \{4\}, \{6\}$

0-element subset: $\{\}$

(b) The number of subsets of A is 8. This is found by either listing out all the subsets as in part **(a)** or from finding the value of $2^{(\text{number of elements in the set})}$. As there are 3 elements in set A then the number of subsets of A is $2^3 = 8$.

Remember

The number of subsets of a set = $2^{(\text{number of elements in the set})}$

Describing a set

Points to note

There are three different ways to describe a set:

1 **The written method**

P is the set of natural numbers less than 6.

2 **The list method**

$P = \{1, 2, 3, 4, 5\}$

Note: In the list method, we separate the elements by commas, enclose the set in chain (curly) brackets { } and list each element **once only**.

3 **The set builder notation or rule method**

$P = \{x \mid x < 6, x \in \mathbb{N}\}$

How to read the rule method

P is the set of all values of x, such that x is a natural number less than 6.

Venn diagrams

Key Terminology

Symbol / description	Example
U Universal set	The set of all elements for a given context.
$A \cap B$ A intersection B (Elements common to both sets)	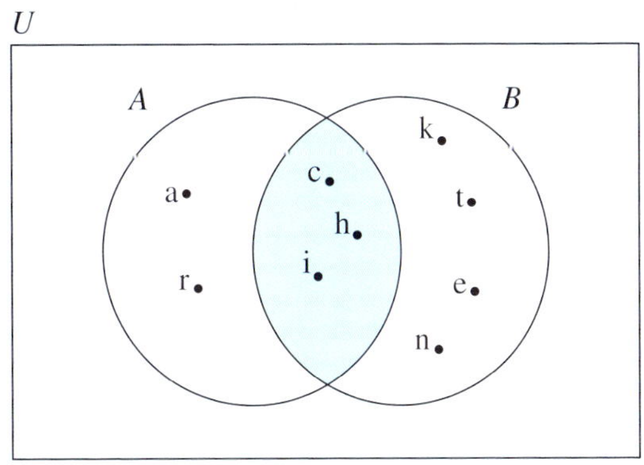 $A = \{c, h, a, i, r\}$ and $B = \{k, i, t, c, h, e, n\}$. $A \cap B = \{c, h, i\}$
$A \cup B$ A union B (Elements which are in both A and B)	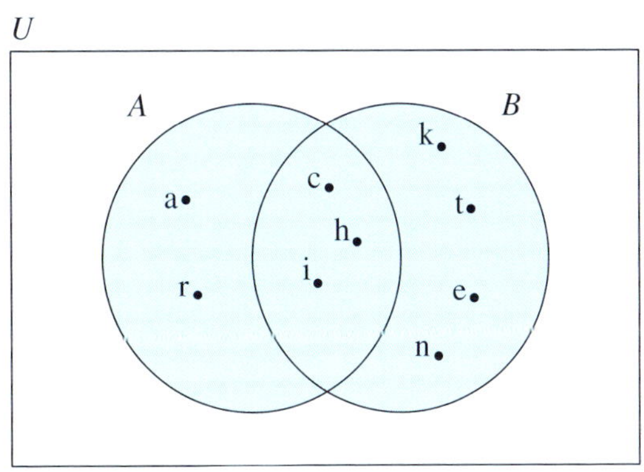 $A = \{c, h, a, i, r\}$ and $B = \{k, i, t, c, h, e, n\}$. $A \cup B = \{a, r, c, h, i, k, t, e, n\}$ Note: The elements c, h, and i which are common to both sets are listed only once.

Set difference

Key Terminology

Symbol / description	Example
$A \setminus B$ A less B (Elements which are in A but not in B)	U 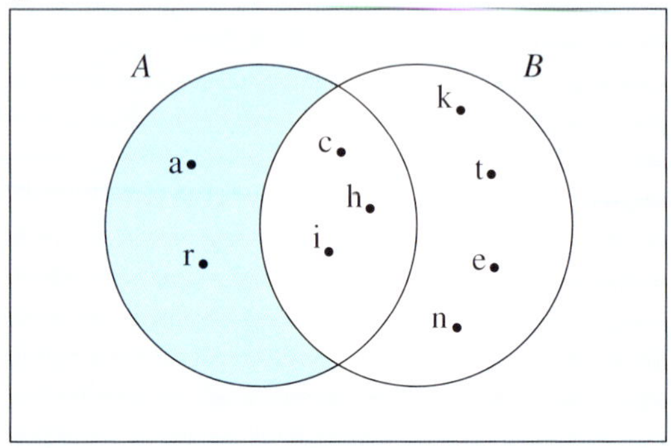 $A = \{c, h, a, i, r\}$ and $B = \{k, i, t, c, h, e, n\}$. $A \setminus B = \{a, r\}$
$B \setminus A$ B less A (Elements which are in B but not in A)	U 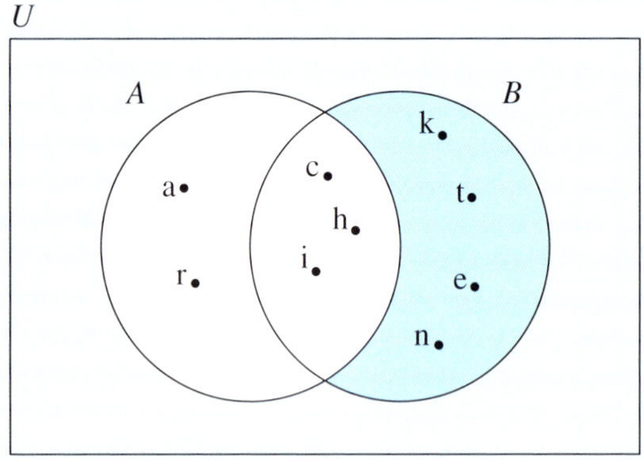 $A = \{c, h, a, i, r\}$ and $B = \{k, i, t, c, h, e, n\}$. $B \setminus A = \{k, t, e, n\}$
Note: $A \setminus B \neq B \setminus A$	(not commutative)

Complement of a set

Key Terminology

Symbol / description	Example
A' A complement (Elements which are **not** in A)	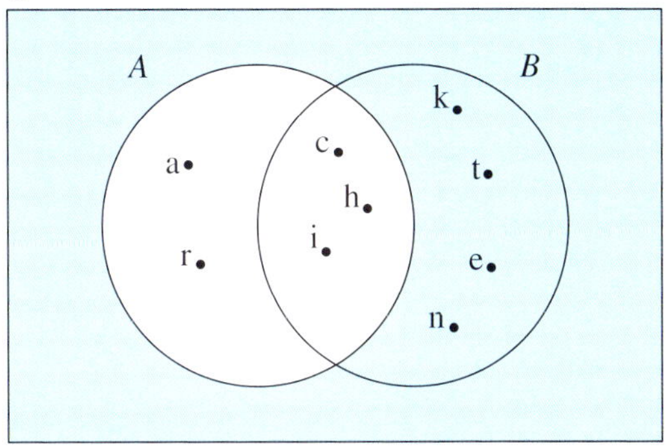 $A = \{c, h, a, i, r\}$ and $B = \{k, i, t, c, h, e, n\}$. $A' = \{k, t, e, n\}$

Remember

1 Elements are never repeated when listed or represented on a Venn diagram.

2 The order in which the elements of a set are listed is not important.

Example

List the elements in each of the following sets:

(a) U

(b) C

(c) D

(d) $C \cup D$

(e) $C \cap D$

(f) C'

(g) $D \backslash C$

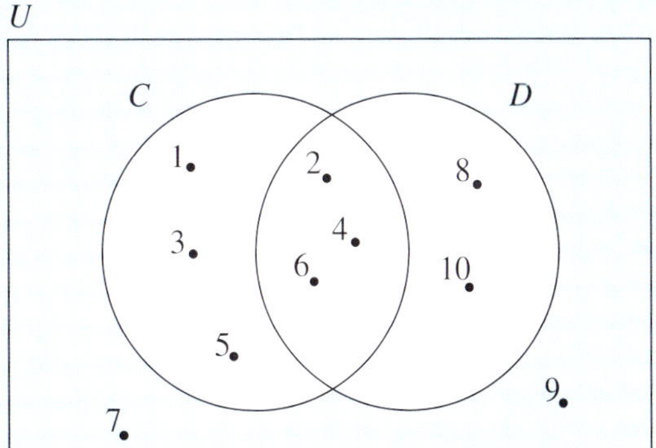

Solution

From inspection of the given Venn diagram we can see that:

(a)	$U = \{1, 2, 3, 4, 5, 6, 7, 8, 9, 10\}$	Elements in the universal set.
(b)	$C = \{1, 2, 3, 4, 5, 6\}$	Elements in set C.
(c)	$D = \{2, 4, 6, 8, 10\}$	Elements in set D.
(d)	$C \cup D = \{1, 2, 3, 4, 5, 6, 8, 10\}$	Elements in both set C and/or set D.
(e)	$C \cap D = \{2, 4, 6\}$	Elements common to both set C and set D.
(f)	$C' = \{7, 8, 9, 10\}$	Elements not in set C.
(g)	$D \setminus C = \{8, 10\}$	Elements in set D but not set C.

Top Tip

When representing information on a Venn diagram, follow these steps:

1. Find the elements in $A \cap B$.
2. Find the remainder of elements in the sets 'A only' and 'B only'.
3. Find the remainder of elements in the universal set $U \setminus (A \cup B)$.
4. Represent all information on a Venn diagram as shown below.

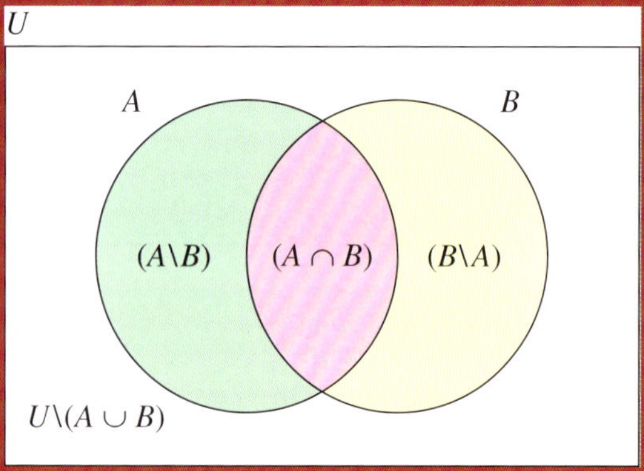

Note: $U \setminus (A \cup B)$ can also be written as $(A \cup B)'$ which is 'the complement of the union of sets A and B'.

Example

$U = \{1, 2, 3, \ldots, 13\}$

$A = \{x \mid x$ is an even number between 1 and 13$\}$

$B = \{x \mid x$ is a multiple of 4$\}$.

(a) Draw a Venn diagram to represent sets U, A and B.

(b) Find the value of each of the following:

(i) $\#A$ **(iii)** $\#(A \setminus B)$ **(v)** $\#(A \cup B)'$

(ii) $\#B$ **(iv)** $\#(A \cap B)'$

Solution

(a) $U = \{1, 2, 3, 4, 5, 6, 7, 8, 9, 10, 11, 12, 13\}$

$A = \{2, 4, 6, 8, 10, 12\}$

$B = \{4, 8, 12\}$.

Represent the information on a Venn diagram.

1 Find the elements in $A \cap B = \{4, 8, 12\}$.

2 Find the remainder of elements in set 'A only' $= \{2, 6, 10\}$ and set 'B only' $= \{\,\}$.

3 Find the remainder of elements in the set: $U \setminus (A \cup B) = \{1, 3, 5, 7, 9, 11, 13\}$.

4 Fill all information into a Venn diagram as shown below:

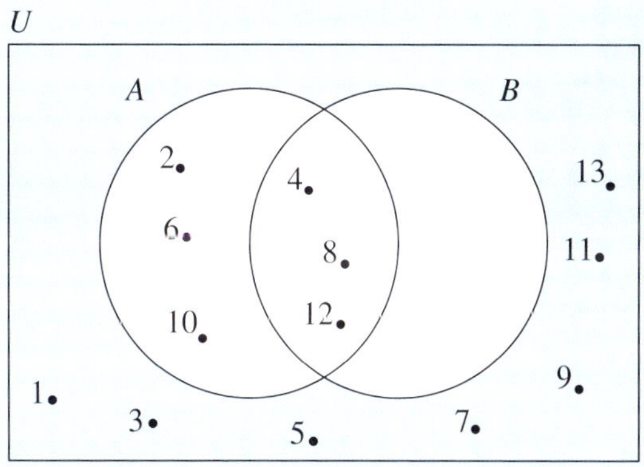

(b) From inspection of the Venn diagram we can see that:

(i) $\#A = 6$	Number of elements in A.
(ii) $\#B = 3$	Number of elements in B.
(iii) $\#(A \setminus B) = 3$	Number of elements in A less B.
(iv) $\#(A \cap B)' = 10$	Number of elements in A intersection B complement (elements not common to A and B).
(v) $\#(A \cup B)' = 7$	Number of elements in A union B complement (elements not in A and / or B).

Solving word problems using two-set Venn diagrams

Top Tip

When solving word problems using two-set Venn diagrams, follow these steps:

1. Label all information given in the question.
2. Find the cardinal number for the members that are common to both sets: $\#(A \cap B) = x$
3. Find the cardinal numbers for the members that remain in each set: $\#(A \setminus B) = \#A - x$ and $\#(B \setminus A) = \#B - x$
4. Find the cardinal number for any of the remaining members listed in the universal set that have not been used: $\#(A \cup B)'$ or $\# U \setminus (A \cup B)$
5. Fill all information into a Venn diagram as shown below:

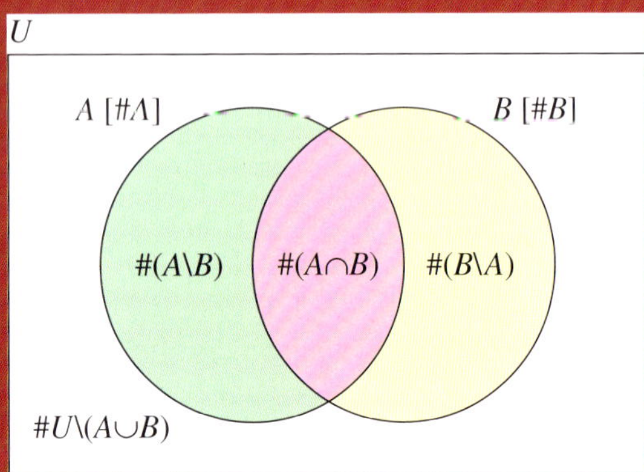

Example

In a group of 95 first year students, 47 students play a musical instrument, 52 students play a sport, and 25 students play neither a sport nor a musical instrument.

(a) Draw a Venn diagram to represent this information.

(b) How many students play both a musical instrument and a sport?

Solution

(a) **1** Label all information given:

$\#U = 95$, the number of first year students

$\#M = 47$, the number of students who play a musical instrument

$\#S = 52$, the number of students who play a sport

$\#(M \cup S)' = 25$, the number of students who play neither a sport nor a musical instrument.

Let $\#(M \cap S) = x$, the number of students who play both a sport and a musical instrument.

Now complete the Venn diagram as follows:

2 Find the cardinal number for the members that are common to both sets:
$\#(M \cap S) = x$

3 Find the cardinal numbers for the members that remain in each set.
$\#(M \backslash S) = 47 - x$
$\#(S \backslash M) = 52 - x$

4 Find the cardinal number for any of the remaining members listed in the universal set not already used.
$\#(M \cup S)' = 25$

5 Fill in all information into a Venn diagram.

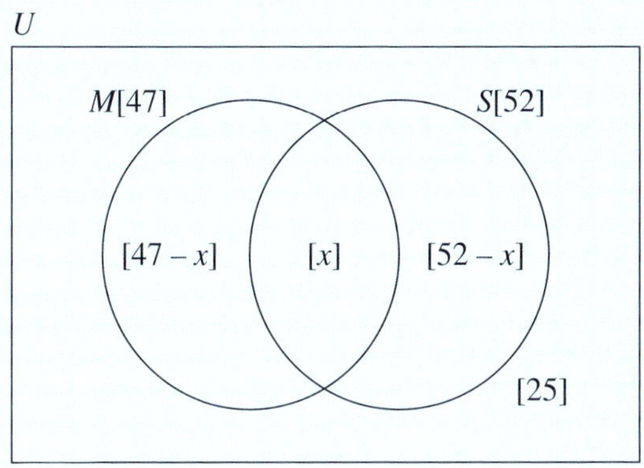

Solve for x:

$\#U = [47 - x] + [x] + [52 - x] + [25] = 95$

$124 - x = 95$

$\therefore x = 29$

$\Rightarrow$ 29 students play both.

Alternative method:

$\#M + \#S = 47 + 52 = 99$

$99 + 25$(neither sport) $= 124$

Extra: $124 - 95 = 29$ students

(b) Filling our answer from part **(a)** into the Venn diagram we can see that there are 29 students in the school who play both a musical instrument and sport.

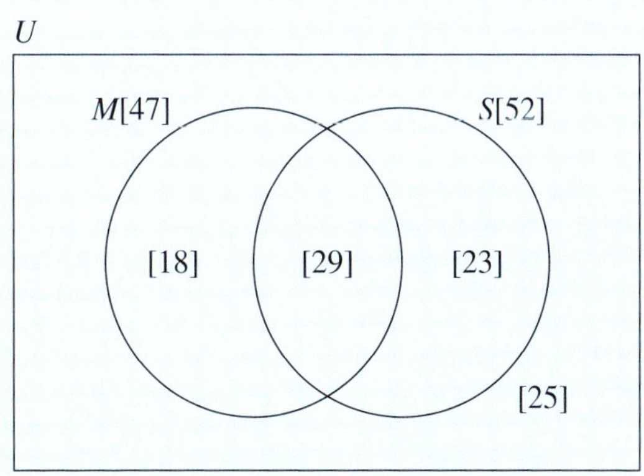

Points to note

When dealing with minimum and maximum problems involving two sets, draw a Venn diagram and let $\#(A \cap B) = x$.

Then follow these points:

1 To get a minimum value for $\#(A \cup B)$, we must maximise the value of $\#(A \cap B)$.

2 To get a maximum value for $\#(A \cup B)$, we must minimise the value of $\#(A \cap B)$.

Example

In a survey of shoppers leaving a shopping centre, 736 people said they bought food in the shopping centre, 431 said they bought clothes in the shopping centre, and 121 said they bought neither food nor clothes.

(a) What is the smallest number of shoppers that could have taken part in the survey?

(b) What is the largest number of shoppers that could have taken part in the survey?

Solution

Draw a Venn diagram.

1 Find the cardinal number for the members that are common to both sets.
$\#(\text{food} \cap \text{clothes}) = x$

2 Find the cardinal numbers for the members that remain in each set.
$\#(\text{food} \setminus \text{clothes}) = 736 - x$
$\#(\text{clothes} \setminus \text{food}) = 431 - x$

3 Find the cardinal number for any of the remaining members listed in the universal set that have not been used.
$\#U \setminus (\text{food} \cup \text{clothes}) = \#(\text{food} \cup \text{clothes})' = 121$

4 Fill all information into a Venn diagram.

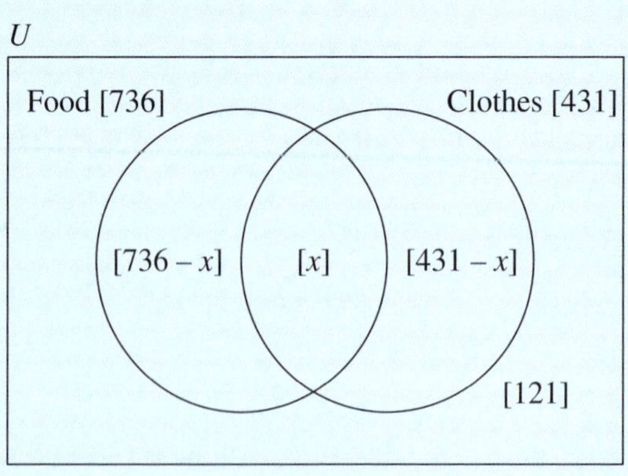

(a) To get a minimum value for #(food $\cup$ clothes), we must maximise the value of #(food $\cap$ clothes).

$\therefore$ #(food $\cap$ clothes) $= x = 431$. This is the largest possible value for x.

The total number of shoppers in the survey is given by:

$\#U = [736 - x] + [x] + [431 - x] + [121]$

$\#U = 1288 - x$

Given that #(food $\cap$ clothes) $= x = 431$

$\#U = 1288 - 431 = 857$

The smallest number of shoppers that could have taken part in the survey is 857.

(b) To get a maximum value for #(food $\cup$ clothes), we must minimise the value of #(food $\cap$ clothes).

$\therefore$ #(food $\cap$ clothes) $= x = 0$ which is the smallest possible value for x.

The total number of shoppers in the survey is given by:

$\#U = (736 - x) + (x) + (431 - x) + (121)$

$\#U = 1288 - x$

Given that #(food $\cap$ clothes) $= x = 0$

$\#U = 1288 - 0 = 1288$

The largest number of shoppers that could have taken part in the survey is 1288.

Example

U is the universal set, and sets A and B are two subsets of U.

$\#U = u$

$\#A = a$

$\#B = b$

$\#(A \cap B) = x$

$\#(A \cup B)' = y$.

(a) Represent this information on a Venn diagram and hence express u in terms of a, b, x and y.

(b) Show that if $a > b$, then the minimum possible value of u is $y + a$.

Solution

(a) To represent information on a Venn diagram:

1 Find the cardinal number for the members that are common to both sets.
$\#(A \cap B) = x$

2 Find the cardinal numbers for the members that remain in each set.
$\#(A \backslash B) = a - x$
$\#(B \backslash A) = b - x$

3 Find the cardinal number for any of the remaining members listed in the universal set that has not been used.
$\#(A \cup B)' = y$

4 Fill all information into a Venn diagram.

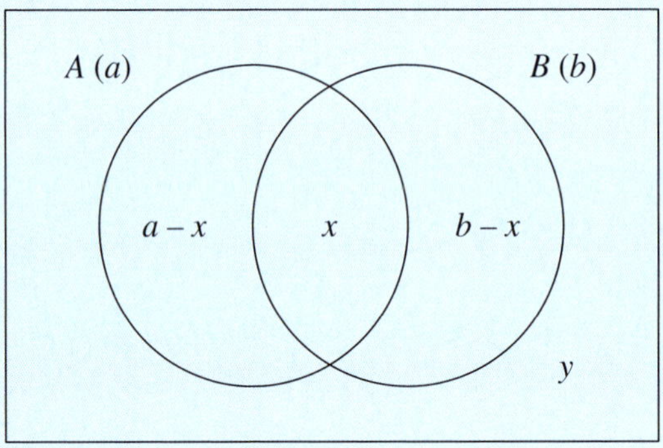

Solve for u in terms of a, b, x and y.

$u = a - \cancel{x} + \cancel{x} + b - x + y$
$\quad = a + b - x + y$

(b) If $a > b$, then the minimum value for $x = b$, is given by:

$u = a - x + x + b - x + y$
$\quad = a - \cancel{x} + \cancel{x} + \cancel{x} - \cancel{x} + y$
$\quad = a + y$

Venn diagrams with three sets

We solve Venn diagrams with three sets in the same way as we solve Venn diagrams involving two sets. However, there are more regions to deal with.

Top Tip

When asked to represent three sets on a Venn diagram, follow these steps:

1 Find the elements that are common to all three sets.

$$A \cap B \cap C$$

2 Find the elements that remain common to two sets.

$$(A \cap B)\setminus C$$
$$(A \cap C)\setminus B$$
$$(B \cap C)\setminus A$$

3 Find the elements that are unique to each set.

$$A\setminus(B \cup C)$$
$$B\setminus(A \cup C)$$
$$C\setminus(A \cup B)$$

4 Find any remaining elements in the universal set that have not been used.

$$U\setminus(A \cup B \cup C) \text{ or } (A \cup B \cup C)'$$

5 Fill all information into a Venn diagram as shown:

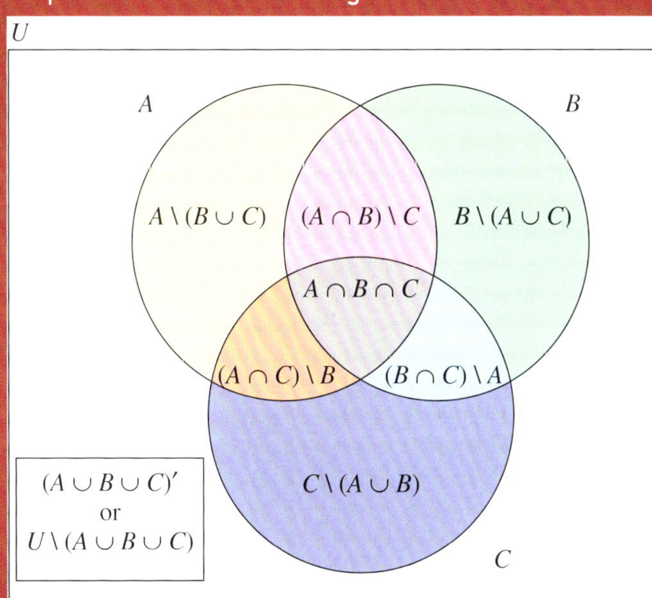

Example

$U = \{1, 2, 3, 4, 5, 6, 7, 8, 9, 10, 11, 12, 13, 14\}$ is the universal set.

$X = \{1, 2, 3, 5, 7, 11, 13\}$,

$Y = \{5, 6, 7, 8, 9, 10, 11\}$ and

$Z = \{1, 3, 4, 7, 11\}$ are three subsets of U.

(a) Represent the above information on a Venn diagram.

(b) Use your Venn diagram to list the elements of:

(i) X' **(ii)** $(X \cup Y) \cap Z$ **(iii)** $(X \backslash Y) \backslash Z$ **(iv)** $(Z \backslash Y) \cap X$

(c) Write down a null set, in terms of X, Y and Z.

Solution

(a) Draw a Venn diagram.

1 Find the elements that are common to all three sets.

$X \cap Y \cap Z = \{7, 11\}$

2 Find the elements that remain common to two sets.

$(X \cap Y) \backslash Z = \{5\}$

$(Y \cap Z) \backslash X = \{\}$

$(X \cap Z) \backslash Y = \{1, 3\}$

3 Find the elements that are unique to each set.

$Z \backslash (X \cup Y) = \{4\}$

$X \backslash (Y \cup Z) = \{2, 13\}$

$Y \backslash (X \cup Z) = \{6, 8, 9, 10\}$

4 Find any remaining elements in the universal set that have not been used.

$U \backslash (X \cup Y \cup Z) = \{12, 14\}$

5 Represent all the information on a Venn diagram.

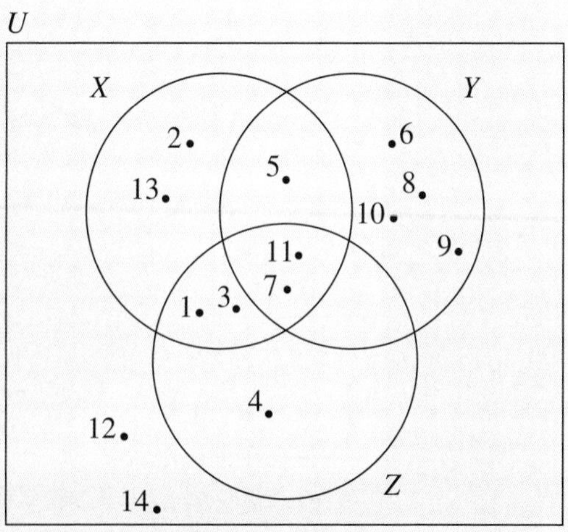

(b) From inspection of the Venn diagram we can see that:

(i) $X' = \{4, 6, 8, 9, 10, 12, 14\}$

(ii) $(X \cup Y) \cap Z = \{1, 3, 7, 11\}$

(iii) $(X \backslash Y) \backslash Z = \{2, 13\}$

(iv) $(Z \backslash Y) \cap X = \{1, 3\}$

(c) Write down a null set, in terms of X, Y, and Z. $(Y \cap Z) \backslash X = \{\}$

Set operations

The commutative property of two sets

Symbols	Descriptions
• $A \cup B = B \cup A$	Union is a commutative operation.
• $A \cap B = B \cap A$	Intersection is a commutative operation.
• $A \backslash B \neq B \backslash A$	Set difference is **not** a commutative operation.

The associative property of three sets

Symbols	Descriptions
$(A \cup B) \cup C = A \cup (B \cup C)$	Union is an associative operation.
$(A \cap B) \cap C = A \cap (B \cap C)$	Intersection is an associative operation.
$(A \backslash B) \backslash C \neq A \backslash (B \backslash C)$	Set difference is **not** an associative operation.

The distributive property of three sets

Symbols	Descriptions
$A \cup (B \cap C) = (A \cup B) \cap (A \cup C)$	Union of sets is distributive over intersection.
$A \cap (B \cup C) = (A \cap B) \cup (A \cap C)$	Intersection of sets is distributive over union.
$A \backslash (B \cup C) \neq (A \backslash B) \cup (A \backslash C)$	Set difference over union is **not** distributive.
$A \backslash (B \cap C) \neq (A \backslash B) \cap (A \backslash C)$	Set difference over intersection is **not** distributive.

Remember

When proving that a mathematical statement is true, we must prove that the sides of the statement are equal.

Left hand side (LHS) = right hand side (RHS)

Example

Let $P = \{1, 2, 3, 4, 5\}$, $Q = \{3, 5, 7\}$ and $R = \{2, 3, 4, 5, 6\}$.
Prove that the following identity is true:

$P \cap (Q \cup R) = (P \cap Q) \cup (P \cap R)$

Solution

To prove $P \cap (Q \cup R) = (P \cap Q) \cup (P \cap R)$ is true, we must prove that the sides of the equation are equal (left hand side = right hand side).

- LHS $= P \cap (Q \cup R)$
  $(Q \cup R) = \{3, 5, 7\} \cup \{2, 3, 4, 5, 6\} = \{2, 3, 4, 5, 6, 7\}$
  $\therefore P \cap (Q \cup R) = \{1, 2, 3, 4, 5\} \cap \{2, 3, 4, 5, 6, 7\} = \{2, 3, 4, 5\}$
- RHS $= (P \cap Q) \cup (P \cap R)$
  $(P \cap Q) = \{1, 2, 3, 4, 5\} \cap \{3, 5, 7\} = \{3, 5\}$
  $(P \cap R) = \{1, 2, 3, 4, 5\} \cap \{2, 3, 4, 5, 6\} = \{2, 3, 4, 5\}$
  $\therefore (P \cap Q) \cup (P \cap R) = \{3, 5\} \cup \{2, 3, 4, 5\} = \{2, 3, 4, 5\}$
  Therefore, $P \cap (Q \cup R) = (P \cap Q) \cup (P \cap R)$ as both sides of the equation equal the set $\{2, 3, 4, 5\}$.

Solving word problems using three-set Venn diagrams

When solving word problems using Venn diagrams, we generally use the same method to work out each region in the three-set Venn diagram as given earlier in this chapter. However there is one key difference, which is that when we are dealing with a word based problem we work with the cardinal number of each set rather than each element of the set.

Top Tip

When dealing with a Venn diagram for (word) problems involving three sets, follow these steps:

1 Find the cardinal number for the members that are common to all three sets.

$$\#(X \cap Y \cap Z)$$

2 Find the cardinal numbers for the members that are common to two sets.

$$\#(X \cap Y)\backslash Z$$

$$\#(X \cap Z)\backslash Y$$

$$\#(Y \cap Z)\backslash X$$

3 Find the cardinal numbers for the members that are unique to each set.

$$\#X\backslash(Y\cup Z)$$

$$\#Y\backslash(X\cup Z)$$

$$\#Z\backslash(X\cup Y)$$

4 Find the cardinal number for any remaining members listed in the universal set that have not been used.

$$\#U\backslash(X\cup Y\cup Z) \text{ or } \#(X\cup Y\cup Z)'$$

5 Represent all information on a Venn diagram like the one below:

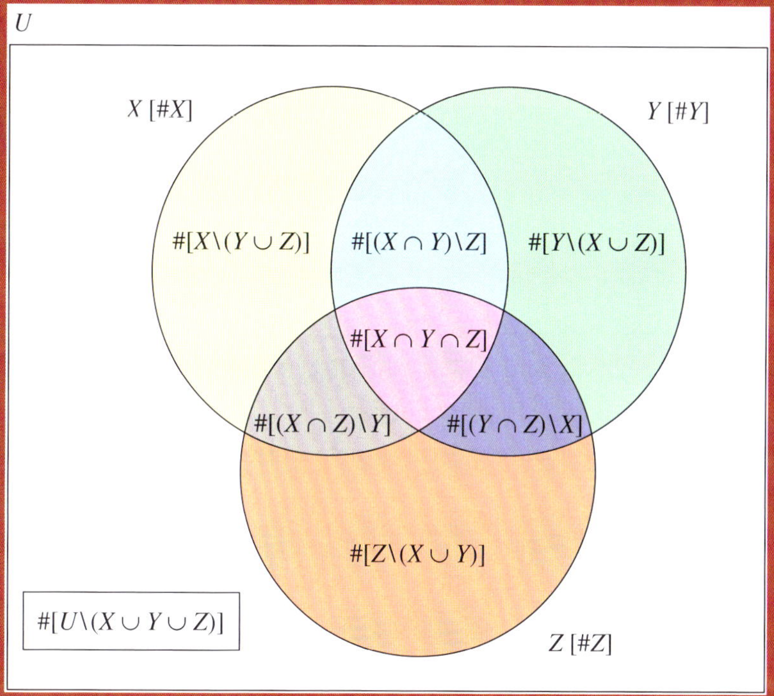

Example

U = {the number of students in a class}

L = {the number of students in the class who have a laptop at home}

S = {the number of students in the class who have a smart tablet at home}

P = {the number of students in the class who have a PC at home}

Describe in your own words the members of the following sets:

(a) $(L\cup S)$

(b) $(P\cap L)$

(c) $(L\cup S\cup P)'$

(d) $L\backslash P$

(e) $(L\cap S)\backslash P$

Solution

(a) $(L \cup S)$ = The number of students in the class who have a laptop and/or a smart tablet.

(b) $(P \cap L)$ = The number of students in the class who have a PC and a laptop.

(c) $(L \cup S \cup P)'$ = The number of students in the class who do not have a laptop, nor a smart tablet, nor a PC.

(d) $L \backslash P$ = The number of students in the class who have a laptop but do not have a PC.

(e) $(L \cap S) \backslash P$ = The number of students in the class who have a laptop and a smart tablet but do not have a PC.

Example

70 teenagers responded to a survey about holiday destinations.

30 had travelled to France.

26 had travelled to Spain, and 28 had travelled to Italy.

12 had travelled to both France and Spain.

8 had travelled to both Spain and Italy, while x had travelled to France and Italy only.

4 teenagers had travelled to all three countries.

Twice as many had never travelled to any of these destinations as had travelled to France and Italy only.

(a) Represent the above information on a Venn diagram.

(b) Find the number of teenagers who had travelled to France only.

(c) What is the probability that a teenager drawn at random from the group has been to at least two of these countries?

(SEC 2006)

Solution

(a) **1** Find the cardinal number for the members that are common to all three sets.

$\#(F \cap S \cap I) = 4$

2 Find the cardinal numbers for the members that are common to two sets

$\#(F \cap S) \backslash I = 12 - 4 = 8$

$\#(F \cap I) \backslash S = x$

$\#(S \cap I) \backslash F = 8 - 4 = 4$

3 Find the cardinal numbers for the members that are unique to each set.

$\#F \backslash (S \cup I) = 30 - (8 + 4 + x) = 18 - x$

$\#S \backslash (F \cup I) = 26 - (8 + 4 + 4) = 10$

$\#I \backslash (F \cup S) = 28 - (4 + 4 + x) = 20 - x$

4 Find the cardinal number for any remaining members listed in the universal set that have not been used.

$\#U\backslash(A \cup B \cup C) = 2x$

5 Represent all information on a Venn diagram.

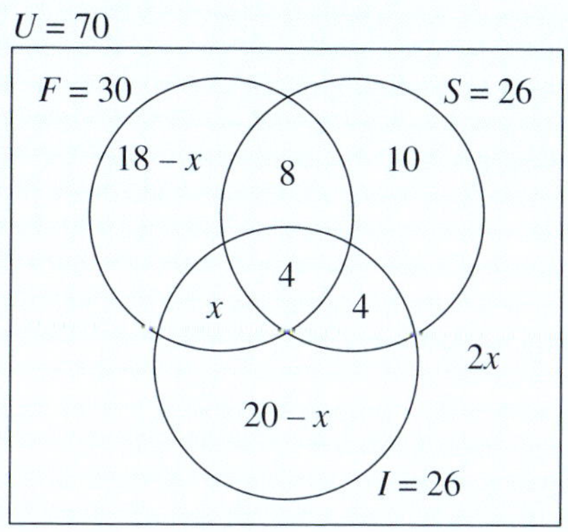

(b) Solve for x:

$\#U = 26 + (18 - x) + (x) + (20 - x) + (2x) = 70$

$64 + x = 70$

$\therefore x = 70 - 64 = 6$

The number of teenagers who travelled to France only = $18 - x = 18 - 6 = 12$.

(c) From the diagram, we can see that 22 teenagers have been to at least two of these countries, so the probability is $\frac{22}{70}$ or $\frac{11}{35}$.

Exercise

Q1 (a) List all the subsets for the set:

$A = \{10, 20\}$.

(b) From the Venn diagram shown, list the elements in each of the following sets:

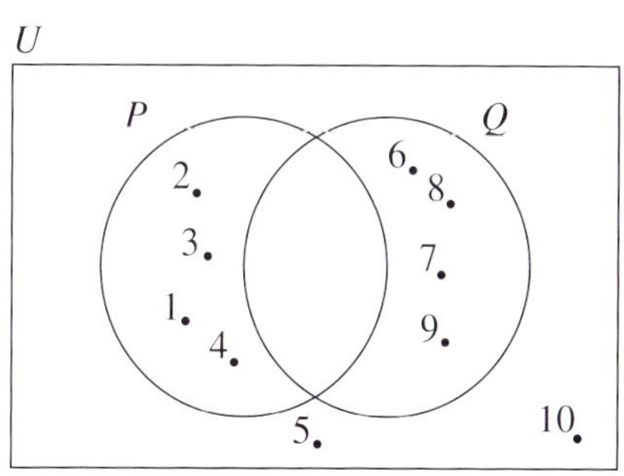

(i) P

(ii) Q

(iii) $P \cup Q$

(iv) $P \cap Q$

(v) $P\backslash Q$

(vi) $Q\backslash P$

(vii) P'

(viii) Q'

(ix) $(P \cap Q)'$

(x) $(Q\backslash P)'$

Q2 (a) List all the subsets for the following set:
$B = \{$red, green, blue$\}$.

(b) Copy the Venn diagram four times and shade in the regions that represent each of the following:

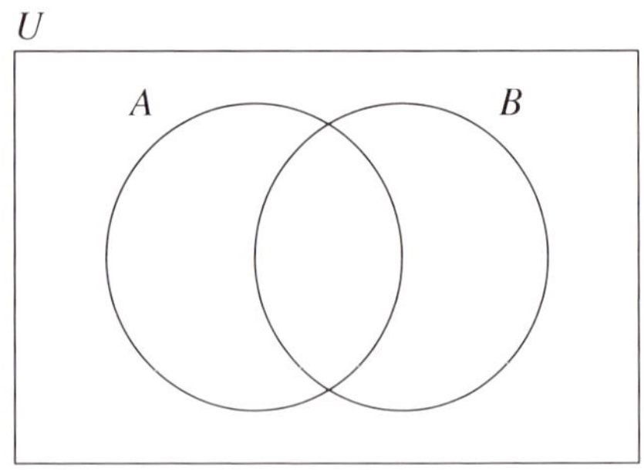

(i) $(A \cup B)'$

(ii) $U \setminus (B \setminus A)$

(iii) $(A \setminus B)'$

(iv) $U \setminus (A \cap B)$

(c) Given the following sets:

$U = \{a, b, c, d, e, f, g, h, i, j\}$, $A = \{a, b, c, d\}$ and $B = \{c, d, e, f, g\}$,

list the elements in:

(i) A'

(ii) $U \setminus (A \cap B)$

(iii) $(A \cup B)'$

(iv) $(A \setminus B)'$

Q3 You are given the following sets:

$U = \{1, 2, 3, 4, 5, 6, 7, 8, 9, 10, 11, 12\}$,

$X = \{1, 2, 3, 4, 5, 6\}$ and $Y = \{2, 3, 5, 7, 9, 11\}$.

(a) Describe each set given using the **rule** method.

(b) Find the cardinal number for each of the following:

(i) $\#(X \cup Y)$

(ii) $\#(X \cap Y)$

(iii) $\#Y'$

(iv) $\#(X \cup Y)'$

(v) $\#(X \setminus Y)$

(vi) $\#(Y \setminus X)$

(c) In a school of 430 students, 250 students study History and 240 students study Geography. Let x represent the number of students who study neither History nor Geography. The number of students who study both History and Geography is three times the number who study neither of these subjects.

(i) Represent this information on a Venn diagram.

(ii) Find the number of students who study neither History nor Geography.

Q4 **(a)** Using set notation, describe the shaded region in each of the following Venn diagrams.

(i)

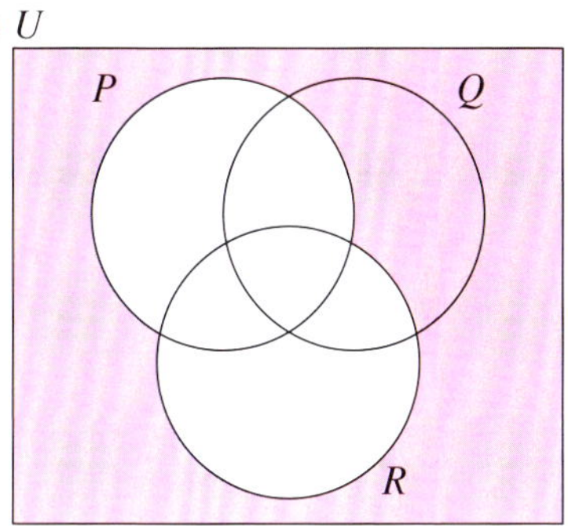

(iii)

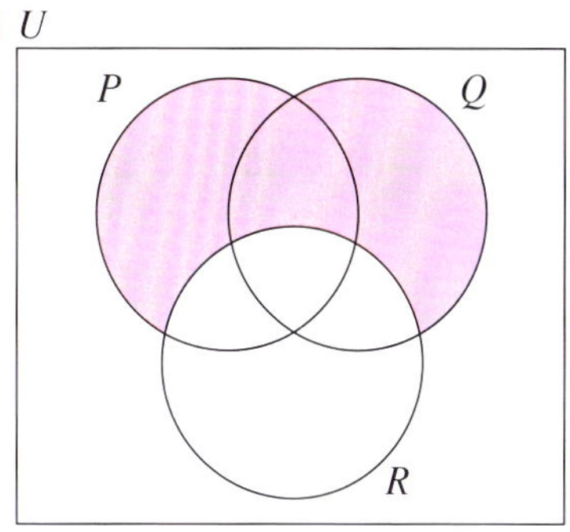

(ii)

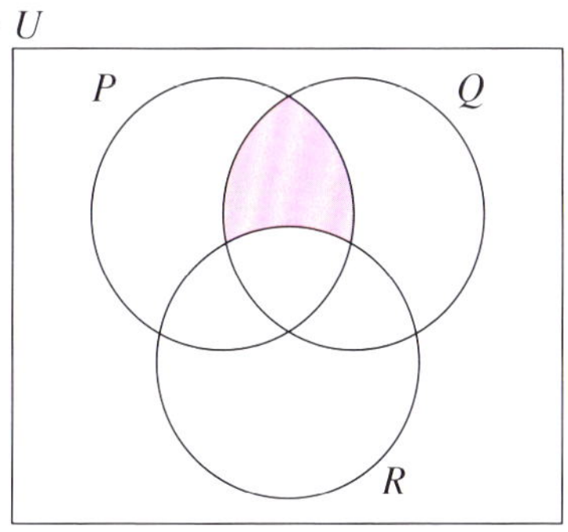

(iv)

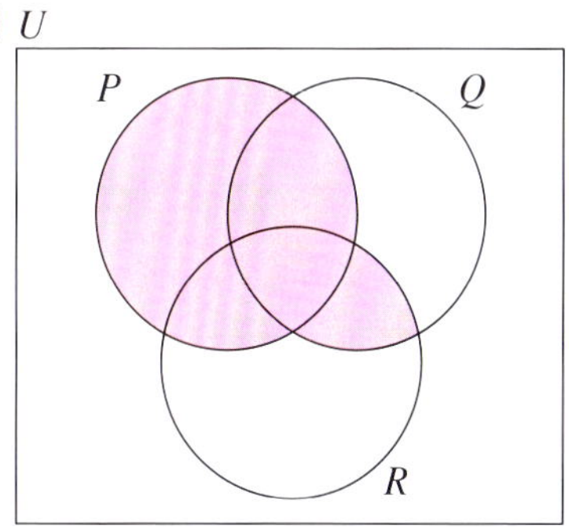

(b) A class of 29 students were asked if they had ever been to England or France.

15 students said they had been to England, 22 said they had been to France, and 13 said they had been to both countries.

(i) Draw a Venn diagram to represent this information.

(ii) How many students in the class have not been to either country?

Q5 **(a)** Copy the Venn diagram below four times and shade in the regions that represent each of the following:

(i) $(A \cap B) \cup C$ **(iii)** $(A \cup C)' \backslash B$

(ii) $(A \backslash B) \backslash C$ **(iv)** $(A \backslash B) \cap (C \backslash B)$

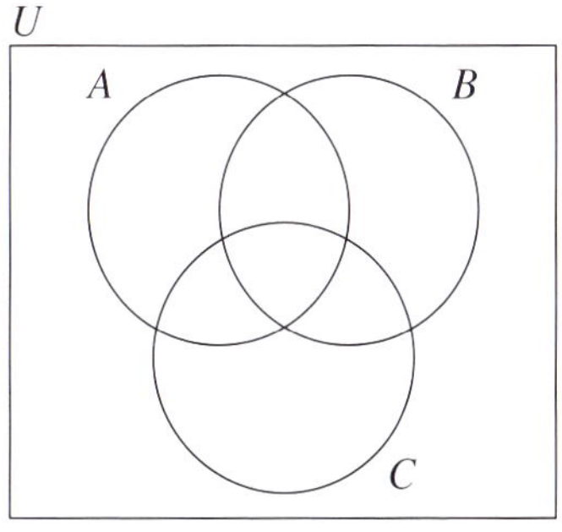

(b) In a survey, school students were asked if they travelled home by bus, by car, or neither.

88 students said they travelled by bus, 95 said they travelled by car, and 46 said they didn't use either.

(i) What is the smallest number of students that could have taken part in the survey?

(ii) What is the largest number of students that could have taken part in the survey?

Q6 In a survey, 220 people were asked if they like tea, coffee or hot chocolate.

The results were as follows:

98 people said they like tea.

112 said they like coffee.

100 said they like hot chocolate.

57 said they like tea and coffee.

32 said they like coffee and hot chocolate.

29 said they like tea and hot chocolate.

12 said they do not like any of these drinks.

How many people like all three drinks?

Q7 **(a)** Given the following sets:

$F = \{1, 2, 3, 4\}$, $G = \{2, 3, 5\}$ and $H = \{1, 3, 4, 5, 6\}$,

list the elements of:

(i) $(F \setminus G) \cup (H \cap F)$ **(ii)** $(F \cap G) \cup (H \setminus F)$

(b) A group of second year students were asked if they like tennis, badminton and/or golf.

43 like tennis, 36 like badminton and 31 like golf.

18 like tennis and badminton, 14 like tennis and golf, and 21 like badminton and golf.

6 like all of these activities, and 18 like none of these activities.

How many second year students are in the group?

Q8 A survey of 40 students was carried out to find how many owned an MP3 player, a digital camera or a CD player.

1 student does not own any of these.

x students own all three, and $2x$ own an MP3 player and a digital camera but not a CD player.

10 own an MP3 player and a CD player, while 11 own a digital camera and a CD player.

22 own an MP3 player, 22 own a digital camera and 24 own a CD player.

(a) Construct a Venn diagram and solve for x.

(b) Hence, calculate the percentage of students who own one item only.

(SEC 2007)

Solutions

Q1 (a) {}, {10}, {20}, {10, 20}

(b) From observation of the Venn diagram:

(i) $P = \{1, 2, 3, 4\}$

(ii) $Q = \{6, 7, 8, 9\}$

(iii) $P \cup Q = \{1, 2, 3, 4, 6, 7, 8, 9\}$

(iv) $P \cap Q = \{\ \}$

(v) $P \setminus Q = \{1, 2, 3, 4\}$

(vi) $Q \setminus P = \{6, 7, 8, 9\}$

(vii) $P' = \{5, 6, 7, 8, 9, 10\}$

(viii) $Q' = \{1, 2, 3, 4, 5, 10\}$

(ix) $(P \cap Q)' = \{1, 2, 3, 4, 5, 6, 7, 8, 9, 10\}$

(x) $(Q \setminus P)' = \{1, 2, 3, 4, 5, 10\}$

Q2 (a) {}, {red}, {green}, {blue}, {red, green}, {red, blue}, {green, blue}, {red, green, blue}

(b) **(i)** $(A \cup B)'$

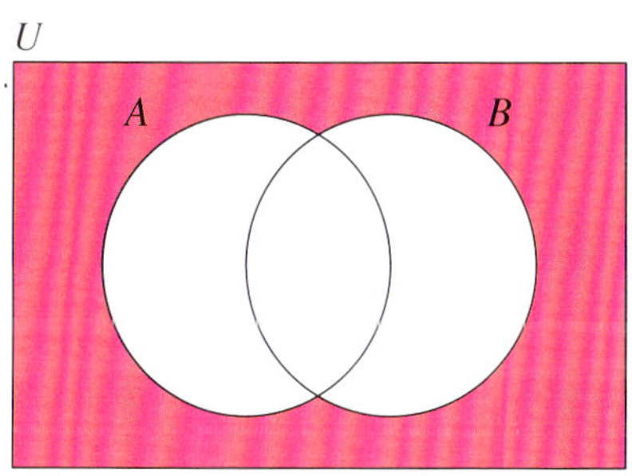

(iii) $(A \setminus B)'$

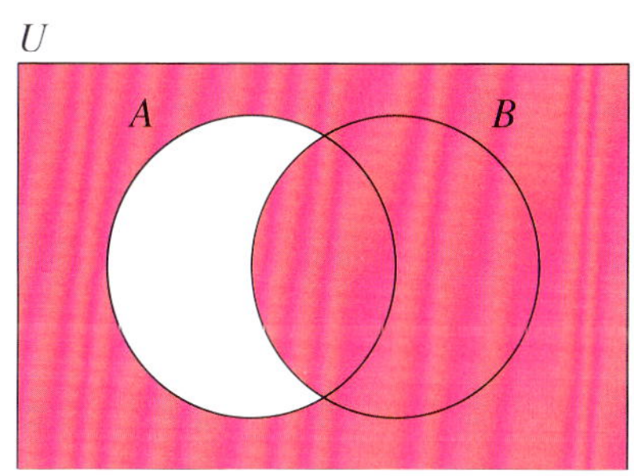

(ii) $U \setminus (B \setminus A)$

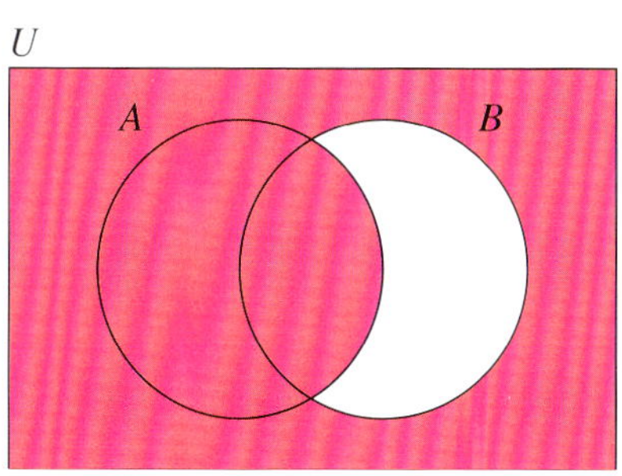

(iv) $U \setminus (A \cap B)$

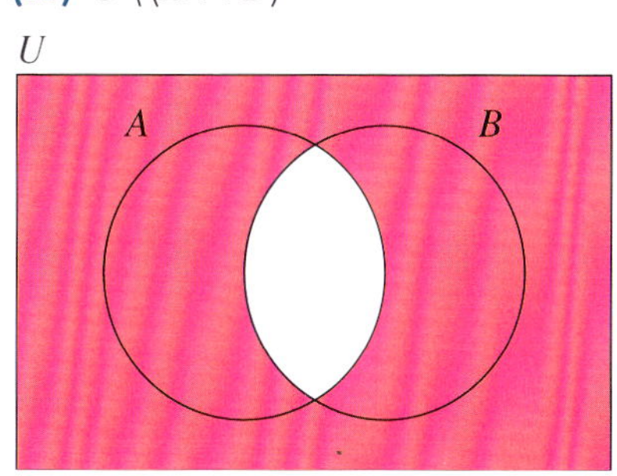

(c) $U = \{a, b, c, d, e, f, g, h, i, j\}$

$A = \{a, b, c, d\}$

$B = \{c, d, e, f, g\}$

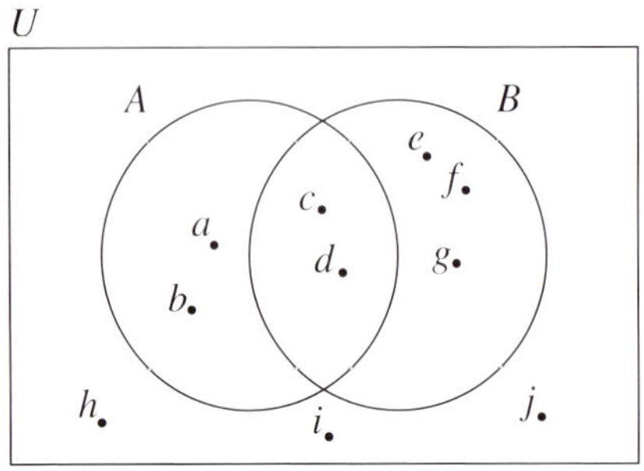

(i) $A' = \{e, f, g, h, i, j\}$

(ii) $U \backslash (A \cap B) = \{a, b, e, f, g, h, i, j\}$

(iii) $(A \cup B)' = \{h, i, j\}$

(iv) $(A \backslash B)' = \{c, d, e, f, g, h, i, j\}$

Q3 (a) $U = \{x \mid x < 13, x \in \mathbb{R}\}$

$X = \{x \mid x < 7, x \in \mathbb{R}\}$

$Y = \{x \mid x$ is one of the first five prime numbers$\}$

(b)

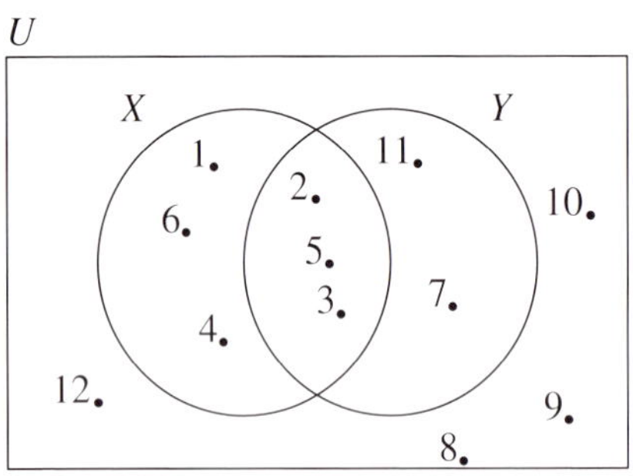

(i) $\#(X \cup Y) = 8$

(ii) $\#(X \cap Y) = 3$

(iii) $\#Y' = 7$

(iv) $\#(X \cup Y)' = 4$

(v) $\#(X \backslash Y) = 3$

(vi) $\#(Y \backslash X) = 2$

(c) (i)

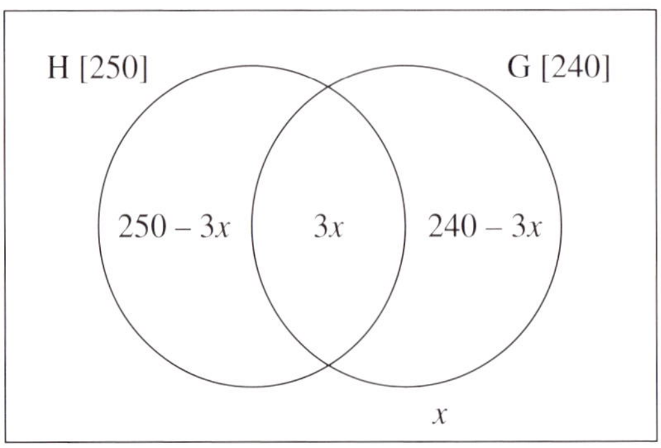

(ii) $\#U = 430$

$\#U = [250 - 3x] + [3x] + [240 - 3x] + [x] = 430$

$490 - 2x = 430$

$490 - 430 = 2x$

$60 = 2x$

$\therefore x = 30$

30 students study neither History nor Geography.

Q4 (a) (i) $(P \cup R)'$

(ii) $(P \cap Q) \setminus R$

(iii) $(P \cup Q) \setminus R$

(iv) $P \cup (Q \cap R)$

(b) (i) Let $\#(E \cup F)' = x$, the number of students who have not been to either country. Now complete the Venn diagram as follows:

Find the cardinal number for the members that are common to both sets.

$\#(E \cap F) = 13$

Find the cardinal numbers for the members that remain in each set.

$\#(E \setminus F) = 15 - 13 = 2$

$\#(F \setminus E) = 22 - 13 = 9$

Find the cardinal number for any of the remaining members listed in the universal set that have not been used

$\#(E \cup F)' = x$

Fill in all information into a Venn diagram.

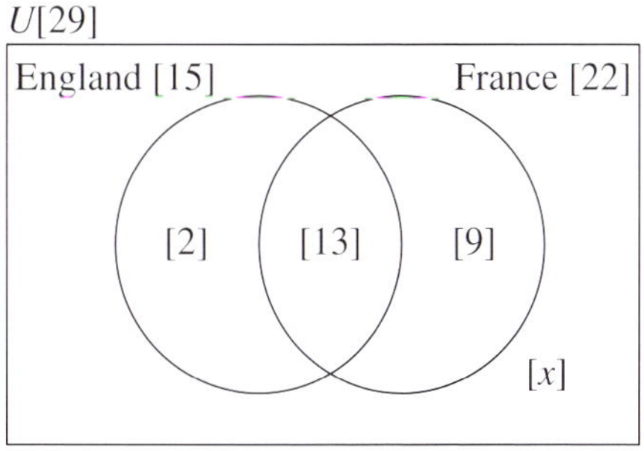

(ii) Solve for x:

$\#(E \cup F)' = x$

$\#U = 29$

$\#U \setminus (E \cup F) = \#(E \cup F)' = x$

$2 + 13 + 9 + x = 29$

$24 + x = 29$

$\therefore x = 5$

5 students in the class have not been to either country.

Q5 (a) (i) $(A \cap B) \cup C$

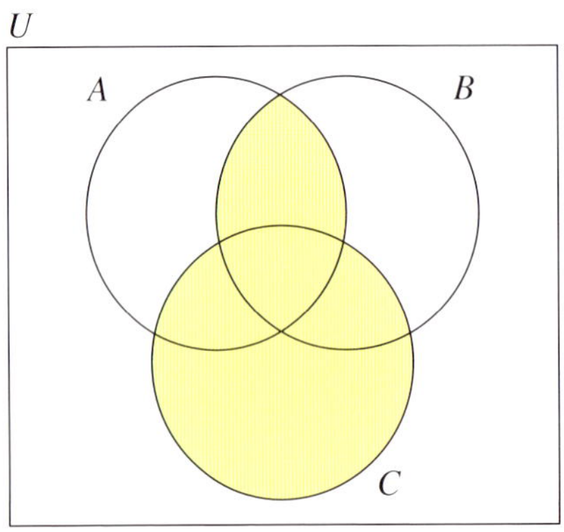

(iii) $(A \cup C)' \setminus B$

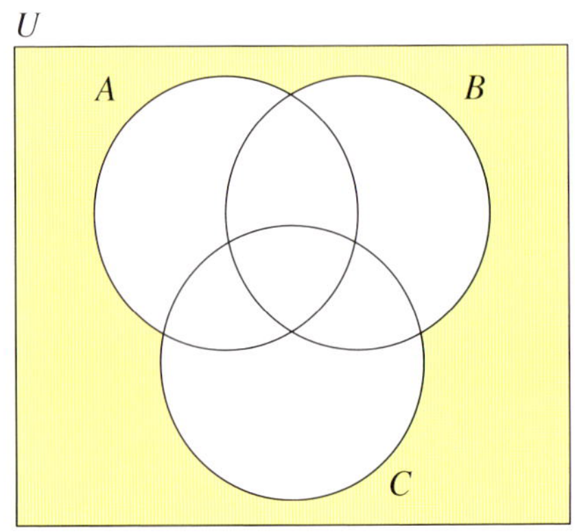

(ii) $(A \setminus B) \setminus C$

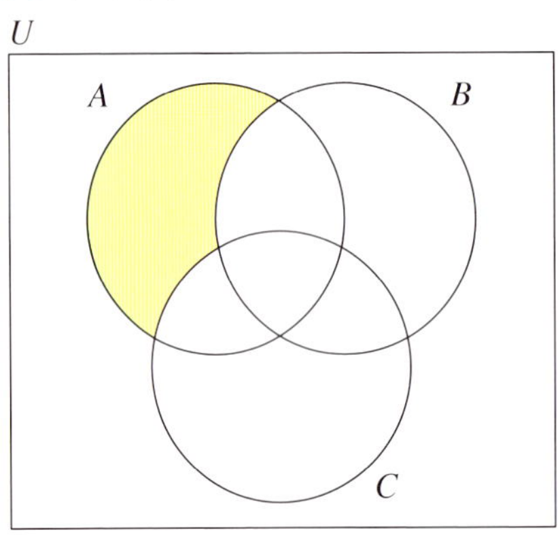

(iv) $(A \setminus B) \cap (C \setminus B)$

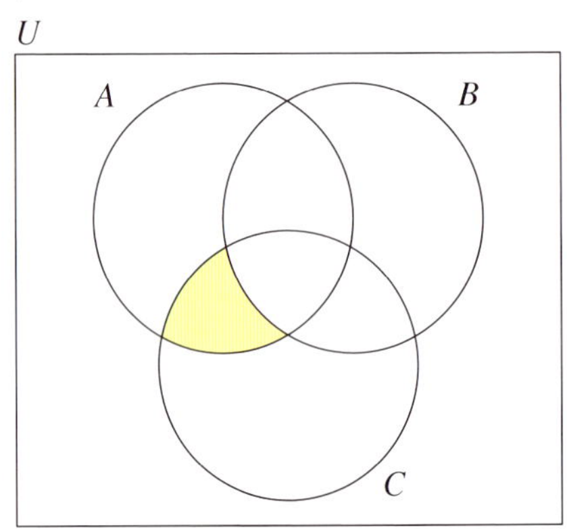

(b) 1 Find the cardinal number for the members that are common to both sets

$\#(B \cap C) = x$

2 Find the cardinal numbers for the members that remain in each set.

$\#(B \setminus C) = 88 - x$

$\#(C \setminus B) = 95 - x$

3 Find the cardinal number for any of the remaining members listed in the universal set that have not been used.

$\#U \setminus (B \cup C) = \#(B \cup C)' = 46$

4 Fill all information into a Venn diagram.

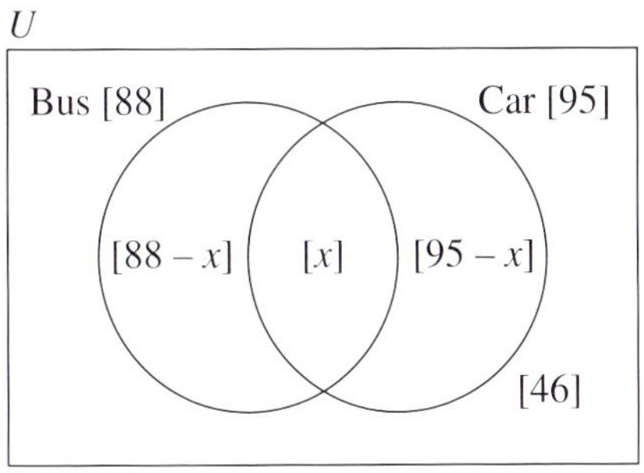

(i) To get the value for the smallest number of students that could have taken part in the survey, $\#(B \cup C)$, we must maximise the value of $\#(B \cap C)$.

$\therefore \#(B \cap C) = 88$ This is the largest possible value for x.

The total number of students in the survey is given by:

$\#U = [88 - x] + [x] + [95 - x] + [46]$

$\#U = 229 - x$

Given that $\#(B \cap C) = x = 88$,

$\#U = 229 - 88 = 141$

The smallest number of students that could have taken part in the survey is 141.

(ii) To get the value for the largest number of students that could have taken part in the survey, $\#(B \cup C)$, we must minimise the value of $\#(B \cap C)$.

$\therefore \#(B \cap C) = x = 0$ This is the smallest possible value for x.

The total number of students in the survey is given by:

$\#U = [88 - x] + [x] + [95 - x] + [46]$

$\#U = 229 - x$

Given that $\#(B \cap C) = x = 0$,

$\#U = 229 - 0 = 229$

The largest number of students that could have taken part in the survey is 229.

Q6 **1** Find the cardinal number for the members that are common to all three sets.

$\#(T \cap C \cap H) = x$

2 Find the cardinal numbers for the members that are common to two sets.

$\#(T \cap C) \setminus H = 57 - x$

$\#(C \cap H) \setminus T = 32 - x$

$\#(T \cap H) \setminus C = 29 - x$

3 Find the cardinal numbers for the members that are unique to each set.

$\#T\backslash(C \cup H) = 98 - [57 - x + x + 29 - x] = 12 + x$

$\#C\backslash(T \cup H) = 112 - [57 - x + x + 32 - x] = 23 + x$

$\#H\backslash(T \cup C) = 100 - [29 - x + x + 32 - x] = 39 + x$

4 Find the cardinal number for any remaining members listed in the universal set that have not been used.

$\#U\backslash(T \cup C \cup H) = 12$

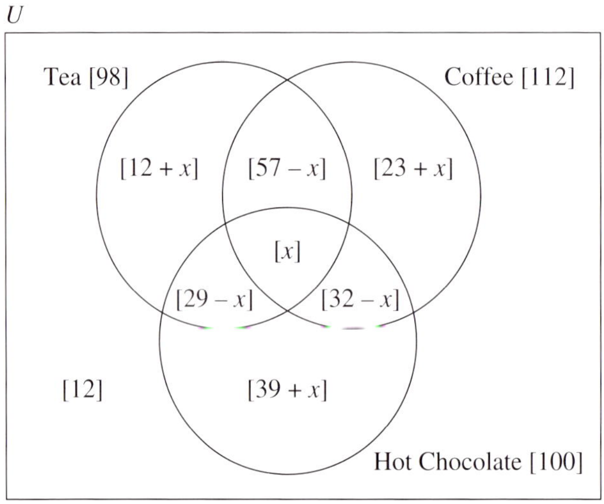

$\#U = 220$

$\#U = [12 + x] + [57 - x] + [23 + x] + [29 - x] + [x] + [32 + x] + [39 + x] + 12$

$204 + x = 220$

$\therefore x = 16$

Q7 (a) (i) $(F\backslash G) \cup (H \cap F)$

$= \{1, 4\} \cup \{3, 4\}$

$= \{1, 3, 4\}$

(ii) $(F \cap G) \cup (H\backslash F)$

$= \{2, 3\} \cup \{5, 6\}$

$= \{2, 3, 5, 6\}$

(b) Draw a Venn diagram:

$\#(T \cap B \cap G) = 6$

$\#(T \cap B)\backslash G = 18 - 6 = 12$

$\#(T \cap G)\backslash B = 14 - 6 = 8$

$\#(B \cap G)\backslash T = 21 - 6 = 15$

$\#T \setminus (B \cup G) = 43 - [12 + 6 + 8] = 17$

$\#B \setminus (T \cup G) = 36 - [12 + 6 + 15] = 3$

$\#G \setminus (T \cup B) = 31 - [8 + 6 + 15] = 2$

$\#U \setminus (T \cup B \cup G) = 18$

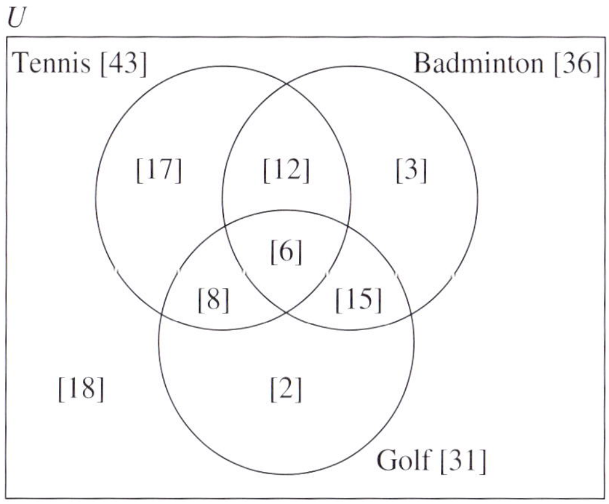

From the Venn diagram,

$\#U = 17 + 12 + 3 + 8 + 6 + 15 + 2 + 18$

$\#U = 81$

Q8 (a) Draw a Venn diagram and solve for x.

$\#(M \cap D \cap C) = x$

$\#(D \cap C) \setminus M = 11 - x$

$\#(T \cap C) \setminus D = 10 - x$

$\#(M \cap D) \setminus C = 2x$

$\#M \setminus (D \cup C) = 22 - [10 - x + x + 2x] - 12 - 2x$

$\#C \setminus (M \cup D) = 24 - [10 - x + x + 11 - x] = 3 + x$

$\#D \setminus (C \cup M) = 22 - [2x + x + 11 - x] = 11 - 2x$

$\#U \setminus (M \cup D \cup C) = 1$

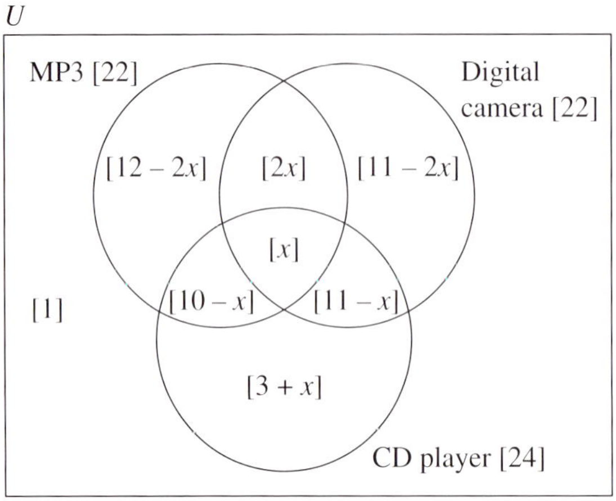

Solve for x:

$\#U = 40$

$\#U = 12 - 2x + 2x + 11 - 2x + 10 - x + x + 11 - x + 3 + x + 1$

$\#U = 48 - 2x = 40$

$2x = 8$

$\therefore\ x = 4$

(b) From the Venn diagram we can see the number of students who own one item only is:

$12 - 2x + 11 - 2x + 3 + x$

$= 26 - 3x$

$= 26 - 3(4) = 14$

Hence the percentage of students who own one item only is:

$\frac{14}{40} \times 100\% = 35\%$

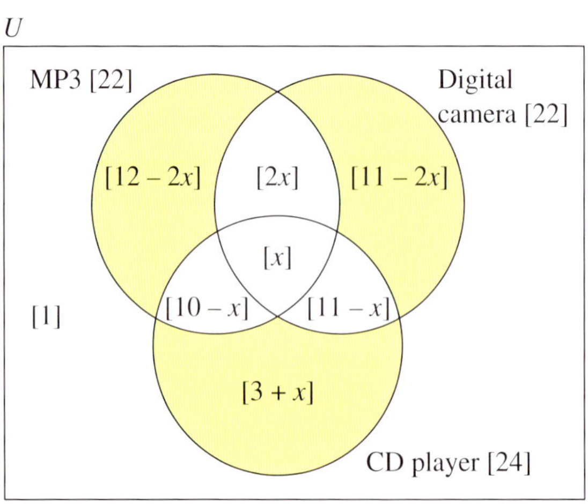

Functions 1

13

Learning objectives

In this chapter you will learn about:

- The definition of a function
- How to identify a function
- How to solve function-based problems algebraically
- How to solve function-based problems, given the graph of a function.

Functions

One way of illustrating the concept of a function is the function machine. We input something into the function machine, a rule is applied, and then we get an output.

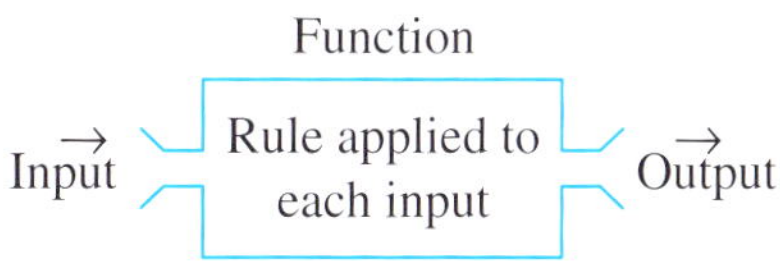

Key Terminology

Word	Meaning	Example
Function	A **function** is a special relationship where a set of inputs relates directly to a set of outputs. In particular, each input corresponds only to one output.	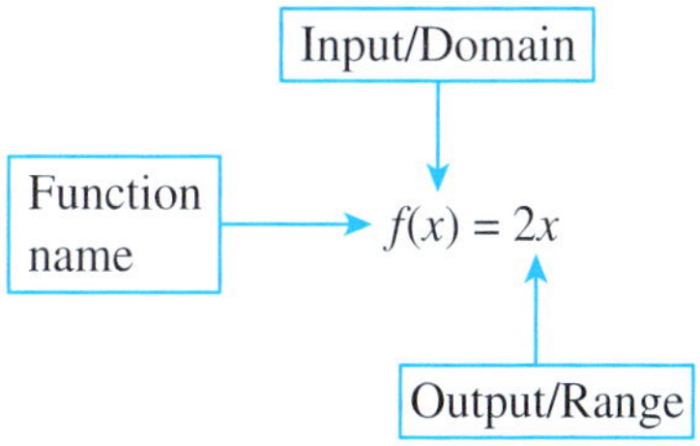

Word	Meaning	Example
Arrow diagram	Functions can be represented graphically on an **arrow diagram**. Each input value is mapped onto its corresponding output value.	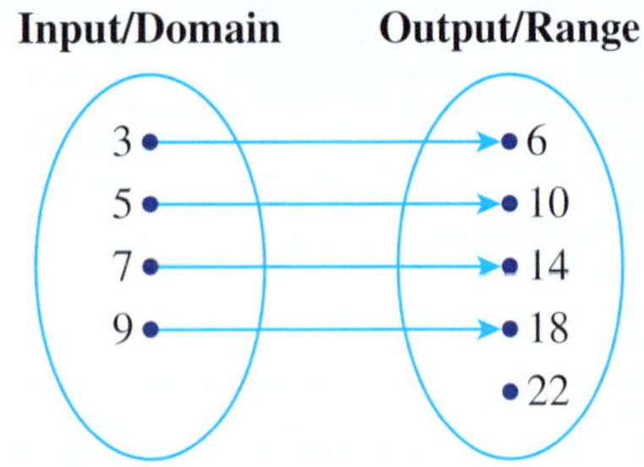
Input/ Domain	The number that goes into the function is the **input value**, also known as the x value. The set of input values is called the **domain**.	Domain = {3, 5, 7, 9}
Output/ Range	The **output** or **range** is the resulting values from the function that correspond to each input value. These are also known as the y values.	Range = {6, 10, 14, 18}
Couples	A **couple** refers to the pairing of an input value and its corresponding output value as (x, y) for a given function.	The function as a set of couples: $\{(3, 6), (5, 10), (7, 14), (9, 18)\}$
Codomain	The **codomain** is the set of all possible outputs for the given function.	Codomain = {6, 10, 14, 18, 22}
Function notation	Functions can be written in three different ways.	$f(x) = 2x$ or $f: x \to 2x$ or $y = 2x$

Example

The arrow diagram represents the function $g(x) = x^2 - 2$.

(a) List the set of elements in the domain.

(b) List the set of elements in the range.

(c) List the set of elements in the codomain.

(d) Write the function as a set of couples.

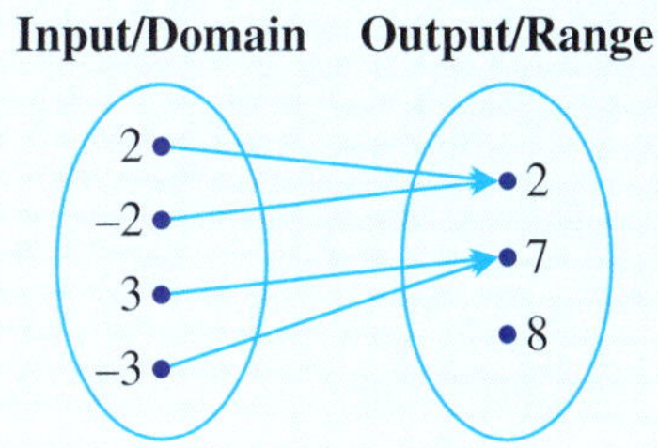

Solution

(a) The set of elements in the domain = $\{-3, -2, 2, 3\}$.

(b) The set of elements in the range = $\{2, 7\}$.

(c) The set of elements in the codomain = $\{2, 7, 8\}$.

(d) The function as a set of couples = $\{(2, 2), (-2, 2), (3, 7), (-3, 7)\}$.

How to identify a function

Not all relationships represented on arrow diagrams are functions. A relationship is a function **only if** each input value has **one and only one** output value.

	Arrow diagram	Function or not?
A	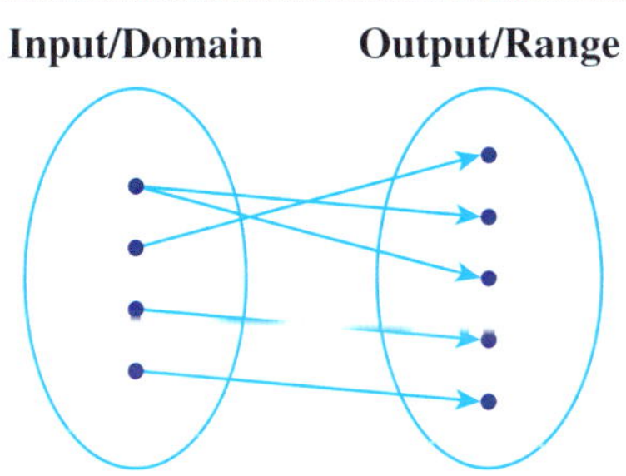	This is **not** a representation of a function as one of the input values has two different corresponding outputs.
B	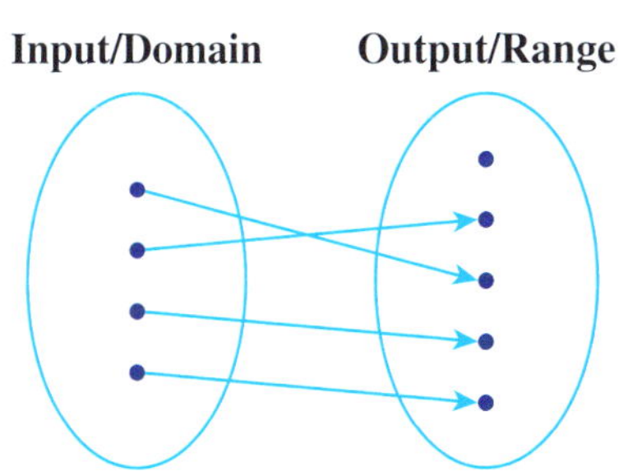	This is a representation of a function as each input has **one and only one** corresponding output.

C

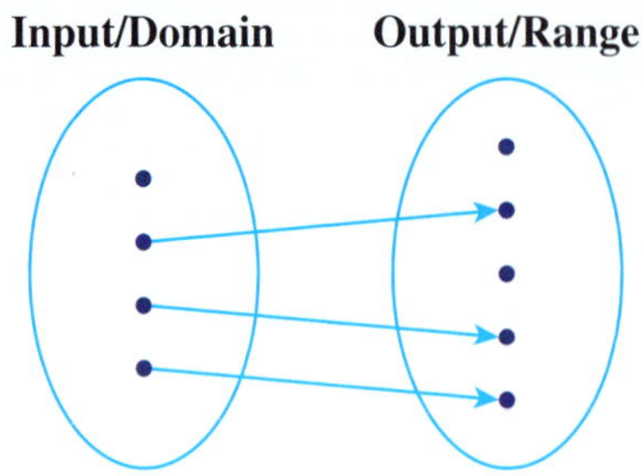

This is **not** a representation of a function as one of the input values has no corresponding output.

D

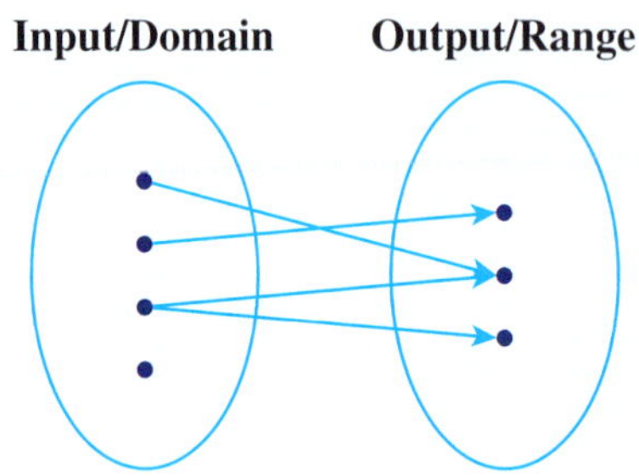

This is **not** a representation of a function as one of the input values has two different corresponding outputs, and one input value has no corresponding output.

Solving function problems algebraically

When solving different function problems, we use the same techniques as we use in algebra. Therefore it is important that you have successfully completed Chapters 3 to 10 of this book first.

Example

Given that the arrow diagram represents the function h such that $h : x \rightarrow 6x - 4, x \in \mathbb{N}$, find the values of a and b.

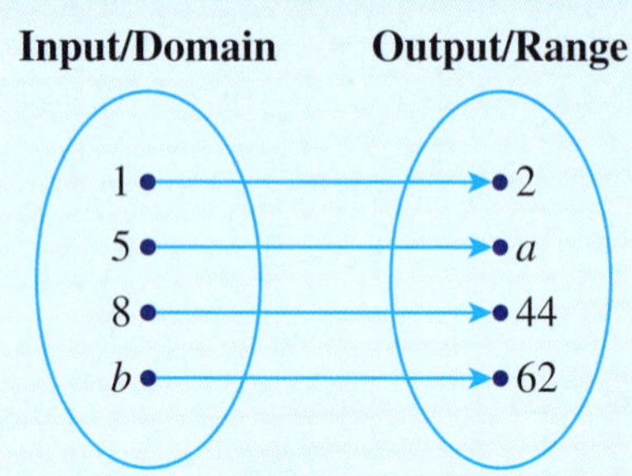

Solution

To solve for a, given the input value of 5:

$h : x \rightarrow 6x - 4$

$h(x) = 6x - 4$ Substitute $x = 5$ into the given function and solve.

$h(5) = 6(5) - 4$

$h(5) = 30 - 4 = 26$

$\therefore a = 26$

To solve for b, given an output value of 62:

$h : x \rightarrow 6x - 4$

Solve using the rules of algebra:

$h(b) = 6b - 4 = 62$

$6b = 62 + 4$

$6b = 66$

$\frac{6b}{6} = \frac{66}{6}$

$b = 11$

$\therefore b = 11$

Example

The function g is defined as $g : x \to 4x - 2,\ x \in \mathbb{N}$.

(a) Find the value of $g(3)$. **(b)** Find the value of x given that $g(x) = 30$.

Solution

(a) To find the value of $g(3)$:

$g : x \to 4x - 2$

$g(x) = 4x - 2$

$g(3) = 4(3) - 2$ Substitute $x = 3$ into the given function and solve.

$g(3) = 12 - 2 = 10$

(b) To find the value of x given that $g(x) = 30$ using the rules of algebra:

$g(x) = 4x - 2 = 30$

$4x = 30 + 2$

$4x = 32$

$x = 8$

Example

If $f(x) = x^2 + 5$, find the value of each of the following:

(a) $f(2)$ **(b)** $f(-3)$

Express each of the following in terms of p.

(c) $f(p)$ **(d)** $f(p + 2)$

Solution

(a) $f(2) = (2)^2 + 5$ Substitute $x = 2$ into the given function and solve.

$f(2) = 4 + 5 = 9$

(b) $f(-3) = (-3)^2 + 5$ Substitute $x = -3$ into the given function and solve.

$f(-3) = 9 + 5 = 14$

(c) $f(p) = (p)^2 + 5$ — Substitute $x = p$ into the given function and simplify.

$f(p) = p^2 + 5$

(d) Substitute $x = p + 2$ into the given function and simplify.

$$
\begin{aligned}
f(p+2) &= (p+2)^2 + 5 \\
&= (p+2)(p+2) + 5 \\
&= p(p+2) + 2(p+2) + 5 \\
&= p^2 + 2p + 2p + 4 + 5 \\
&= p^2 + 4p + 9
\end{aligned}
$$

Example

Let the functions $g(x)$ and $h(x)$ be defined as:

$g : x \to x^2 + 2x - 4$

$h : x \to 3x - 2$

Find the value of x if $g(x) = h(x)$.

Solution

$g(x) = h(x)$ — At the point of intersection the equations are equal.

$x^2 + 2x - 4 = 3x - 2$

$x^2 - x - 2 = 0$ — Factorise and solve for x.

$(x - 2)(x + 1) = 0$

$\therefore x = 2$ or $x = -1$

Graphical representation of functions

Sometimes we are given the graphical representation of a function and asked to solve a number of different types of questions.

Linear functions

Linear functions are in the form $f(x) = ax + b$, where $a, b \in \mathbb{R}$.

A straight line on a graph represents a linear function.

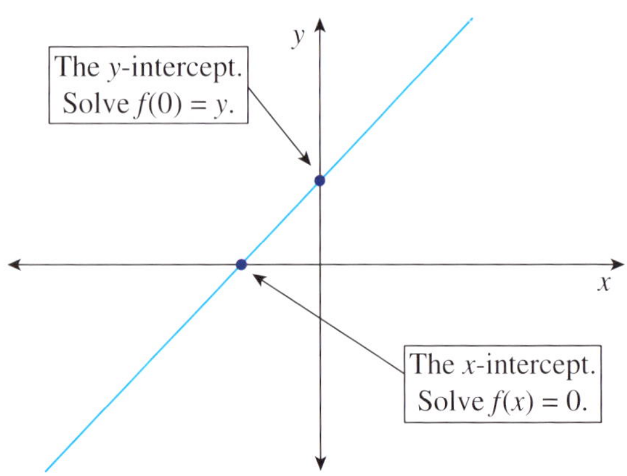

Example

Graph of the function $f(x) = 2x + 4$

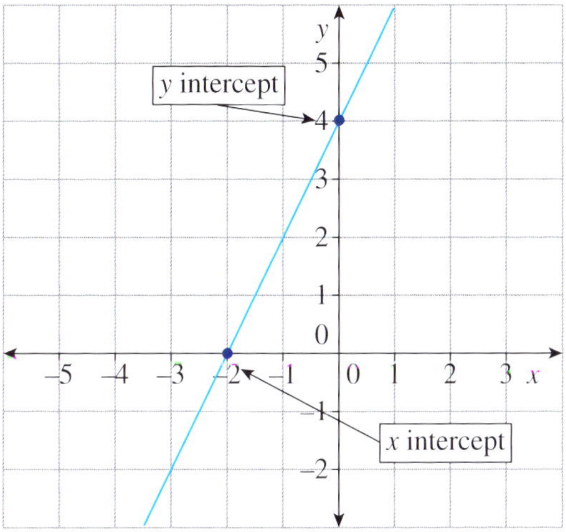

Typical questions asked

1 Find the value of the y-intercept.

Solution

Find the value of y such that $f(0) = y$.

$\therefore y = 4$

2 Find the value of the x-intercept.

Solution

Find the value of x such that $f(x) = 0$.

$\therefore x = -2$

Quadratic functions

Quadratic functions are in the form $f(x) = ax^2 + bx + c$, where $a, b, c \in \mathbb{R}$.

A $\cup$-shaped or $\cap$-shaped curve on a graph represents a quadratic function.

Positive quadratic function
($\cup$-shaped curve)
$f(x) = x^2 - x - 2$

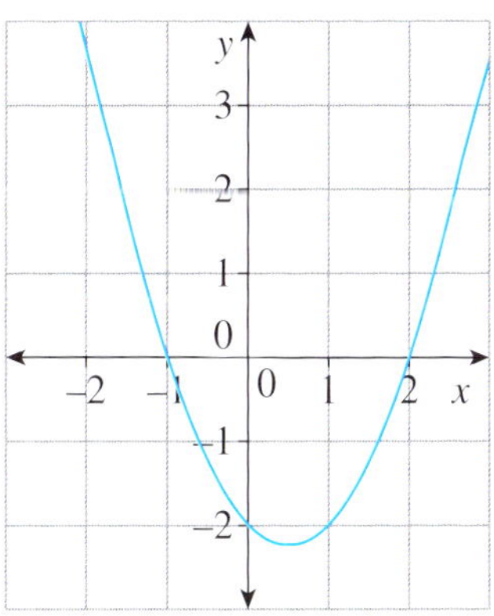

Negative quadratic function
($\cap$-shaped curve)
$f(x) = -x^2 + x + 2$

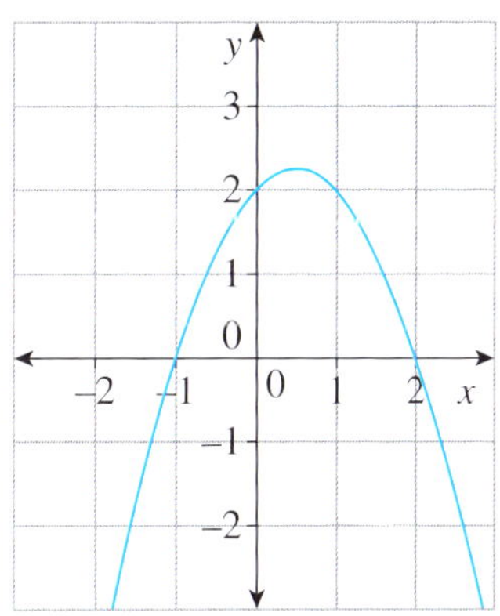

Example

Graph of the function $f(x) = x^2 - 2x - 3$

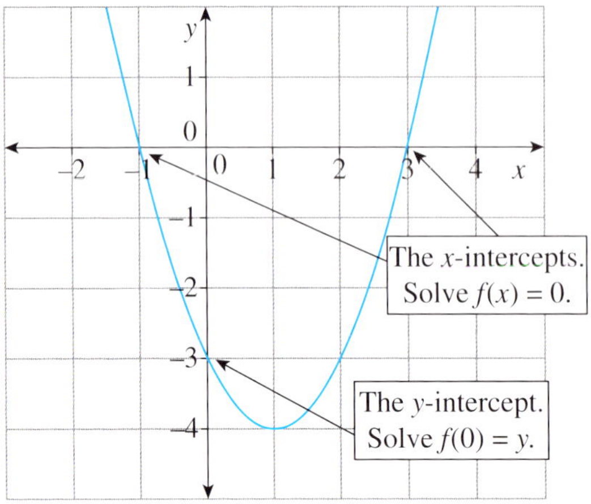

Typical questions asked

1 Find the values of the x-intercepts.

or:

Find the roots of the function.

Solution

Find the values of x such that $f(x) = 0$.

$f(x) = x^2 - 2x - 3 = 0$

$x^2 - 2x - 3 = 0$ Factorise.

$(x - 3)(x + 1) = 0$

$\therefore x = 3$ or $x = -1$

The points of intersection with the x-axis are $(-1, 0)$ and $(3, 0)$.

2 Find the value of the y-intercept.

Solution

Find the value of y such that $f(0) = y$.

$f(x) = x^2 - 2x - 3$

$f(0) = (0)^2 - 2(0) - 3$

$f(0) = -3$

The point of intersection with the y-axis is $(0, -3)$.

Graph of the function $f(x) = x^2 + 2x - 4$

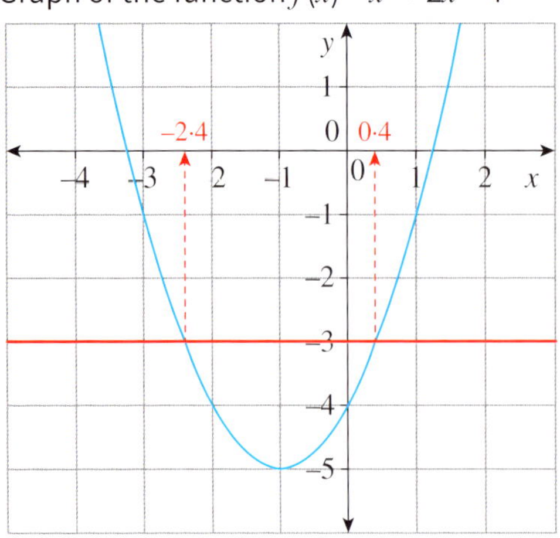

1 Find the values of x such that $f(x) = -3$.

Solution

Draw a horizontal line at the given value of $f(x) = y$.

Where this line meets the curve, draw perpendicular lines to the x-axis to find the corresponding y values.

At $f(x) = -3$, the line intersects the curve at $x = -2{\cdot}4$ and $x = 0{\cdot}4$.

Graph of the function $f(x) = x^2 - 2x - 3$

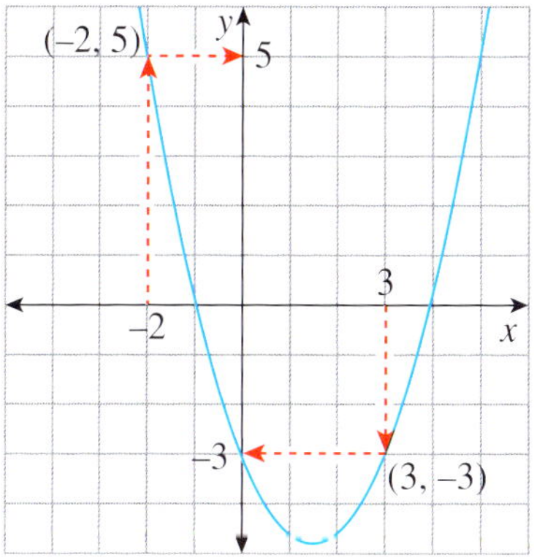

1 Find the values of $f(-2)$.

Solution

Find the value of y such that $x = -2$.

Draw a vertical line from $x = -2$ until it meets the curve. Then draw a horizontal line until it meets the y-axis to find the corresponding y value. $f(-2) = 5$

2 Find the value of $f(3)$.

Solution

Find the value of y such that $x = 3$.

Draw a vertical line from $x = 3$ until it meets the curve. Then, draw a horizontal line until it meets the y-axis to find the corresponding y value. $f(3) = -3$

Graph of the function $f(x) = x^2 - 2x - 1$

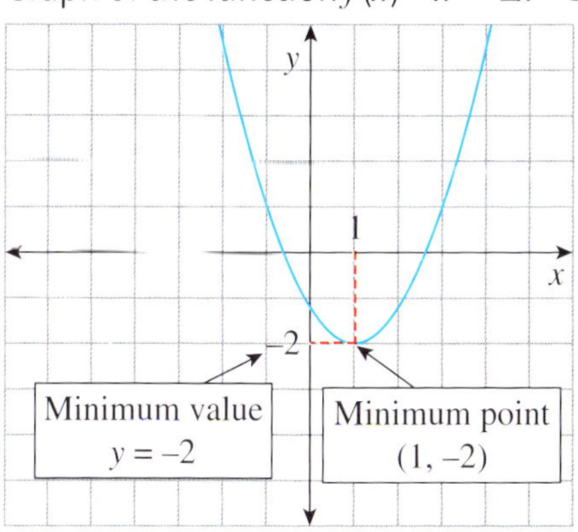

1 What is value of the minimum point of the function $f(x) = x^2 - 2x - 1$?

Solution

Draw a vertical line from the x-axis to the minimum point on the curve. Then draw a horizontal line to the y-axis to find the corresponding y value.
The minimum point is $(1, -2)$.

2 What is the minimum value of the function?

Solution

Draw a horizontal line to the y-axis from the minimum point on the curve.
Minimum value is $y = -2$.

Graph of the function $f(x) = -x^2 - 2x + 3$

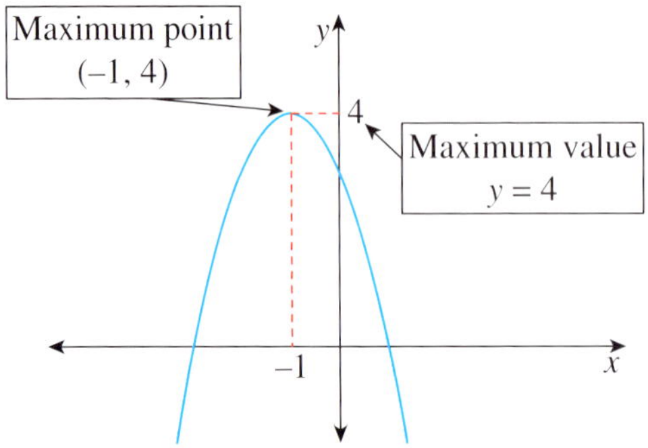

1 What is the maximum point of the function $f(x) = -x^2 - 2x + 3$?

Solution

Draw a vertical line from the x-axis to the maximum point on the curve. Then draw a horizontal line to the y-axis to find the corresponding y value. Maximum point is $(-1, 4)$.

2 What is the maximum value of the function?

Solution

Draw a horizontal line to the y-axis from the maximum point on the curve.
Maximum value is $y - 4$.

Graph of the function $f(x) = -x^2 - 2x + 3$

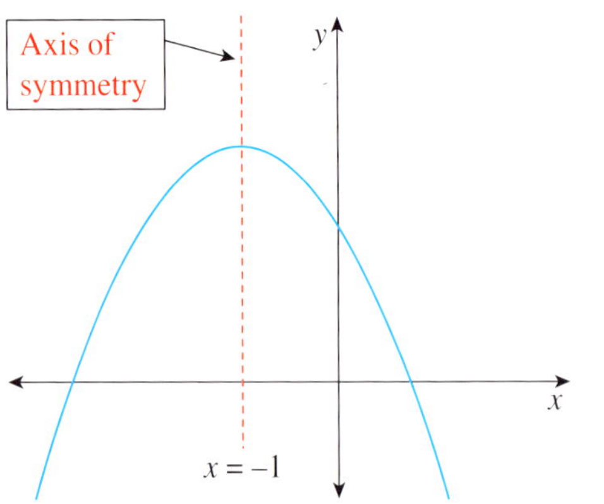

1 Write down the equation of the axis of symmetry of the function.

Solution

Draw a vertical line through the maximum or minimum point of the function.
The equation of the axis of symmetry is $x = -1$.

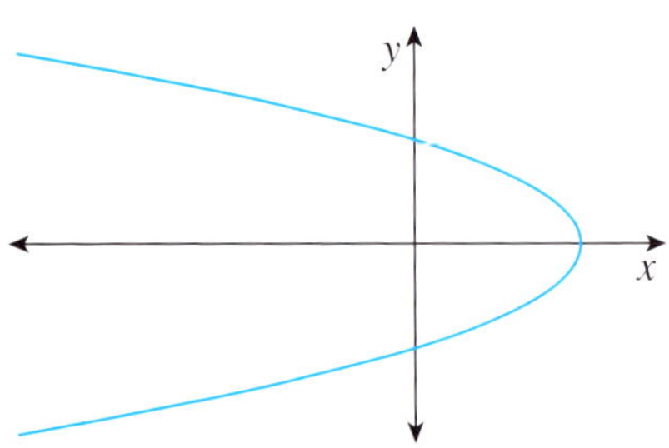

1 Explain why this graph is **not a representation of a function**.

Recall:

- A relationship is a function, if each input value has **one and only one** output value.
- Input value = x-coordinate.
Output value = y-coordinate.
This graph does not represent a function, as we can see that some of the x-coordinates correspond with two y-coordinates.

Example

The function h is defined as $f(x) = x^2 + 3x - 2, x \in \mathbb{R}$.

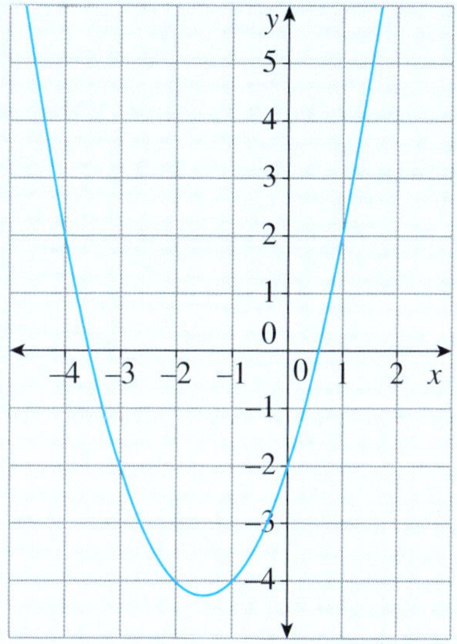

Use the graph to answer each of the following:

(a) Find the values of x such that $f(x) = -3$.

(b) Estimate the value of $f(-2)$.

(c) What are the roots of the function?

(d) Estimate the minimum point of the function.

(e) Write down the equation of the axis of symmetry of the function.

Solution

From the graph:

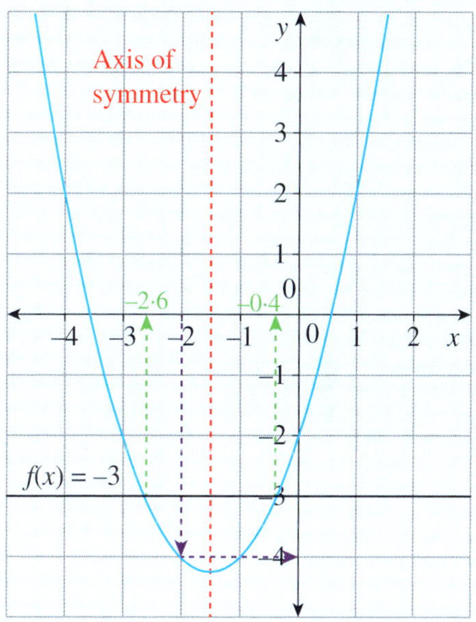

(a) To find the values of x, draw a horizontal line at the given value of $f(x) = -3$.

Where this line meets the function, draw perpendicular lines to the x-axis to find the corresponding y values.

At $f(x) = -3$, the line intersects the curve at $x = -2{\cdot}6$ and $x = -0{\cdot}4$.

(b) 'Estimate the value of' $f(-2)$ means 'Find the value of y such that $x = -2$'.

Draw a vertical line from $x = -2$ until it meets the curve. Then draw a horizontal line until it meets the y-axis to find the corresponding y value. $f(-2) = -4$

(c) 'What are the roots of the function?' means solve $f(x) = x^2 + 3x - 2 = 0$.

The graph cuts the x-axis at $x = -3{\cdot}5$ and $x = 0{\cdot}5$.

(d) To estimate the minimum point of the function, draw a vertical line from the x-axis to the minimum point on the curve. Then draw a horizontal line to the y-axis to the corresponding y value.

Minimum point $= (-1{\cdot}5, -4{\cdot}2)$

(e) Draw a vertical line through the maximum or minimum point of the function. The equation of the axis of symmetry of the graph is $x = -1{\cdot}5$.

Example

Let f be the function $f(x) = x^2 - 3x - 4$ and h be the function $h(x) = -x - 1$ as shown on the graph.

Find the coordinates of A, B, C and D on the graph.

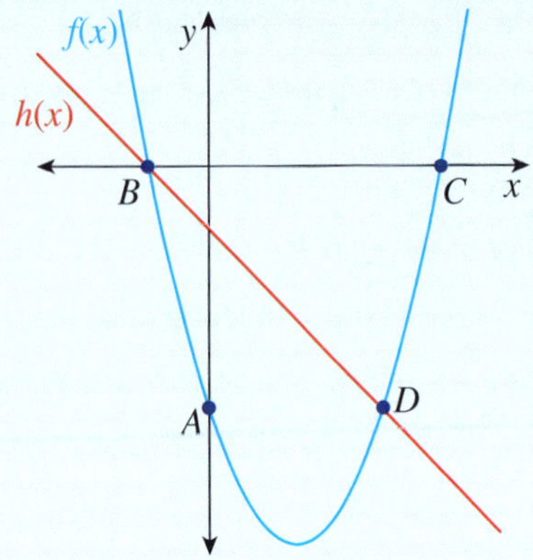

Solution

A represents the y-intercept of the function $f(x) = x^2 - 3x - 4$.

To find the value of the y-intercept, find the value of y such that $f(0) = y$:

$f(x) = x^2 - 3x - 4$

$f(0) = (0)^2 - 3(0) - 4$

$f(0) = -4$

The point of intersection with the y-axis (A) is $(0, -4)$.

B and C represent the roots or x-intercepts of the function $f(x) = x^2 - 3x - 4$.

Find the values of x such that $f(x) = 0$:

$f(x) = x^2 - 3x - 4 = 0$

$x^2 - 3x - 4 = 0$ Factorise.

$(x - 4)(x + 1) = 0$

$\therefore x = 4$ or $x = -1$

The points of intersection with the x-axis are $C(4, 0)$ and $B(-1, 0)$.

D represents one of the points of intersection of the two functions.

$f(x) = h(x)$

$x^2 - 3x - 4 = -x - 1$

$x^2 - 2x - 3 = 0$

$(x - 3)(x + 1) = 0$

$\therefore x = 3$ or $x = -1$

Now substitute $x = 3$ and $x = -1$ into $f(x)$ or $h(x)$ to solve for y.

$h(x) = -x - 1$

$h(3) = -3 - 1 = -4$

$h(x) = -x - 1$

$h(-1) = -(-1) - 1 = 0$

The points of intersection $f(x) = h(x)$ are $D(3, -4)$ and $B(-1, 0)$.

Example

Part of the graph of the function $y = x^2 + ax + b$ where $a, b \in \mathbb{Z}$ is shown.

The points $R(2, 3)$ and $S(-5, -4)$ are on the curve.

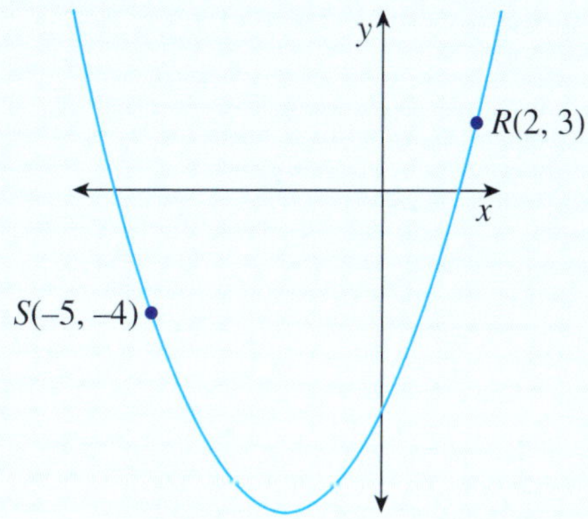

(a) Use the given points to form two equations in a and b.

(b) Solve your equations to find the value of a and the value of b.

(c) Write down the coordinates of the point where the curve crosses the y-axis.

(d) Find the points where the curve crosses the x-axis. Give your answers correct to one decimal place.

(SEC 2015)

Solution

(a) Form two equations in a and b using the points given.

Given $R(2, 3)$ satisfies the equation $y = x^2 + ax + b$, substitute the point R into the equation:

$y = x^2 + ax + b$

$3 = (2)^2 + a(2) + b$

$3 = 4 + 2a + b$

$2a + b = -1$ (1)

Given $S(-5, -4)$ satisfies the equation $y = x^2 + ax + b$, substitute the point S into the equation:

$y = x^2 + ax + b$

$-4 = (-5)^2 + a(-5) + b$

$-4 = 25 - 5a + b$

$5a - b = 29$ (2)

(b) Given two equations with two unknown variables, we use the simultaneous equations method to solve for the two unknown variables a and b.

Add the two equations together to solve for one of the unknown variables.

$2a + b = -1$ (1)

$+ \quad 5a - b = 29$ (2)

$7a = 28$

$a = \frac{28}{7} = 4$

Substitute $a = 4$ into Equation (1) or (2) to find the other unknown variable.

Using Equation (1):

$2a + b = -1$

$2(4) + b = -1$

$8 + b = -1$

$b = -1 - 8$

$b = -9$

Therefore the function is $y = x^2 + 4x - 9$.

(c) The curve crosses the y-axis when $x = 0$.

$y = x^2 + 4x - 9$

$y = (0)^2 + 4(0) - 9$

$y = -9$

Therefore the coordinates of the point where the curve crosses the y-axis = (0, −9).

(d) The curve crosses thc x-axis when $y - 0$.

$y = x^2 + 4x - 9$

$0 = x^2 + 4x - 9$

$x^2 + 4x - 9 = 0$

Using the quadratic formula:

$$x = \frac{-b \pm \sqrt{b^2 - 4ac}}{2a}$$

Substitute $a = 1$, $b = 4$ and $c = -9$ into the quadratic formula.

$$\Rightarrow x = \frac{-(4) \pm \sqrt{(4)^2 - 4(1)(-9)}}{2(1)}$$

$$\Rightarrow x = \frac{-4 \pm \sqrt{16 + 36}}{6}$$

$$\Rightarrow x = \frac{-4 + \sqrt{52}}{2} \quad \text{or} \quad x = \frac{-4 - \sqrt{52}}{2}$$

Simplify $\sqrt{52} = 2\sqrt{13}$ using a calculator.

$$\Rightarrow x = \frac{-4 + 2\sqrt{13}}{2} \quad \text{or} \quad x = \frac{-4 - 2\sqrt{13}}{2}$$

$$\Rightarrow x = 1{\cdot}6055... \quad \text{or} \quad x = -5{\cdot}6055...$$

Therefore the curve crosses the x-axis at $x = 1{\cdot}6$ and $x = -5{\cdot}6$, correct to one decimal place.

Exercise

Q1 For each of the arrow diagrams given, state:

(a) The domain

(b) The codomain

(c) The range

(d) The set of couples for the given function.

A **Input/Domain** **Output/Range**

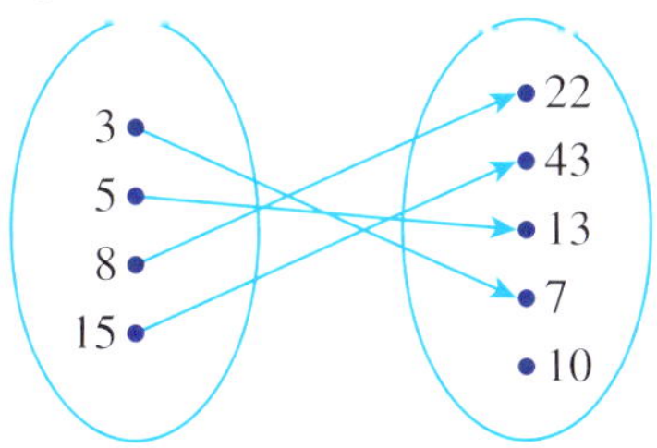

B **Input/Domain** **Output/Range**

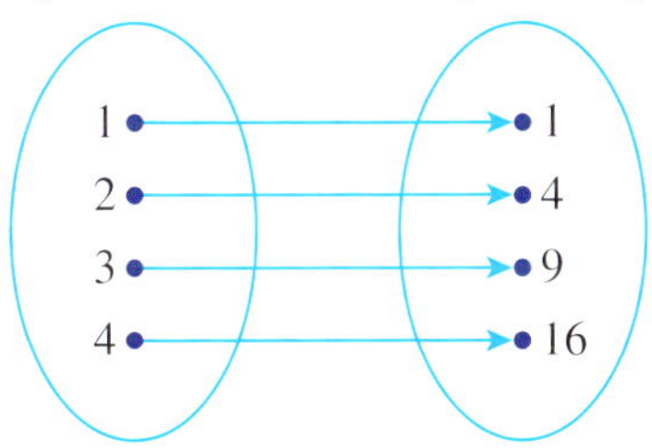

C **Input/Domain** **Output/Range**

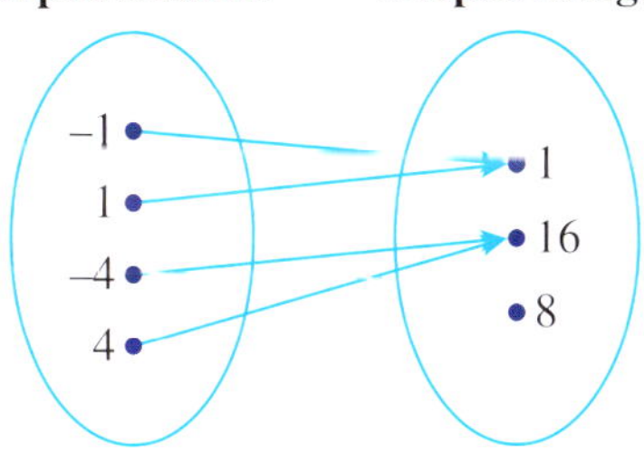

Q2 State whether or not each of the following arrow diagrams represents a function. Give a reason for each answer.

A **Input/Domain** **Output/Range**

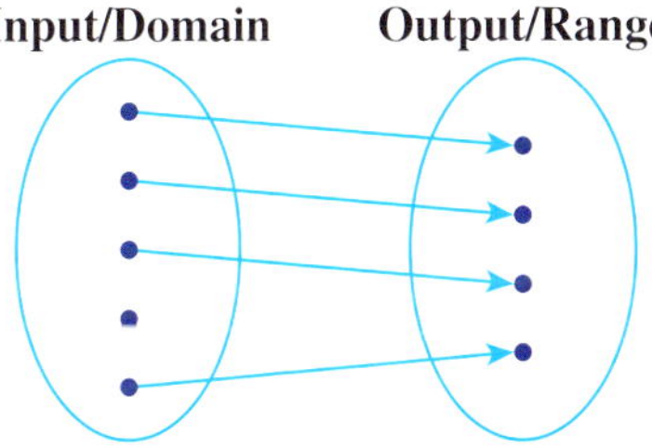

B **Input/Domain** **Output/Range**

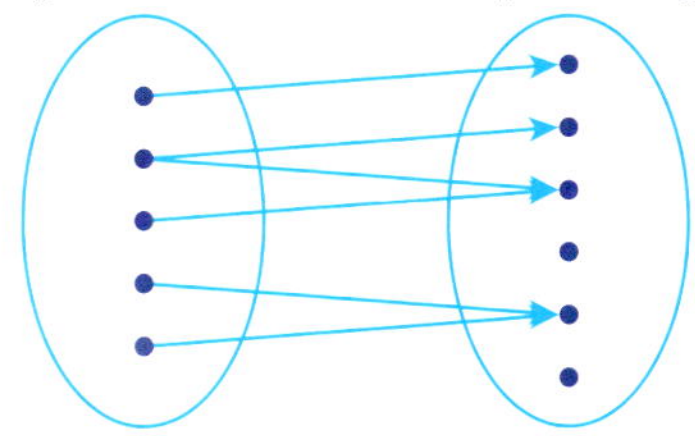

C **Input/Domain** **Output/Range**

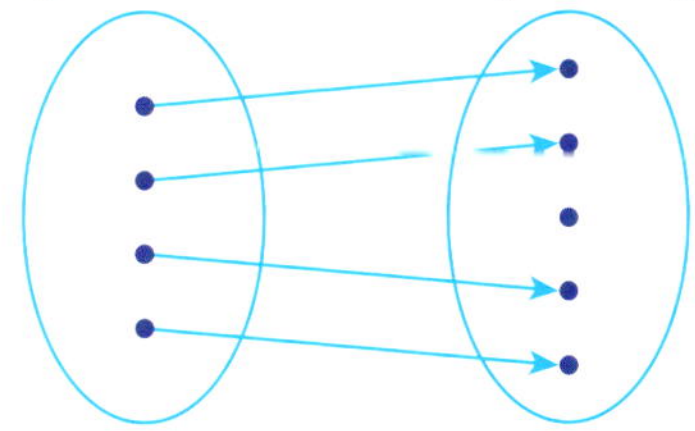

D **Input/Domain** **Output/Range**

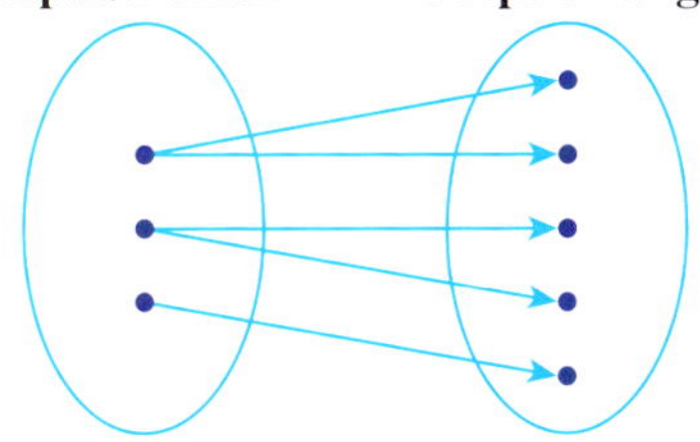

Q3 Given the arrow diagram represents the function h such that $h : x \to 10 - 2x, x \in \mathbb{N}$, find the values of a and b.

Input/Domain **Output/Range**

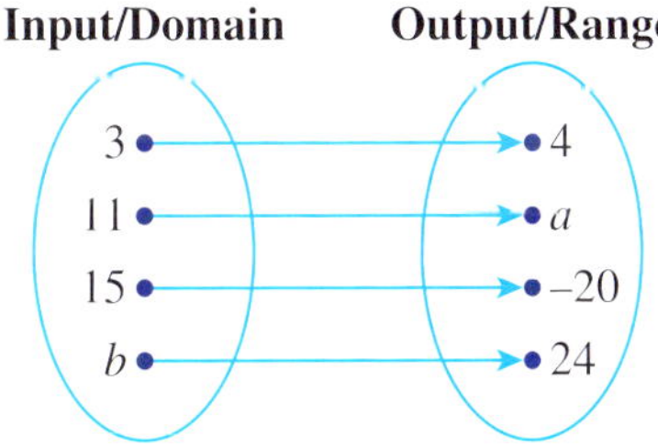

Q4 Given the function $f(x) = 5x + 7$:

(a) Find the value of each of the following.

(i) $f(5)$ **(ii)** $f(-5)$

(b) Express each of the following in terms of q.

(i) $f(q)$ **(ii)** $f(q - 4)$

Q5 The function h is defined as $h : x \rightarrow 2x - 4, x \in \mathbb{R}$.

(a) Find the value of each of the following.

(i) $h(-2)$ **(ii)** $h(6)$ **(iii)** $h(12)$

(b) Find the value of x for each of the following given that:

(i) $h(x) = 2$ **(ii)** $h(x) = -14$

(iii) $h(x) = -3$

Q6 The function f is defined as $f(x) = -x^2 + x + 6, x \in \mathbb{R}$.

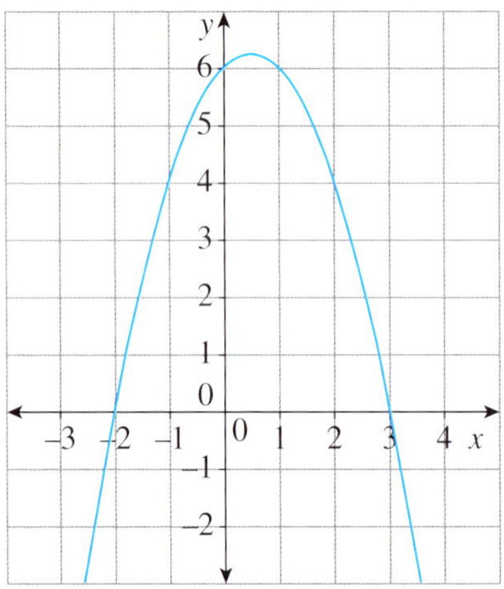

Use the graph to answer each of the following:

(a) Find the value(s) of x such that $f(x) = 4$.

(b) Estimate the value of $f(1)$.

(c) What are the roots of the function?

(d) Estimate the maximum point of the function.

(e) Write down the equation of the axis of symmetry of the function.

Q7 The diagram represents part of the function $f(x) = -x^2 + ax + b$, $x \in \mathbb{R}$ and $a, b \in \mathbb{Z}$.

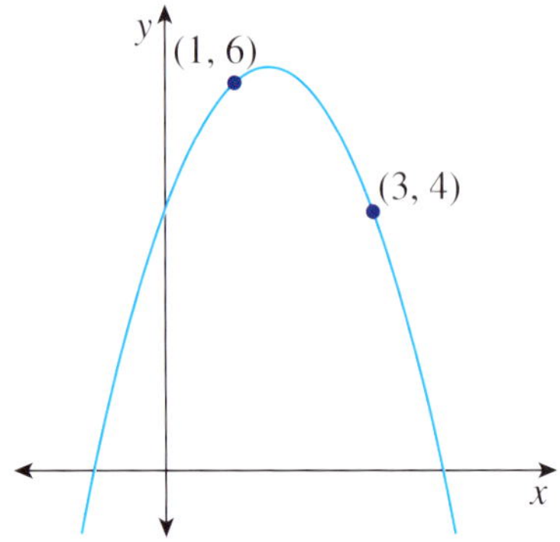

Find the value of a and the value of b.

Q8 The diagram shows part of the graph of the function $f : x \mapsto x^2 - 2x - 8, x \in \mathbb{Z}$.

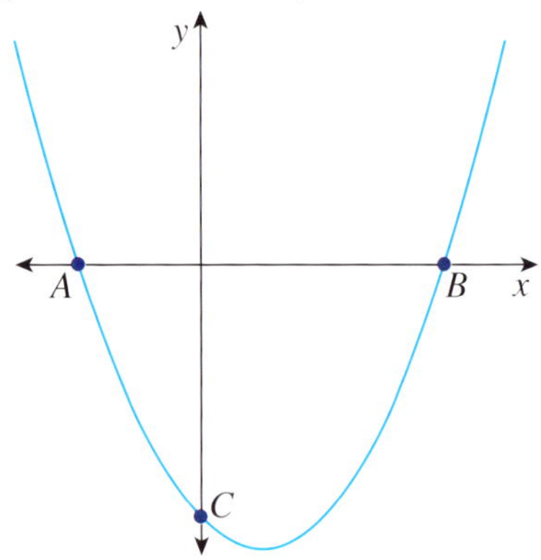

The graph intersects the x-axis at A and B, and the y-axis at C.

Find the coordinates of A, B and C.

Q9 Give a reason why the graph below does not represent a function of x.

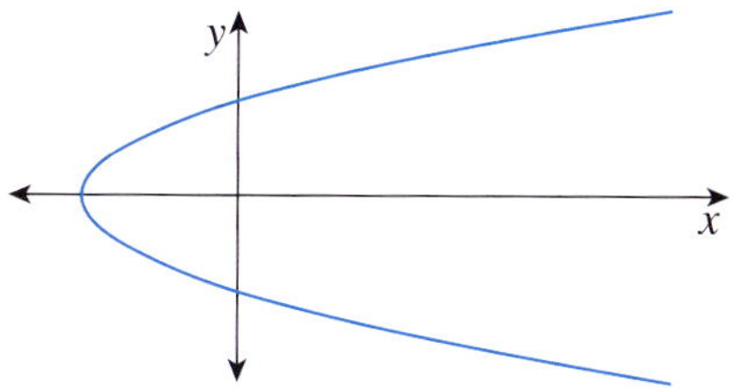

(SEC 2015)

Solutions

Q1 A **(a)** The domain = {3, 5, 8, 15}

(b) The codomain = {7, 10, 13, 22, 43}

(c) The range = {7, 13, 22, 43}

(d) The set of couples for the function = {(3, 7), (5, 13), (8, 22), (15, 43)}

B **(a)** The domain = {1, 2, 3, 4}

(b) The codomain = {1, 4, 9, 16}

(c) The range = {1, 4, 9, 16}

(d) The set of couples for the function = {(1, 1), (2, 4), (3, 9), (4, 16)}

C **(a)** The domain = {−4, −1, 1, 4}

(b) The codomain = {1, 8, 16}

(c) The range = {1, 16}

(d) The set of couples for the function = {(−4, 16), (−1, 1), (1, 1), (4, 16)}

Q2 **A** does **not** represent a function as one input has no output.

B does **not** represent a function as one input has two different outputs.

C represents a function as each input has only one output.

D does **not** represent a function as two different inputs have more than one output.

Q3 To solve for a, given the input value of 11:

$h : x \rightarrow 10 - 2x$

$h(x) = 10 - 2x$

$h(11) = 10 - 2(11) = 10 - 22 = -12$

$\therefore a = -12$

To solve for b, given the output value of 24:

$h : x \rightarrow 10 - 2x$

$h(b) = 10 - 2b = 24$

$-2b = 24 - 10$

$-2b = 14$

$\frac{-2b}{-2} = \frac{14}{-2}$

$b = -7$

$\therefore b = -7$

Q4 (a) (i) $f(x) = 5x + 7$

$f(5) = 5(5) + 7 = 32$

(ii) $f(x) = 5x + 7$

$f(-5) = 5(-5) + 7 = -18$

(b) (i) $f(x) = 5x + 7$

$f(q) = 5(q) + 7$

$= 5q + 7$

(ii) $f(x) = 5x + 7$

$f(q - 4) = 5(q - 4) + 7$

$= 5(q) - 5(4) + 7$

$= 5q - 20 + 7$

$= 5q - 13$

Q5 (a) (i)

$h : x \rightarrow 2x - 4$

$h(x) = 2x - 4$

$h(-2) = 2(-2) - 4 = -8$

(ii)

$h : x \rightarrow 2x - 4$

$h(x) = 2x - 4$

$h(6) = 2(6) - 4 = 8$

(iii)

$h : x \rightarrow 2x - 4$

$h(x) = 2x - 4$

$h(12) = 2(12) - 4 = 20$

(b) (i)

$h(x) = 2x - 4 = 2$

$2x = 2 + 4$

$2x = 6$

$\frac{2x}{2} = \frac{6}{2}$

$x = 3$

(ii)

$h(x) = 2x - 4 = -14$

$2x = -14 + 4$

$2x = -10$

$\frac{2x}{2} = \frac{-10}{2}$

$x = -5$

(iii)

$h(x) = 2x - 4 = -3$

$2x = -3 + 4$

$2x = 1$

$\frac{2x}{2} = \frac{1}{2}$

$x = \frac{1}{2}$

Q6

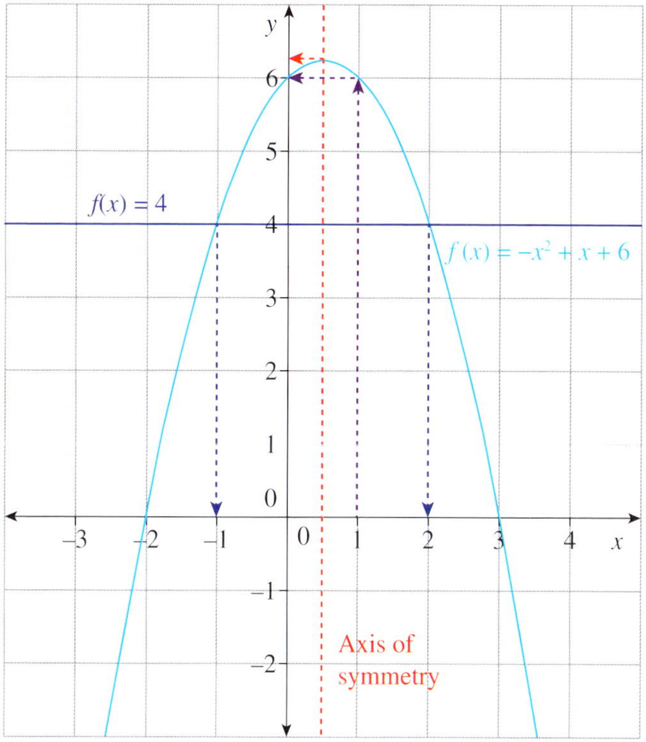

From the graph:

(a) Draw a horizontal line at the given value of $f(x) = 4$.

Where this line meets the curve, draw perpendicular lines to the x-axis to find the corresponding y values.

At $f(x) = 4$, the line intersects the curve at $x = -1$ and $x = 2$.

(b) Draw a vertical line from $x = 1$ until it meets the curve. Then, draw a horizontal line until it meets the y-axis to find the corresponding y value.

$f(1) = 6$

(c) The roots of the function are the solutions when $f(x) = x^2 + x + 6 = 0$.

The graph cuts the x-axis at $x = -2$ and $x = 3$.

(d) To estimate the maximum point of the function, draw a vertical line from the x-axis to the maximum point on the curve. Then draw a horizontal line to the y-axis to the corresponding y value.
Maximum point = $(0{\cdot}5, 6{\cdot}2)$

(e) To find the equation of the axis of symmetry of the function, draw a vertical line through the maximum or minimum point of the function.

The equation of the axis of symmetry of the graph is $x = 0{\cdot}5$.

Q7 At the point (1, 6), $f(1) = 6$.

$f(x) = -x^2 + ax + b$

$f(1) = -(1)^2 + a(1) + b = 6$

$-1 + a + b = 6$

$a + b = 7 \qquad (1)$

At the point (3, 4), $f(3) = 4$.

$f(x) = -x^2 + ax + b$

$f(3) = -(3)^2 + a(3) + b = 4$

$-9 + 3a + b = 4$

$3a + b = 13 \qquad (2)$

Subtract Equation (1) from Equation (2):

$$\begin{array}{rl} 3a + b = 13 & (2) \\ -\quad a + b = 7 & (1) \\ \hline 2a = 6 & \\ \therefore \quad a = 3 & \end{array}$$

Substitute $a = 3$ into Equation (1) or (2) to solve for b.

$a + b = 7 \qquad (1)$

$3 + b = 7$

$b = 4$

Therefore the function is $f(x) = -x^2 + 3x + 4$.

Q8 C represents the y-intercept.

Let $x = 0$:

$f(0) = (0)^2 - 2(0) - 8$

$= -8$

Point $C = (0, -8)$

A and B represent the roots of the function.

Let $f(x) = 0$

$x^2 - 2x - 8 = 0$

$(x - 4)(x + 2) = 0$

$x - 4 = 0$ or $x + 2 = 0$

$x = 4$ or $x = -2$

The coordinates are $A(-2, 0)$ and $B(4, 0)$.

Q9 This graph does **not** represent a function, as we can see that some of the x-coordinates correspond to two y-coordinates.

Functions 2 14

Learning objectives

In this chapter you will learn about:

- How to graph linear, quadratic and exponential functions
- How to solve questions based on the constructed graph
- How to transform linear, quadratic and exponential graphs.

Graphing linear, quadratic and exponential functions

Linear graphs

Linear functions are in the form $f(x) = ax + b$, where $a, b \in \mathbb{Z}, x \in \mathbb{R}$.

Link

RW Book 2 Chapter 9 Coordinate Geometry of the Line

Graphical representations of linear functions always form a straight line.

If $a > 0$, then the graph is increasing. For example: the function $f(x) = x + 2$, in the domain $-4 < x < 4$ as shown below.

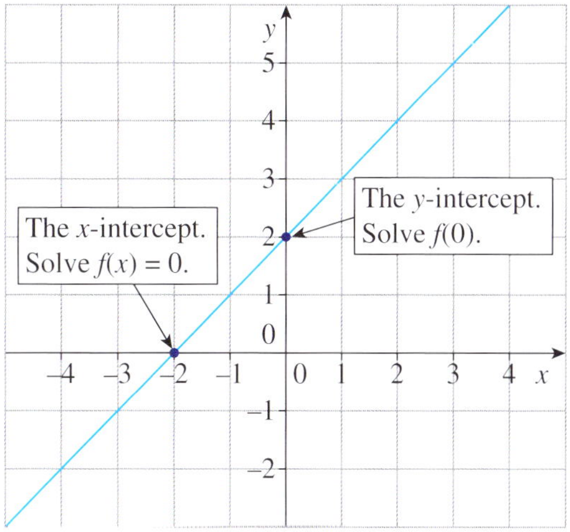

If $a < 0$, then the graph is decreasing. For example: the function $f(x) = -x + 2$, in the domain $-4 \leq x \leq 4$ is shown below.

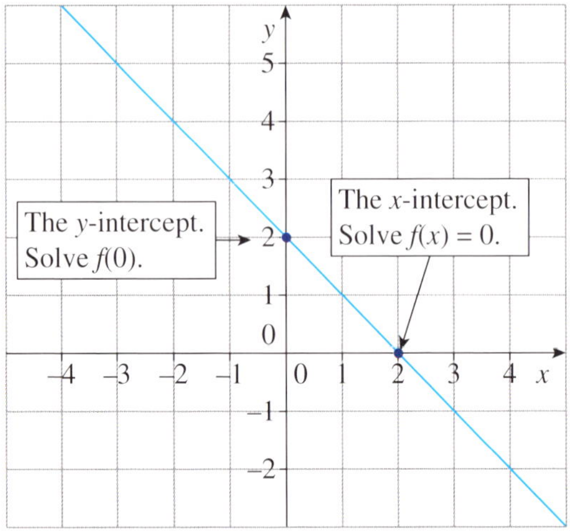

Top Tip

When graphing a linear function, we need a minimum of two points that satisfy the function.

We can find these points using either of these two methods:

Method 1

Solve for:

1 $(0, y)$ by setting $x = 0$, to find $y = f(0)$.

This means let $x = 0$ and find the corresponding y value by substituting into the given function.

2 $(x, 0)$ by setting $y = f(x) = 0$ and solve for x.

This means let $y = 0$ and find the corresponding x value by substituting into the given function.

Note: We could use any two points that satisfy the graphed function.

Method 2

1 Set up a table with the following headings and complete for the given domain.

Domain x	Function $f(x) = ax + b$	Range y	Coordinates (x, y)

Note: you can use the table mode on your calculator to check all values.

2 Plot these points on an x–y graph in the given domain.

3 Draw in the line joining these points (extending the line in both directions).

Example

(a) Graph the functions $f: x \to -2x + 7$ and $g: x \to x - 2$ using the same axes and scale, in the domain $-1 \le x \le 6$.

(b) From your graph, estimate each of the following:

(i) $g(4)$

(ii) $f(x) = 3$

(iii) Estimate the value of x such that $f(x) = g(x)$.

Solution

(a) We need a minimum of two points that satisfy the function $f: x \to -2x + 7$.

Using Method 1:

1 Solve for $(0, y)$ by setting $x = 0$, to find $y = f(0)$.

$f: x \to -2x + 7$

$f(x) = -2x + 7$

$f(0) = -2(0) + 7$

$f(0) = 7$

Therefore, the 1st coordinate is (0, 7).

2 Solve for $(x, 0)$ by setting $y = f(x) = 0$ and solve for x.

$f(x) = -2x + 7 = 0$

$-2x + 7 = 0$

$-2x = -7$

$x = 3{\cdot}5$

Therefore, the 2nd coordinate is (3·5, 0).

The function $g: x \to x - 2$ using **Method 2:**

1 Create a table and complete for the given domain.

Domain	$g(x) = x - 2$	Range	Coordinates
−1	(−1) − 2	−3	(−1, −3)
0	(0) − 2	−2	(0, −2)
1	(1) − 2	−1	(1, −1)
2	(2) − 2	0	(2, 0)
3	(3) − 2	1	(3, 1)
4	(4) − 2	2	(4, 2)
5	(5) − 2	3	(5, 3)
6	(6) − 2	4	(6, 4)

2 Plot these points on an x–y graph for the given domain.

3 Draw in the line joining these points (extending the line in both directions).

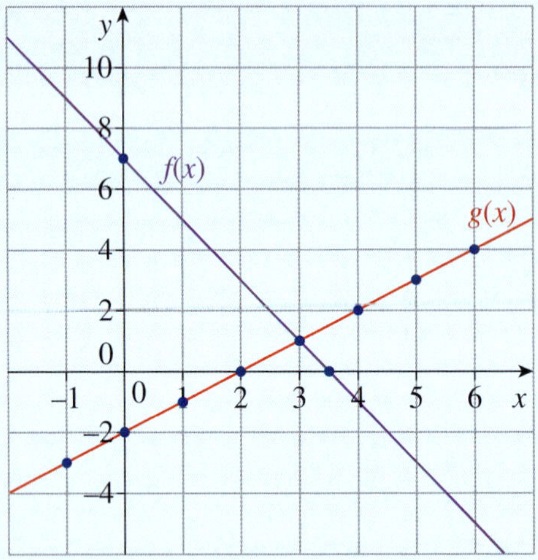

(b)

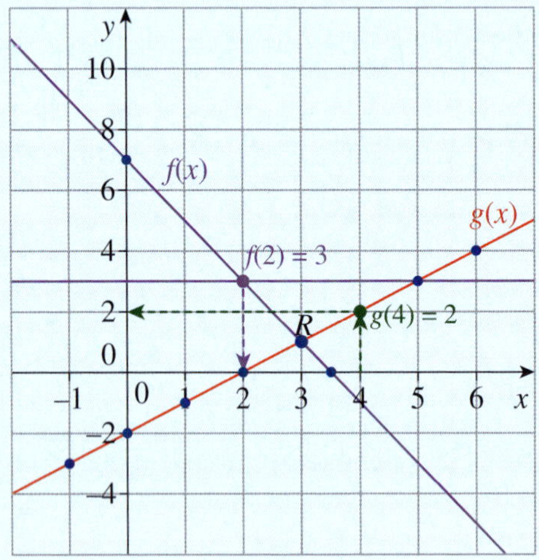

(i) $g(4)$ means find the value of y when $x = 4$.

$g(4) = 2$

(ii) $f(x) = 3$ means find where the function cuts the line $y = 3$.

$f(2) = 3$

(iii) $f(x) = g(x)$ means find the point of intersection, R, of the two functions.

R is $(3, 1)$.

Quadratic graphs

Quadratic functions are in the form $f(x) = ax^2 + bx + c$, where $a, b, c \in \mathbb{Z}, x \in \mathbb{R}$.

Graphical representations of quadratic functions

If $a > 0$, the graph will always have a minimum point, so it will be ∪-shaped.

For example, the graph of the function $f(x) = x^2 - 4x - 5$ in the domain $-3 \leq x \leq 6$ is shown below.

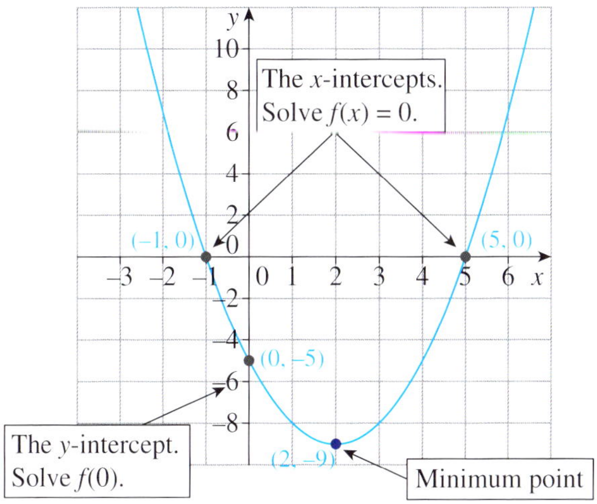

If $a < 0$, the graph will always have a maximum point, so it will be ∩-shaped.

For example, the graph of the function $f(x) = -x^2 - 4x + 5$, in the domain $-6 \leq x \leq 3$ is shown below.

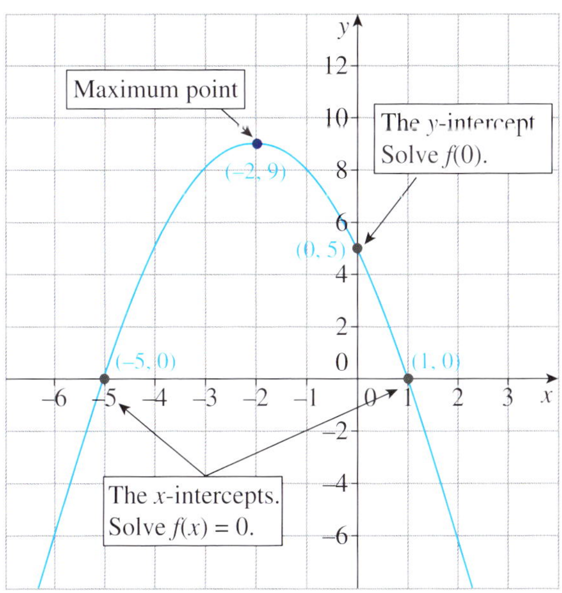

Top Tip

When graphing a quadratic function, we generally follow these steps:

1 Set up a table using the following headings and complete for the given domain.

Domain x	Function $f(x) = ax^2 + bx + c$	Range y	Coordinates (x, y)

2 Plot these points on an x–y graph (use an appropriate scale).

3 Draw in the curve by joining these points (extending the curve in both directions).

Example

The function h is defined as $h: x \to x^2 - 2x - 3$.

(a) Draw a graph of the function in the domain $-2 \le x \le 4$.

(b) From your graph, estimate:

(i) The values of x for which $h(x) = 3$

(ii) The value of $h(2)$

(iii) The coordinates of the minimum point of the function

(iv) The values of the roots of the function

(v) The values of x such that $h(x) > 0$

(vi) The values of x such that $h(x) < 0$.

Solution

(a)

Domain	$h(x) = x^2 - 2x - 3$	Range	Coordinates
−2	$(-2)^2 - 2(-2) - 3$	5	(−2, 5)
−1	$(-1)^2 - 2(-1) - 3$	0	(−1, 0)
0	$(0)^2 - 2(0) - 3$	−3	(0, −3)
1	$(1)^2 - 2(1) - 3$	−4	(1, −4)
2	$(2)^2 - 2(2) - 3$	−3	(2, −3)
3	$(3)^2 - 2(3) - 3$	0	(3, 0)
4	$(4)^2 - 2(4) - 3$	5	(4, 5)

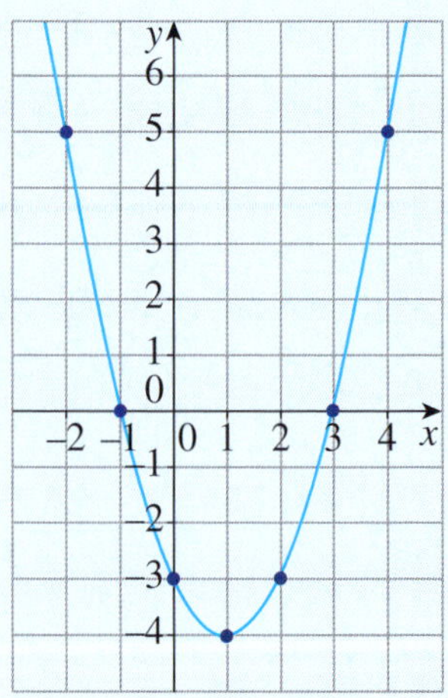

(b) **(i)** $h(x) = 3$ means where the graph cuts the line $y = 3$.

$\therefore h(x) = 3$ at $x = -1{\cdot}7$ and $x = 3{\cdot}7$.

(ii) $h(2)$ means find the value of y when $x = 2$.

$h(2) = -3$

(iii) The minimum point of the function is the lowest point of the graph, which is $(1, -4)$.

(iv) The roots of the function are where the function cuts the x-axis at $h(x) = 0$.

The roots of the function are $x = -1$ and $x = 3$.

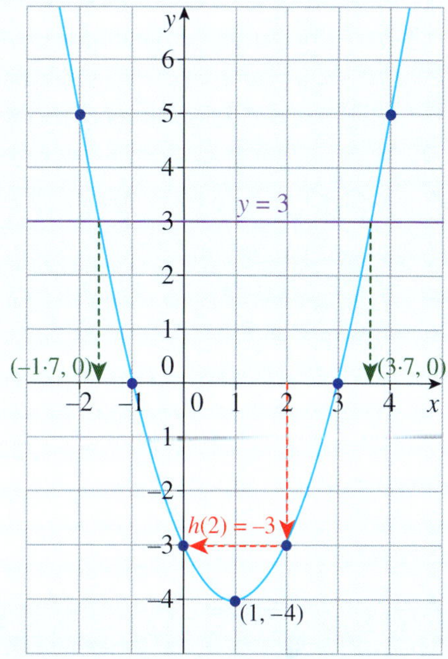

(v) $h(x) > 0$ means the values of x where the function is above the x-axis (i.e. when y is greater than 0).

$x < -1$ or $x > 3$, which can also be written as $-1 > x > 3$.

(vi) $h(x) < 0$ means the values of x where the function is below the x-axis.

$x > -1$ or $x < 3$, which can also be written as $-1 < x < 3$.

Using graphs to solve inequalities

The graph of $f(x) = x^2 - 2x - 8$, in the domain $-6 \leq x \leq 10$ is shown.

1 Find the values of $f(x) > 0$.

$f(x) > 0$ means where the graph is above the x-axis (illustrated by the green shaded areas).

This is when $x < -2$ or $x > 4$, which can also be written as $-2 > x > 4$.

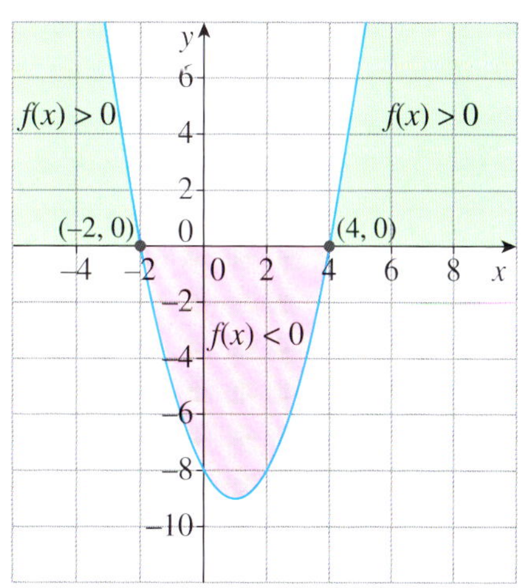

2 Find the values of $f(x) < 0$.

$f(x) < 0$ means where the graph is below the x-axis (illustrated by the pink shaded area).

This is when $x > -2$ or $x < 4$, which can also be written as $-2 < x < 4$.

The graphs of $f(x) = x^2 - 2x - 8$ and $g(x) = -2x - 4$ are shown below.

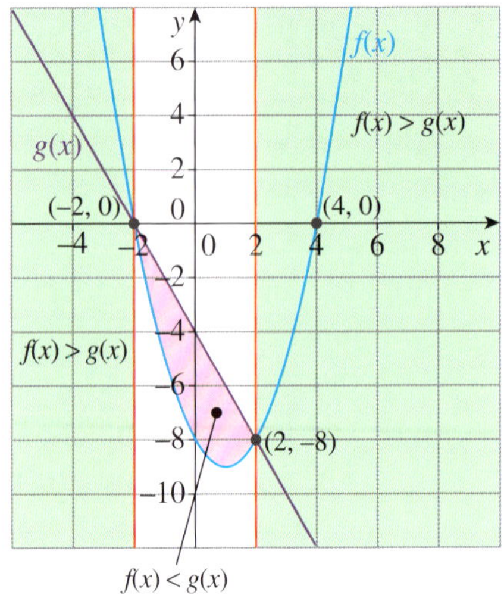

1 $f(x) > g(x)$ means the values of x where $f(x)$ is greater than $g(x)$, as illustrated by the green shaded areas of the graph.

This occurs when $x < -2$ or $x > 2$, which can also be written as $-2 > x > 2$.

2 $f(x) < g(x)$ means the values of x where $f(x)$ is less than $g(x)$, as illustrated by the pink shaded area of the graph.

This occurs when $x > -2$ or $x < 2$, which can also be written as $-2 < x < 2$.

Example

Let f be the function $f: x \rightarrow 2x + 3$ and g be the function $g: x \rightarrow -x^2 + 2x + 7$.

(a) Using the same axes and scale, draw the graph of f and the graph of g, for $-2 \leq x \leq 4, x \in \mathbb{R}$.

(b) Use your graphs to estimate:

(i) the maximum point of $g(x)$

(ii) the values of x such that $f(x) = g(x)$

(iii) the values of x such that $g(x) > f(x)$.

Solution

(a) We need a minimum of two points that satisfy the function $f: x \rightarrow 2x + 3$.

Solve for $(0, y)$ by setting $x = 0$, to find $y = f(0)$.

$f: x \rightarrow 2x + 3$

$f(x) = 2x + 3$

$f(0) = 2(0) + 3$

$f(0) = 3$

First point = (0, 3)

Solve for $(x, 0)$ by setting $y = f(x) = 0$ and solve for x.

$f: x \rightarrow 2x + 3$

$f(x) = 2x + 3 = 0$

$2x + 3 = 0$

$2x = -3$

$x = \frac{-3}{2} = -1{\cdot}5$

Second point = (−1·5, 0)

Set up a table for the function $g(x) = -x^2 + 2x + 7$:

Domain	$g(x) = -x^2 + 2x + 7$	Range	Coordinates
−2	$-(-2)^2 + 2(-2) + 7$	−1	(−2, −1)
−1	$-(-1)^2 + 2(-1) + 7$	4	(−1, 4)
0	$-(0)^2 + 2(0) + 7$	7	(0, 7)
1	$-(1)^2 + 2(1) + 7$	8	(1, 8)
2	$-(2)^2 + 2(2) + 7$	7	(2, 7)
3	$-(3)^2 + 2(3) + 7$	4	(3, 4)
4	$-(4)^2 + 2(4) + 7$	−1	(4, −1)

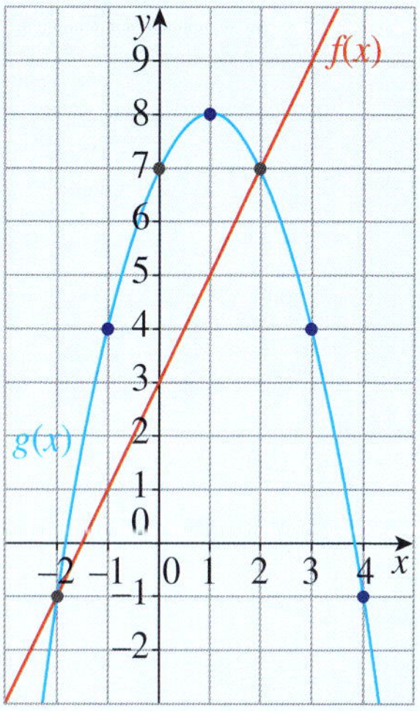

(b)

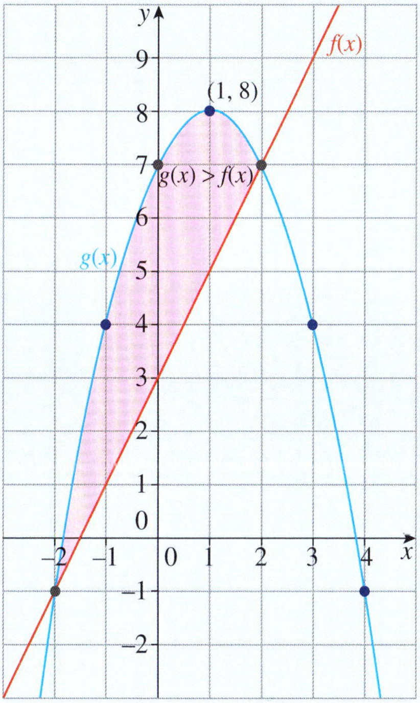

(i) The maximum point of $g(x)$ is (1, 8).

(ii) $f(x) = g(x)$ means find the points of intersection of the two functions.

The points of intersection are (−2, −1) and (2, 7).

(iii) $g(x) > f(x)$ means find the values of x where $f(x)$ is less than $g(x)$ (illustrated by the pink shaded area of the graph).

Answer: $-2 < x < 2$

Exponential graphs

Exponential functions

An **exponential function** is a function whose value is a constant raised to the power of x.

On the Junior Certificate course we will focus on exponential functions in the form $f(x) = a(2^x)$ or $f(x) = a(3^x)$, where $a \in \mathbb{N}, x \in \mathbb{R}$.

Exponential graphs

For exponential functions on the Junior Certificate course, an **exponential graph** will always:

1. Pass through the point $(0, a)$
2. Stay above the x-axis
3. Have an upward slope.

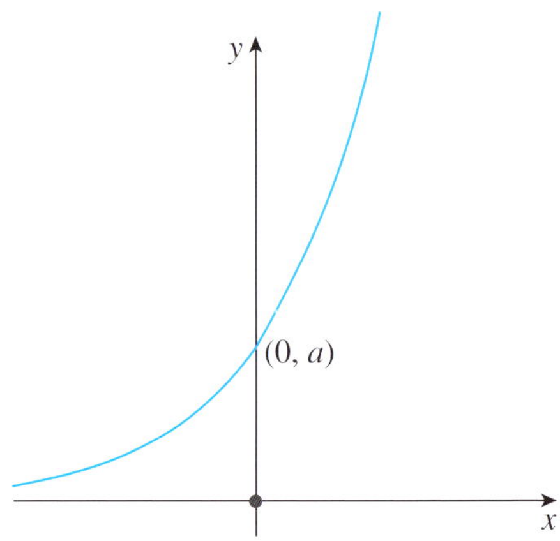

Top Tip

When graphing an exponential function, we generally follow these steps:

1. Set up and complete a table, solving the function $f(x) = a(2^x)$ or $f(x) = a(3^x)$, for a given domain / values of x.

Domain x	Function $f(x) = a(2^x)$ or $f(x) = a(3^x)$	Range y	Coordinates (x, y)

2. Plot these points on an x–y graph (use an appropriate scale).
3. Draw in the curve joining these points (extending the curve in both directions, making sure not to go below the x-axis).

Example

Draw a graph of the function $p(x) = 2^x$, in the domain $-3 < x < 3$.

Solution

Set up and complete a table in the given domain.

Domain	$f(x) = 2^x$	Range	Coordinates
−3	2^{-3}	$\frac{1}{8}$	$\left(-3, \frac{1}{8}\right)$
−2	2^{-2}	$\frac{1}{4}$	$\left(-2, \frac{1}{4}\right)$
−1	2^{-1}	$\frac{1}{2}$	$\left(-1, \frac{1}{2}\right)$
0	2^0	1	(0, 1)
1	2^1	2	(1, 2)
2	2^2	4	(2, 4)
3	2^3	8	(3, 8)

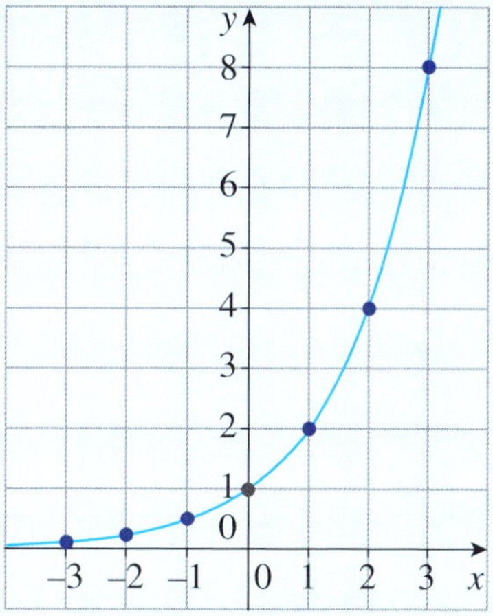

Transformations of linear, quadratic and exponential graphs

Transformations involve taking a parent function (original function) and moving it in some way to produce a new image.

Transformations of a linear function

Linear functions are in the form $f(x) = ax + b$, where $a, b \in \mathbb{Z}$, $x \in \mathbb{R}$.

Vertical shift

The new function will shift up or down the graph depending on its y-intercept and it will be parallel to the original linear function.

The function will:

1. Shift vertically up if the constant is positive.

   In general, if $y = f(x)$, then $y = f(x) + n$, where $n \in \mathbb{R}$, means the function $y = f(x)$ will move vertically **up** by n units.

2. Shift vertically down if the constant is a negative.

   In general, if $y = f(x)$, then $y = f(x) - n$, where $n \in \mathbb{R}$, means the function $y = f(x)$ will move vertically **down** by n units.

Example

Copy the graph of the function $y = f(x)$ in the domain $-4 < x < 4$, and on the same graph sketch the following translations:

(a) $f(x) + 4$ **(b)** $f(x) - 3$

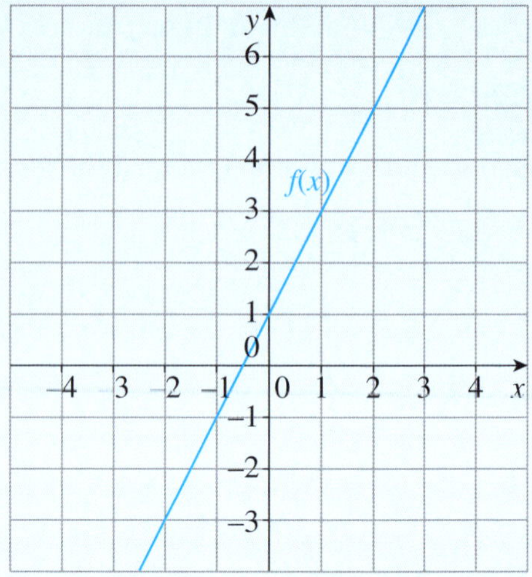

Solution

(a) The function $y = f(x)$ will move vertically **up** by 4 units and it will be parallel to the original function.

(b) The function $y = f(x)$ will move vertically **down** by 3 units and it will be parallel to the original function.

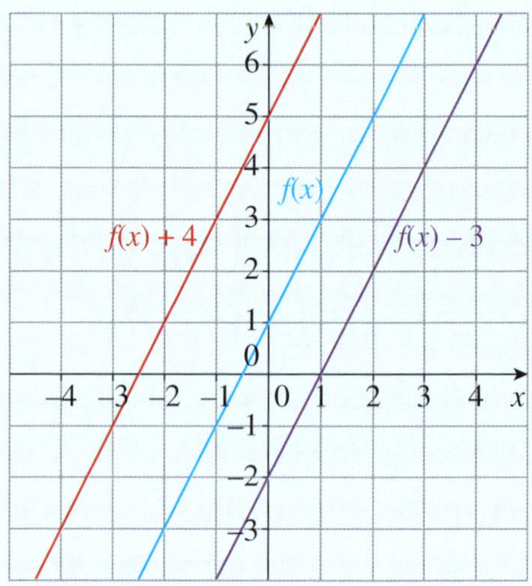

Transformations of a quadratic function

Quadratic functions are in the form $f(x) = ax^2 + bx + c$, where $a, b, c \in \mathbb{Z}, x \in \mathbb{R}$.

Vertical shift

When we add or subtract a constant to a quadratic function, the graph will remain the same shape but will:

1 Shift **up** if the constant is **positive**.

In general, if $y = f(x)$, then $y = f(x) + n$, where $n \in \mathbb{R}$, means the function $y = f(x)$ will move vertically **up** by n units.

2 Shift **down** if the constant is a **negative**.

In general, if $y = f(x)$, then $y = f(x) - n$, where $n \in \mathbb{R}$, means the function $y = f(x)$ will move vertically **down** by n units.

Example

Copy the graph of the function $y = f(x)$, in the domain $-3 < x < 4$ and on the same graph sketch the following translations:

(a) $f(x) + 5$

(b) $f(x) - 2$

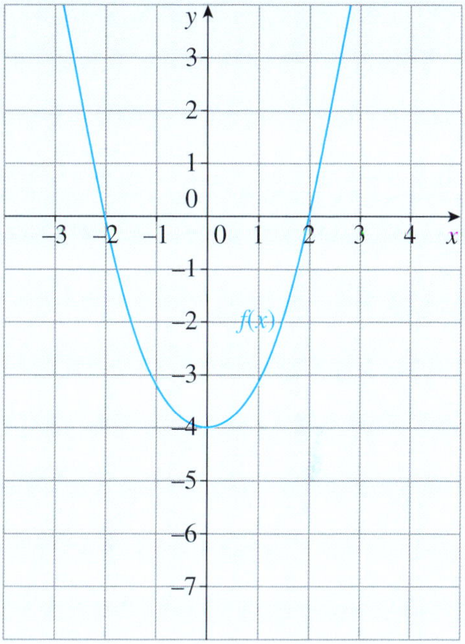

Solution

(a) Sketch $f(x) + 5$, means the function $y = f(x)$ will move vertically **up** by 5 units and will remain the **same shape**.

(b) Sketch $f(x) - 2$, means the function $y = f(x)$ will move vertically **down** by 2 units and will remain the **same shape**.

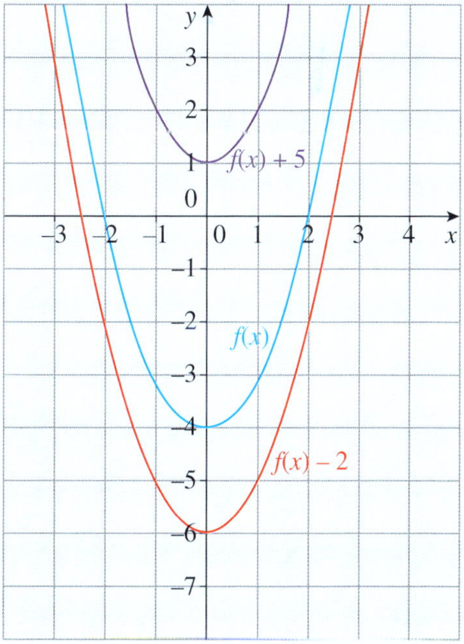

Horizontal shift

When we add or subtract a constant to the input of a quadratic function, the graph will remain the same shape but will:

1. Shift to the left, if the constant is positive.

   In general, if $y = f(x)$, then $y = f(x + n)$, where $n \in \mathbb{R}$, means the function $y = f(x)$ will move **horizontally to the left by n units**.

2. Shift to the right, if the constant is a negative.

   In general, if $y = f(x)$, then $y = f(x - n)$, where $n \in \mathbb{R}$, means the function $y = f(x)$ will move **horizontally to the right by n units**.

Example

Copy the graph of the function $y = f(x)$ and on the same graph sketch the following translations:

(a) $f(x + 3)$

(b) $f(x - 2)$

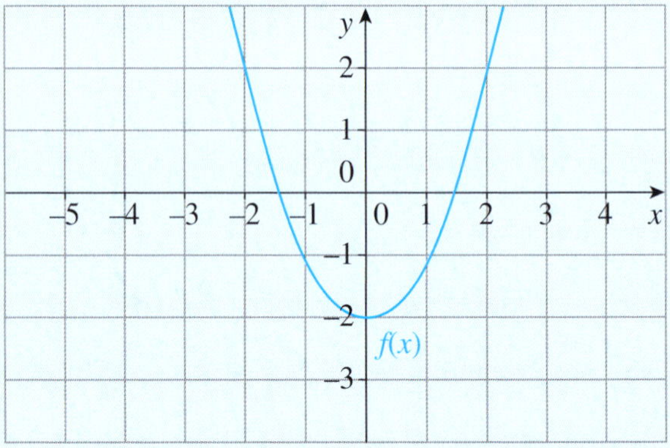

Solution

(a) The function $y = f(x)$ will move horizontally to the **left** by 3 units.

(b) The function $y = f(x)$ will move horizontally to the **right** by 2 units.

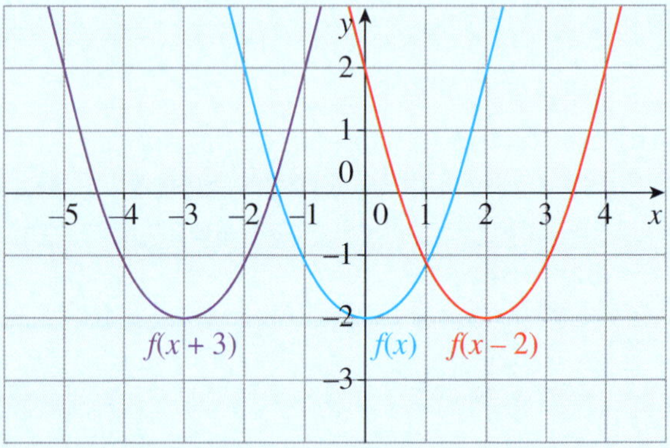

Exercise

Q1 **(a)** Graph the functions $f: x \rightarrow 4x + 8$ and $g: x \rightarrow -x - 2$ using the same axes and scale, in the domain $-1 \leq x \leq 6$.

(b) From your graphs, estimate each of the following:

(i) The values of g such that $g(x) = 2$

(ii) $f(-4)$

(iii) The value of x, such that $f(x) = g(x)$.

Q2 Let h be the function $h: x \rightarrow -x + 3$, and g be the function $g: x \rightarrow -x^2 + 4x + 3$.

(a) Using the same axes and scale, draw the graph of h and the graph of g, for $-2 \leq x \leq 6, x \in \mathbb{R}$.

(b) Use your graph to estimate:

(i) the maximum point of $g(x)$

(ii) the values of x such that $h(x) = g(x)$

(iii) the values of x such that $h(x) \leq g(x)$.

Q3 Draw a graph of the function $q(x) = 2(3^x)$, in the domain $-2 \leq x \leq 1, x \in \mathbb{R}$.

Q4 Copy the graph of the function $y = g(x)$ in the domain $-3 < x < 4$, and on the same graph sketch the following translations:

(a) $g(x) - 5$

(b) $g(x) + 3$

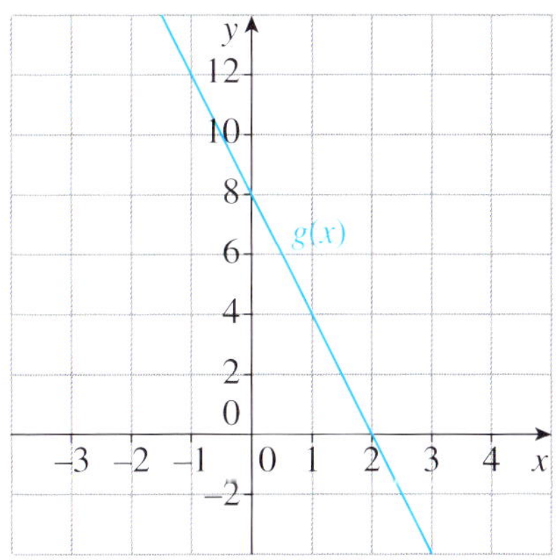

Q5 Copy the graph of the function $y = q(x)$ in the domain $-3 < x < 3$, and on the same graph sketch the following translations:

(a) $q(x) - 4$

(b) $q(x) + 4$

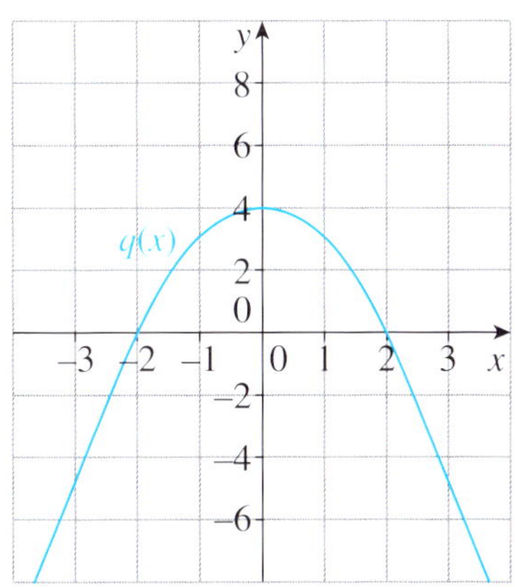

Q6 Copy the graph of the function $y = f(x)$, and on the same graph sketch the following translations:

(a) $f(x - 3)$

(b) $f(x + 2)$

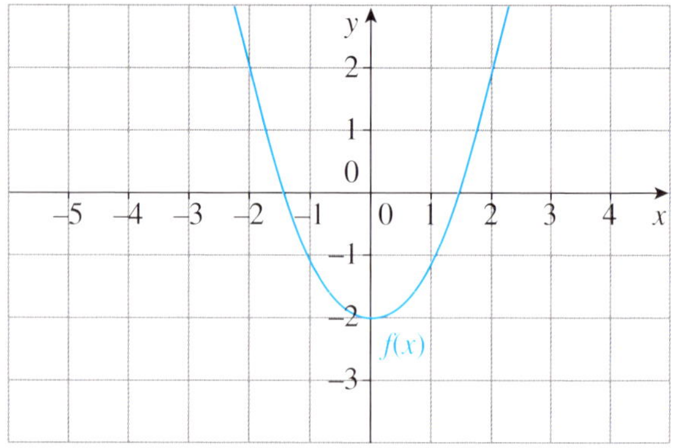

Q7 **(a)** Let f be the function $f: x \rightarrow 5x - 4$, and g be the function $g: x \rightarrow 3x + 1$.

Using the same axes and scale, draw the graph of f and the graph of g, for $0 \leq x \leq 3, x \in \mathbb{R}$.

(b) From your graphs, write down the coordinates of the point of intersection of the two lines.

Q8 Let f be the function $f(x) = 2x^2 + x - 15$.

(a) Draw the graph of f for $-4 \leq x \leq 3, x \in \mathbb{R}$.

(b) Use your graph to find the minimum value of $f(x)$.

(c) Use your graph to find the range of values of x for which $f(x) \geq 0$.

Solutions

Q1 **(a)** For each function, we need a minimum of two points that satisfy it.

For the function $f: x \rightarrow 4x + 8$:

- Solve for $(0, y)$ by setting $x = 0$, to find $y = f(0)$.

  $f(x) = 4x + 8$

  $f(0) = 4(0) + 8 = 8$

  The 1st point is (0, 8).

- Solve for $(x, 0)$ by setting $y = f(x) = 0$ and solve for x.

  $f(x) = 4x + 8 = 0$

  $4x + 8 = 0$

  $4x = -8$

  $x = -2$

  The 2nd point is (−2, 0).

For the function $g: x \rightarrow -x - 2$:

- Solve for $(0, y)$ by setting $x = 0$, to find $y = g(0)$

  $g(x) = -x - 2$

  $g(0) = -(0) - 2 = -2$

  The 1st point is (0, −2).

- Solve for $(x, 0)$ by setting $y = g(x) = 0$ and solve for x.

  $g(x) = -x - 2 = 0$

  $-x - 2 = 0$

  $x = -2$

  The 2nd point is (−2, 0).

- Plot these points on an x–y graph in the given domain.
- Draw in the line joining these points (extending the line in both directions).

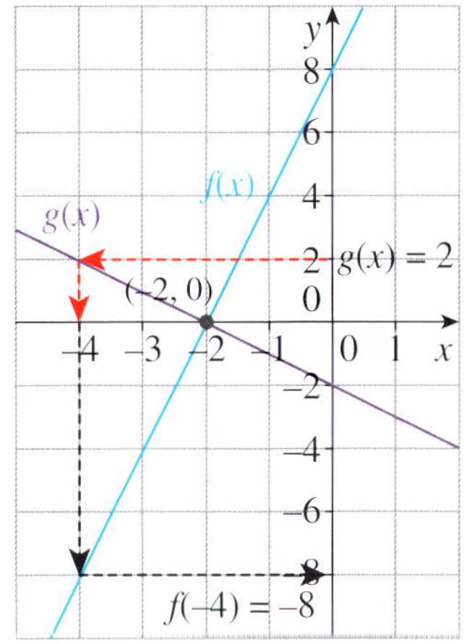

(b) **(i)** $f(-4)$ means find the value of y when $x = -4$.

$f(-4) = -8$

(ii) $g(x) = 2$ means find where the function cuts the line $y = 2$.

$g(-4) = 2$

(iii) $f(x) = g(x)$ means find the point of intersection of the two functions.

The point of intersection is $(-2, 0)$.

Q2 **(a)** For each function, we need a minimum of two points that satisfy it.

For the function $h : x \to -x + 3$:

- Solve for $(0, y)$ by setting $x = 0$, to find $y = h(0)$

$h(x) = -x + 3$

$h(0) = -(0) + 3 = 3$

The 1st point is $(0, 3)$.

- Solve for $(x, 0)$ by setting $y = h(x) = 0$ and solve for x.

$h(x) = -x + 3 = 0$

$-x + 3 = 0$

$x = 3$

The 2nd point is $(3, 0)$.

For the function $g : x \to -x^2 + 4x + 3$:

Domain	$g : x \to -x^2 + 4x + 3$	**Range**	**Coordinates**
−2	$-(-2)^2 + 4(-2) + 3$	−9	(−2, −9)
−1	$-(-1)^2 + 4(-1) + 3$	−2	(−1, −2)
0	$-(0)^2 + 4(0) + 3$	3	(0, 3)
1	$-(1)^2 + 4(1) + 3$	6	(1, 6)
2	$-(2)^2 + 4(2) + 3$	7	(2, 7)
3	$-(3)^2 + 4(3) + 3$	6	(3, 6)
4	$-(4)^2 + 4(4) + 3$	3	(4, 3)
5	$-(5)^2 + 4(5) + 3$	−2	(5, −2)
6	$-(6)^2 + 4(6) + 3$	−9	(6, −9)

(b) **(i)** The maximum point of $g(x)$ is (2, 7).

(ii) $h(x) = g(x)$ means find the points of intersection of the two functions.

The points of intersection are (0, 3) and (5, −2).

(iii) $h(x) \leq g(x)$ means find the values of x for which $h(x)$ is less than or equal to $g(x)$.

Answer: $0 \leq x \leq 5$

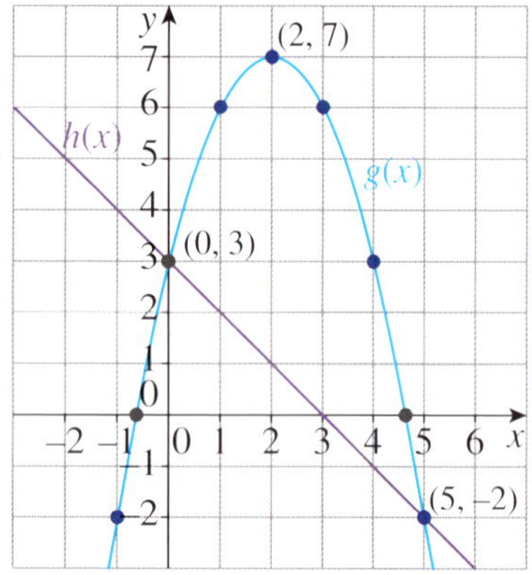

Q3 Set up and complete a table in the given domain.

Domain	$q(x) = 2(3^x)$	Range	Coordinates
−2	$2(3^{-2})$	$\frac{2}{9}$	$\left(-2, \frac{2}{9}\right)$
−1	$2(3^{-1})$	$\frac{2}{3}$	$\left(-1, \frac{2}{3}\right)$
0	$2(3^{0})$	2	(0, 2)
1	$2(3^{1})$	6	(1, 6)

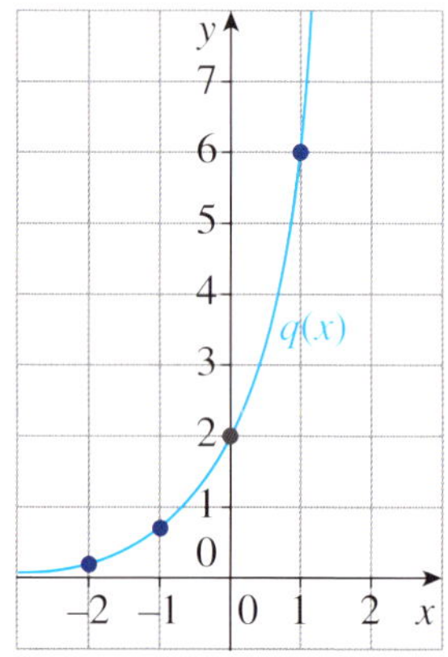

Q4 **(a)** The function $y = g(x)$ will move vertically down by 5 units and it will be parallel to the original function.

(b) The function $y = g(x)$ will move vertically up by 3 units and it will be parallel to the original function.

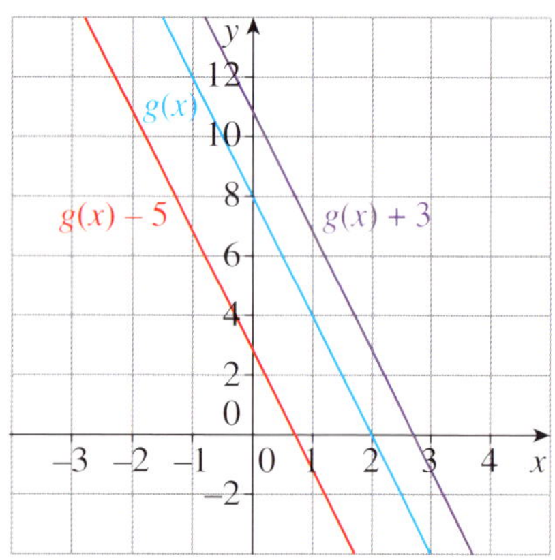

Q5 **(a)** The function $y - q(x)$ will move vertically down by 4 units and it will remain the same shape as the original function.

(b) The function $y = q(x)$ will move vertically up by 4 units and it will remain the same shape as the original function.

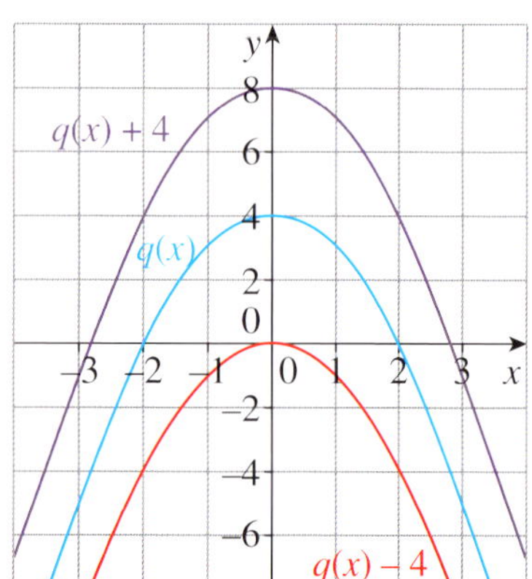

Q6 (a) The function $y = f(x)$ will move horizontally to the right by 3 units.

(b) The function $y = f(x)$ will move horizontally to the left by 2 units.

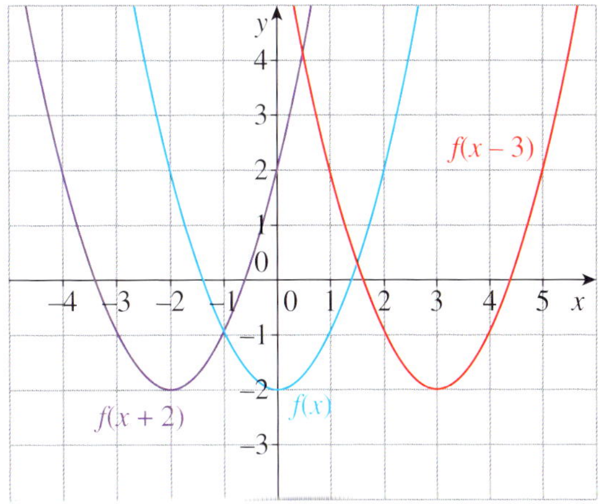

Q7 (a)

Domain	$f(x) = 5x - 4$	Range	Coordinates
0	5(0) – 4	–4	(0, –4)
1	5(1) – 4	1	(1, 1)
2	5(2) – 4	6	(2, 6)
3	5(3) – 4	11	(3, 11)

Domain	$g(x) = 3x + 1$	Range	Coordinates
0	3(0) + 1	1	(0, 1)
1	3(1) + 1	4	(1, 4)
2	3(2) + 1	7	(2, 7)
3	3(3) + 1	10	(3, 10)

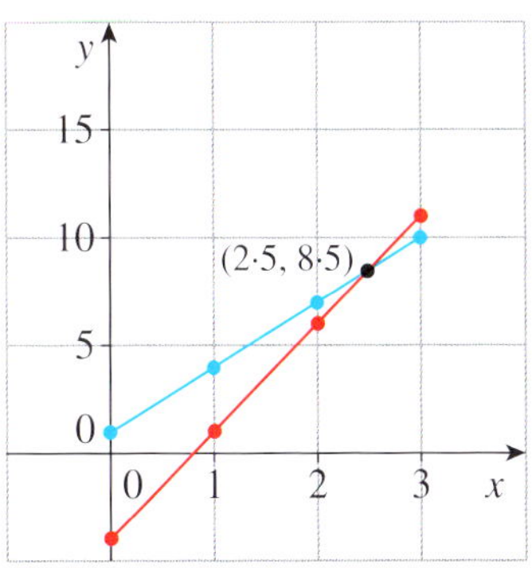

(b) Point of intersection: (2·5, 8·5)

Q8 (a)

Domain	$f(x) = 2x^2 + x - 15$	Range	Coordinates
−4	$2(-4)^2 + (-4) - 15$	13	(−4, 13)
−3	$2(-3)^2 + (-3) - 15$	0	(−3, 0)
−2	$2(-2)^2 + (-2) - 15$	−9	(−2, −9)
−1	$2(-1)^2 + (-1) - 15$	−14	(−1, −14)
0	$2(0)^2 + (0) - 15$	−15	(0, −15)
1	$2(1)^2 + (1) - 15$	−12	(1, −12)
2	$2(2)^2 + (2) - 15$	−5	(2, −5)
3	$2(3)^2 + (3) - 15$	6	(3, 6)

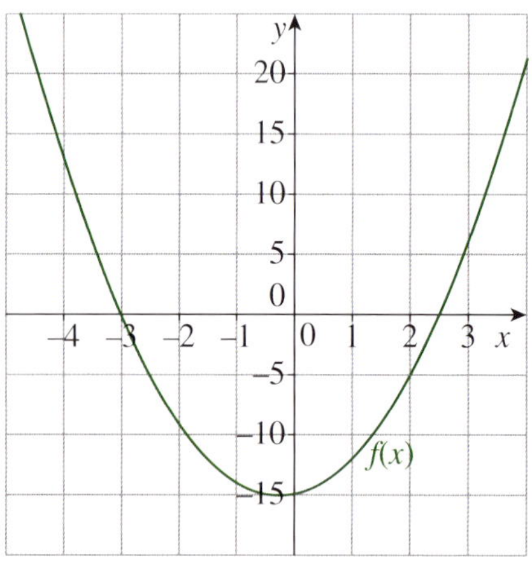

(b) Minimum value of $f(x) \simeq -15{\cdot}1$

(c)

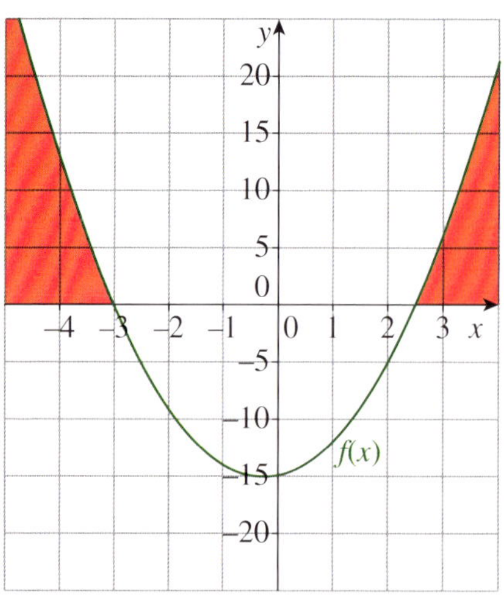

$f(x) \geq 0$ when $x \leq -3$ and $x \geq 2{\cdot}5$

Patterns 15

Learning objectives

In this chapter you will learn about:

- Patterns and number sequences
- How to recognise linear, quadratic and exponential patterns
- How to represent patterns using tables, diagrams and graphs
- How to generate arithmetic expressions from repeating patterns
- How to generate formulae from patterns or terms in a sequence.

Patterns

Point to note

A pattern is a set of objects, numbers, letters, shapes, pictures, symbols or diagrams which repeat in a set way.

Example

Complete the following patterns:

(a)  __

(b) 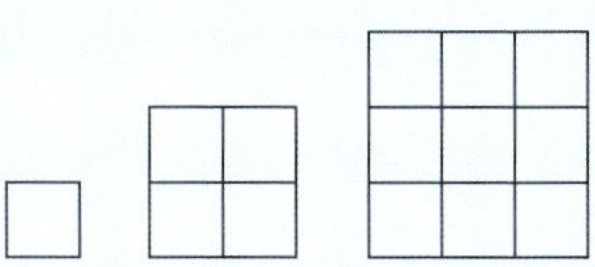 _____ _____

(c)  _____ _____

(d) Mary, Paul, Peter, Sean, Mary, ____, Peter, ____

Solution

(a) 

(b)

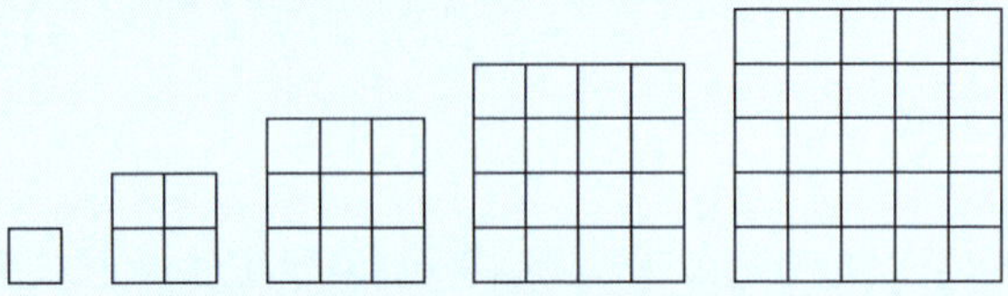

(c)

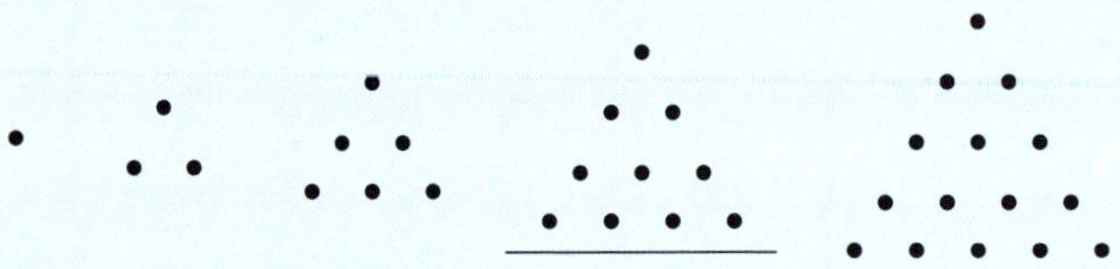

(d) Mary, Paul, Peter, Sean, Mary, <u>Paul</u>, Peter, <u>Sean</u>

Example

A four-shape repeating pattern is shown below:

(a) If the pattern continued, what would the 12th shape be?

(b) If the pattern continued, what would the 130th shape be?

(c) If the pattern continued, what would the 53rd shape be?

(d) If the pattern continued, what would the 963rd shape be?

Solution

The pattern repeats every 4th shape, so the pattern shape is found from the remainder:

Remainder	Shape
$\frac{1}{4}$	
$\frac{2}{4}$	
$\frac{3}{4}$	
0	

(a) $\frac{12}{4} = 3$. There is no remainder, so the shape is .

(b) $\frac{130}{4} = 32\frac{2}{4}$. The shape is 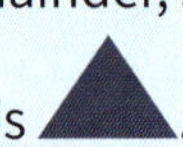.

(c) $\frac{53}{4} = 13\frac{1}{4}$. The shape is .

(d) $\frac{963}{4} = 240\frac{3}{4}$. The shape is .

Link
Chapter 1: Number

Example

In a number pyramid we add the two numbers in the lower blocks to find the number in the block above.

Complete the number pyramid by filling in the empty spaces.

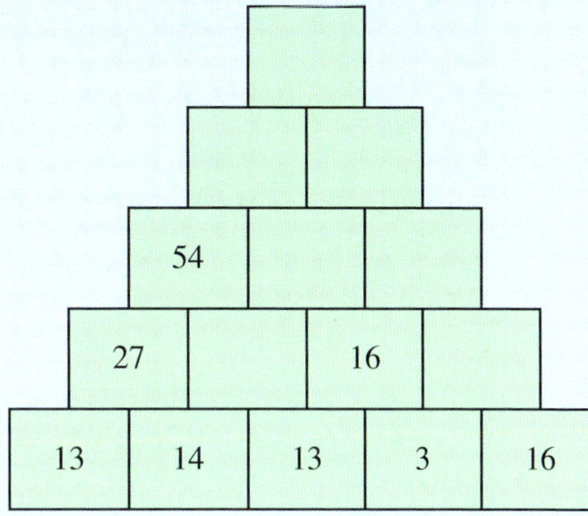

Solution

Start from the bottom row of blocks and work up to the top of the pyramid.

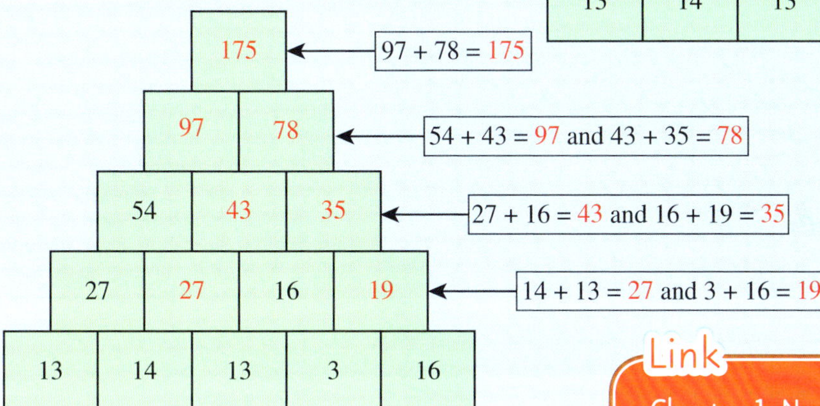

Link
Chapter 1: Number

Number sequences

Points to note

A **number sequence** is a pattern of numbers given in a definite order and connected by some rule.

A **linear/arithmetic sequence** is a sequence where:

- each term after the first term is found by adding or subtracting a constant
- the first difference is a constant value, d. The value of d is found from:

$$\text{Any term} - \text{previous term} = T_n - T_{n-1} = d$$

- the general term can be found using the formula: $T_n = a + (n - 1)d$ (given in the *Formulae and Tables* booklet), where: T_n = nth term, a = first term, n = term number and d = common difference.

Example: 1, 4, 7, 10, 13, 16…

A **quadratic sequence** is a sequence where:

- the nth term contains n^2 as the highest power
- the general form is $T_n = an^2 + bn + c$, where $a, b, c \in \mathbb{R}$
- the second difference is a constant value
- the value of a is: $a = \dfrac{\text{second difference}}{2}$.

Example: 1, 4, 9, 16, 25, 36...

An **exponential sequence** is a sequence where:

- the nth term contains n as the highest power, e.g. a^n
- the general form is $T_n = ar^{n-1}$, where $a, r, n \in \mathbb{R}$
- each consecutive term can be found by multiplying the previous term by a constant.

Example: 1, 2, 4, 8, 16, 32, 64...

Note: The Junior Certificate course only examines doubling and trebling exponential sequences.

Example

(a) Complete the following number sequences:

(i) 103, 93, 83, ___, 63, ___, ___, 33

(ii) 3, 6, 9, 12, 15, 18, 21, ___, 27, ___

(iii) 1, 2, 4, 8, 16, ___, 64, ___, 256

(iv) 1, 1, 2, 3, 5, ___, 13, 21, ___

(v) 1, 4, 9, 16, ___, 36, 49, ___, 81

(vi) 1, 3, ___, 27, 81, ___, 729

(b) Hence, state whether each sequence is linear, quadratic, exponential or none of these.

Solution

(a) **(i)** 103, 93, 83, <u>73</u>, 63, <u>53</u>, <u>43</u>, 33 — Starting with 103, subtract 10 to get the next number.

(ii) 3, 6, 9, 12, 15, 18, 21, <u>24</u>, 27, <u>30</u> — Starting with 3, add 3 to get the next number.

(iii) 1, 2, 4, 8, 16, <u>32</u>, 64, <u>128</u>, 256 — Starting with 1, multiply by 2 to get the next number.

(iv) 1, 1, 2, 3, 5, <u>8</u>, 13, 21, <u>34</u> — Add the two previous numbers together to get the next number.

(v) 1, 4, 9, 16, <u>25</u>, 36, 49, <u>64</u>, 81 — Square each consecutive natural number to get the terms in the sequence.

(vi) 1, 3, <u>9</u>, 27, 81, <u>243</u>, 729 — Starting with 1, multiply by 3 to get the next number.

(b) Sequences **(i)** and **(ii)** are linear or arithmetic sequences, as we add or subtract the same number each time.

Sequences **(iii)** and **(vi)** are exponential sequences, as we multiply each consecutive term by 2 and 3, respectively. Sequence **(iii)** is 2^{n-1} and sequence **(vi)** is 3^{n-1}.

Sequence **(iv)** is neither linear, quadratic nor exponential. The numbers in this sequence are called the **Fibonacci numbers** and they are found by adding the two previous numbers together to get the next one.

Sequence **(v)** is a quadratic sequence, as each term is found by squaring each natural number.

Link
Chapter 1: Number
Chapter 14: Functions 2

Example

List the first three terms of each sequence:

(a) $T_n = 3n - 1$ **(b)** $T_n = n^2 + 2n - 5$ **(c)** $T_n = \frac{1}{2}(3^n)$

Solution

(a) $T_n = 3n - 1$

$n = 1 \Rightarrow T_1 = 3(1) - 1$
$\Rightarrow T_1 = 3 - 1$
$\Rightarrow T_1 = 2$

$n = 2 \Rightarrow T_2 = 3(2) - 1$
$\Rightarrow T_2 = 6 - 1$
$\Rightarrow T_2 = 5$

$n = 3 \Rightarrow T_3 = 3(3) - 1$
$\Rightarrow T_3 = 9 - 1$
$\Rightarrow T_3 = 8$

Answer: 2, 5, 8

(b) $T_n = n^2 + 2n - 5$

$n = 1 \Rightarrow T_1 = (1)^2 + 2(1) - 5$
$\Rightarrow T_1 = 1 + 2 - 5$
$\Rightarrow T_1 = -2$

$n = 2 \Rightarrow T_2 = (2)^2 + 2(2) - 5$
$\Rightarrow T_2 = 4 + 4 - 5$
$\Rightarrow T_2 = 3$

$n = 3 \Rightarrow T_3 = (3)^2 + 2(3) - 5$
$\Rightarrow T_3 = 9 + 6 - 5$
$\Rightarrow T_3 = 10$

Answer: −2, 3, 10

(c) $T_n = \frac{1}{2}(3^n)$

$n = 1 \Rightarrow T_1 = \frac{1}{2}(3^1)$
$\Rightarrow T_1 = \frac{3}{2}$

$n = 2 \Rightarrow T_2 = \frac{1}{2}(3^2)$
$\Rightarrow T_2 = \frac{9}{2}$

$n = 3 \Rightarrow T_3 = \frac{1}{2}(3^3)$
$\Rightarrow T_3 = \frac{27}{2}$

Answer: $\frac{3}{2}, \frac{9}{2}, \frac{27}{2}$

Link
Chapter 3: Algebra 1

How to recognise and represent linear, quadratic and exponential patterns

Points to note

To recognise linear, quadratic and exponential patterns using differencing:

Pattern type	How to recognise this pattern type
Linear	First difference is constant.
Quadratic	Second difference is constant.
Exponential	Each consecutive term is multiplied by a common factor.

Example

Fiona finds the volumes of five different cylinders. Each has a height of K centimetres.

(a) Complete the table to show the volume of each of the five cylinders.
Give each answer in terms of π and K.

Radius of cylinder (cm)	Height of cylinder (cm)	Volume of cylinder (cm^3)
1	K	
2	K	
3	K	$9\pi K$
4	K	
5	K	

(b) Is the sequence of volumes in the table linear, quadratic, exponential, or none of these? Justify your answer fully.

(SEC 2016)

Solution

(a) The formula for the volume of a cylinder is given in the *Formulae and Tables* booklet as $V = \pi r^2 h$.

Radius of cylinder (cm)	Height of cylinder (cm)	Volume of cylinder (cm^3)
1	K	$1\pi K$
2	K	$4\pi K$
3	K	$9\pi K$
4	K	$16\pi K$
5	K	$25\pi K$

(b)

Radius of cylinder (cm)	Height of cylinder (cm)	Volume of cylinder (cm^3)	First difference	Second difference
1	K	$1\pi K$		
2	K	$4\pi K$	$3\pi K$	
3	K	$9\pi K$	$5\pi K$	$2\pi K$
4	K	$16\pi K$	$7\pi K$	$2\pi K$
5	K	$25\pi K$	$9\pi K$	$2\pi K$

The sequence of volumes of the cylinder:

- is **not** linear as the first difference is not constant
- is **quadratic** as the second difference is constant
- is **not** exponential as each consecutive term is not multipled by a constant, thus each term in the sequence cannot be written in the form a^n.

Link

RW2 Chapter 13: Applied Measure

Point to note

A question on patterns was examined in both Papers 1 and 2 in 2016.

How to recognise linear, quadratic or exponential patterns from a graph

If a pattern is:

- **linear**, the graph will be a straight line.
- **quadratic**, the graph will be a curve/parabola. It will either be '∪-shaped' or '∩-shaped' and will be symmetrical about the maximum/minimum turning point.
- **exponential**, then the graph will be a curve where the slope will begin less steep and get increasingly steeper as the value of x increases, or the slope will start off steep and get less steep as the value of x increases.

Each sequence type is shown on the graph.

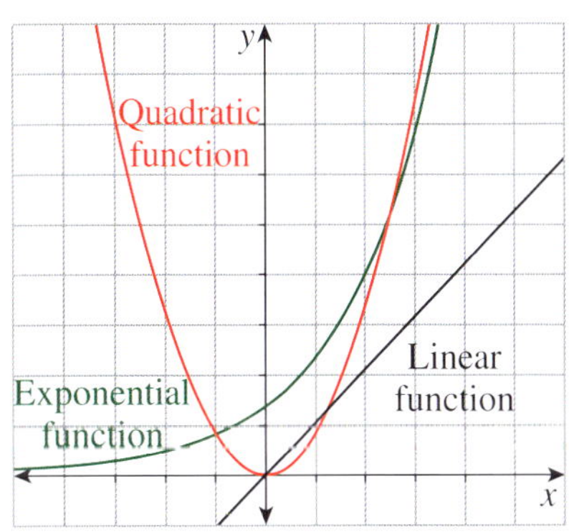

Example

Three experiments on temperature are done in the science lab. Pupils record and plot the temperature of each experiment each hour, for five hours. In experiment A, the temperature doubles every hour. In experiment B, the temperature increases by 2° every hour. In experiment C, the temperature increases by 3° each hour for three hours and then remains constant. Identify each experiment by its number.

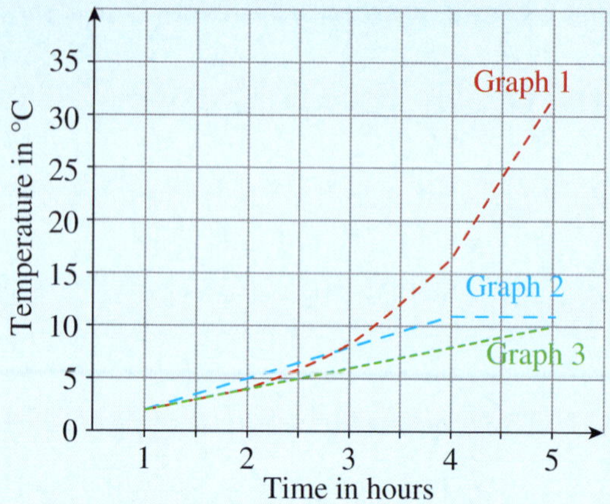

Experiment	Graph
A	
B	
C	

Solution

- In experiment A, the temperature doubles every hour. This indicates that the pattern is exponential. The exponential graph is Graph 1.
- In experiment B, the temperature increases by 2° every hour. This indicates that the pattern is linear. The linear graph is Graph 3.
- In experiment C, the temperature increases by 3° each hour for three hours and then remains constant. This indicates that the pattern is linear for three hours and then the temperature remains constant (the same). The graph which is linear for the first three hours and then stops increasing (flattens) thereafter is Graph 2.

Experiment	Graph
A	1
B	3
C	2

(SEC 2012)

Generating formulae from repeating patterns

Example

The following patterns are made of toothpicks.

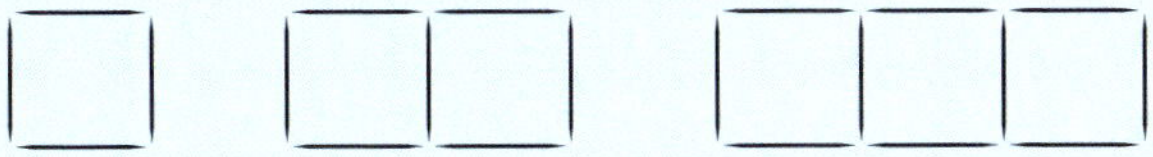

(a) Draw pattern 4.

Look at the pattern of the toothpicks.

(b) How many extra toothpicks do you add each time?

(c) Complete this sentence: 'One rule for the number of toothpicks in a pattern is to start with 4 and add ____ toothpicks for every additional term.'

(d) How many toothpicks will there be in pattern 6?

(e) How many toothpicks will there be in pattern 10?

(f) How many toothpicks will there be in pattern 100?

(g) Can you give a rule for the number of toothpicks if you are given any pattern number?

(h) What is the pattern in symbols? Let m = number of toothpicks and n = the pattern number.

(i) Copy and complete this table:

Pattern number	Toothpicks	
	Number	Pattern
1		
2		
3		
4		
Any number		
50		
200		

(j) Sarah suggested that another rule for the toothpicks is: '3 times the number of the pattern and add 1.' Verify this for the first four patterns. Is it true?

(k) Peter used 34 toothpicks to make a pattern. Find the number of the pattern.

Solution

(a) Pattern 4:

(b) Add 3 toothpicks each time.

(c) One rule for the number of toothpicks in a pattern is to start with 4 and add 3 toothpicks for every additional term.

(d) $4 + 3 + 3 + 3 + 3 + 3 = 19$ toothpicks in pattern 6.

(e) $4 + 9(3) = 4 + 27 = 31$ toothpicks in pattern 10.

(f) $4 + (100 - 1)(3) = 4 + (99)(3) = 4 + 297 = 301$ toothpicks in pattern 100.

(g) Rule: number of toothpicks = 4 + 3 × (number of the pattern less 1).

(h) Rule using symbols: $m = 4 + 3(n - 1)$.

(i)

Pattern number	Toothpicks	
	Number	**Pattern**
1	4	4
2	7	$4 + 3$
3	10	$4 + 3 + 3$
4	13	$4 + 3 + 3 + 3$
Any number, n	$4 + 3(n - 1)$	4 + 3 × (number of the pattern less 1)
50	151	$4 + (3 \times 49) = 151$
200	601	$4 + (3 \times 199) = 601$

(j) Check to see if Sarah's rule works for the first 4 patterns.

Pattern number	Actual number of toothpicks	Number of toothpicks using Sarah's rule: '3 times the number of the pattern and add 1'
1	4	$3(1) + 1 = 4$ ✓
2	7	$3(2) + 1 = 7$ ✓
3	10	$3(3) + 1 = 10$ ✓
4	13	$3(4) + 1 = 13$ ✓

Sarah's rule works for the first four patterns, so it is true.

(k) Let $m = 34$ (number of toothpicks) and n = the pattern number.

$m = 4 + 3(n - 1)$ Substitute $m = 34$ into the formula and expand the RHS.

$\Rightarrow 34 = 4 + 3n - 3$

$\Rightarrow 34 = 1 + 3n$ Subtract 1 from both sides.

$\Rightarrow 34 - 1 = 3n$

$\Rightarrow 33 = 3n$ Divide by 3.

$\Rightarrow n = \frac{33}{3} = 11$

The pattern number is 11.

Example

The first five numbers in a pattern of numbers are given in the table.

(a) (i) Follow the pattern in the table to write the next three numbers into the table.

(ii) Use the data in the table to show that the pattern is quadratic.

(b) $T_n = n^2 + bn + c$, where $b, c \in \mathbb{Z}$. Find the values of b and c.

Term	Number
T_1	13
T_2	15
T_3	19
T_4	25
T_5	33
T_6	
T_7	
T_8	

Solution

(a) (i) To fill in the table:

- Insert two columns and label them: 'First difference' and 'Second difference'.
- Find the first and second differences.
- Find the values of T_6, T_7 and T_8.

	Term	Number	First difference	Second difference
	T_1	13		
	T_2	15	+2	
	T_3	19	+4	+2
	T_4	25	+6	+2
	T_5	33	+8	+2
33 + 10 = 43	T_6	43	+10	+2
43 + 12 = 55	T_7	55	+12	+2
55 + 14 = 69	T_8	69	+14	+2

(ii) The pattern is quadratic as the second difference is constant, as shown in the table.

(b) The sequence is of the form $T_n = n^2 + bn + c$, where the values of b and c need to be found.

Note: $a = \frac{\text{second difference}}{2} = \frac{2}{2} = 1$. This shows that the coefficient of n^2 is 1.

Use the information given in the table and $T_n = n^2 + bn + c$ to write two equations in b and c.

For equation 1:
Substitute $T_1 = 13$ and $n = 1$.

$(1)^2 + b(1) + c = 13$

$\Rightarrow b + c = 12 \qquad (1)$

For equation 2:
Substitute $T_2 = 15$ and $n = 2$.

$(2)^2 + b(2) + c = 15$

$\Rightarrow 4 + 2b + c = 15$

$\Rightarrow 2b + c = 11 \qquad (2)$

- Solve the simultaneous equations, to find the values of b and c.
- Eliminate c: equation (1) × −1, plus equation (2):

$$\begin{array}{rll} & -b - c = -12 & (1) \times -1 \\ + & \underline{2b + c = 11} & (2) \\ & b = -1 & \end{array}$$

- Find the value of c:

$b + c = 12$ Substitute $b = -1$ into equation (1).

$\Rightarrow -1 + c = 12$

$\Rightarrow c = 12 + 1$

$\Rightarrow c = 13$

The quadratic sequence is of the form $T_n = n^2 - n + 13$.

Exercise

Q1 List the next three terms in each pattern below:

(a) 

(b) 

(c) 

Q2 For each of the sequences below:

(a) List the next term in the sequence.

(b) Write down the 10th term in the sequence.

(c) Write down the general formula for the nth term.

(d) State whether the sequence is linear, quadratic, exponential or none of these.

(i) 11, 22, 33, 44, … **(iii)** 1, 4, 9, 16, …

(ii) 3, 7, 11, 15, … **(iv)** 2, 4, 8, 16, …

Q3 A four-card repeating pattern is shown below, where the Ace represents the number 1:

(a) Describe how the pattern repeats in words.

(b) Predict the 9th card if this pattern continues.

(c) Predict the 16th card if this pattern continues.

(d) Predict the 202nd card if this pattern continues.

(e) Predict the 503rd card if this pattern continues.

Q4 In the 100-square grid here, some of the squares are coloured green.

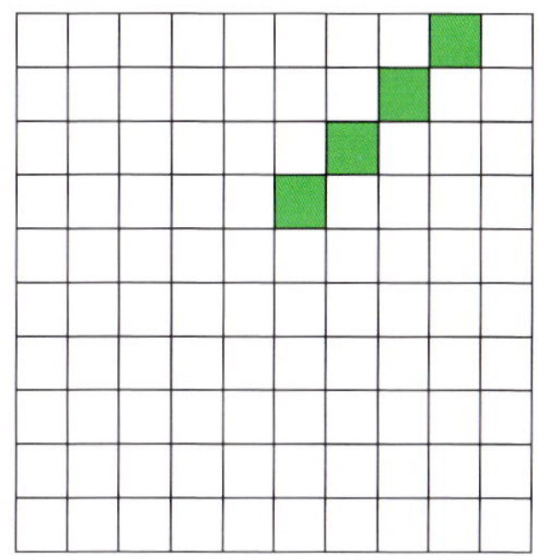

(a) Copy the grid and continue the pattern.

(b) Counting the grid from left to right, write down the numbers that represent the green squares.

(c) In words, write down what you notice about the numbers in the green squares.

If the grid was to expand and continue:

(d) What colour would the 118th square be?

(e) What colour would the 180th square be?

(f) What colour would the 903rd square be?

Q5 Complete the number pyramid by filling in the empty spaces.

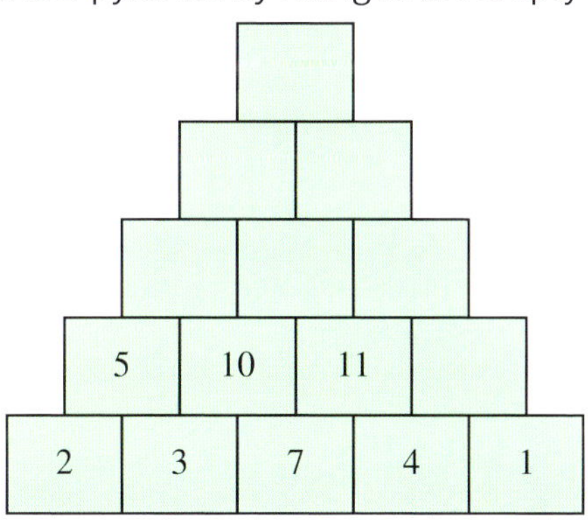

Q6 (a) Fill in all empty spaces in the number pyramid in terms of x.

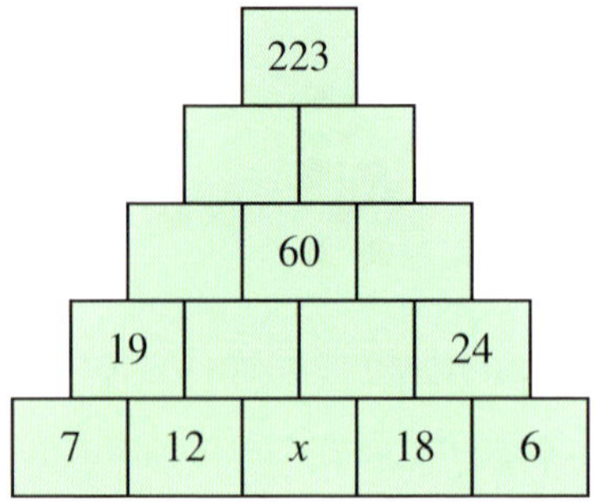

(b) Solve for x.

(c) Substitute x for all unknown values to complete the number pyramid.

Q7 List the first three terms of each sequence:

(a) $T_n = 2n^2 - 3$ **(b)** $T_n = 5n - 7$ **(c)** $T_n = 3(2^n)$

Q8 (a) Fill in the first difference and the second difference for each pattern.

(i) Pattern 1: 2 4 9 17 28

First difference: (Change) ☐ ☐ ☐ ☐

Second difference: (Change of change) ☐ ☐ ☐

(ii) Pattern 2: −1 2 5 8 11

First difference: (Change) ☐ ☐ ☐ ☐

Second difference: (Change of change) ☐ ☐ ☐

(iii) Pattern 3: 6 12 24 48 96

First difference: (Change) ☐ ☐ ☐ ☐

Second difference: (Change of change) ☐ ☐ ☐

(b) State whether each pattern is linear, quadratic or exponential. Give a reason for each answer.

(SEC 2014)

Q9 The first three stages of a pattern are shown below. Each stage is made up of a certain number of shaded discs and a certain number of white discs.

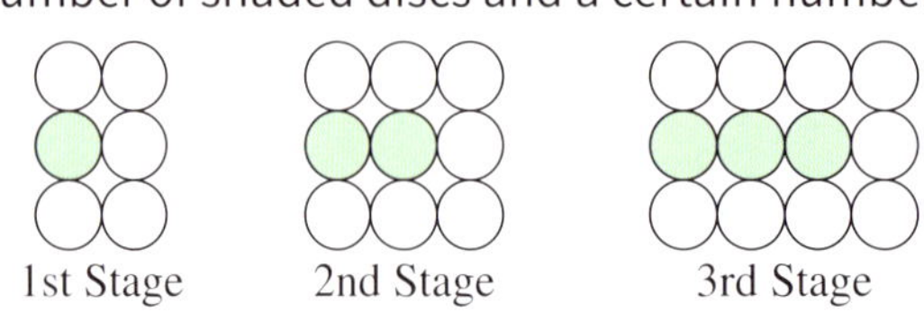

(a) Shade in the appropriate discs to show the 4th stage of the pattern.

(b) Complete the table to show how the pattern continues.

(c) In a particular stage of the pattern, there are 21 white discs. How many shaded discs are there in this stage of the pattern?

(d) Write down the relationship between the number of shaded discs and the number of white discs in each stage of the pattern. State clearly the meaning of any letters you use.

Number of shaded discs	Number of white discs
1	5
2	
3	
4	
5	
6	

(SEC 2014)

Q10 Melissa bought a horse in 2007 for €500. She took the horse to the sales each year for three years to have it valued but did not sell. She recorded the values on the graph shown.

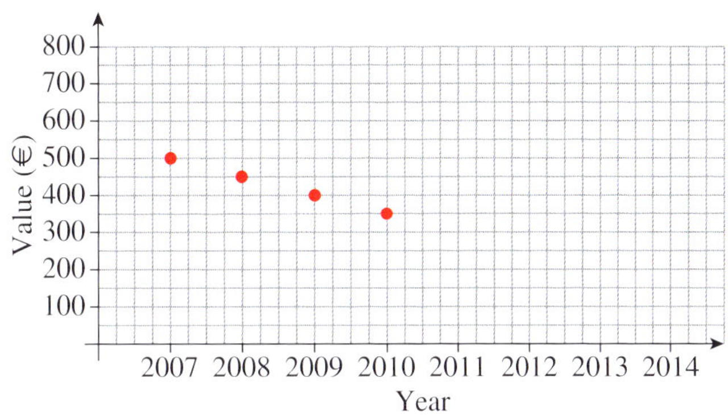

(a) Use a line to join the points on the graph.

(b) If the pattern continued, what was the horse worth in 2011?

(c) How much did the horse lose in value each year?

(d) Melissa will sell the horse when it reaches a value of €200. If the pattern continues, in what year will she sell the horse?

(e) James bought a horse for €700 in 2007. His horse loses value at a constant rate. It was worth €100 in 2011. Mark these two points on the graph above, and join them with a straight line.

(f) In what year will the two horses have the same value? What is that value?

(g) Louise examines the graph and says, 'Looking at the slopes of the lines, I can tell which horse loses value faster'. Explain in your own words what Louise means.

(SEC 2012)

Solutions

Q1 **(a)** 

(b) 

(c) 

Q2 **(i)** 11, 22, 33, 44, …

(a) $5(11) = 55$

(b) $11(10) = 110$

(c) $11n$

(d) Linear

(ii) 3, 7, 11, 15, …

(a) $3 + 4(5 - 1) = 3 + 4(4) = 3 + 16 = 19$

(b) $3 + 4(10 - 1) = 3 + 4(9) = 3 + 36 = 39$

(c) $3 + 4(n - 1)$

(d) Linear

(iii) 1, 4, 9, 16, …

(a) $(5)^2 = 25$

(b) $(10)^2 = 100$

(c) n^2

(d) Quadratic

(iv) 2, 4, 8, 16, …

(a) $2^5 = 32$

(b) $2^{10} = 1024$

(c) 2^n

(d) Exponential

Q3 **(a)** The pattern repeats in words as below:

The first card in the pattern is the Ace of Hearts.

The second card in the pattern is the 2 of Hearts.

The third card in the pattern is the 4 of Hearts.

The fourth card in the pattern is the 8 of Hearts.

(b) The pattern repeats every 4th card, so the card pattern is found from the remainder:

Remainder	Card
$\frac{1}{4}$	
$\frac{2}{4}$	
$\frac{3}{4}$	
0	

Hence, the 9th card in this pattern would be: $\frac{9}{4} = 2\frac{1}{4}$. The remainder is $\frac{1}{4}$, so the 9th card is the Ace of Hearts.

(c) Hence, the 16th card in this pattern would be: $\frac{16}{4} = 4$. There is no remainder, so the 16th card is the 8 of Hearts.

(d) Hence, the 202nd card in this pattern would be: $\frac{202}{4} = 50\frac{2}{4}$. The remainder is $\frac{2}{4}$, so the 202nd card is the 2 of Hearts.

(e) Hence, the 503rd card in this pattern would be: $\frac{503}{4} = 125\frac{3}{4}$. The remainder is $\frac{3}{4}$, so the 503rd card is the 4 of Hearts.

Link
Chapter 1: Number

Link
RW2 Chapter 2: Probability

Q4 (a)

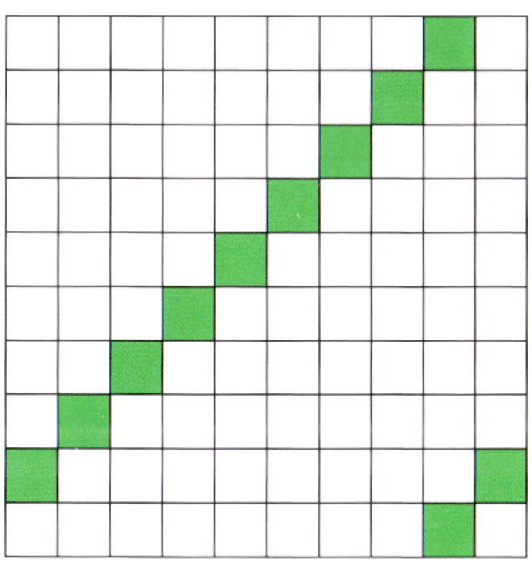

(b) 9, 18, 27, 36, 45, 54, 63, 72, 81, 90, 99.

(c) The green squares are multiples of 9.

(d) $\frac{118}{9} = 13\frac{1}{9}$. Therefore, the square is white, as 118 is not a multiple of 9.

(e) $\frac{180}{9} = 20$. Therefore, the square is green, as 180 is a multiple of 9.

(f) $\frac{903}{9} = 100\frac{1}{3}$. Therefore, the square is white, as 903 is not a multiple of 9.

Link
Chapter 1: Number

Q5 Start from the bottom row of blocks and work up to the top of the pyramid.

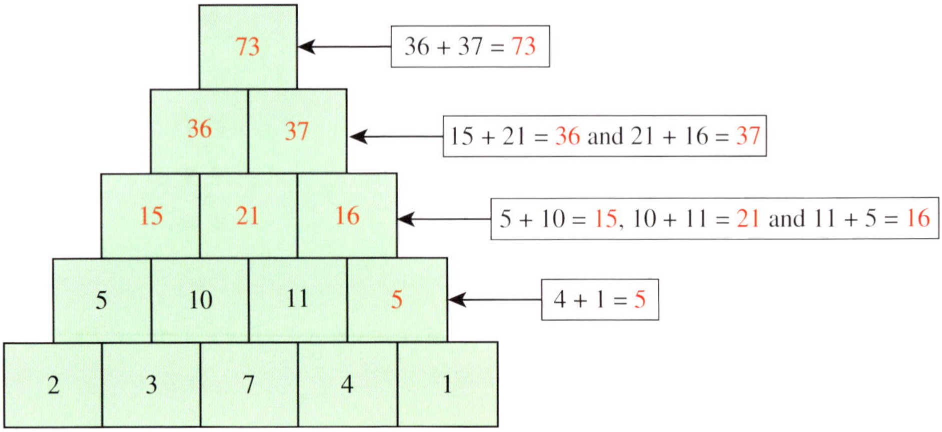

Link
Chapter 1: Number

Q6 **(a)** Start from the bottom row of blocks and work up to the top of the pyramid.

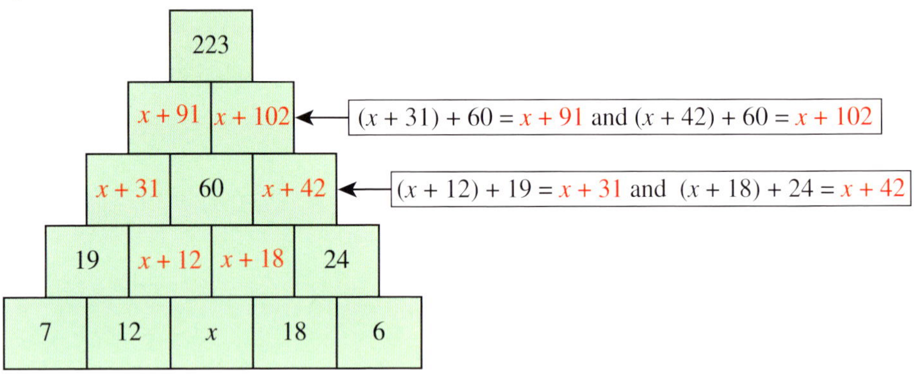

(b) We can find the value of x, using either:

$(x + 91) + (x + 102) = 223$

$\Rightarrow \; 2x + 193 = 223$

$\Rightarrow \; 2x = 30$

$\Rightarrow \; x = 15$

or

$(x + 12) + (x + 18) = 60$

$\Rightarrow \; 2x + 30 = 60$

$\Rightarrow \; 2x = 30$

$\Rightarrow \; x = 15$

Link
Chapter 6:
Linear Equations

(c)

				223				
			106		117			
		46		60		57		
	19		27		33		24	
7		12		15		18		6

Q7 (a) $T_n = 2n^2 - 3$

$n = 1 \Rightarrow T_1 = 2(1)^2 - 3$

$\Rightarrow T_1 = 2 - 3$

$\Rightarrow T_1 = -1$

$n = 2 \Rightarrow T_2 = 2(2)^2 - 3$

$\Rightarrow T_2 = 8 - 3$

$\Rightarrow T_2 = 5$

$n = 3 \Rightarrow T_1 = 2(3)^2 - 3$

$\Rightarrow T_3 = 18 - 3$

$\Rightarrow T_3 = 15$

Answer: −1, 5, 15

(b) $T_n = 5n - 7$

$n = 1 \Rightarrow T_1 = 5(1) - 7$

$\Rightarrow T_1 = 5 - 7$

$\Rightarrow T_1 = -2$

$n = 2 \Rightarrow T_2 = 5(2) - 7$

$\Rightarrow T_2 = 10 - 7$

$\Rightarrow T_2 = 3$

$n = 3 \Rightarrow T_3 = 5(3) - 7$

$\Rightarrow T_3 = 15 - 7$

$\Rightarrow T_3 = 8$

Answer: −2, 3, 8

(c) $T_n = 3(2^n)$

$n = 1 \Rightarrow T_1 = 3(2^1)$

$\Rightarrow T_1 = 3(2)$

$\Rightarrow T_1 = 6$

$n = 2 \Rightarrow T_2 = 3(2^2)$

$\Rightarrow T_2 = 3(4)$

$\Rightarrow T_2 = 12$

$n = 3 \Rightarrow T_2 = 3(2^3)$

$\Rightarrow T_3 = 3(8)$

$\Rightarrow T_3 = 24$

Answer: 6, 12 and 24.

Q8 (a) (i)

Pattern 1:	2		4		9		17		28
First difference: (Change)		+2		+5		+8		+11	
Second difference: (Change of change)			+3		+3		+3		

(ii)

Pattern 2:	−1		2		5		8		11
First difference: (Change)		+3		+3		+3		+3	
Second difference: (Change of change)			0		0		0		

(iii)

Pattern 3:	6		12		24		48		96
First difference: (Change)		+6		+12		+24		+48	
Second difference: (Change of change)			+6		+12		+24		

(b) **(i)** Pattern 1 is quadratic as the second difference is constant.

(ii) Pattern 2 is linear as the first difference is constant.

(iii) Pattern 3 is exponential as the general form is $3(2^n)$.
We know the pattern is exponential, as each consecutive term is found by multiplying the previous term by 2.

Q9 **(a)**

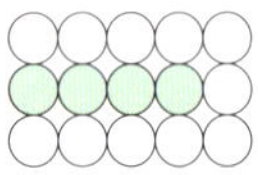

(b)

Number of shaded discs	Number of white discs
1	5
2	**7**
3	**9**
4	**11**
5	**13**
6	**15**

(c) If we continue the pattern in the table:

Number of shaded discs	Number of white discs
1	5
2	**7**
3	**9**
4	**11**
5	**13**
6	**15**
7	**17**
8	**19**
9	**21**

We see that there are 9 shaded discs when there are 21 white discs.

(d) Let n = number of shaded discs.

Number of shaded discs	Number of white discs	First difference
1	5	
2	**7**	**+2**
3	**9**	**+2**
4	**11**	**+2**
5	**13**	**+2**
6	**15**	**+2**

From the table we see that the common difference is +2. So we can state that there are 2 extra white discs for each extra shaded disc. When there are 0 shade discs there would be 3 white discs (subtract 2 from 5); this is the starting value.
Number of white discs = $3 + 2n$.

Q10 (a)

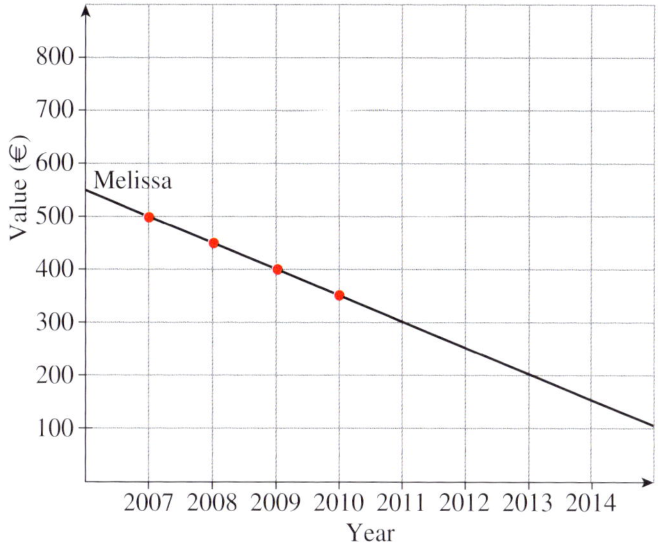

(b) €300

(c) €500 − €450 = €50

(d) Melissa will sell the horse in 2013, when it reaches a value of €200.

(e) Plot the points (2007, 700) and (2011, 100) and join the points with a straight line, as the pattern is linear.

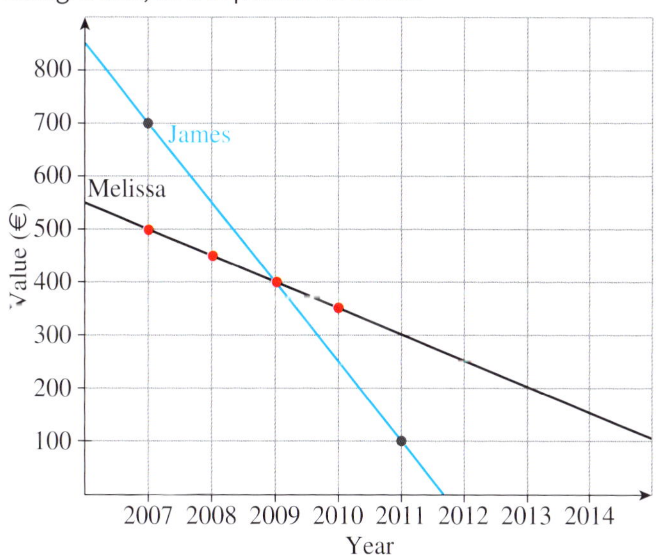

(f) The value of the horses is the same where the two lines intersect. This happens in 2009 when both horses are valued at €400.

(g) The line with the steepest slope indicates which horse loses value faster. From the graph, we can see that James' horse loses value faster.

16 Graphs and Real-life Problems

Learning objectives

In this chapter you will learn about:

- Linear graphs
- Quadratic graphs
- Exponential graphs
- Graphs without formulae.

Linear graphs – real-life problems

A linear graph represents a linear function or pattern which always forms a straight line. The equation of the line has the form $y = mx + c$, where $m, c \in \mathbb{Q}, x \in \mathbb{R}$.

Link

RW Book 2 Chapter 9
Coordinate Geometry of the Line

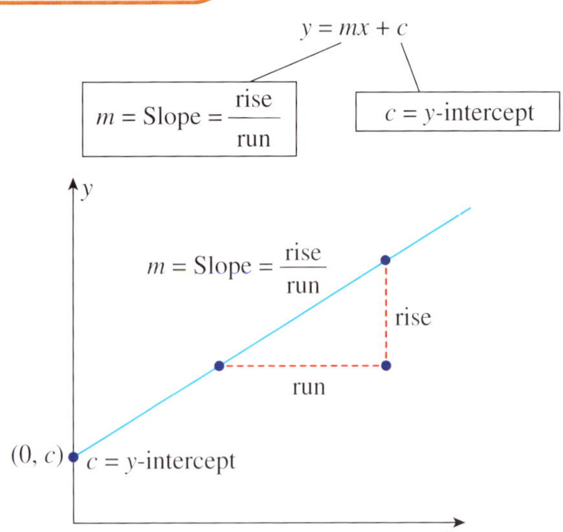

Directly proportional and non-proportional graphs

Top Tip

Two quantities are directly proportional if:

- one quantity increases as the second quantity increases at a constant rate.
- when graphed, the information forms a straight line which passes through the origin (0, 0) of the graph.

The equation of a line for two quantities that are **directly proportional**:

$$y = mx$$

where m represents the rate of change (slope) of the line.

Example:

$y = 2x$ where $m = 2$.

This means that the rate of change (slope) is 2.

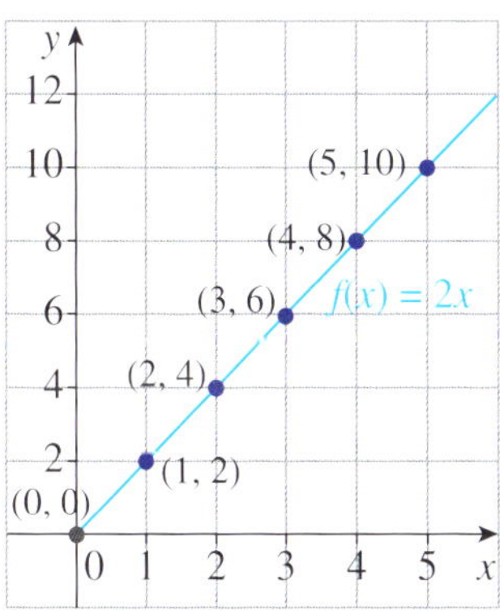

The equation of a line for two quantities that are **not directly proportional**:

$$y = mx + c$$

where m represents the rate of change (slope) of the line and c represents the y-intercept.

Example:

$y = 2x + 4$ where $m = 2$, $c = 4$.

This means that the rate of change (slope) is 2 and the y-intercept is 4.

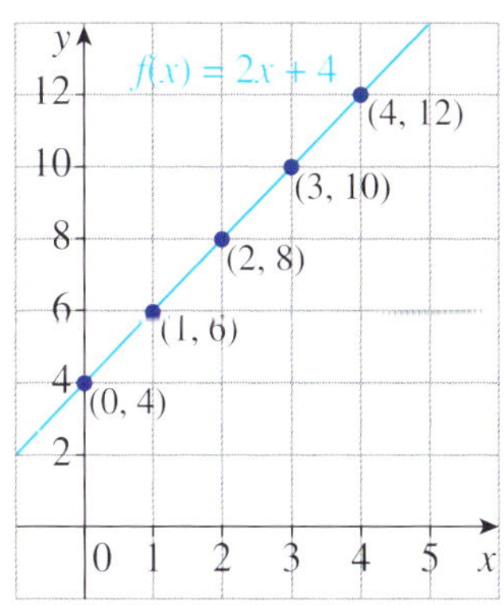

Example

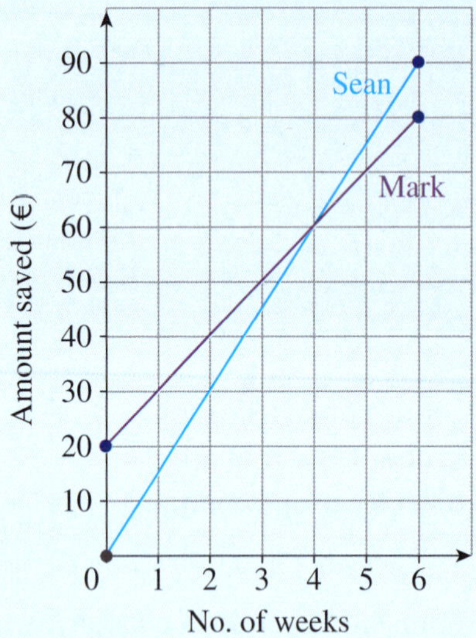

Sean and his brother Mark decide to save some of their pocket money each week for six weeks as shown on the graph.

Use the graph to answer the following questions.

(a) How much has Mark saved by week 3?

(b) In which week did Sean and Mark have the same amount saved?

(c) Write down a formula to represent Sean's savings each week.

(d) Write down a formula to represent Mark's savings each week.

(e) Identify which of the graphs is directly proportional and give a reason for your answer.

Solution

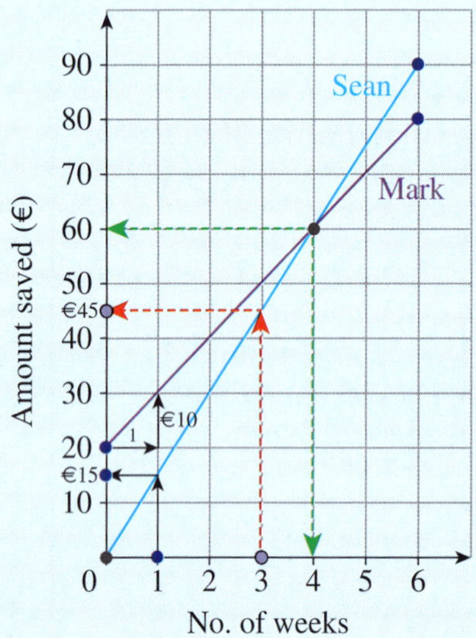

(a) From the graph, Mark saved €45 by week 3.

(b) From the graph, by week 4 Sean and Mark had each saved €60.

(c) Use the equation of the line $y = mx + c$, where m is the slope (rate of change) and c is the y-intercept.

Find the slope (rate of change) using the coordinates (0, 0) and (1, 15).

$$m = \text{slope} = \frac{\text{rise}}{\text{run}} = \frac{y_2 - y_1}{x_2 - x_1} = \frac{15 - 0}{1 - 0} = \frac{15}{1} = 15$$

$c = y\text{-intercept} = 0$

Substituting into $y = mx + c$ gives $y = 15x + 0$.

$\therefore y = 15x$ (The equation of the line is **directly proportional**.)

This equation represents the relationship between the number of weeks and the amount saved per week by Sean.

(d) Use the equation of the line $y = mx + c$, where m is the slope (rate of change) and c is the y-intercept.

Find the slope (rate of change) using the coordinates (0, 20) and (1, 30).

$$m = \text{slope} = \frac{\text{rise}}{\text{run}} = \frac{y_2 - y_1}{x_2 - x_1} = \frac{30 - 20}{1 - 0} = \frac{10}{1} = 10$$

$c = y\text{-intercept} = 20$

Substituting into $y = mx + c$ gives $y = 10x + 20$.
(The equation of the line is **not** directly proportional.)

This equation represents the relationship between the number of weeks and the amount saved each week by Mark.

(e) The graph representing the relationship between number of weeks and amount saved per week by Sean is directly proportional as it passes through the origin (0, 0) and is a straight line.

Quadratic graphs – real-life problems

Questions that involve finding the maximum area of a rectangle or square, or the flight of an object through the air, will all form quadratic functions or patterns which, when graphed, will form a ∩-shaped or a ∪-shaped graph.

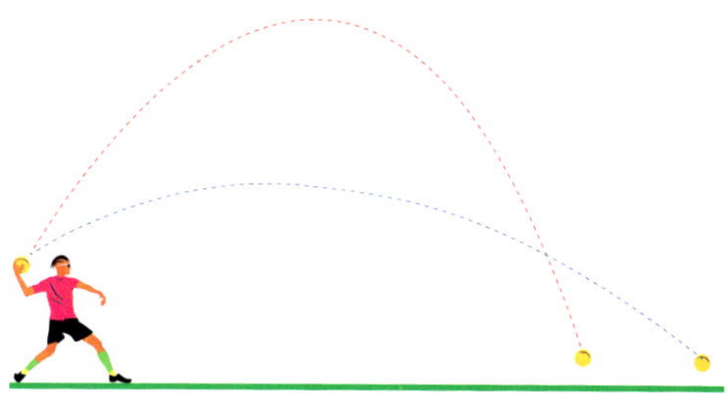

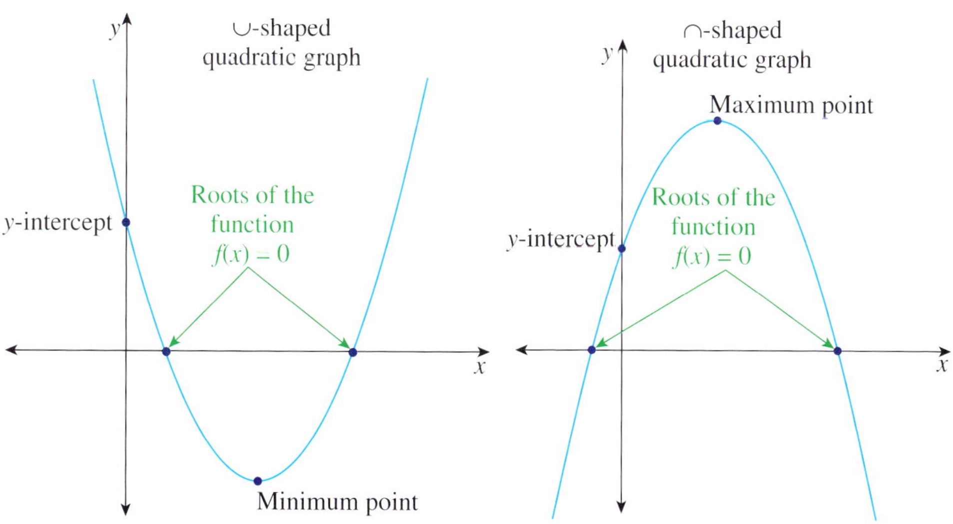

Example

A square sheet of cardboard measures 6 cm by 6 cm.

A square of side x cm is removed from each corner.

The remaining piece of cardboard is folded to form an open box as shown.

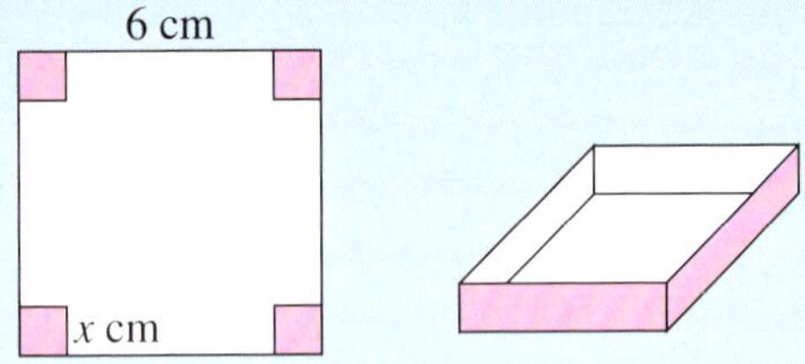

(a) Show that the area, in cm^2, of each side of the box is $6x - 2x^2$.

(b) Let f be the function $f: x \rightarrow 6x - 2x^2$.

(c) Hence, draw the graph of f for $0 \leq x \leq 4, x \in \mathbb{R}$, and use your graph to estimate:

- **(i)** the area of a side when $x = 0{\cdot}5$
- **(ii)** the maximum possible area of a side
- **(iii)** the value of x that gives sides of maximum area
- **(iv)** the length and height of a side of maximum area.

(SEC 2003)

Solution

(a) Area = length × height

$= (6 - 2x) \times (x)$

$= 6x - 2x^2$

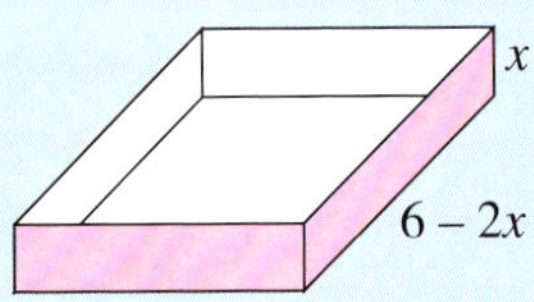

(b) Table for $f: x \rightarrow 6x - 2x^2$

Domain x	$f(x) = 6x - 2x^2$	**Range** y	**Coordinates** (x, y)
0	$f(0) = 6(0) - 2(0)^2$	0	(0, 0)
1	$f(1) = 6(1) - 2(1)^2$	4	(1, 4)
2	$f(2) = 6(2) - 2(2)^2$	4	(2, 4)
3	$f(3) = 6(3) - 2(3)^2$	0	(3, 0)
4	$f(4) = 6(4) - 2(4)^2$	−8	(4, −8)

(c)

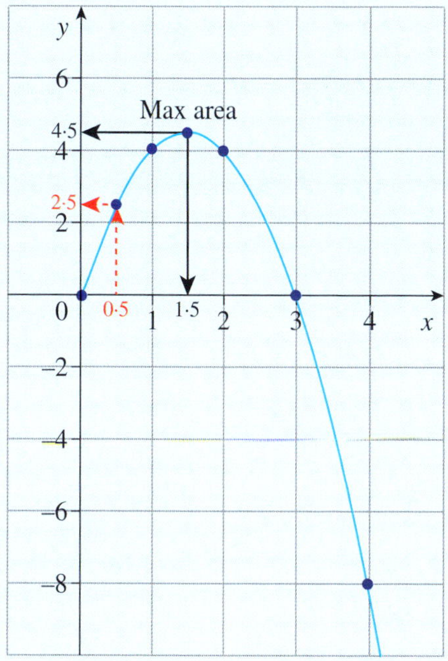

(i) From the graph, the area of a side when $x = 0{\cdot}5$ is $f(0{\cdot}5) = 2{\cdot}5$ cm^2.

(ii) From the graph, the maximum possible area of a side = $4{\cdot}5$ cm^2.

(iii) From the graph, $f(1{\cdot}5) = 4{\cdot}5$ cm^2, i.e. $x = 1{\cdot}5$.

(iv) Length of a side of maximum area $= 6 - 2x$

$= 6 - 2(1{\cdot}5)$

$= 3$.

Height of a side of maximum area $= x = 1{\cdot}5$.

Exponential graphs – real-life problems

An exponential function or pattern is a function or pattern whose value is a constant raised to the power of x.

On the Junior Certificate course we will focus on exponential functions in the form $f(x) = a(2^x)$ or $f(x) = a(3^x)$, where $a \in \mathbb{N}, x \in \mathbb{R}$.

Exponential graphs of the forms $f(x) = a(2^x)$ or $f(x) = a(3^x)$, where $a \in \mathbb{N}, x \in \mathbb{R}$, will always:

- pass through the point $(0, a)$
- stay above the x-axis
- have an upward slope.

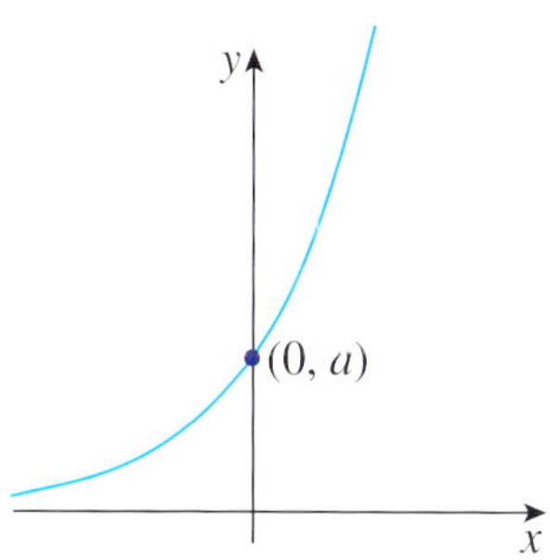

Example

A scientist is studying the growth rate of bacteria in a food sample. The number of bacteria N in the sample after t days is given by $N(t) = 40(2^t)$.

(a) Graph the growth rate of bacteria over four days.

(b) Use the graph to estimate how long it will be before 200 bacteria are present in the sample.

(c) Use the graph to estimate the number of bacteria present after three days.

Solution

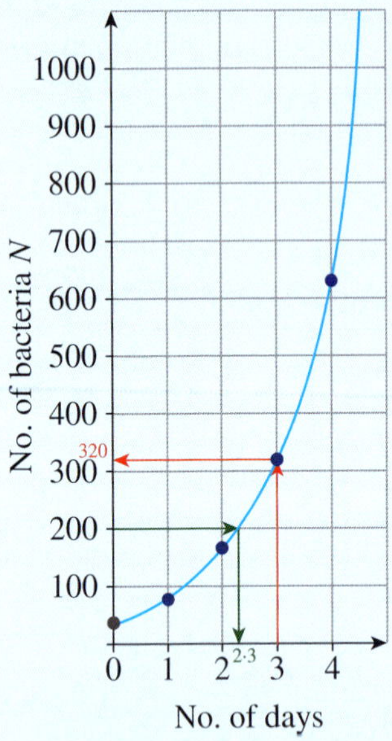

(a) Set up and complete a table for $N(t) = 40(2^t)$ in the given domain.

Domain	$N(t) = 40(2^t)$	Range	Coordinates
0	$40(2^0)$	40	(0, 40)
1	$40(2^1)$	80	(1, 80)
2	$40(2^2)$	160	(2, 160)
3	$40(2^3)$	320	(3, 320)
4	$40(2^4)$	640	(4, 640)

(b) From the graph, we can see that '200 bacteria' corresponds to approximately 2·3 days.

(c) From the graph, we can see that after three days the number of bacteria is approximately 320.

Graphs without formulae

Rates of change

A rate of change is a rate that defines how one quantity changes in relation to another quantity. When the rate of change is constant, the graph will form a straight line.

Positive

When the value of x increases, the value of y increases.

The graph slants upward (positive slope).

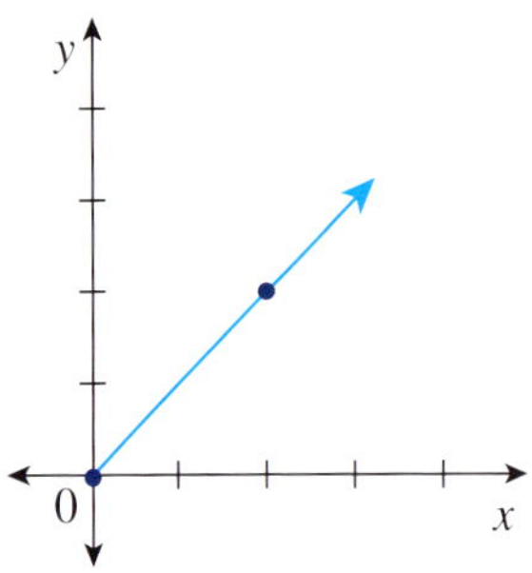

Horizontal

When the value of x increases, the value of y remains constant.

The graph will be a horizontal line.

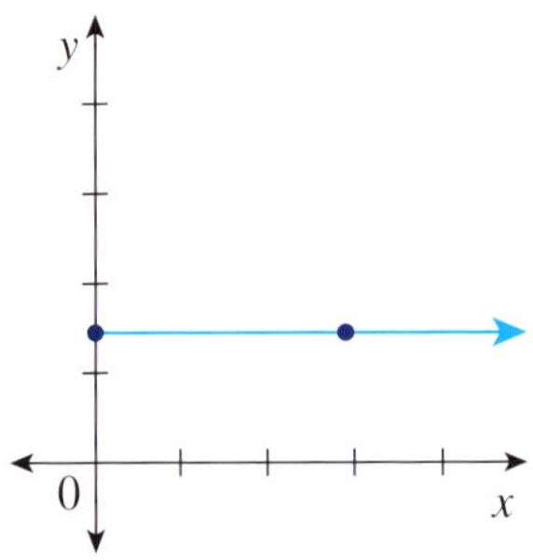

Negative

When the value of x increases, the value of y decreases.

The graph slants downward (negative slope).

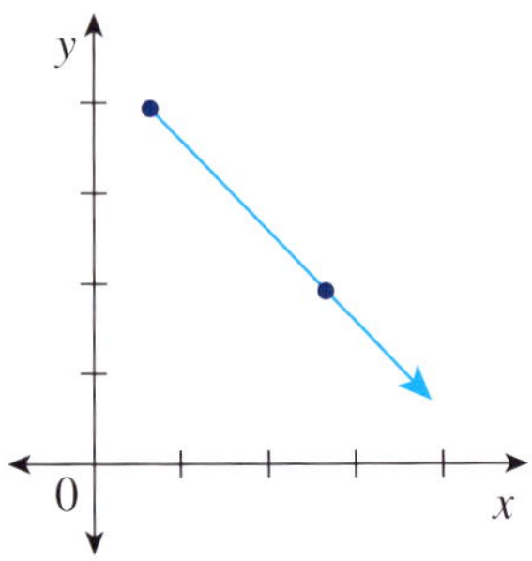

Distance–time graphs

Top Tip

A distance–time graph represents the distance travelled by an object over a given period of time.

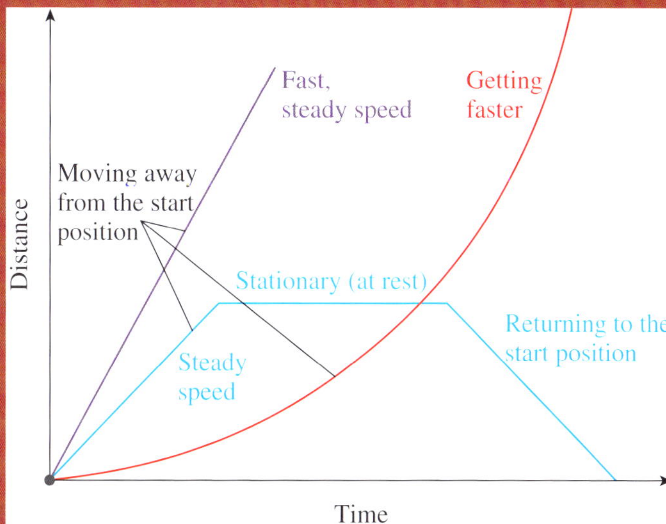

Points to note

1 The steeper the graph, the faster the object is moving.

2 A horizontal line means the object is not changing its position. In other words, the object is at rest.

3 An upward-sloping line means the object is moving away from the start position.

4 A downward-sloping line means the object is returning to the start position.

Example

The graph shows information about a journey taken by a bus on its morning route to and from a bus terminal.

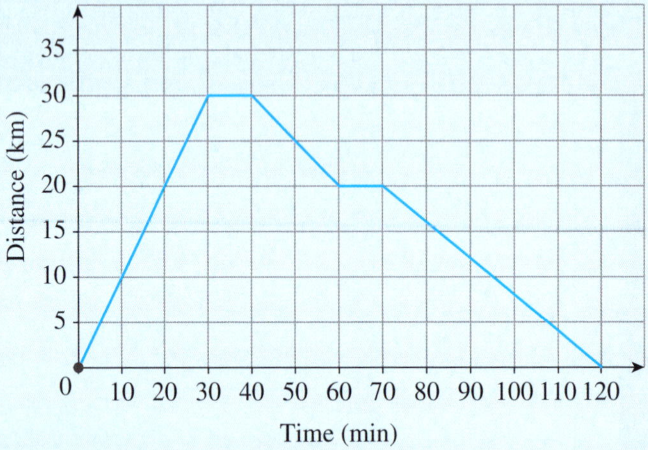

Use the graph to answer the following questions:

(a) What was the rate of change for the first part of the journey?

(b) In total, how long was the bus stopped for, over the journey?

(c) At which two times is the bus 10 km from the bus terminal?

(d) What is the average speed of the bus over the last 20 km of the journey?

Solution

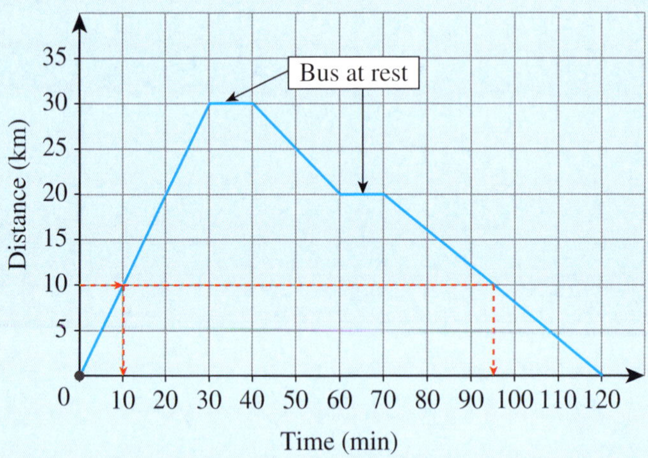

(a) From the graph, the rate of change for the first part of the journey is represented as the slope of the line.

$m = \text{slope} = \frac{\text{rise}}{\text{run}} = \frac{10}{10} = 1 \text{ km/min}$

(b) From the graph, the bus had stopped:

for 10 minutes, between 30 and 40 minutes, and

for 10 minutes, between 60 and 70 minutes

Therefore the bus stopped for a total of 20 minutes.

(c) From the graph, the bus is 10 km from the bus terminal at both 10 minutes and 95 minutes into the journey.

(d) The average speed of the bus over the last 40 km of the journey:

$$\text{Average speed} = \frac{\text{distance travelled}}{\text{time taken}}$$

$$= \frac{40\text{ km}}{(120 - 70)\text{ min}} = \frac{20}{50} = 0{\cdot}4\text{ km/min}$$

Speed–time graphs

Top Tip

- Speed–time graphs are also called velocity–time graphs.
- A speed–time graph shows how the speed of an object changes over time.

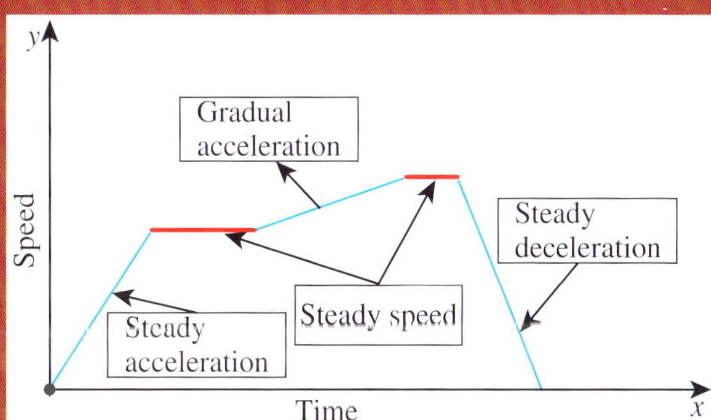

Points to note

1 The steeper the graph, the greater the acceleration of the object.

2 A horizontal line means the object is moving at a constant speed.

3 An upward sloping line means that the object is accelerating (speeding up).

4 A downward sloping line means that the object is decelerating (slowing down).

Example

The graph below shows some details about a journey Alex made by bicycle.

Alex's journey

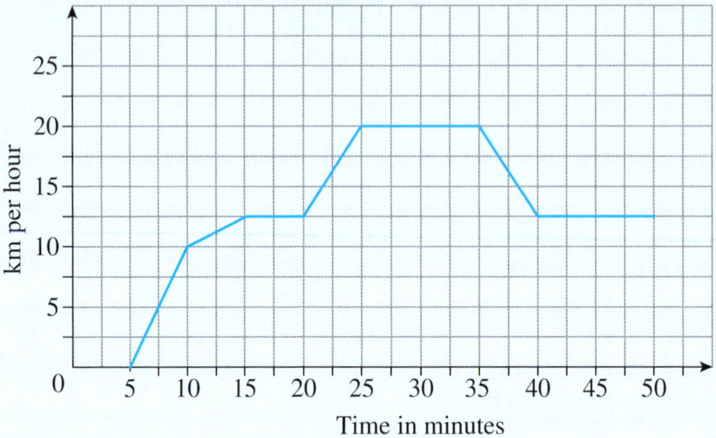

Alex waited for his friend before he set off on his journey.

(a) How long did he wait before setting out?

(b) What was Alex's highest speed during the journey?

(c) For what length of time was Alex travelling at the highest speed?

(d) How far did Alex travel at the highest speed?

(SEC 2013)

Solution

(a) From the graph, Alex waited 5 minutes before setting out.

(b) From the graph, Alex's highest speed was 20 km/h.

(c) From the graph, Alex travelled at his highest speed for 10 minutes $(35 - 25 = 10)$.

(d) Using the graph to calculate how far Alex travelled at the highest speed:

Distance = speed × time

$= 20 \times 10$ min   Convert min to hours by dividing by 60.

$= 20 \times \frac{1}{6}$ of an hour

$= 3\frac{1}{3}$ km

Height–time graphs

We use height–time graphs to examine how various containers are filled with a liquid flowing at a constant rate. We compare the depth (height) of the liquid in the container over time.

Example

Three containers are shown. Water is poured into each container at a constant rate, until it is full. The three graphs represent the height of the water, h, in the containers after time t. Match each container with its corresponding graph.

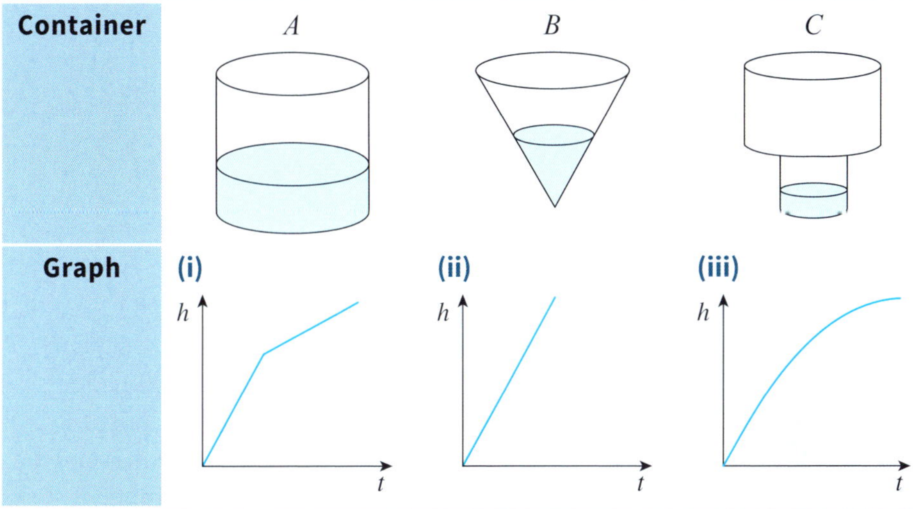

Solution

- Container A corresponds to graph **(ii)**.

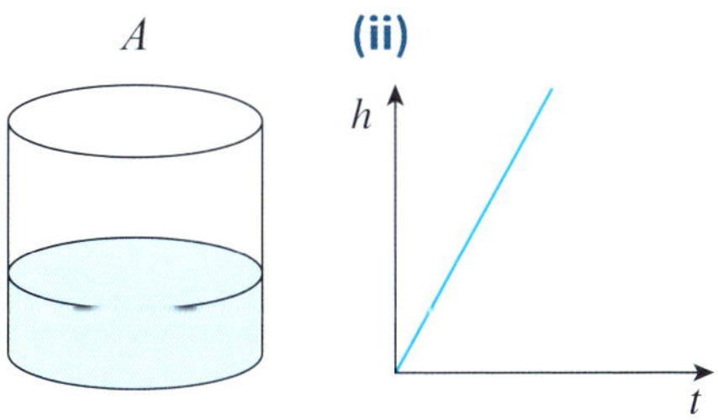

Reason – As the radius of the container doesn't change, it fills at a uniform rate, thus the height of the water flowing into the container increases at a steady rate.

- Container B corresponds to graph **(iii)**.

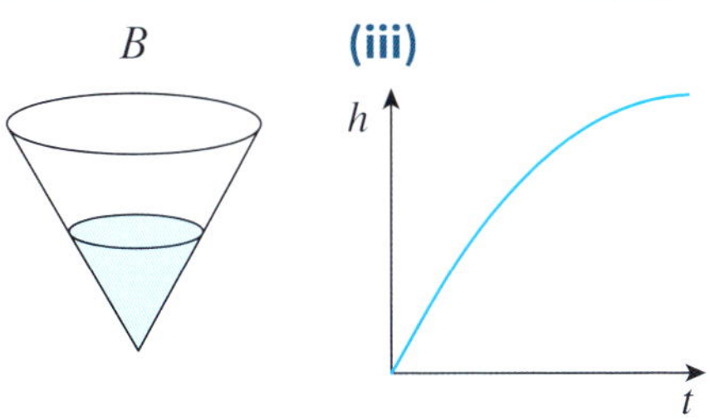

Reason – The shape is not uniform. As the radius of the container widens, the height of the water flowing into the container will increase more slowly. The rate the water flows into the container starts off very fast; then, as the container is filled, the rate slows down. This is why the graph starts with a steep slope and then gradually gets less steep as the height increases.

- Container C corresponds to graph **(i)**.

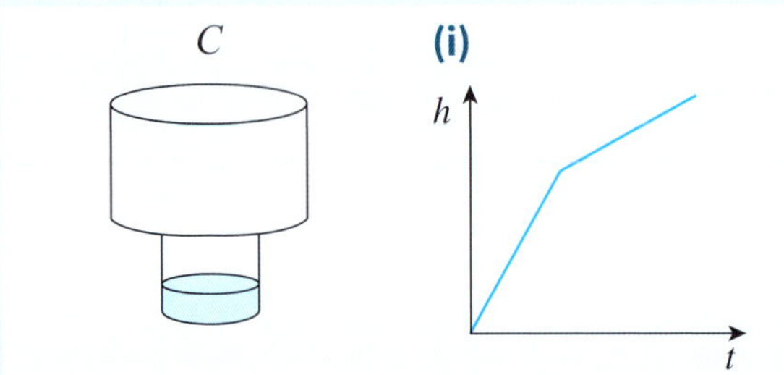

Reason – The container is a combination of two uniform shapes. To begin with, the water flows into the container at a uniform rate, then when the width of the container increases the water will continue to flow into the container, but at a slower rate. This is illustrated on the graph by the fact that the slope is steeper for the first part of the graph, then less steep for the second part of the graph.

Exercise

Q1 Two mobile phone companies, Cellulon and Mobil, offer price plans for mobile internet access. A formula, in x, for the total cost per month for each company is shown in the table below. x is the number of MB of data downloaded per month.

Phone company	Total cost per month (cents)
Cellulon	$c(x) = 4x$
Mobil	$m(x) = 1000 + 2x$

(a) Draw the graphs of $c(x)$ and $m(x)$ on a coordinate grid to show the total cost per month for each phone company, for $0 \leq x \leq 700$. Label each graph clearly.

(b) Which company charges no fixed fee? Justify your answer, with reference to the relevant formula or graph.

(c) Write down the point of intersection of the two graphs.

Fergus wants to buy a mobile phone from one of these two companies, and wants his mobile internet bill to be as low as possible.

(d) Explain how your answer to part **(c)** would help Fergus choose between Cellulon and Mobil.

(SEC 2015)

Q2 The height, h, of a tennis ball thrown into the air is given by the formula $h(t) = 10t - t^2$ which is graphed below.

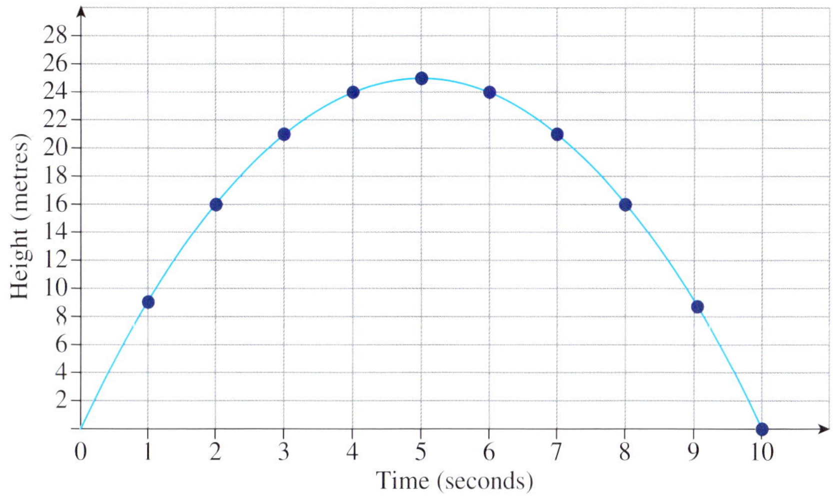

Use the graph to estimate answers to each of the following.

(a) What was the height of the tennis ball after 2·5 seconds?

(b) At what times is the height of the tennis ball 12 metres above the ground?

(c) What is the maximum height of the tennis ball?

Q3 James is planting a rectangular flower bed that has a perimeter of 12 m.

(a) If the width of the flower bed is x m, find an equation, in terms of x, for the length of the flower bed.

(b) Show that the area of the flower bed is given by $A(x) = 6x - x^2$.

(c) Draw a graph to represent the area of the flower bed $A(x) = 6x - x^2$ as the width, x, changes from 0 m to 6 m.

(d) What is the width that corresponds to the maximum area?

Q4 A new app was launched during the first week in January. The number of users is estimated by the function $u(n) = 100(2^n)$, where $u(n)$ means the number of users and n means the number of months since the launch date.

(a) Draw a graph to represent the number of users over the first four months.

(b) How many users does the company expect after three months?

(c) How many months does the company expect it will take for the new app to reach 300 users?

Q5 The speed–time graph given represents the speed of a car travelled on a given day.

(a) What is the car's highest speed over the journey?

(b) How far did the car travel at its highest speed?

(c) How long (in minutes) is the car travelling for?

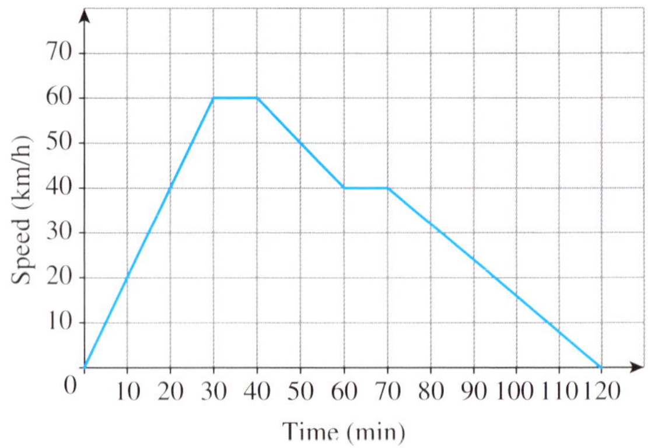

Q6 Match each distance–time graph with its corresponding speed–time graph.

Distance–time graphs

(a) **(b)** **(c)** **(d)**

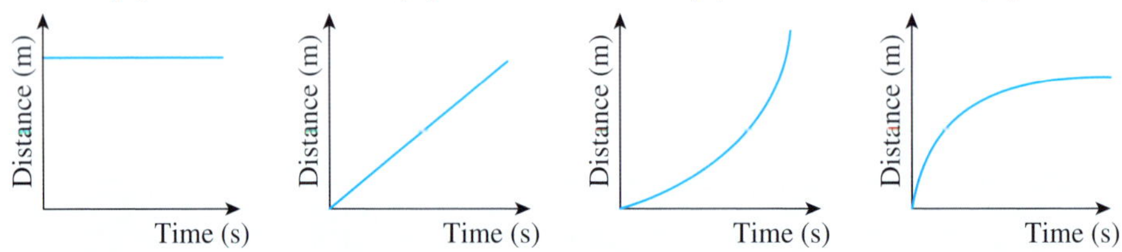

Speed–time graphs

(i) **(ii)** **(iii)** **(iv)**

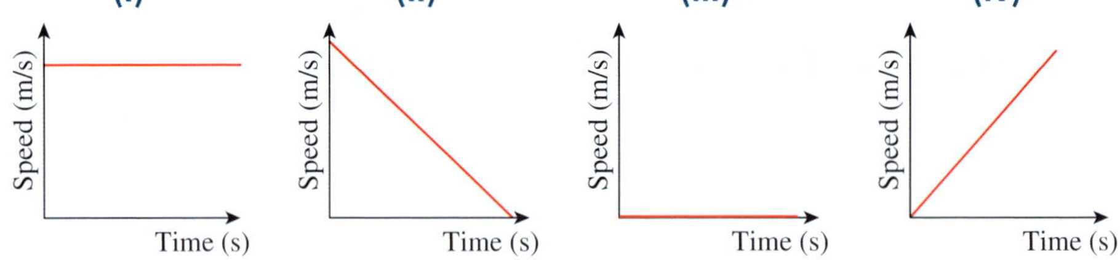

Q7 Water is poured at a constant rate into each container shown, until they are full. The graphs represent the height of the water, h, in the containers after time t. Match each container with its corresponding graph.

Container

A *B* *C*

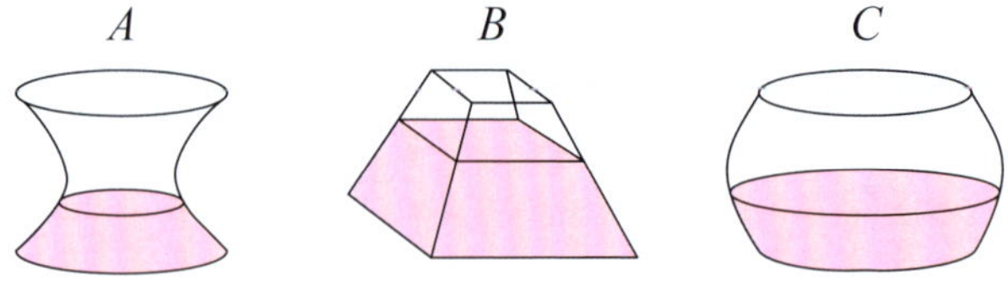

Graph

(i) **(ii)** **(iii)**

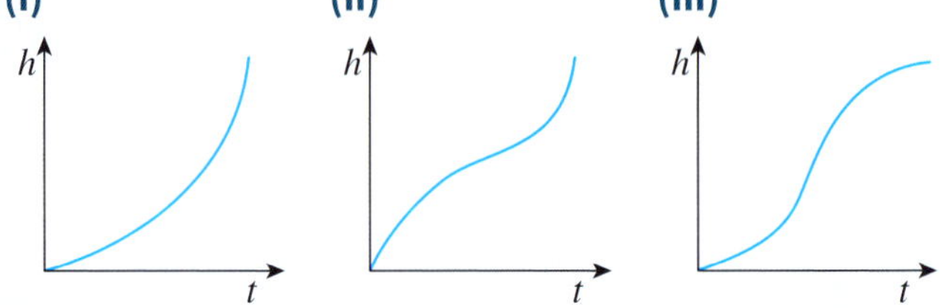

Q8 Match each description of motion with its corresponding distance–time graph.

Description of motion	**(a)** Object is moving at a slow pace and then moves at a faster pace for a certain period of time.	**(b)** Object is moving at a fast pace, slows down and then speeds up again.	**(c)** Object is moving at a steady pace, then it comes to a stop and remains at rest for a certain period of time.
Distance-time graph	**(i)** 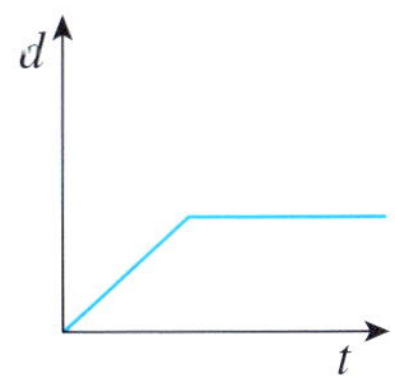	**(ii)** 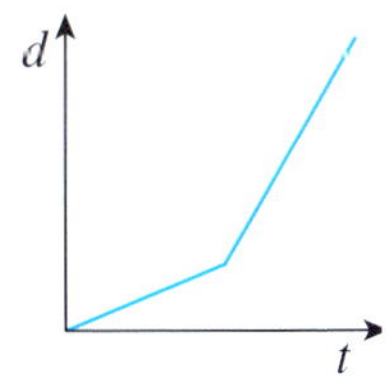	**(iii)** 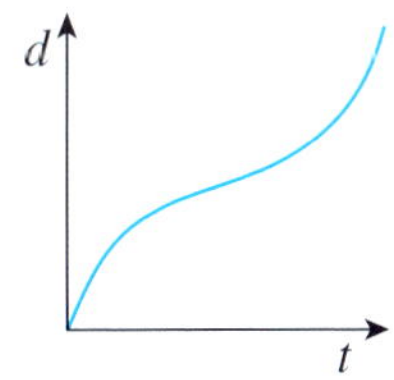

Q9 Paul and Marie have been studying the growth of a particular bacterium.

They each come up with a function to predict the number of bacteria in a colony, in thousands, after t days. They both assume that there are 1000 bacteria in the colony at the beginning ($t = 0$).

Paul comes up with the function: $f : t \rightarrow 2^t$

Marie comes up with the function: $g : t \rightarrow t^2 + 2t + 1$.

(i) On a grid, draw the graphs of $y = f(t)$ and $y = g(t)$ in the domain $0 \leq t \leq 5, t \in \mathbb{R}$. For parts **(ii)**, **(iii)**, and **(iv)**, you must show your working out on the diagram.

(ii) Use your graphs to find the difference in the number of bacteria predicted by Paul and the number of bacteria predicted by Marie after 2·5 days.

(iii) Use your graphs to estimate the range of values of t for which both Paul and Marie predict that there will be at least 20 000 bacteria in the colony.

(iv) By extending your graphs, estimate the value of t (other than $t = 0$) for which the number of bacteria predicted by Paul and the number of bacteria predicted by Marie will be the same.

(v) The actual number of bacteria after two weeks (14 days) is roughly $1{\cdot}6 \times 10^7$. Based on this, which formula would you say gives the better prediction for the number of bacteria? Explain your answer.

(SEC 2014)

Solutions

Q1

Phone company	Total cost per month (cents)
Cellulon	$c(x) = 4x$ $c(0) = 4(0) = 0$ $c(700) = 4(700) = 2800$ Plot (0, 0) and (700, 2800).
Mobil	$m(x) = 1000 + 2x$ $m(0) = 1000 + 2(0) = 1000$ $m(700) = 1000 + 2(700) = 2400$ Plot (0, 1000) and (700, 2400).

(a)

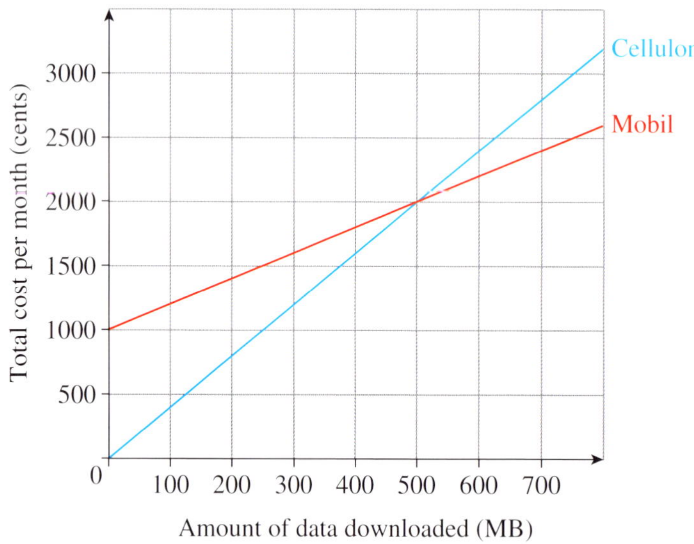

(b) Answer: Cellulon

Using the graph: We can see that the line goes through (0, 0), so there is no cost if no data is used.

or

Using a formula: Given $c(0) = 0$; so there no cost if no data is used.

(c) The point of intersection of the graphs is (500, 2000).

(d) If the data used is less than 500 MB per month, Cellulon is cheaper. If the data used is more than 500 MB per month, Mobil is cheaper.

Q2

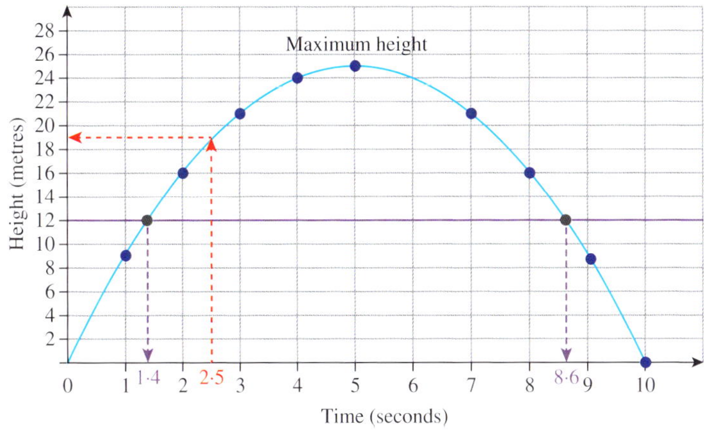

(a) From the graph, the height of the tennis ball after 2·5 seconds is 19 m.

(b) From the graph, the height of the tennis ball is 12 m above the ground at $t = 1{\cdot}4$ seconds and at $t = 8{\cdot}6$ seconds.

(c) From the graph, the maximum height of the tennis ball is 25 m.

Q3 (a) If the width of the flower bed is x m, an equation, in terms of x, for the length of the flower bed is derived as follows:

Total perimeter = 2(width) + 2(length) = 12 m

$\Rightarrow$ (width) + (length) = 6 m

$\Rightarrow x + l = 6$

Therefore $l = 6 - x$

(b) Proof that the area of the flower bed is given by $A(x) = 6x - x^2$:

Area = length × height

$= (6 - x) \times (x)$

$= 6x - x^2$

(c) To draw a graph to represent the area of the flower bed $A(x) = 6x - x^2$ as the width, x, changes from 0 m to 6 m, first construct a table for $A(x) = 6x - x^2$, then use the table to draw the graph.

Domain	$A(x) = 6x - x^2$	Range	Coordinates
0	$6(0) - (0)^2$	0	(0, 0)
1	$6(1) - (1)^2$	5	(1, 5)
2	$6(2) - (2)^2$	8	(2, 8)
3	$6(3) - (3)^2$	9	(3, 9)
4	$6(4) - (4)^2$	8	(4, 8)
5	$6(5) - (5)^2$	5	(5, 5)
6	$6(6) - (6)^2$	0	(6, 0)

(d) From the graph, a width of 3 m corresponds to the maximum area of 9 m^2.

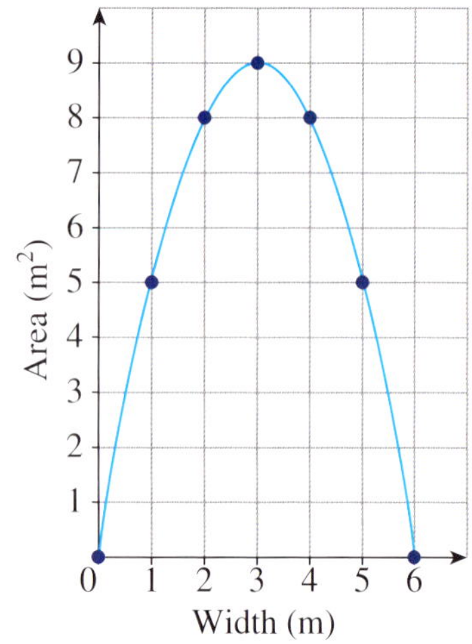

Q4 (a) Set up and complete a table for $u(n) = 100(2^n)$ in the given domain.

Domain	$u(n) = 100(2^n)$	Range	Coordinates
0	$100(2^0)$	100	(0, 100)
1	$100(2^1)$	200	(1, 200)
2	$100(2^2)$	400	(2, 400)
3	$100(2^3)$	800	(3, 800)
4	$100(2^4)$	1600	(4, 1600)

(b) From the graph, the company can expect 800 users after three months.

(c) The company can expect the app to reach 300 users after 1·5 months.

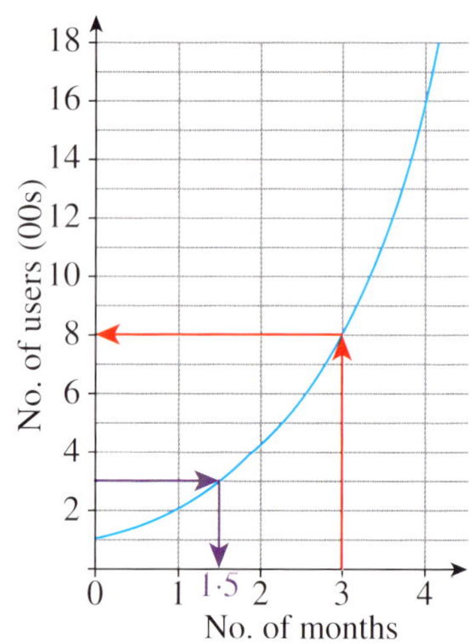

Q5 (a) The car's highest speed is 60 km/h.

(b) To calculate how far the car travelled at its highest speed:

Distance = speed × time

= 60 × 10 min

= 60 × $\frac{1}{6}$ of an hour

= 10 km

(c) From the graph, the car is travelling for 120 minutes (= 2 hours).

Q6

Distance–time graph **(a)** corresponds to speed–time graph **(iii)**.

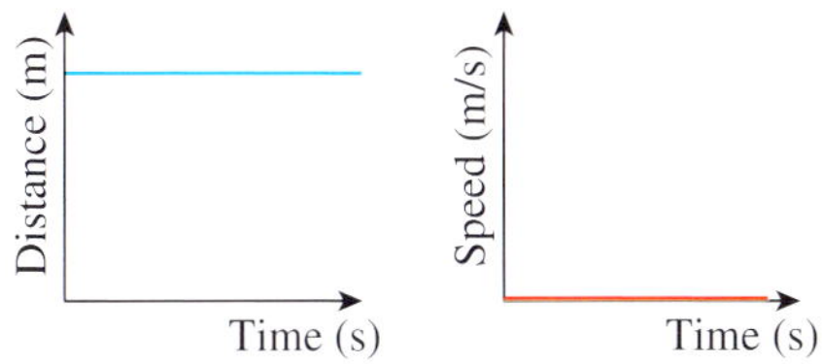

Distance–time graph **(b)** corresponds to speed–time graph **(i)**.

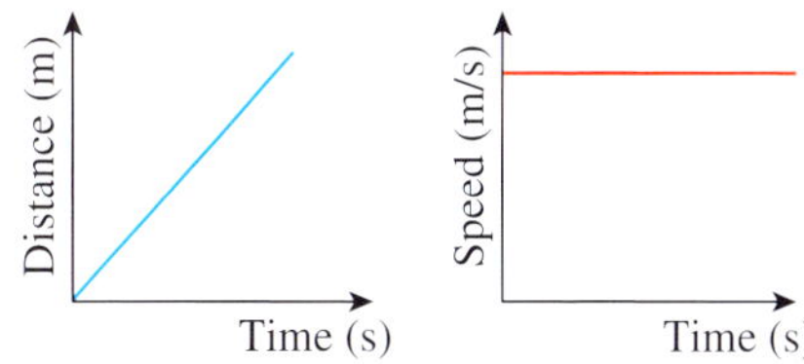

Distance–time graph **(c)** corresponds to speed–time graph **(iv)**.

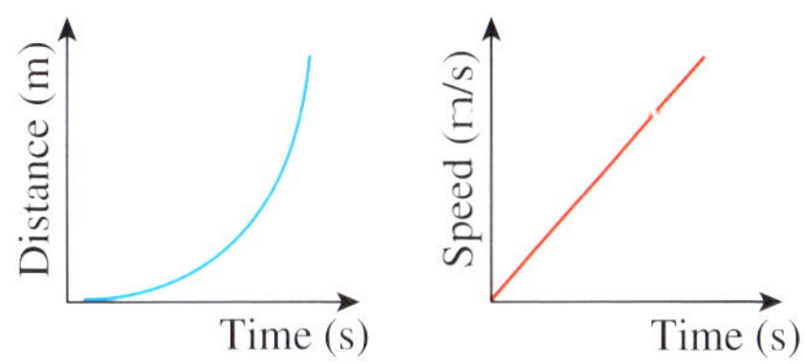

Distance–time graph **(d)** corresponds to speed–time graph **(ii)**.

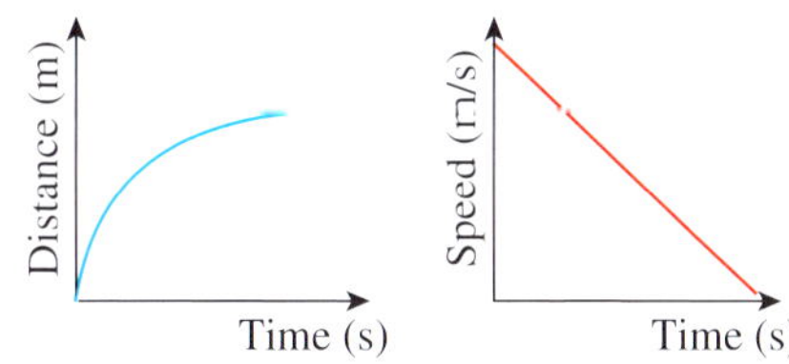

Q7 Container A corresponds to graph **(iii)**.

Container B corresponds to graph **(i)**.

Container C corresponds to graph **(ii)**.

Q8 Description **(a)** corresponds to graph **(ii)**.

(a) The object is moving at a slow pace, and then moves at a faster pace for a certain period of time.

(ii)

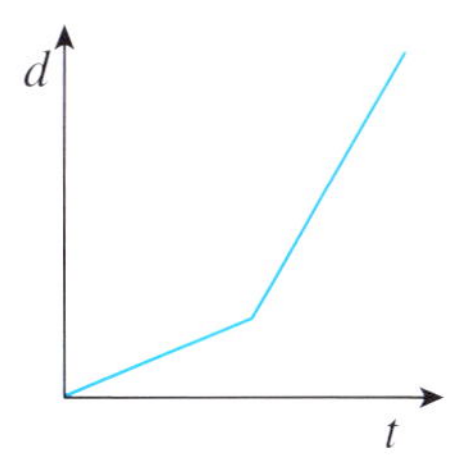

Description **(b)** corresponds to graph **(iii)**.

(b) The object is moving at fast pace, slows down, and then speeds up again.

(iii)

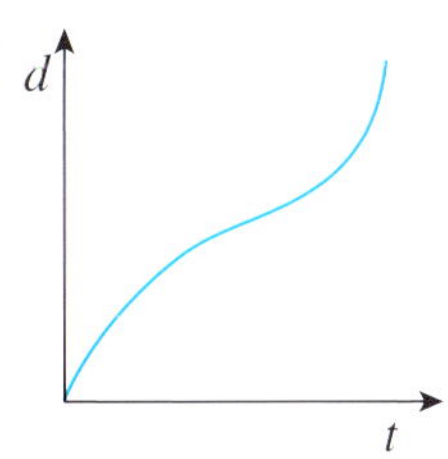

Description **(c)** corresponds to graph **(i)**.

(c) The object is moving at a steady pace, then it comes to a stop and remains at rest for a certain period of time.

(i)

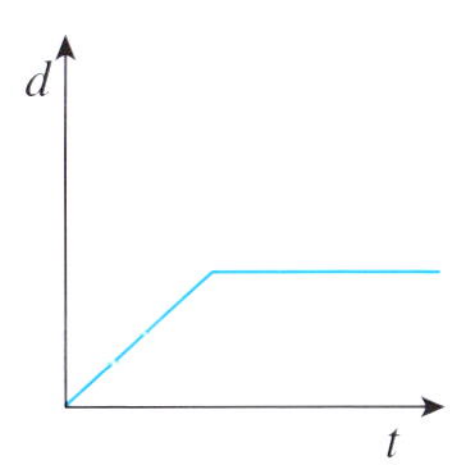

Q9 (i) Table for $f(t) = 2^t$

Domain	$f(t) = 2^t$	Range	Coordinates
0	$2^{(0)}$	1	(0, 1)
1	$2^{(1)}$	2	(1, 2)
2	$2^{(2)}$	4	(2, 4)
3	$2^{(3)}$	8	(3, 8)
4	$2^{(4)}$	16	(4, 16)
5	$2^{(5)}$	32	(5, 32)

Table for $g(t) = t^2 + 2t + 1$

Domain	$g(t) = t^2 + 2t + 1$	Range	Coordinates
0	$(0^2) + 2(0) + 1$	1	(0, 1)
1	$(1^2) + 2(1) + 1$	4	(1, 4)
2	$(2^2) + 2(2) + 1$	9	(2, 9)
3	$(3^2) + 2(3) + 1$	16	(3, 16)
4	$(4^2) + 2(4) + 1$	25	(4, 25)
5	$(5^2) + 2(5) + 1$	36	(5, 36)

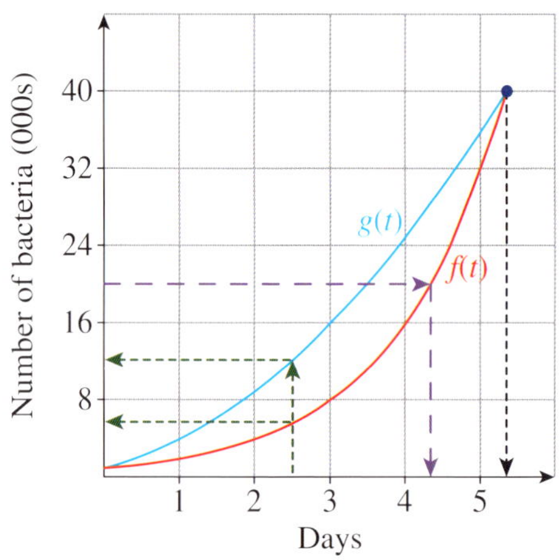

(ii) Marie after 2·5 days: 12 000 bacteria, approximately.
Paul after 2·5 days: 6000 bacteria, approximately.
Difference: 12 000 – 6000 = 6000 bacteria.

(iii) $t \geq 4{\cdot}3$ days

(iv) $t = 5{\cdot}3$ days

(v) Paul's prediction of $f(x)$ is better:

Paul: $f(x)$ gives $f(14) = 16\,384 \approx 1{\cdot}6 \times 10^4$,
so Paul predicts $1{\cdot}6 \times 10^4 \times 1000 = 1{\cdot}6 \times 10^7$

Marie: $g(x)$ gives $g(14) = 225 \approx 2{\cdot}3 \times 10^2$,
so Marie predicts $2{\cdot}3 \times 10^2 \times 1000 = 1{\cdot}6 \times 10^5$

STUDY GUIDE

Date:				
Time:				
Section to be revised:				
Date:				
Time:				
Section to be revised:				
Date:				
Time:				
Section to be revised:				
Date:				
Time:				
Section to be revised:				
Date:				
Time:				
Section to be revised:				
Date:				
Time:				
Section to be revised:				

Night before exam:

Sections to be revised:

Date:				
Time:				
Section to be revised:				
Date:				
Time:				
Section to be revised:				
Date:				
Time:				
Section to be revised:				
Date:				
Time:				
Section to be revised:				
Date:				
Time:				
Section to be revised:				
Date:				
Time:				
Section to be revised:				

Night before exam:	
Sections to be revised:	

Date:				
Time:				
Section to be revised:				
Date:				
Time:				
Section to be revised:				
Date:				
Time:				
Section to be revised:				
Date:				
Time:				
Section to be revised:				
Date:				
Time:				
Section to be revised:				
Date:				
Time:				
Section to be revised:				

Night before exam:	
Sections to be revised:	

Date:				
Time:				
Section to be revised:				
Date:				
Time:				
Section to be revised:				
Date:				
Time:				
Section to be revised:				
Date:				
Time:				
Section to be revised:				
Date:				
Time:				
Section to be revised:				
Date:				
Time:				
Section to be revised:				

Night before exam:	
Sections to be revised:	

Date:				
Time:				
Section to be revised:				
Date:				
Time:				
Section to be revised:				
Date:				
Time:				
Section to be revised:				
Date:				
Time:				
Section to be revised:				
Date:				
Time:				
Section to be revised:				
Date:				
Time:				
Section to be revised:				

Night before exam:	
Sections to be revised:	

Date:				
Time:				
Section to be revised:				
Date:				
Time:				
Section to be revised:				
Date:				
Time:				
Section to be revised:				
Date:				
Time:				
Section to be revised:				
Date:				
Time:				
Section to be revised:				
Date:				
Time:				
Section to be revised:				

Night before exam:	
Sections to be revised:	